Cumberland Island: A History

A Wormsloe

FOUNDATION
PUBLICATION

Cumberland
ISLAND

A HISTORY

Mary R. Bullard

THE UNIVERSITY OF GEORGIA PRESS
Athens and London

University of Georgia Press paperback edition, 2005
© 2003 by the University of Georgia Press
Athens, Georgia 30602
www.ugapress.org
All rights reserved
Designed by Sandra Strother Hudson
Set in Monotype Walbaum by Graphic Composition, Inc.

Most University of Georgia Press titles are
available from popular e-book vendors.

Printed digitally

The Library of Congress has cataloged the cloth edition of this book as follows:
Bullard, Mary Ricketson.
Cumberland Island : a history / Mary R. Bullard.
xx, 415 p., [32] p. of plates : ill., maps ; 25 cm.—(Wormsloe Foundation
publications ; no. 22)
Includes bibliographical references (p. 351–392) and index.
ISBN 0-8203-2267-9 (hardcover : alk. paper)
1. Cumberland Island (Ga.)—History. 2. Cumberland Island (Ga.)—
History—Pictorial works. I. Title. II. Publications
(Wormsloe Foundation) ; no. 22.
F292.C94 B86 2003
975.8746—dc21   2002004783

Paperback ISBN-13: 978-0-8203-2741-9
ISBN-10: 0-8203-2741-7

British Library Cataloging-in-Publication Data available

To my brother, Oliver G. Ricketson III

CONTENTS

PREFACE

I began work on a history of Cumberland Island in 1969 by making a few desultory notes. My husband, Bill Bullard, an archaeologist, had taken up a new position as curator of social sciences at the Florida Museum of Natural History, and we had recently moved to the University of Florida, in Gainesville. In 1970 the Fernandina Historical Society invited him to give a short talk on Cumberland's history. Bill read my scanty notes in preparation for his talk. My notes were too slight to be of much use, and we both noticed that very little had been written about Cumberland Island. He gave instead a good talk about the Florida Museum. The Fernandina Historical Society may not have been disappointed, but its interest in getting an insider's picture of Cumberland was illusory. Although we were insiders, we didn't know much about the island's past.

My grandmother was Margaret Carnegie Ricketson, one of the nine children of Thomas Morrison Carnegie and his wife, Lucy Coleman. From 1881 to 1972 the Carnegie presence on Cumberland Island, in Camden County, Georgia, had been splendid if somewhat reclusive. However, between 1964 and 1970 various forces were tearing apart a concept that we once entertained—that the future of family property was ours to decide. United to take it from us seemingly stood Camden County, the state of Georgia, internal family pressures, and perhaps even the U.S. government. We were analyzed in the press, we were pilloried in the legislature. In response, we hired lawyers and met among ourselves to determine each person's wishes and needs. Finally—and most wisely—we united to create the Cumberland Island Company. It was a temporary tool, but with it we accomplished two primary aims. First, we divided the property, a lengthy process in itself. Second, we maintained the property during the interim period before making final decisions.

All the details of our time of troubles were known to my husband. When we Carnegies met, our preoccupation with division of the property made conversation on other subjects almost impossible. My Bostonian husband was puzzled by the pent-up emotions unveiled in these family meetings. When I at last obtained a piece of land on Cumberland in 1970, my husband and I made plans to build a small cabin by the side of a creek called Lanes Landing. Gainesville was only a hundred miles from Fernandina, in a straight line on a good highway. All our island troubles were over, we thought.

Sadly, our future differed greatly from our happy visions. Bill Bullard never saw the house we planned. Diagnosed with cancer, he resigned his job. I closed up our house in Gainesville and sent its furnishings to a storage warehouse in Florida. Then we flew home to New England. Shortly before his death, Bill said I should continue with the construction of the little cabin at Lanes Landing. He said, "Cumberland Island means more to you than you think it does." In this he was correct. I did complete the cabin and spent many months between jobs there over the following eighteen years.

After my husband's death, I was pleased to be invited to join a University of Pennsylvania archaeological project in Guatemala. Fieldwork was performed on a seasonal basis. Each year, once the four months were up and I was back in Massachusetts, I read the *Georgia Historical Quarterly* and all the standard histories of Georgia on which I could lay my hands. I also made forays to the Georgia Historical Society in Savannah, where I met the impressive and charming Lilla M. Hawes, then its director. I soon created the beginnings of a massive filing system. When my work with the Quirigua Project ended in 1976, I began to go more frequently to the Georgia Department of Archives and History in Atlanta. Following the advice of its director at the time, Carroll Hart, who counseled me to complete the title search for the whole island, I began to study the colonial grants and plats. "If you complete the title search," said Carroll, "everything else will fall into place." That was good advice.

More and more I realized how little had been written about the island. What little there was skipped lightly over the Spanish occupation, omitted the American Revolution, tore through the Civil War, and hurried on to describe the Carnegie administration, which was always presented as little short of princely. With the advent of the Cumberland Island National Seashore, Louis Torres, a historian on contract to the National Park Service, completed an excellent short history of the island. By this time, with the assistance of J. Edwin Godley, then clerk of the county commissioners, I had introduced myself to Camden County's courthouse, where the county records are kept. The court officers and staff treated me with great kindness. Although Camden County's records had

already been microfilmed, I am glad now that I took the time to look at the
original records.

By 1980 a three-by-five-inch card file that I called "Personal Biographical"
contained notes on more than two hundred people who had inhabited the island at one time or another, many of them almost totally obscure. No matter. If
I thought someone had ever set foot on Cumberland, he or she went into my
magic file. My proudest catch was Aboo, a slave of Louisa Shaw in the 1820s
who was mentioned only once in Shaw's will. I was astonished to find three letters written in the 1850s by Mrs. Aboo Shaw of Hartford, Connecticut, a prac-
titioner of homeopathic nursing, at the Southern Historical Collection at the
University of North Carolina at Chapel Hill.

Finding such information is not easy; using it is even harder. I kept thinking,
"What about all these obscure people I now know who lived on Cumberland?
Isn't anyone interested in them? Can I write about them?" Kenneth H. Thomas
Jr. of the Georgia Department of Natural Resources encouraged me to consider
publication. Diffident about my own abilities, I took his advice. On the as-
sumption that island residents and their lives could be made interesting if they
appeared in their proper historical settings, I published three titles on my own.
Each book was a small contribution to the history of Cumberland.

I have not wanted until now to write about my own family. We Carnegies,
torn away from our land, realize instinctively that its loss means the partial dis-
solution of our family. Cumberland Island fed into each of our lives. Therefore,
I can imagine that the island was just as important for others. The Carnegies
are no more or less alien to Cumberland than all the others who resided here.
Although we loved Cumberland, it wasn't always perfect. There were disappointments here. Still, it was our island. The timelessness of this small and isolated island, which seems never to change, creates this intimacy.

The island itself is enlisted as a character. Its overgrown fields and muddy
landing places are as familiar to Cumberland Islanders as their own homes. All
of the island's roads and trails bear local names, some of them more than two
hundred years old. We know these paths and trails, and we resent changes.
Early island residents were startled, as we still are today, by the unexpected appearance of Lake Whitney's blue water and brilliantly white sand hills. Cumberland's long, empty Atlantic beach, with its crowds of sandpipers and ring-
necked plovers skittering before the surf, amazed American Revolutionary
officers and amazes present-day visitors. Little has changed. Time stands still.
But there is another dimension in addition to timelessness.

Contemporary islanders are not alone on the island. We share Cumberland's terrain with its fauna, with which we sometimes live on almost intimate terms. Once, in 1975, I began to climb down a steep trail from the high bluff where Fort St. Andrew once stood. My cautious descent was terrifyingly interrupted by a wild horse scrambling upward. Horse and human were utilizing an old horse path to the great marshes extending to the southwest below Cumberland's High Point. It was a humbling experience. While land use on the island has varied considerably, Cumberland has always been home to animals, birds, and insects. Human residents have learned to live with these other creatures. Cumberland is more than a beautiful landscape; it is a landscape with figures. Despite our difficulty accommodating rattlesnakes and sandflies, we coexist.

Not all the people who came to Cumberland found sanctuary there, and some, quite frankly, were anxious to leave. The hardship of field labor by Cumberland's slave population did not make island residence endearing to them. Yet even so, a freedmen's settlement put down roots during Reconstruction, and its members grew to be especially close to the island.

I have never lived on Cumberland for long periods of time; nevertheless, I feel I know its rhythms well. Visitors coming nowadays to the national seashore feel it still. Lawrence Durrell, the English poet and essayist, found vivid words for *islomania*, a pathology that he said afflicted him and his friends. "There are people," he wrote, "who find islands somehow irresistible. The mere knowledge that they are on an island fills them with an indescribable intoxication. . . . we all of us, by tacit admission, knew ourselves to be islomanes."[1]

In the early 1970s, shortly before he sold his island land, my brother, Oliver G. Ricketson III, wrote a poignant letter to his children. He lamented his inability to write the island's history.

> Cumberland Island has been an influential factor in the lives of your father, grandfather and great-grandfather, and undoubtedly will be an influence in your lives, even if, as is likely, it soon becomes part of the public domain. It is perhaps fit and proper that it once again revert to the public domain, for the original inhabitants, Indians, had no concept of the private ownership of land as do we. . . . My generation of cousins has been profoundly influenced by the island, some for the better and some for the worse. . . . None of them seemed to have either the ability or the time to write of Cumberland. As if we were watching a boat which had been washed ashore on Cumberland and disappears into the sand in a week, our own lives are so brief that the sands of time overwhelm us as remorselessly as the tide on the beach.

We all shared what Oliver felt. The first to sell his home land, he recognized its importance to him. When we leave our land, something leaves us, and like a beached boat, we fear that we may disappear from Cumberland without leaving a trace. Perhaps my brother's chief omission was that he had never realized how many other Cumberland Islanders entertained the same proprietary feelings long before the Carnegies. Here is a new version of Cumberland's history, with a tip of the hat to the island for enriching our lives. Human, beetle, bobcat, otter, horse—we are islomanes, and we call Cumberland Island our home.

ACKNOWLEDGMENTS

My first book was *An Abandoned Black Settlement on Cumberland Island, Georgia*, about a freedmen's community at Brick Hill. I called it a *settlement* because the blacks' title to the land was not fully valid. The book dealt with a short period during Reconstruction in which freedmen's actions were greatly influenced by their family relationships. Extrapolating from Herbert Gutman's *The Black Family in Slavery and Freedom, 1750–1925,* I suggested that just like the white families who lived on plantations, many freedmen often became closely attached to their homes and closely identified with the same land as did the whites. Some of Cumberland's freedmen had lived on the island before the Civil War. Slave ownership affected kinship patterns and interfamily relationships. Since kinship was the motivating factor for the little Brick Hill community, I wish to express my gratitude to some descendants of slave owners, foremost among them Mary Miller of Brunswick, Georgia, who granted access to the Bible of her great-grandfather, John Clubb, in which were written the names of Clubb slaves, and Mildred Frazier of St. Simons Island. Their personal kindnesses were greatly appreciated.

I am also greatly indebted to descendants of former slaves from Cumberland Island, especially George Merrow of Kingsland, whose patience with me was aided by the kindness of his wife, Audrey. Bob Rischarde and Nate Lane contributed mightily in giving me new insights into Stafford's character. Finally, I acknowledge my debt to Cumsie Commodore, born a slave. Although I never met her, Cumsie's words have been drilled into me since childhood by Lucy R. Ferguson, my aunt. I have since met some of Cumsie's descendants, who confirm some of her acute observations.

Kenneth H. Thomas Jr. of the Georgia Department of Natural Resources gave me the idea for my second book, *Black Liberation on Cumberland Island in 1815.* In 1976 Thomas told me that the admiralty logs at the Manuscript

xvii

Division, Library of Congress, were full of information about British Admiral Sir George Cockburn's occupation of Cumberland Island. I left for Washington within a month. During the same visit, I spent ten days at the National Archives at the suggestion of the Library of Congress's Virginia Steele Wood, who shared with me much of her material on Georgia claims after the War of 1812. For assistance at the National Archives, I thank Sally Marks of the Diplomatic Section. I am very grateful to Mary Lyman Cammann of Philadelphia for sharing her research on the Jackson family correspondence. I am also grateful to Lilla M. Hawes for directing my attention to the Blackshear correspondence.

By 1984 I felt I had gathered enough information about Cumberland Island's wealthiest planter to justify pulling together various facets of his previously undocumented life. The result was my third book, *Robert Stafford of Cumberland Island: Growth of a Planter*. I thank three professional researchers: genealogist Gerald M. Cruthers, for his indefatigable labors in Connecticut's probate courts and its state library and in the National Whaling Bank Collection, Mystic Seaport Museum; and Dale Foster and Harold E. Mahan, for their work at the National Archives to determine what, if any, Confederate business transactions Stafford undertook during the Civil War. I also express my appreciation to Virginia Steele Wood and to John E. Ehrenhard of the National Park Service for their critical readings of the manuscript. For assistance on specific legal cases and definitions, I am deeply indebted to lawyers John Scott Talbott and Lyman G. Bullard Jr. For photographic assistance I thank Gerald M. Cruthers, Dorsey Harris, Gerald LePage, Nicholas Whitman, and Anne C. Wyman. Assistance from various institutions, libraries, agencies, and departments referred to within the text came from many persons. I express particular thanks to Elizabeth Alexander, former director of the P. K. Yonge Library of Florida History at the University of Florida, Gainesville; Virginia Shadron, specialist in Georgia law, Georgia Department of Archives and History, Atlanta; Melvin G. Crandall, formerly of the Jekyll Island State Authority; Kenneth H. Thomas, Georgia Department of Natural Resources; Mark A. Mastromarino, Baker Library, Harvard University Business School, Cambridge, Massachusetts; Marion R. Hemperley, surveyor-general's office, secretary of state, Georgia; Anthony R. Dees, Hawes's successor as director of the Georgia Historical Society; and Theresa Ann Singleton, anthropologist, Smithsonian Institution. I also thank Superintendent Kenneth Morgan, Cumberland Island National Seashore, who commissioned a report on Pierre Bernardey that stimulated my research on

Georgia's French residents in the 1790s. I also particularly thank Elias B. Bull of Charleston, whom I first met in the Microfilm Library, South Carolina Historical Society, where I asked him if he had ever heard of an obscure South Carolinian named Peter Belin. He said, "Of course," which floored me, and generously shared his extensive research on this Cumberland Island planter.

I am grateful to friends and colleagues who have cheered me up, helped with transportation, showed great curiosity about the nature of my research, and, for one reason or another, indicated their strong belief that work on a Cumberland Island history was worth doing. No one has been more helpful than my friend Virginia Steele Wood. Others include Chet Benson, Matilda Bridges, the late Joseph Copp, Nancy and Dan Copp, Eugenia W. Howard, Richard C. Kugler, Nate Lane, Helen G. Litrico, Barbara Lutz, Mary Miller, Bernard Nicolau Nightingale, Madena Proctor, Burt Rhyne, Bob Rischarde, Merita Rozier, Anne Shelander, the late Richard K. Showman, Gordon B. Smith, Margaret R. Sprague, and Eloise Y. Bailey Thompson. In the spring of 1982 I was invited to go through a collection at the Coastal Georgia Historical Society. A visitor asked me what I was doing. When I said that I was working on a history of Cumberland Island, with a sly grin he asked me if I had ever heard of Mrs. James Shaw of Dungeness. I am greatly indebted to Professor J. K. Johnson, Carleton University, Ottawa, for illuminating a hidden aspect of Phineas M. Nightingale's financial life.

Many agencies, libraries, and societies gave generously of their time and skills for this project. I could not have worked without the resources of the library of the Boston Athenaeum and particularly without the assistance of Stephen Nonack and Cynthia English of its reference library and Sally Pierce of its print department. For issuing an invitation to lecture on Stafford, I thank the Athenaeum's director at the time, Rodney Armstrong, and staff member Donald Kelley. My gratitude goes to Bruce S. Chappell of the P. K. Yonge Library of Florida History, who provided me with a dictionary of eighteenth-century Spanish so I could read documents from the library's East Florida Papers, Spanish Borderlands Collection, and to archaeologist Jerald Milanich of the University of Florida's Department of Anthropology. One of this project's greatest surprises was a telephone call from England identifying a living descendant of an 1815 slave refugee. For information about Polydore McNish, I wish to thank Althea McNish and her husband, John Weiss, both of London. I am grateful to composer Walter H. Robinson for alerting me to a Howard University alumni yearbook that provided additional information about Stafford.

For architectural advice about Dungeness, I am greatly indebted to Robert G. Neiley, AIA, and Ellen Ehrenhard, Newnan Historical Society. S. F. D. Hughes, visiting professor at Harvard University, generously shared his knowledge of old Scandinavian languages and helped me understand the origin of the name *Dungeness*. I am grateful to Richard A. Shrader, Southern Historical Collection, University of North Carolina at Chapel Hill, for his help. The entire staff of the Georgia Department of Archives and History in Atlanta have been extraordinarily helpful over the many years I did research there, including giving me rides back to my hotel when walking became too hard for me: I am particularly grateful to Elizabeth Knowlton of the manuscripts department for her kindness and thoroughness in sharing her comprehensive knowledge of the Carnegie Estate Records. And finally, I acknowledge with gratitude all responses from the Cumberland Island National Seashore office in St. Marys, relayed to me with humor and accuracy by Janis H. Davis, secretary to the superintendent.

Cumberland Island: A History

ONE

Cumberland:
A Sea Island

Waterways

A chain of islands extends along the Atlantic coast from Cape Hatteras, North Carolina, to Talbot Island, Florida. Almost 24,000 acres, Cumberland Island is one of the largest of these barrier islands, the southernmost Sea Island in Georgia, lying almost adjacent to the Florida border and about 17.5 miles long by 3 miles wide. It is often called Great Cumberland to distinguish it from its smaller neighbor, 1,400-acre Little Cumberland Island.

Great Cumberland is a continental island, meaning that its core or inland portion consists of Pleistocene sediments. Deposited prior to the last ice age, this section of the coast was cut off from the mainland by a slow rise in sea level. Great and Little Cumberland Islands together form a good example of what geologists call a composite barrier island. Meanderings and channel erosion of the St. Andrews and St. Marys estuaries have reworked the northern and southern extremities of this composite island into a series of seaward sand spits. Little Cumberland, a beach ridge island, can be reached from its "parent island" by crossing a wide tidal creek, now called Christmas Creek, which may once have been an inlet. The two islands are still separating from each other as a result of the rising sea level.[1]

Almost one-third of Cumberland Island is salt marsh. Its ocean beach is thirteen miles long. Rarely since the disappearance of the Spanish mission in the seventeenth century has its population numbered more than 500 persons. In 1850 the island's population peaked at 520 persons, of whom 65 were white and 455 were black slaves, some of them leased to work on county road and canal projects or to private landowners "off island," a term used for the mainland. When such projects were finished, these slaves returned to their homes and gardens on Cumberland. The island's chief products from the mid-eighteenth to mid–nineteenth century were horses and cattle, live oak for shipbuilding, indigo, corn, cotton, and, less certainly, rice. In the 1780s the abundant timber on both Cumberland and Little Cumberland was valued more highly than cotton.

From the perspective of early mariners, the low coastal islands of Georgia and Florida formed a long barrier against the open sea. Like all such islands, Cumberland has always benefited and suffered because of the sea and the tides. In 1753 Jonathan Bryan, a South Carolina planter in the process of moving to Georgia, described Cumberland and its neighboring waters in glowing terms:

> It is separated from the Main by Rivers and Marshes, about two or three miles distant from the Mainland. . . . St. Marys River vents itself into Amelia Inlet, between the South End of Cumberland and the North End of Amelia Island. . . . We were informed by a Person who had been four days row up the River that there were several fine high Bluffs upwards and there was the greatest quantity of fine cedar that he had seen . . . that on the sides of [St. Marys] River was fine swamps for rice. . . . The Lands on and near the head of this River is very open and Grassy so that a Person may see Miles before him. . . . these lands are full of wild cattle and Buffalo.[2]

However, in a 1785 letter to French diplomat Compte de la Forest, American surveyor Benjamin Hawkins gave a more negative view:

> In your American Atlas you have a tolerable good map of the seacoast islands, harbors and depth of water; but I do not recollect any treatise which describes the soil and timber of the islands or the lands bordering on the inland navigation. The latter are very low and everywhere sandy except the salt marsh and swamp on the rivers. The larger growth is yellow pine with some fine groves (called in [Georgia] Hammocks) of the live-oak. [The largest islands in Georgia—Cumberland, St. Simons, St. Catharines, and Sapelo—]are edged . . . with Liveoak, the soil where this grows is always the best and very good for corn or indigo; [in] the middle of them or bordering on the sea the soil is sandy and apparently of no other use than of being a barrier against the waves of the sea, the growth is small scrubby pine, brush and palmetto. I believe there is not more than one third of the land capable of cultivation on any of the islands situated out of the freshes.[3]

Through the inlets—or "lets," as they were called—that separated the barrier islands, early sailing vessels slipped away from the ocean, either to ride at anchor in such deep water as they could find amid the wide salt marshes of Georgia's coast or to sail the long, relatively narrow bodies of water that separated the coastal islands from the mainland. These bodies of water comprised river mouths, bays, and sounds. All together, they made the Inland Navigation, a riverlike passage that winds through a wide belt of salt marsh, ranges in width from four to six miles, and is broken by the various lets and sounds. Known today as the Inland Waterway, in the eighteenth century it was often called the Inland Passage. Early travelers noted that by taking advantage of the Inland Passage, one could sail from Fernandina to Philadelphia without once venturing into the open ocean, a great advantage in the days of small sailing vessels. The portion of the Inland Passage that passes Cumberland Island is called Cumberland River, although it is not technically a river.

At the southern tip of Cumberland, where the island narrows to a half mile, sailing vessels entered the Inland Navigation by passing through St. Marys Inlet. This inlet was vital in human utilization of the island; significantly, European occupation of Cumberland almost surely began at its south point because of this let. Artesian springs once percolated up through its waters, providing a source of fresh water for mariners.[4] By 1800 the inlet was well known to navigators as the best way to enter the St. Marys Basin, whose broad, interior waterways separate eastern Florida and southeast Georgia and thus constitute the most efficient way to exploit the area's vast timber stands. At Cumberland's northern end lies St. Andrew Sound. The Cumberland River connects St. Marys Basin and the sound.

All the Sea Islands have what are called *dividings,* shoal areas behind the barrier islands where the tides meet and divide. The resulting ebb and flow creates sand deposition that in turn creates unexpected sandbanks and sandbars. These dividings were serious drawbacks in the days of small sailing craft, canoes and piraguas, and rowing galleys. Even now, the dividings require periodic dredging. Nineteenth-century maps of the barrier islands nearly always show points in the Inland Navigation marked by names such as "Mud Creek," "the Divide," or "the Narrows."

The Cumberland Dividings are the point in the Cumberland River where the tides reverse themselves. At this line the daily tides flow out in opposite directions at an ebb tide and flow toward one another at a flood tide. Contrary winds at an ebb tide often forced sailing vessels to wait as long as six hours until the tide changed.

The Cumberland Dividings hindered eighteenth-century sailing vessels. In 1742 two attacking Spanish fleets from St. Augustine sailed north to destroy Fort Frederica on St. Simons Island. The sea fleet was instructed to tack back and forth far out to sea to synchronize its arrival at St. Simons Bar with the slower inland flotilla. Edward Kimber, who went with James Oglethorpe's expedition to attack St. Augustine, departed Frederica on 27 February 1743 on one of the small fleet of schooners ordered south. In the Cumberland River on 1 March, Kimber's ship "struck on a Bank near the Dividers." The next day the ship struck on another mud bank, where it lay until the tide changed, allowing the oarsmen to heave off with the flood. Kimber reported, "The reason of our so frequently running aground, was the extreme Length of our Vessell, which was too long to tack in these Inland Straits, where the Channel is very narrow."[5] Island inhabitants frequently provided visitors with expert local pilotage through the various "Mud Creeks" and "Narrows" of the Inland Passage. Travelers sometimes used the locals' marks. William Gerard DeBrahm, a British mapmaker, indicated a narrows on his 1770 map of Amelia Island, marking it by the words "Pine tree—a mark to go through the Narrows," adding, "At this point the Tides meet."[6]

All of coastal Georgia is subject to considerable tidal variation, in some places ranging from seven to ten feet. The inlets nearly always were fronted by bars, large underwater spits of sand formed by wind, current, and tidal action. At best, these bars formed obstacles to easy entrance; at worst, they created distinct hazards. Breakers—waves breaking in shoal water—signaled the presence of sandbars. Inlets often were called by the names of their bars; hence, St. Marys Bar may be equated with St. Marys Inlet, although they are not the same feature.

The width of St. Marys Inlet varied but was generally under a mile. Although its depth was highly variable until modern jetty construction, early-nineteenth-century maps and charts indicate that the inlet was approximately fourteen feet deep at low water. Being narrow, St. Marys Inlet had a natural tendency to scour, providing a moderately deep channel at all tides. However, tidal currents at the entrance to this inlet have considerable velocity and can be dangerous, especially at flood tide. Prolonged onshore winds sometimes generate unusually high tides. The mean range of tide is 6.8 feet, but when winds reach fifty knots or more, tidal surges of 8 to 10 feet above normal can occur. Once safely across St. Marys Bar and inside its inlet, sailing vessels could proceed north through the Cumberland River, south to Florida through the Jolly and Nassau Rivers, or west upstream more than sixty miles to the head of navigation on the St. Marys River.

St. Marys Inlet now merely separates Georgia from Florida, but for centuries the inlet and the St. Marys River formed an international frontier border between Spain and Britain. When European mariners first touched New World coasts, they sought inlets through which they could sail to seek meat and fresh water and to repair and clean their ships. The first foreigners to visit the Sea Islands generally intended to return to St. Augustine and Havana or directly to Europe. Rarely did they plan settlement on an isolated island such as Cumberland, although in the mid–sixteenth century French and Spanish ships visited it to gather sassafras, then thought by Europeans to cure venereal diseases. To early mapmakers, inlets were useful in marking the location of a given island, but since inlets can open and close, early French and Spanish shipmasters have left little in the way of charts for St. Marys Inlet. Sailors and fishermen gave human value to inlets, seeking harbors of refuge within the Inland Navigation.

Both the Cumberland River's length and the Cumberland Dividings presented real obstacles to coastal navigation. In addition, the entrance to St. Andrew Sound from the ocean was considered dangerous. Mariners are often reluctant to cross the bar or the sound because both are full of shoals. About five miles wide, the depth of St. Andrew Sound ranged from forty-two to sixty feet. St. Andrew Sound is entered over a shifting bar that extends about five miles offshore. Two large rivers, the Great and Little Satillas, empty into the sound, carrying thousands of pounds of silt, which means the sound changes its underwater configuration with dangerous rapidity. Sandbars appear and disappear with no particular surface evidence. When the Little Satilla River, which enters Jekyll Sound from the west, is in freshet, the entrance to St. Andrew Sound is affected. Its shifting bar moves, lengthens, and diminishes in proportion to the river freshets. In St. Andrew Sound's extensive shoals lie submerged three channels that lead to its principal tributaries: Jekyll Sound to the north, Satilla River to the west, and Cumberland River to the south. Since Cumberland River empties into St. Andrew Sound at a point just inside Little Cumberland Island, it is almost impossible for sailing vessels to travel through the channel leading to the Cumberland River at ebb tide.

No other way exists to enter St. Andrew Sound from the north. Great Cumberland is separated from Little Cumberland by a salt marsh through which winds a tidal waterway called Christmas Creek. At one time it was wider and deeper, but sand deposition has silted up its ocean mouth. Even the smallest canoes or piraguas have long been unable to sail or paddle through the creek to the ocean.[7]

In the eighteenth century the Spanish referred to Fort St. Andrews as a settlement on the "Isla de Vejeces," also spelled *Bejeces* or *Bajeses*. Since the Spanish words *bajezas*, *bajos*, and *bajiales* mean "low places," "shoal places," or "sandbars," these early charts were calling St. Andrew Sound the "Sound of Shoals." The Sound of Shoals provided a home for certain sea mammals, most notably pilot whales.[8] From the 1790s to the present, humans have dredged, canalled, and cut through the great marshes in an effort to straighten the Inland Navigation, but the waterways remain essentially the same as they were in the 1560s.

The inland water routes were rarely used for long-distance north-south shipments. It was generally quicker and cheaper to make long transports by sea. Naval stores; red oak for ships, staves, and shingles; and other forms of lumber from the Chesapeake region generally continued to reach New York and New England by coasting schooner. For coastal shipping and for getting goods to a port, the southern states, with their numerous lengthy but shallow rivers, made the greatest efforts at improving inland navigation. By the late 1780s many southern legislatures subsidized canal companies. After the War of 1812 the upland sections of Georgia began to demand better means of transportation to ship out their cotton, and in 1817 Georgia made its first appropriations for river improvement. However, actual improvements were slow to come and were disappointing. By 1829, when coastal efforts petered out, river navigation had been little improved. In the South, where there was little to fear from winter storms and ice, the deepening of channels to coastal or river ports constituted the bulk of the project. In the late 1830s the bar obstructing the harbor entrance to Brunswick was tackled with horse- and steam-powered dredging machines. Since the early East Coast projects focused on making harbors accessible to seagoing ships, work on inland waterways was negligible and was hampered by localism.

After 1880, with the buildup of emigration to Florida, coastal businessmen in Georgia and Florida began to see certain advantages to reviving the Inland Navigation, especially their portion of it. In 1884 the channel between the St. Johns River in Florida and St. Marys Harbor in Georgia was one of the first stretches of the Inland Navigation to be improved by federal funding. By the late 1850s the coastal steamer, with a flat-bottomed hull, a keel that protruded only slightly, and a shallow-dipping paddle wheel, was perceived to be even more suited than the schooner to the relatively shoal waters of the Inland Navigation. Between 1870 and 1880 the Cumberland Route—that section of the Inland Navigation that included the Cumberland River and Cumberland Sound—developed as a local response to revived interest in the Inland Passage. The Cumberland Route allowed small steamboats to make rail connections with the Georgia hinterland.

Along with boat traffic and food supply, almost every aspect of life on the Sea Islands is controlled by the sea and particularly by the tides. Their daily rise and fall determine the grazing patterns of island horses and cows as well as many islanders' food-gathering activities, such as oystering, crabbing, and fishing. It takes only a few minutes for an incoming tide to fill a narrow creek. During the short time when the incoming tide stealthily creeps through the steep, dripping-mud banks, herons and raccoons watch for incoming fish and shrimp. At the spring tide in autumn, when high water completely inundates the *spartina* marsh, hunters can go over the marsh in flat-bottomed boats and collect dozens of raccoons clinging to islets of grass and mud.

Settlers used the tides when they could and found deeper, calmer havens for their harbors. By 1800 the principal local harbors were Cumberland Harbor, Amelia Island Harbor, and Lynches Creek at Cumberland as well as the mouths of such rivers as the St. Marys and Great Satilla. The harbor at the city of St. Marys, laid out in 1788, was long considered the best on the southeastern coast, surpassing that of St. Augustine. To land on Cumberland from St. Marys Inlet meant rounding South Point and then tying up at one of the relatively few deepwater landing places along the island's western shore. South Point, a low-lying island with a source of freshwater, is connected to Cumberland by a spine-like sand spit.

Humans harnessed tidal power to suit their needs. The first sawmills to appear in the St. Marys Basin were tidal sawmills or wind and tidal sawmills, at least one of them on Cumberland Island. Various Spanish charts of the 1790s show *molinos* (mills) on some of the larger, inhospitable tidal islands on which there was almost no agricultural activity. In 1796 Nathaniel Pendleton described thriving St. Marys and its burgeoning sawmills:

> There are a few . . . streams on the St. Marys and on Great Satilla, where saw mills may be erected for cutting timber to supply the West Indies and where vessels may come and carry it away. . . . for ship building there are a great number of creeks on which are situations proper for framing and launching ships into the water. . . . No river in America has pine timber equal to that on St. Marys, nor so many situations convenient for shipping it away, on account of the great number of Bluffs, and the depth of the water.[9]

Even though diplomatic relations between Spain and the United States were sometimes tense, on the local level Spanish and Georgian authorities frequently cooperated, putting out *balizas* (buoys) to mark the entrance to

St. Marys Inlet or repairing the harbor entrance after abnormal weather conditions, such as hurricanes. Because of the privateers and smugglers who plied Florida and Georgia's waterways, Americans and Spanish alike did their share to mark the entrance to Fernandina. When a state boundary is formed by a river, its midchannel is taken as the center of the boundary. As every boatman knows, however, the deepest part of a channel is found not in midriver but generally toward the outermost part of a bend. During the period of U.S. history when various Embargo Acts cut off American trade with warring European powers, ships from all nations used Fernandina as a port because through it they could obtain American cargoes in Spanish waters. A narrow back river called Spanish Creek, which cut through the marshes at the back of Tiger Island, divided the Spanish waters of St. Marys River from the main U.S. channel. Historical archaeologist John W. Griffin credited this creek with Fernandina's sudden prosperity in 1817: "Through this communication was conveyed the produce of the southern of the United States . . . for shipment at Amelia. So great was the trade of that island during the operation of [the U.S. Embargo Acts] that three hundred sail of square-rigged vessels were seen in the Spanish waters waiting for cargoes."[10]

Seaman Jacob Nagle wrote in his journal in 1807 that Spanish Fernandina had become the destination for British ships seeking American cotton smuggled from the nearby Sea Islands to St. Marys Basin, technically neutral.

> The Amelia Island then belong'd to the Spaniard, but at this time was the Embargo in America, therefore the English came to this place for cotton, smugled over in schooner from the main[land], where the English ships lay'd and loaded. Cape St. Mares [St. Marys] lays opposite, where a Merican gun boat was stationed as a guard ship. It is very shoal water coming into this harbor. . . . In about three weeks we receiv'd cotton as fast as we could stow it away.[11]

Sovereignty over Cumberland's waterways greatly influenced local trade patterns. Cumberland Island was situated at the point where two national jurisdictions met. For example, Americans were prohibited during the early 1800s from buying European iron. A Swedish ship loaded with iron ingots from the Baltic could cross the Atlantic and anchor in Spanish waters off Fernandina. If the ship paid a tax (called the *trasbordo*) to the Spanish customs officials, the cargo could be off-loaded in Spanish waters. The local American entrepreneur could then load up his vessel, which might be as small as a sailing skiff or even a cotton flat, and slip through Spanish Creek to the United States to sell the iron ingots to St. Marys blacksmiths. In this way, American traders successfully avoided the U.S. gunboats guarding St. Marys Inlet.

During the years of the Napoleonic Wars and the continental blockade (1799–1815), an enormous number of foreign vessels came to Spanish Fernandina, partly because of these opportunities. Proximity to St. Marys gave Fernandina a feeling of complacency about its business future; unfortunately, these hopes for continued prosperity were not realized in later years. Many undercapitalized St. Marys merchants easily increased their capital by opening small stores selling contraband European goods to commission agents from Savannah and Augusta.

Cumberland Island is not far offshore. Although, as Bryan wrote, Cumberland Island is "about two or three miles distant from the Mainland," his statement needs amplification. The broad expanse of salt marsh that borders high land on either side of the Inland Navigation effectively blocks direct east-west passage. Ships had to wind through the marshes to find a channel. The marshes hid suitable landing places for cargo. Ships looked for bluffs where they could unload, even if they had to use a lighter to ferry their shipments ashore. From a landing on the island, such as Lynches Creek, to the port of St. Marys, about four miles from the river's mouth, the distance is six miles. But to animals that swim across the Inland Passage, the Cumberland Dividings is the narrowest point. Between Crooked River and Black Point the open waterway narrows considerably, and the distance between high land on the mainland and high land on Cumberland Island is about three hundred yards. Deer, bear, and horses could easily swim that far.

Cumberland Island's waterways influenced human and animal utilization of the island. Until the advent of airplanes, access to the island depended completely on water passage.

Coastal Indians and Spanish Values

In the 1550–60s Indian and European cultures may have first met in peaceful trade. Although European traders often visited the Sea Islands, these visitors have left little in the historic record. In 1932 an aboriginal Indian canoe was excavated from the mud flats of Cumberland Island. Constructed from a single pine log, its interior had been hollowed out by fire. Finishing work was probably done with shell tools. One end had been broken off, possibly by the weight of the mud that had preserved it. Coastal tribes were already familiar with intra-Indian trading techniques and could travel great distances both on land and at sea.[12] A crew of nine or ten Indians could man an oceangoing canoe, some of which were twenty-five or thirty feet long. Thoroughly exposed to customs and trade far beyond their boundaries, they were certainly aware of passing European vessels and must often have observed beached ships. For Europeans coasting in unfamiliar waters, careening their ships—pulling vessels out of water to get at their hulls to make structural repairs—was a necessary activity. European mariners sought fresh water not only to fill their water barrels but also to rid their ships' hulls of marine growths. When ships were careened, the sailors pitched tents or made huts for shelter, hunted game, fished, or explored the anchorage for future use. Sometimes finding shipboard life beyond endurance, mariners occasionally sought relief by jumping ship. From time to time, sailors were put ashore as punishment, but written records for Cumberland were scanty. Cumberland Island undoubtedly saw some runaway mariners. Beach Creek was an especially good landing site for careening ships.[13] Conflicts began when traders cheated or abused the natives.

When the first Europeans arrived in the 1550s, the Timucua Indians occupied most of the northern third of peninsular Florida and a small portion of southeastern Georgia. The Timucua who occupied the coastal marshes and oak hammocks of Cumberland Island and its adjacent mainland were called the Tacatacuru.[14]

As a whole, the Timucua could hardly be called a nation. About seven Timucuan tribes lived in or near northeastern coastal Florida and southeastern coastal Georgia. When the eastern Timucua first encountered French adventurers in 1562, the Indians retained a way of life unchanged from that of at least a millennium earlier. It took only one hundred years, however, for the effects of European contact to reduce—and ultimately to eliminate—the Indian culture. In 1620 Father Francisco Pareja identified nine Timucuan dialects, one of which, the Mocamo dialect, was spoken by Indians from Cumberland to St. Augustine and was sometimes referred to as the main language of the Timucua. When the large Spanish Church of San Pedro was built on Cumberland Island in 1603, it was named San Pedro de Mocamo. Thus, Mocamo was Cumberland's original name. Mocamo-speaking Indians were found at least as far north as the mission of San Buenaventura de Guadalquini on Jekyll Island in the 1670s.[15]

It is not known how many Timucua lived on Cumberland or on the Georgia coast. Some French comments made in 1568 suggest coastal populations between fifteen and twenty thousand, but the Timucuan population declined when epidemics struck in 1613–17, 1649–50, and 1672. Spanish missionary efforts redoubled in the mid-1600s, and after 1650 the archaeological evidence indicates that eastern Timucuan culture was replaced by elements of the Guale culture.[16]

The Guale Indians lived on most of Georgia's coast as well as on some coastal islands and possibly as far north as South Carolina. Guale control of the coast, and consequently of Cumberland, hindered Spanish expansion. Although more scattered than the Timucua, the Guale may have been culturally more homogeneous. Distinguished archaeologist Lewis H. Larson has suggested that the Altamaha River was the southern limit of Guale territory, observing that "it may not be entirely coincidental" that this mighty river marks the southern boundary of the range of *Quercus alba L,* a white oak of major importance for natives of the Georgia coast, who sought its acorn crop.[17]

Between 1560 and 1600 the Guale and the Mocamo had a large number of settlements scattered among the coastal islands and on the neighboring mainland. As late as the first years of the seventeenth century, most of the Guale settlements and missions were on the mainland rather than on the Sea Islands, to which they migrated later. The Tacatacuru, conversely, appear to have been largely an island people. With the exception of the Tacatacuru, all the eastern Timucuan tribes of the southeast Georgia mainland occupied and exploited environmental zones of the coastal plain. They utilized the freshwater marshes, rivers, and lakes as well as the pine forests. The Tacatacuru, however, are believed to have exploited the salt-marsh lagoons and live oak hammocks of the coastal islands. They depended on shellfish, fish, and the mammals of the live oak hammocks.[18]

European contact with the Tacatacuru was long and intensive. Among the first export items noticed by European traders was sassafras, and the island of San Pedro Mocamo was described as the center of the sassafras trade.[19] After the Guale rebellion, which began in 1582 and was subdued by Governor Gonzalo Méndez de Canzo in the mid-1590s, French sassafras traders came and went unhindered, occasionally dropping off a crew member as a factor to make up the next cargo.[20]

Europeans were greatly interested in Indian medicinal techniques. In 1569 Nicolás Monardes, a Spanish physician, wrote a book entitled *Joyful News from the New Found World.* One of the medicinal plants that he described at length was "the Tree that is Brought from the Florida, which is called Sassafras." He understood that it grew only in certain places, in Santa Elena (Port Royal) in Carolina and in San Mateo on the St. Johns River in Florida. But stands of sassafras trees also grew in other estuarine areas, where the trees were conspicuous as a second growth. Indians used the sassafras tree for house frames, for fire sticks, for bows, and as a valuable deep yellow dye. When steeped in boiling water and made into a sort of tea, its fleshy, sticky root brought relief to sick sailors. The infusion was supposed to be particularly useful for reducing fevers, curing headaches, stopping colds, helping lameness, and relieving constipation. In 1682 an Englishman wrote that sassafras "profits in all Diseases of the blood, and Liver, particularly in all Venereal and Scorbutick Distempers." The root was so valuable that Florida sassafras sold in Spain for £18 per ton. Such prices lured European mariners to find investors for a sassafras trade. Possibly because of its success as a center for sassafras trade, San Pedro was described as "the head of the other maritime pueblos, even larger than the presidio at St. Augustine."[21] Because it was a safe harbor, Cumberland's South End became the site of the most prominent marketplace for French and Spanish coastal traders.

After the Spanish established a colony at St. Augustine in 1565, the Tacatacuru were the object of one of the earliest attempts at conversion. Governor Pedro Menéndez de Avilés's agreement with the king of Spain expressly stipulated that the spiritual welfare of the Indians be carefully guarded. The Tacatacuru originally had sought to identify with the French: in fact, in 1567 a cacique pledged support to the Frenchman Dominique de Gourges. In 1566 a ship was dispatched from Spain with supplies for Florida, and at that date, in response to repeated requests, the Jesuits sent three missionaries, the first sent to convert the native Floridians. A storm prevented the ship from reaching St. Augustine in September of that year. Instead, the Flemish shipmaster had Father Pedro Martinez and a party of sailors put ashore on Cumberland Island. The castaways' subsequent wanderings are difficult to follow, but it appears that they went some distance up the St. Marys River, retraced their steps, and reached the vicinity of Fort George Island before being attacked by Indians, who killed Father Martinez and many of the other Europeans.[22]

In 1572 the Crown ordered the Jesuit friars in Florida to go to Mexico. Their departure left Florida without Christian instruction. Franciscan friars, hoping to succeed where the Jesuits had failed, entered the field soon after their predecessors abandoned it. In the mid-1570s the Franciscan order received permission to missionize Florida, and by the late 1570s they took up missionary work in this coastal area. They encountered considerable resistance, culminating in the Guale rebellion of 1582. Not until 1583, with the arrival of Father Alonzo de Reynoso, did the Franciscans begin to meet with something like success in the missionary movement. In 1587 a Franciscan priest, Father Baltazar López, arrived on Cumberland to administer to the Tacatacuru and to reestablish the San Pedro mission. Henceforth, the largest Spanish mission on Cumberland Island was often called San Pedro de Tacatacuru.[23]

Establishing their various stations about 1590, the Franciscans prospered for several years. In 1597, however, the Indians revolted under the leadership of Juanillo, a young *mico* (chieftain) whose political aspirations had been discouraged by the friars. The revolt collapsed after an unsuccessful attempt to storm the island of San Pedro, where the local chief remained loyal to the Spaniards. As soon as he could organize a punitive expedition, Governor Méndez de Canzo marched into Guale territory, burned the towns and cornfields, and forced most of the Indians into submission, although Juanillo remained at large. In 1601 a second punitive expedition set out, and the chiefs who had surrendered were called on to conquer their former allies. During this period Juanillo was killed. For almost three-quarters of a century (1601–70) after the second uprising, the Indians of Guale submitted to Spanish rule.[24]

In addition to converting the Indians, the Franciscan missions were expected to link the dispersed coastal Spanish garrisons. Documents indicate that the friars also provided help to distressed mariners. Luis Jeronimo de Oré reported stopping for supplies at Cumberland Island on his return from a 1588 voyage of exploration that had taken him almost to Chesapeake Bay. He visited the island of San Pedro, which he said "at that time was thickly populated by the Indians." The Christian (baptized) Indians received the navigators and replenished their supplies, as they had arrived in great need.[25]

The religious orders that settled coastal Georgia built missions intended to become centers of market life. It is possible that the San Pedro de Mocamo mission was situated at an already well known sassafras trading area. From 1587 to 1689 Cumberland Island was the site of several Franciscan missions. The largest, San Pedro (named for Saint Peter, the first of the apostles and a fisherman), was occasionally called the capital of Mocamo Province. Its success came in part because a local paramount chief, with authority over certain mainland caciques, became an enthusiastic convert to Christianity, thereby recruiting influential native followers. He may have resided on the island.

San Pedro de Mocamo was almost surely built at the southern end of Cumberland Island, a site determined by St. Marys Inlet. Because all missions were

supposed to conform to a uniform plan, the mission's appearance can be de-
duced from a rare 1691 plan view of a mission compound on nearby Isla de
Santa María (Amelia Island). The Spanish Royal Ordinances (1573) dictated all
practical aspects of New World site selection, city planning, and political organization. Towns were to be established only on vacant lands or where Indians had consented freely to the establishment of settlements. The Crown declared that the ideal town site should be within easy reach of fresh water, fuel,
timber, and native people (presumably for labor purposes).[26]

Each town was supposed to have a plaza, an empty space in the center that
was surrounded by but separated from the *pueblo* (town). Plazas were laid out
first, and the rest of the town was oriented accordingly. In coastal towns the
principal plaza was to be located near the landing place. However, Spanish settlers and friars were not always able to build the mission compounds according
to the Royal Ordinances. The rigid urban plan developed in Spain sometimes
usurped the highest, most desirable residential land for a centralized plaza. Because this was not always practical in New Spain, some settlements grouped the
public buildings, including the church, at the northern end of town rather than
in the center.[27]

In addition to the plaza, the typical Franciscan mission compound contained
three main features, the *convento,* the mission church, and the *atrio.* The complex known as the *convento* was a cloistered building for the friars. Separated
from other mission buildings, it generally consisted of very small, sparsely furnished rooms, usually in a single row facing an interior garden. The *convento*
contained a refectory, where monks ate in silence; their sleeping cells; and a few
specialized rooms, such as a kitchen, granary, offices, and workshops. In many
missions, especially those in the tropics, the *cocina* (kitchen) was a detached
building, although it too faced the *convento*'s central enclosure. Some friaries
also contained a slightly larger room that served as either a library or some form
of communal room.[28]

The second feature was the mission church, a long, rectangular building that
usually took up one whole side of the central plaza. Its facade often was made
of wattle and daub. Since it was important to the friars to symbolize the difference between church nave and *sanctuario,* different building techniques
sometimes were used to distinguish the two. Fronting the church was the third
important feature, a square churchyard (*atrio*), a low-walled enclosure that
marked the public entrance to the church and served as an outdoor chapel for
overflow congregations. The principal church was called the *doctrina.*[29]

Church orientation was an important concern. According to the rigid grid pattern stipulated by the Royal Ordinances, the church was supposed to be "separated from any nearby building . . . and ought to be seen from all sides." The church building was always to dominate the mission compound. Ordinance 120 urged that the temple of the cathedral "where the town is situated on the coast shall be built in part so that it may be seen on going out to sea and in a place where its buildings may serve as a means of defense for the port itself."[50] Even a humble structure, such as a one-story wattle-and-daub church, would be visible for miles over the marshes if it was brilliantly whitewashed.

Local topography sometimes influenced the long axis of the church. At St. Catherines Island, archaeologists noticed that the long axis of the mission church paralleled the intracoastal waterway, a layout that may well have been duplicated on Cumberland Island, since the Inland Passage was the major transportation route along the Georgia coast. From the *pueblo,* Indian converts walked out to tend the fields. Georgia colonists later frequently mentioned "Indian old fields" on the barrier islands.[51]

Before the arrival of the friars, aboriginal Indians had occupied the Sea Islands only sporadically, probably mostly during the winter. The Indians generally made cyclical or seasonal visits to the islands for fish, shellfish, turtles, deer, and other such provisions. By the time the Spanish abandoned the missions (between 1690 and 1702), however, the Timucua were well on their way to becoming accomplished farmers. They had learned that a market existed for their produce, and they had learned to desire European goods. Aboriginal Indians on the Georgia coastal strand evidently had become horticulturists slowly and reluctantly. The first missionaries in the Guale area complained bitterly about how the Indians neglected agriculture in favor of hunting and fishing. Long seasonal junkets in pursuit of game mitigated against a settled populace, and the fathers wanted settlements. After the first contacts with Spanish friars, Indians were observed cultivating small orchards near their villages. As Cumberland Island was said to have been thickly settled by mission Indians (those who had converted to Christianity), it may be supposed that the island had many fields, gardens, and orchards. Orange groves require much care. Since Indian women generally attended to agricultural activities, it may well be that Indian or mestiza women cared for orange groves on Cumberland.[52]

Cacique Don Juan, a Timucuan convert, was a devout Christian supporter. During the Guale rebellion in September 1597, pagans attacked the San Pedro mission, burning it and its church. The Timucuan mission Indians not only sounded the alarm but, led by Don Juan, successfully repelled the attack. In addition, he and his people frequently celebrated mass. Five hundred natives were reported converted before 1593, and Don Juan even asked for more friars. Converts at San Pedro de Mocamo celebrated *Semana Santa* (Holy Week) as lavishly as in Seville itself: Organized into *cofradías* (religious fraternities) to appear in ornate public procession, San Pedro's Christians carried images of the Virgin and Christ. Holy Thursday was spent entirely in religious celebration and revelry, Good Friday in mourning and gloom. Partly as the result of the friars' success with the cacique, a new Mission San Pedro de Mocamo on Cumberland Island, located between Old Tower and Abraham Point, was dedicated on 10 March 1603. Its *doctrina*, made of boards, was said to be remarkably splendid. It may even have had a bell tower. Governor Ibarra reported in 1608 that the new church was as large as the cathedral in St. Augustine and had cost the Indians more than three hundred ducats. Bishop Juan de las Cabezas Altamirano paid his first episcopal visit to San Pedro de Mocamo in 1606, when he baptized 308 natives.[33]

The friars taught the Indians to read and write Spanish, and as early as 1595, villagers at San Pedro de Mocamo were speaking that language. Father Francisco Pareja used his method of writing down the Timucua language to translate primers and devotional books into the native language. Some of the Indians began writing letters to one another. In addition to the responses to the questions of the catechism, the Indians learned the Pater Noster, Ave Maria, and Salve Regina in Latin as well as the sign of the cross and the credo. They memorized the Ten Commandments, the seven deadly sins, the fourteen works of mercy, and other doctrines. Some of the Catholic rites were even translated into Timucua, and a wedding ceremony could easily have included words in Timucua, Spanish, and Latin.[34]

In the early 1660s powerful British investors, subsidized by the British Crown, wanted to encourage Scottish and English settlers. Because Spain maintained no garrison north of the Savannah River after 1657, nothing prohibited English sailors from exploring the coastal area, and several English expeditions reached the Carolinas in an effort to explore lands to the south. The English explorers were instructed to report on agricultural conditions, soil fertility, potential crops, and trade items and to advertise Carolina's advantages. The distinction between English exploration and piracy was very slight, however, and Spanish officials immediately perceived that they would have to do something to forestall English threats beginning to emanate from Carolina.

Even though the Timucuan rebellion of 1656 had interrupted the Spanish mission program, increased missionary activity on Cumberland was the answer. By 1675 a second Franciscan mission, San Felipe de Athulteca, was established on the island.[35]

Anglo-Spanish rivalry between St. Augustine and Cape Fear took many forms. The two nations occasionally cooperated with one another in obtaining the release of European captives. The Indians quickly learned that foreigners sometimes would pay ransoms and that it was possible to play one European nation off another. The Spanish and English were competing for control on Cumberland Island. Increasing Catholic missionary work was one way for the Spanish to keep away the "godless" English.[36]

San Felipe de Athulteca is thought to have been served by two churches— the *doctrina*, which almost certainly remained at the southern end of the island, and a smaller *visita* church, where mass was celebrated only when the presiding priest was able to make his rounds. The *visita* may have been much nearer the island's northern end and likely had only three walls, an open nave for communicants, and a thatched roof. Some historians think it may have been at Brick Hill Bluff or perhaps at Table Point. The presence of two churches on Cumberland suggests a rather large Indian population. In 1688 a stone tower at Table Point was projected to serve as a refuge for the natives, but the six thousand pesos were diverted in St. Augustine, and the tower was never built.[37]

By 1695 the Mocamo and Guale mission settlements were reduced to a few villages: Santa Clara de Tupiqui at the northern end of Amelia Island; Santa María de Guale, the head village, at Harrison Creek in the St. Marys Basin; and San Felipe de Athulteca, a mission settlement on Amelia Island, thought to have moved there during the troubled 1680s from the mission of the same name on Cumberland Island.[38]

When the English settled in Savannah in 1733, they encountered a small group of Yamassee Indians, who greeted the foreigners hospitably. Although the Yamassee Indians originally did not live on Isla San Pedro, pressure from the Yamassees contributed mightily to the downfall of the Franciscan missions. This aggressive group came from "Wallie" (the English spelling for the Guale region), loosely defined as southeastern Georgia. The Yamassees were found over most of the Georgia coast, on some of the coastal islands, and possibly in South Carolina. They spoke a Muskhogean language and are believed to have had other affinities with the inland Indians later known as the Creeks. Comparatively little is known of Yamassee history prior to English settlement. From the beginning of British occupation of coastal Carolina, other Indian groups, especially in the Port Royal area, greatly feared them. Calling them "Yamases, Spanish Comeraros," or "partners of the Spanish," the Port Royal Indians urged the incoming English and Scottish traders to shoot the Yamassees.

Because the Europeans used Indian alliances to further continental diplomatic and military objectives, the terms *Spanish Indians* and *British Indians* soon came into general use. British missionaries for the Propagation of the Gospel in Foreign Parts, arriving in Carolina as early as 1702, noted that the Yamassees were at war with Spain and all its Indian allies.

Mission Indians became victims of both sides. The Creeks joined British interests in burning and destroying all traces of Spanish civilization, including the island missions. In the 1680s–90s British settlers in Carolina comprised a mix of rough privateers and traders, both groups deeply interested in the profits of the slave trade. Reports, letters, and official documents of the period often mention captured seamen who were associated with specific privateers. Race and skin color of all prisoners were important considerations in terms of their potential sale as slaves. Of two Spanish prisoners, for example, the governor of South Carolina wrote in 1720, "One of them seems to be a mestiza, and in trueth the other is not white, but being a liver in St. Augustine for 16 years and has a wife & 8 Children there, I told ye Indians to carry him to your Honour."[39]

San Pedro's mission was heavily fortified, although such was not the case with all Spanish mission complexes. Some merely had a barracks building for the soldiers and quarters of the simplest sort for the commanding officer, with a stockade surrounding the fortification. The Spanish fort on Isla San Pedro appears to have been considerably more than mere barracks, however, and was built in the first half of 1569. Lieutenant Governor Esteban de las Alas had gone to the island of Tacatacuru to punish the Indians for killing Spaniards. For this purpose he chartered the frigate *Nuestra Senora del Piñar* to carry 150 soldiers to lay waste to the "lands of our enemies." In March 1569 four cannon were shipped to Tacatacuru to make up the main battery of artillery. Witnesses to an interrogatory in the Archives of the Indies describe how a company sent from St. Augustine built Fort San Pedro de Tacatacuru from its foundations, with much physical labor.[40]

Two descriptions of the Cumberland Island Spanish fort exist, and therefore something is known about its appearance. It was evidently quite large. A Spanish geographer, López de Velasco, said that the fort of San Pedro was at the bar of "Sena," the Spanish name for the Seine River, once the French name for

St. Marys River. He said the fort maintained about eighty soldiers and had four artillery pieces carrying a total weight of four thousand pounds. The fort was surrounded by a wooden ditch. In 1569 a Spanish military officer, urging repair and increased manpower for Spain's four principal fortifications in Florida, went into considerable detail about San Pedro. He said the fort needed at least one hundred soldiers because the island was so long. The fort was triangular in shape, with wooden casemates and moats. "The soldiers work each day . . . morning and afternoon to put them in perfect condition and to open the moats." Their intensive work may have included bringing more landfill to the plaza, using both earth and the contents of nearby shell middens. The fill would then be compacted by tamping down the soil by using mallets and water.[41]

Life in the missions aimed at making the natives Spanish and Catholic. By the seventeenth century, a system of labor tribute had developed with the Spanish as recipients. The "labor draft" meant that mission Indians were required to serve as burden bearers, transporting foodstuffs, and as stockmen and field laborers. They were required to provide ferry service between the Sea Islands. The mission Indians often complained about not being paid. Mission Indians particularly disliked being forced to provide foodstuffs for soldiers stationed at the presidio. Spanish soldiers were apt to brutalize the mission Indians. This abuse drove away many Indians, both Christian and pagan, who sometimes went over to the English.[42]

Before 1569 the Spanish had envisaged a gradual northward shift of their colonists in *La Florida*. As a result, a large body of Spanish settlers arrived that year in Santa Elena, the new capital, in Carolina. To safeguard their northernmost settlement, the Spanish determined to protect the Inland Navigation from Santa Elena all the way south to St. Augustine by building fortifications along the route. A fort was planned at one of the most endangered points, the island of the hostile Tacatacuru. A Spanish garrison was established on Cumberland in 1569.

Even though the royal government strongly supported colonization, money from the Spanish treasury to pay for the colonists' food and defense was persistently slow in coming. In spite of the Spanish Crown's strong support, supply ships from Spain did not arrive, the garrison could not be supported, adequate clothing and arms for the soldiers were not available, and fortifications began to fall into disrepair, San Pedro among them. Despite recommendations from his engineers and officers for increased fortifications, in 1570 Pedro Menéndez de Avilés ordered a reduction in troop strength at the garrison. Spanish colonists did not settle on Cumberland, and for the next seventeen years there seems to have been little Spanish-Tacatacuru contact.

A 1681 census of Cumberland showed seventy-five adult men, not all Christianized. Because the census was created to show how many able-bodied natives were eligible for the Spanish labor draft, all Indian children and elderly invalids were omitted. Caciques and certain *principales* (married heads of household)—some twenty-nine of them—were also exempted from the labor draft. Mission San Felipe had seventy-one persons associated with it, while Mission San Pedro had fifty-three. Eleven Yamassees were counted separately. If an estimated fifty children and/or elderly people are added, then Cumberland's adult population, both Christian and pagan, in 1681 consisted of around two hundred people.[43]

Flight from Pirates

Aggressive Port Royal–based expansion in Carolina forced the Spanish to cut back on their Sea Island settlements. By the 1680s the mission picture had changed considerably. The provinces of Guale and Mocamo shrank both in size and in population to include only a narrow string of mission towns and refugee villages that stretched from the Sea Islands of southern Georgia to northern Florida's coastline and barrier islands. The mission provinces lay wide open to sea-based pirates. The poorly defended but comparatively rich missions were ripe targets for plunderers from the Caribbean. Within the space of eighteen months in 1683–84, two successive pirate raids would finish off the Spanish presence on the Georgia coast.[44]

The first decisive pirate attack took place in the late spring of 1683. The notorious French pirate Grammont led a group of French and English vessels on a raid on St. Augustine and then sailed north in search of provisions. The ferocious sea rovers sacked the Mission San Felipe on Cumberland and probably vandalized and looted the Mission San Pedro. The unconverted, or pagan, Indians, by now mostly Yamassee, fled. The Christianized Indians, unwilling to leave their cultivated fields and groves, tended to remain on the island. Within a month, the population of Guale and Mocamo was cut in half. Following the Grammont raid, a substantial number of Yamassee fugitives took up a political stance between English Carolina and Spanish Florida. To signal their new allegiance to Britain, they resettled in the middle of present-day Hilton Head Island. Their confidence in the Spanish infantry's ability to protect them had been severely shaken. English pirates were as bad as the French, but the Ya-massee fugitives were as yet ignorant of the pirates' close connection with Car-olina. Charles Town, settled in the 1670s by English and Scottish slave traders, was a safe harbor for privateers.[45]

During 1684 Spanish authorities consulted both Yamassee resettlements and mission Indians on Cumberland about where the Indians might best relo-cate for their safety. Spanish officers actively sought agreement about new settlement sites with St. Simons and Ossabaw natives. The pros and cons of em-igration and tribal cohesiveness were discussed at length. Spanish authorities, suggesting Indian removal to barrier islands closer to St. Augustine, proposed an aggregation of mission settlements at San Pedro. The caciques pointed out disadvantages in regard to overcrowding of agricultural land. While not un-willing to move, the Sea Islands' mission Indians suggested assistance from Spanish military forces, including grain shipments while they traveled.[46]

The final blow in the abandonment of the Sea Islands fell in October 1684, when another pirate attack threatened Spanish-occupied islands. The retreat of the missions was even more rapid and drastic than originally contemplated. Even while resettlement was under discussion, fierce pirate attacks terrified the missions. Unknown to Guale residents, in 1684 a body of eleven pirate ships had united off the west coast of Florida and decided to mount another assault on St. Augustine. A sudden storm scattered five of the ships, and the remaining six vessels—including three large ships and three smaller vessels under the command of a pirate known to the Spanish as Thomas Jingle—decided to abandon their plan. They slipped past St. Augustine to sail north and, seeking desperately needed supplies from coastal settlements, were reported stealing corn from Indian-cultivated fields at the Spanish missions. When both friars and Indians reported the pirate sloops and ketches, Spanish detachments came to the rescue of the chief mission on St. Simons Island. Its panic-stricken Indian inhabitants, however, had already fled en masse to the mainland, an exodus that forced the friar at the Asajo mission on St. Simons to leave more abruptly than he had planned. He reported that the enemy had entered Asajo and burned the church, the *convento,* and six houses. Spanish military forces, joined by Indian sentinels and boatmen, were seriously undermanned in their fight against intruders on armed and rapid vessels and soon joined the crowds of In-dian refugees on the mainland.[47]

Native survivors of the island missions regrouped to the south. Although it is not known whether Mission San Felipe was burned, it is known that its inhabitants retreated from Cumberland with the rest of the refugees. With the early November 1684 establishment of Stuarts Town in Carolina by 150 Scottish colonists, a Yamassee-Scots alliance soon formed. The old site of Santa Elena became the scene of Yamassee coalitions, willing to join English raiders against the Spanish. Port Royal Sound and its adjacent shores began to see a massive influx of Yamassee tribes from the interior, mixing with large numbers of former mission Indians. Before the end of 1686 the Yamassee entered into a contract with the colonists of Stuarts Town, who gave cutlasses and shotguns to the Indians in payment for any captured slaves. The English and Yamassee soon organized joint slave-raiding trips. Some slaves were sold to an Englishman from Charles Town, others to an Irish ship carrying incoming colonists.[48]

Abandonment of San Pedro by its Indian settlers was part of the breakdown of the Spanish mission system. The last known reference to Mission San Pedro appeared in 1660. The 1685 removal of mission Indians from San Pedro Island to the St. Marys Basin and later further south down the coast as far as Fort George Island and ultimately to St. Augustine did not by itself introduce the sudden collapse of Indian family and social structure. Because clan relationships had formed the basis of native societies, intermarriage with the Spanish had already contributed to the gradual erosion of Indian society. *Mestizaje,* or the assimilation process of Spanish-Indian intermarriage and descent, was creating a new type of island settler. In addition, new agricultural techniques shortened the natives' life expectancy. Contraction of Indian fields and orchards signified loss of place and identity, although some mestizos may have returned to harvest Cumberland Island corn fields. Only eighteen years after the 1684 raid on Georgia's coastal missions, another truly terrible raid from Carolina decimated the remaining huddled Indian villages. In 1701 Amelia Island was overrun by English forces, accompanied by Indians and blacks, on their way to burn St. Augustine. Spanish and Indians retreated to St. George Island, leaving behind forever the mission system. San Pedro was almost depopulated. Only old Indian fields and their orange groves remained, possibly tended by mestizo owners.[49]

TWO

San Pedro Gives
Way to St. George

"Go Settle in Georgia": The British Arrival

*S*an Pedro Island lay within an area that seemed to be neither Spanish nor British. Between 1702 and 1736, both Spanish and English diplomats nervously eyed their states' claims. When Colonel James Edward Oglethorpe (1696–1785) arrived on Cumberland Island in 1736, it was Spanish territory. To the common soldiers stationed at St. Augustine, all the coast north of Talbott Island (in present-day Florida) was "tierra de San Jorje" (St. George's land), named for the patron saint of Englishmen.[1]

Like many other cultivated English gentlemen, Oglethorpe, an urbane and experienced British officer, was appalled by the indifference of the British judicial system toward the poor. On his motion, in 1728 Parliament appointed a committee to examine barbarities visited on imprisoned debtors and to seek relief for London's indigent. The committee, of which Oglethorpe soon became chairman, grew to include thirty-eight noblemen, the chancellor of the exchequer, the master of rolls, an admiral of the Royal Navy, and a field marshal. By the early 1730s, interest in the project had grown to such an extent that many of these gentlemen petitioned Parliament to create a new proprietary government in the "American plantations." The new province was to be created from lands lying south of the Savannah River, immediately below what is now South Carolina. Promising to support the new colony with private donations, the committee undertook to settle the colony with working-class Englishmen and -women.[2]

The royal charter granting the committee's request was signed on 9 June 1732. At the same time, the committee became a corporation called the Trustees for Establishing the Colony of Georgia in America. The trustees had a president, secretary, and board of council consisting of twenty-four members. Because the colony had been carved from South Carolina, it is not surprising that the trustees resolved to establish a port town on the Savannah River, as near as possible to Port Royal, the nearest navy station.

The first settlers were 114 men, women, and children, chosen from England's "worthy poor." They sailed for Georgia in November 1732. Somewhat to the surprise of the trustees, Oglethorpe volunteered to accompany them. Still a bachelor and always adventurous, Oglethorpe was the ideal escort for the emigrants. Physically strong and energetic, he possessed the forbearance and alertness that the struggling new settlements needed. Between 1732 and 1739, he worked ceaselessly to safeguard the new colony, to plan and supervise the construction of forts, and to deal with the colonists' problems with intemperance, illness, and fecklessness.

His immediate goals included the peaceful cession of land by the native Indians. The barrier islands were the key to the mainland's political, economic, and military welfare. The offshore islands' inlets and tides controlled Europeans' navigation, which, in turn, controlled their effective use of the mainland. The Indians, however, hesitated to give up their rights to the offshore islands, where they had been hunting and fishing for many years. Representing England and speaking on behalf of the trustees, Oglethorpe entered into a 1733 conditional treaty with the Creek nation. Although the treaty did not say so explicitly, both parties understood that the Creek nation had ceded all islands along the coast between Tybee and St. Simons except Ossabaw, Sapelo, and St. Catherines, which were reserved by the Creeks for hunting, bathing, and fishing.[3]

The 1733 treaty was renewed, clarified, and extended by a 1739 treaty that stated that the Creek nation had once been the legal owner of all the land from the Savannah River to the St. Johns River. The Creek nation acknowledged its earlier grant of "all the lands along the sea coast as far as the St. Johns River, as high as the tide flows" as well as of all the islands as far as the St. Johns River, particularly St. Simons, Cumberland, and Amelia. The Creeks reserved for themselves St. Catherines, Ossabaw, and Sapelo.[4]

The Yamacraws, a Creek nation subdivision that occupied lands in southeast South Carolina and northern Georgia, quickly allied themselves with Oglethorpe. The Yamacraws had observed the financial rewards that accrued to cattle and horse owners, and both the Creeks and Oglethorpe recognized the offshore islands' utility for horse breeding. The first English horses on Cumberland may have stepped ashore in the late summer of 1739, apparently put there by Oglethorpe before a November trip home: "[On both Cumberland and

Amelia] Islands I left a stud of the Trust's horses and mares when I went last for England, and the colts bred out of them are very good." Two years later another Englishman praised not only the horses but also the islands for being inexpensive stock farms: "Upon [Amelia Island], as well as Cumberland . . . a stud of Horses and Mares . . . are bred without any expense."[5]

With Oglethorpe's acquisition of Creek land, the stage was set for a new confrontation between Spain and England over the Georgia frontier, a long, narrow arc of coast that consisted almost entirely of wide marshes, inland swamps, and sounds that were "almost large enough to bear the Appellation of Seas."[6] This sheltered inland waterway, extending a hundred miles, made a corridor for transportation and assault.

In early February 1736, Oglethorpe was on St. Simons Island marking out Fort Frederica. By 23 March workmen, provisions, cannon, and a large number of new colonists had arrived; the streets were laid out; the fort was almost finished; and a battery had been erected to command the river, from which Spanish assaults might be expected to come in the event of war.[7]

Also in March 1736, the Creeks confirmed their grants to Great Britain. Tomochichi, a Yamacraw *mico* (minor chieftain), came to Frederica to point out territorial limits and urged Oglethorpe to travel south with him to see the Spanish domain. Oglethorpe was unwilling to leave Frederica at that time, prompting the Indians to say they would go hunt buffalo on the mainland. Fearing that this was a pretext for molesting the Spanish, Oglethorpe agreed to accompany the Creeks along the coast, partly to supervise their activities and partly to lay claim to the islands that were part of the Creek concession.[8]

Since he was on the verge of reporting to the trustees about defensive measures that he hoped would protect the colony, Oglethorpe was anxious to see for himself the frontier "where his Majesty's Dominions and the Spaniards joyn." During this brief reconnaissance, he first saw Cumberland Island. On 28 March Oglethorpe wrote to Thomas Broughton in London on the subject of establishing a garrison on San Pedro's to block the Inland Passage.[9]

Eager to begin construction of a fort on the island (and possibly anxious to forestall criticism from London), Oglethorpe and an entourage departed from Frederica on 18 April. They rendezvoused at the end of that day with a small fleet of piraguas from Darien carrying Captain Hugh Mackay and thirty Scots Highlanders as well as Mackay's nephew, Ensign Hugh Mackay, and his party of ten rangers. McIntosh relatives had solicited Captain Mackay, second son of Baron Reay of Scotland and an officer in the British army, to accompany them on their planned emigration to the New Inverness settlement, located between Cumberland Island and Savannah. Receiving the king's permission to "go and Settle in Georgia," Mackay resigned his commission in 1736 and received a new one in 1737 as a captain in Oglethorpe's new regiment.[10]

For this expedition, the Highlanders wore belted plaids, in which they both worked and slept, and were equipped with saws and entrenching tools such as shovels and spades. Some of them had been so wild and ignorant that prior to leaving New Inverness, their clan leader, John McIntosh Mohr ("Big John"), had been obliged to teach them how to row and to saw wood. Oglethorpe had great respect for their hardihood and willingness. He wrote: "These Servants cannot be put under the direction of any body at Frederica nor any one that does not understand the Highland language. . . . The Trustees engaged not to separate the Highlanders. They are very useful under their own chiefs and nowhere else."[11]

As indentured servants of the trustees, the Highlanders were brought to the island to build the fortification. On 19 April, the day following Oglethorpe's rendezvous with the Mackays, the little fleet landed on San Pedro Island. Francis Moore, Oglethorpe's assistant and secretary, wrote the following account of Britain's formal occupation of San Pedro Island:

> That afternoon they saw an island, which the Indians formerly called Wissoo, in English, Sassafras. This is over against Jekyll island on the south; the northwest of it rises fifty foot or upwards above the water, like a terras, a mile in length, covered with tall pine trees. The western extremity of this hill commands the passage for boats from the southward as the northern end of the island does the entry for ships. Here they met with some bark-huts, which our friendly Indians had some time since built for their lodging when they hunted there. They saw a great many deer and a wide savannah lying at the foot of the hill, extending near two or three miles: so that from the western point they could discover any boat that came from the southward for several miles.
>
> Mr. Oglethorpe upon the extreme western point of the hill, the foot of which is washed on the one side by the bay and by the channel that goes to the southward on the other, marked out a fort to be called St. Andrew's, and gave Captain Hugh Mackay orders to build it.[12]

In gratitude for the Highlanders' work, Oglethorpe decided to name the new settlement Fort St. Andrews and the island the Highlands. The British occupation had begun.[13]

Fort St. Andrews

Tomochichi's nephew, Toonahowie, allegedly named the island *Cumberland* in honor of the Duke of Cumberland: "The Duke gave us this watch that we might know how the time passes. We will remember him at all times, and therefore give this island his name." The authenticity of this story is open to question, however: Oglethorpe was no favorite of the Duke of Cumberland. British officers may have solicited Toonahowie's suggestion, and Oglethorpe may have decided that naming the island after a member of the royal family—as he had already done with Amelia Island—would be a politic move.[14]

The site chosen for Fort St. Andrews is known today as Terrapin Point. It is easily recognizable from Moore's report. Terrapin Point forms a fifty-foot bluff facing on the Inland Passage. The bluff levels off abruptly at the top into a uniform and featureless shelf. Southwest of this high bluff is a vast expanse of marsh extending for several miles from the island to the Inland Passage. Vessels of any sort approaching through the Inland Waterway can be seen from a great distance. The location was virtually unsurpassed as a viewing point for marine traffic.

Fort St. Andrews was built in a star-work configuration, meaning that the fort was built in the form of a four-pointed star, with each of the points a bastion. Excluding the bastions, the inside dimensions of the fort were about 65 by 130 feet. The military reserve surrounding it, a legality that appeared thirty years later in response to the petitions of would-be grantees, was 100 acres; however, such a reserve was not part of Oglethorpe's thinking in 1736, when he thought of the whole island as a reserve.[15]

The only available earthwork material in the area was loose sand and standing timber from the nearby lofty pines. To construct a wall, it was necessary to alternate layers of tree limbs and brush with layers of sand. Classicists among the officers referred to this method as an old Roman technique.[16]

Fort St. Andrews was never large. Its strength lay chiefly in its commanding position. To protect it, there were a fortifying ditch, a parapet or wooden form that was later constructed to contain the sand walls, and a small clearing in the woods for fifty yards around. There was also a plank-sided frame house built as a powder magazine. The outline of the original fort can be indistinctly traced in a more elaborate plan drawn up by Captain André Thomas but never executed. This "Plan d'un petit fort pour l'Isle de St. André" indicates that the fort could have contained stores and barracks for two hundred soldiers.[17]

In June 1736 the trustees, already uneasy with Oglethorpe's expansionist plans, listened in disapproving silence to the report of the Georgia Society's registrar, John Bromfield, who had come from Savannah. Bromfield reported that Oglethorpe "was bent upon a settlement on St. Pedro's Island, 60 miles southward of St. Simond's Island, where Frederica is building, and intended to build a fort and place a garrison there." Bromfield's report greatly worried the trustees, who feared a sharp Spanish retaliation to Oglethorpe's efforts to garrison the frontier. By July the trustees were taking an increasingly gloomy view of Oglethorpe's expansive ideas. After a session with the Georgia Society, the Earl of Egmont took some of its members to dinner at the Cyder House to commiserate:

> We reflected on the ill situation of our affairs, great drafts and little money to answer them. Two forts building to the southward out of our limits, and jealousies given to the Spaniards thereby, and this without the knowledge of the Trust. At the same time no countenance given us by the Government beyond the £10,000 which the Parliament ordered.[18]

Just a week earlier, the board had agreed on a letter to Oglethorpe warning him that it would not allow any further disbursement of public money for construction outside the bounds of the colony. Fort St. Andrews was the kind of public works of which the trustees heartily disapproved, fearing that Oglethorpe might embroil the colony in a war with Spain, for which the trust could provide neither excuses nor funds.[19]

Oglethorpe subsequently sailed to England in a successful effort to placate the trustees. During this visit, he convinced Sir Robert Walpole, the prime minister, that the Georgia settlements needed the protection of British regulars. Although the trustees' original purposes had been philanthropic, London bankers had been keeping a sharp eye on the Georgia colony's commercial value since 1732. The trustees had never known how to seek financial support from British, French, and Dutch merchants, but Walpole's ministry was susceptible to mercantile leadership in both commercial and diplomatic affairs. After these powerful merchants began to support Georgia as a source of raw materials, Parliament learned to appreciate the colony as a significant addition to England's trade.[20]

Although Walpole reportedly offered Oglethorpe the governorship of South Carolina, he evidently preferred to offer his services as a regular soldier, and in June 1737 he received a commission as "General & Commander in Chief of the Forces in South Carolina & Georgia." In August he received an additional commission as colonel of a regiment to be raised for service in Georgia. Oglethorpe's Regiment, as it was called, was the Forty-second Regiment of Foot. To bring it up to strength, 250 men were drafted from the Twenty-fifth Regiment of Foot, stationed at Gibraltar. The men who transferred from Gibraltar became members of Captain Mackay's companies and were stationed at Fort St. Andrews. Most of the soldiers whose families accompanied them lived in a village of huts called Barriemackie on Cumberland Island.[21]

Transferred abruptly from the relative delights of garrison life in Europe, the soldiers soon became surly and mutinous. They were disappointed in their primitive surroundings, were not receiving extra pay for food as they had in Gibraltar, and had not yet received the traditional extra pay for the sea journey to Georgia. Many of the troops had learned at least some Spanish from girl-friends now left behind and could converse with Spanish soldiers, making them susceptible to Spanish recruitment. Perhaps the strongest reason for their mutinous attitude, according to historian Larry E. Ivers, was that when the commander of the Twenty-fifth at Gibraltar selected men for assignment to Oglethorpe's Regiment, he unloaded his misfits. Captain Mackay's company therefore contained an entire regiment's most undesirable men—the slow-witted, the physically and psychologically ill, and the malevolent, who apparently intended to test the courage of their new officers.[22]

Early in November 1738 Oglethorpe took up temporary quarters at Fort St. Andrews so that he could personally superintend some repairs on the fort. Surliness among the troops from Gibraltar suddenly exploded into violence over the issue of provisions. As part of their terms of enlistment, these soldiers had been allowed extra provisions from the king's store, distributed by either the regiment's purser or the sutlers who generally accompanied regiments. When these extra rations were discontinued, the soldiers became extremely discontented. One day while Oglethorpe was breakfasting after having reviewed the two companies at daybreak, numerous men accosted him, demanding a renewal of their allowance. The general responded that rude behavior would not secure a favorable consideration of their application, but the soldiers were not deterred. As the crowd around him grew, Oglethorpe decided to try to draw them away from the fort and magazine, walking "nimbly" out of the gate. The shouting and cursing troops followed him, demanding beds and free provisions.[23]

One soldier cried out, "Now it's your time!" Oglethorpe seized him as a prisoner and pulled him within the barrier. Another soldier immediately shouted, "You shall then take us all!" and was similarly grabbed by a captain. The two officers shouted for the guard to shut the gates of the fort, but the mutineers surged against them, trying to enter. Many of the rebels had already loaded their guns, and the rest were now doing so. Oglethorpe and his second in command, Captain Albert Desbrisay, left the safety of the fort and ran out into the soldiers' camp. Wrote Oglethorpe,

> I no sooner turned into one of the streets of the camp but I saw a great many men with their arms, and one just behind the corner of the hut about five yards from me presented his piece at me. I stept back and called to him, "Down with your arms." At which he cried, "No, by God, I'll down with you!" On which I rushed forward. He fired, the bullet whizzed above my shoulder, and the powder singed my clothes. At the same time I heard another shot fired, and the bullet whizzed by me and struck the mutineer. He strove to club his firelock, but, before he made sure of his blow, I closed in with him with my sword and, seizing his firelock with my left hand, tore it from him, saying, "Wretch, let go your arms, I will not kill you, I'll leave you to the hangman."[24]

Oglethorpe and the officers who came running to his assistance shouted to the mutineers that if further resistance occurred, they would be shot. If they dispersed, however, the general would pardon them. The mutineers immediately broke up, most of them going directly to their huts. After an examination of their quarters, the officers found evidence that twenty-five soldiers had loaded their guns before the early morning review. After events had quieted down somewhat, the general spoke to the assembled men and asked them what their grievances were. The troops replied that the king's pay was not sufficient to keep them fed. They complained that at Gibraltar they received their pay plus their army provisions, which they were not receiving in Georgia. Furthermore, they alleged that Lieutenant Colonel William Cochran had failed to pay them their sea allowance. Oglethorpe then ordered Cochran to provide the sea pay forthwith. Five ringleaders were taken to Fort Frederica, where they were court-martialed and shot. The mutiny was over. Oglethorpe's prompt and skillful actions averted a serious blow to Georgia's defenses, for had the mutineers succeeded, their best recourse would have been to cast their lot with the Spaniards in St. Augustine.[25]

Fighting the Spanish

As early as 1737 Spanish spies had informed St. Augustine of the new British fort's name and exact location, the number of men stationed there, and the size and number of its guns: "On the Point of Bejecez on the Isle of Whales stands a fort which they called Saint Andrew with sixteen or twenty men commanded by Captain Mackay, mounting ten guns of 8-pounders."[26]

Typical of the men who passed along news to Spanish authorities in Florida was a Spaniard named Juan Castelnau, who testified in 1739 before Field Marshal Juan Francisco de Güemes y Horcasitas. In 1737 Castelnau had traveled from Port Royal to Savannah in a piragua. From there he put to sea, presumably down the Inland Navigation, with the master of the piragua. Bad weather compelled them to go ashore on Amelia Island, and four British guards then took him back to St. Simons Island. Castelnau was eventually taken back to Savannah, where Oglethorpe had him put on a ship to Virginia and New York. Castelnau reported that after the troops from Gibraltar arrived under Colonel "Cokran," troop distribution was six hundred men at Fort Frederica and two hundred men at Fort St. Andrews. Castelnau and others like him updated the Spanish on Oglethorpe's defenses.[27]

St. Andrews's earth construction was not very permanent, and in 1739 Oglethorpe wrote to the trustees that the three forts he had ordered to be built were "run to ruin." He estimated the costs of rebuilding at £500 for Frederica, £400 for St. Andrews, and £100 for the small fortification at the northern end of Amelia Island.[28]

The little fort on Amelia Island was abandoned shortly thereafter. In 1739 Britain and Spain began the War of Jenkins's Ear, which subsequently developed into the War of the Austrian Succession. Even before war broke out, the Spanish government in Florida was deeply uneasy about Oglethorpe's defensive measures. Indian raids in November 1739 showed Oglethorpe that his Amelia Island fortification was vulnerable. Although it maintained a small regular garrison for a time and was used as a temporary rest stop for scout-boat crews, it could no longer serve an important role in Georgia's defenses. Hence, the construction of a new fort began at the southern end of Cumberland Island. Fort William, Cumberland's second fort, was begun sometime between December 1739 and January 1740 and was completed in April 1740.[29]

Although not very large at first, Fort William was a stronger fortification than Fort St. Andrews. At first Fort William was a weak structure consisting of a plank-sided house, a stockade with bastions at each corner, and eight cannon. A small detachment of regulars provided the garrison. Its location was superb. From its position at South Point, the extreme southern tip of Cumberland, Fort William commanded St. Marys Inlet, which a part of the Spanish fleet—the inland squadron—would have to enter to travel up the Inland Passage to attack Fort Frederica.[30]

By 1740 Fort William had been rebuilt and was strongly palisaded. Barracks and storehouses were constructed for 220 men. Fort William had two eighteen-pound cannon mounted on moving platforms that could be moved to face in any direction, a very effective early form of swivel gun. With these improvements, Oglethorpe believed that he was ready to take the initiative against the Spanish. Aided by sea forces from South Carolina, he attempted an unsuccessful assault of Fort San Marcos at St. Augustine.[31]

Spain retaliated for the attack on St. Augustine in 1742. In May of that year, fifty-six vessels carrying about seven thousand men left Havana for St. Augustine. Although part of the Spanish fleet was dispersed by storm, Indians and spies quickly carried the news of its arrival to Frederica, causing alarm and hasty preparations to protect the Georgia coast at St. Simons. Fort William received the first wave of attack on 21 June. Fourteen vessels were seen off Cumberland Island, and nine of them attempted to come through St. Marys Inlet. They were repulsed by the cannon at Fort William with the assistance of the guard schooner *Walker*, with fourteen guns and eighty men.[32]

Oglethorpe ordered coastal patrols at St. Simons to watch for a landing and went to the southern end of Jekyll Island, where he boarded a scout boat and ordered a detachment to follow along in a second boat. The Spanish flotilla suddenly tacked about and stood in for St. Andrew Sound, for which Oglethorpe immediately set sail. He nearly was captured. A ranger wrote,

> We were in all three boats, the Genl. stood over the sound for Cumberland, when the Spanish Fleet (being 13 Sail) saw our three Boats going across the Sound they stood for us and having the Wind and a strong Tide with them soon came so near us that a Smart Engagement ensued. We fired very hotly at them and they at us. The General and the other Boats fought Their way through the Spaniards and got to St. Andrews from whence he drew off the Garrison Stores, etc. and reinforced Fort William.

Of his close encounter with death or capture, Oglethorpe wrote, "God blessed us with such Success that the whole 14 Sail stood out to Sea & only 10 of them ever joined their Fleet."[33]

A week later, 28 June 1742, the Spanish flotilla appeared off St. Simons. Troops landed from Spanish ships and marched north to attack the fortified town of Frederica. Oglethorpe and a far smaller force marched out to meet the

Spanish threat, surprising and ambushing the invaders on 7 July 1742 at a place later named Bloody Marsh. The engagement was one of the most decisive battles of North America, ending Spanish claims to all territory north of Florida and ensuring English control of the seacoast down to the St. Johns River.[34]

For six days after the Battle of Bloody Marsh, the Spanish officers argued among themselves about whether to continue. Then, on 13 July, they began their retreat. A contingent of about fifteen hundred Spanish troops was ferried across to Jekyll Island and ordered to march along the beach to its south end for pickup by the Spanish inland flotilla. General Manuel de Montiano accompanied these soldiers, returning by way of St. Andrew Sound to Cumberland Island and stopping at Jekyll Island long enough to burn the English settlement. Spanish troops began arriving on Cumberland on 15 July, as soon as the inland fleet had anchored near Fort St. Andrews, which had been abandoned by its British troops when the Spanish squadron was first sighted several weeks earlier.

> we arrived at 8:00 in the morning and anchored, and at one and the same time all the troops began to go ashore in good order as was permitted by the nature of the ground. We found the fort abandoned and containing only a few things, such as a four-pounder gun spiked, two swivel guns unspiked, fifty hand grenades, six empty jars and a number of iron hoops.
>
> The fort is situated upon an eminence which commands the entire beach and has no other fortification than that afforded by a dense girdle of lofty and large pines and the superiority of its position. Within this enclosure was a house of limited accommodation and in an angle an underground room which appeared to be a powder magazine; about one hundred paces beyond this circle were three houses at a short distance one from the other, the largest of which, from its construction seemed to be a storehouse; the next one was a stable because it was surrounded by a fence inside of which we found fifty to sixty horses. These at first we thought we would take on to Florida with us but as we had no means of doing so, an order was given that they should be immediately killed in order that our enemies might have a taste of the same treatment to which they had subjected us in Florida. At this very moment, however, this order was suspended until we should begin our march. The third house was immediately at the landing which showed that it was a tavern or a low eating house.

This structure may have been where incoming provisions from Frederica were unloaded and weighed. Informal canteens often sprang up at such docking areas.[35]

The Spanish troops formed a camp about two hundred paces from the fort, in an open pine grove on level ground. They were well disciplined until hunger overtook them:

> There seemed to be an abundance of water with which the men refreshed themselves; they managed to resist the scarcity of food from which they suffered on this day until the afternoon, for it occurred to some of the men to obtain relief by killing a few horses and eating their flesh. In the afternoon an issue was ordered of a little rice and of one hardtack apiece and at the same time a return was asked of the stores which were actually on board the boats with us.[36]

Oglethorpe's scout boats followed the retreating Montiano and were able to discern at least eight ships anchored at Fort St. Andrews. Because of the strength of the enemy force, Oglethorpe sent the scout boats back and continued in a cutter to another point on Cumberland. He wrote to Fort-Major Alexander Stuart at Fort William, ordering him to defend himself to the bitter end. The Spanish, however, soon discovered Oglethorpe's boats and hastily set sail on 26 July 1742, having burned the storehouse and cabins at Fort St. Andrews.[37]

Oglethorpe's war was over. Spanish troops left for St. Augustine, never to return to southeast Georgia.

THREE

Early British Settlements

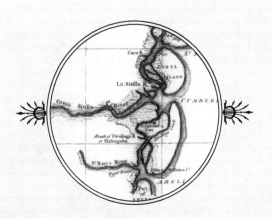

Barriemackie

$\mathcal{D}$uring the 1740s the British and Spanish engaged in lively illicit commerce in southern Georgia, Florida, and the Caribbean. In 1751 the king of Spain ordered that any person in his dominion who was detected to have contraband dealings with the British was to suffer death and the confiscation of property. Nevertheless, the clandestine trade continued to flourish throughout the 1750s. British traders complained vigorously when Spanish *guardacostas* (coast guard vessels) searched and seized ships. British seamen soon learned that flying a flag of truce would enable them to circumvent both Spanish and British government orders and thus to sail directly into Spanish ports. Furthermore, garrison commandants or colonial governors often would connive to admit British vessels. Even more frequently, armed Spanish ships, carrying letters of marque that permitted them to capture enemy vessels, overtook British merchant ships and brought them to Havana.[1]

British shipowners resented the mercantile policy that prevented Spanish colonial trade directly with the British. The Spanish Crown prohibited the payment of gold and silver to foreign nations, insisting that Spanish bullion return to Spain. Even though Cuba and Mexico wanted to buy British manufactured goods, the Spanish government did not permit them to do so directly, requiring instead that such trade pass through Spanish corporations.

Expediency brought exceptions, however. The Spanish had a particular problem in the miserable conditions at St. Augustine, where the garrison frequently ran out of food. During the 1750s the Royal Company of the Island of Cuba was responsible for providing goods for Florida and was permitted to purchase supplies elsewhere when they were unavailable in Cuba. St. Augustine welcomed any source of supply, especially when the colony was in extreme want, but was particularly interested in British goods, which were of high quality, were cheap, and posed relatively few transportation risks. Therefore, the Royal Company began contracting with British merchants in New York and Charleston. Welcoming payment in silver, the merchants hastened to provide British manufactured goods.

Wealthy North American seacoast merchants were not the only participants in contraband trade with the Spanish. British settlers below the Altamaha River discovered that cattle driven into Florida would be heartily welcomed by its governor. The settlers also soon found that the Spanish would buy produce. British authorities did not encourage the development of small agricultural plantations in this area, however.

The British in Georgia were very hesitant to grant land to settlers. Even though the Treaty of Aix-la-Chapelle, signed in 1748, had been designed to establish peace between Britain and Spain, it accomplished very little: both countries continued to claim Georgia. However, Britain could not afford to engage in another war with Spain; therefore, officials were careful not to make firm commitments to any land south of the Altamaha River. As a result, all land in this area, including Cumberland Island, became an "uninhabited tract," to be viewed as neutral ground. Only a few small plantations grew up in this area, most of them operated by British soldiers who were at first primarily interested in supplementing their military allotments. In 1744 a Sergeant Hall deposed that "he had a Plantation on St. Simons Island, and another on Cumberland. . . . That he has himself rais'd Corn Pease Potatoes, and all sorts of Garden stuff. That he saw'd four Acres of Corn that Year." On Jekyll Island, Major William Horton grew grain for both food and beer.[2]

Even though immigration to Georgia continued, no towns grew up south of Frederica during the 1750s, with the exception of the short-lived garrison settlement of Barriemackie (Gaelic for Mackay's Town) on Cumberland Island. Barriemackie, a village of huts inhabited by the families who accompanied the Gibraltar soldiers, was the nearest Cumberland has ever come to a town. During the mutiny at Fort St. Andrews in 1738, the frustrated mutineers ran to "Barrimacke" to get their weapons. In 1741 a regimental surgeon named William Bowler mentioned the same settlement in a letter to the earl of Egmont. Bowler stated that he had gone to Georgia in May 1738 and was stationed at Fort St. Andrews, where he attended two companies of Oglethorpe's Regiment as well as Ensign Hugh Mackay's party of Highlanders at the scout station on Amelia Island. The doctor treated all these people and their families for almost eighteen months without receiving any payment. Among the specific groups that he had helped, Bowler mentioned "80 women and children belonging to the soldiers, and some of them at Mackays town 7 or 8 miles from the Garrison at Cumberland where he most resided." Attending these families had not been part of his regular duties, and he wished reimbursement for his services.[3]

The exact location of Barriemackie is a bit of a mystery. Adjutant Hugh Mackay Jr. (promoted during his kinsman's absence in England), described by nearly all his contemporaries as the commander of a small group of twenty Highland indentured servants but who also may have been one of their clansmen, had supervised the construction of a small village of huts to shelter the regular soldiers at the site of what eventually became Fort St. Andrews. If this assemblage of cabins marks the beginning of a village, then Barriemackie must have been within or very near the fort clearing. Other contemporary observers, like Bowler, however, said that Barriemackie housed soldiers' families, meaning that it must have been a garrison town outside the fort area, perhaps far enough away to have supported planting areas for each family.

Another contemporary observer was an Indian spy, Juan Ygnacio de los Reyes, who described to the Spanish a settlement near the fort in 1738. He said that he saw there "a number of houses, newly built and close together as in Havana, a number of English women, wives of the soldiers, but he could not tell the number of houses in the place." The houses were laid out in squares, with ten houses to each square. Historian William Ramsey believes that four such squares would have been necessary to accommodate the bare minimum of thirty-six houses for the troops, and one or two more squares would have been needed for married soldiers and their families. Oglethorpe referred to the lines between the houses as "streets."[4]

The mutiny at St. Andrews may have been directly responsible for an important 1739 shift in settlement patterns among the married soldiers. Throughout 1738 soldiers' families had lived alongside the garrison in a single camp. Their presence was one of the reasons that during the mutiny, Oglethorpe went "into the midst of the camp at once [rather] than suffer the innocent men and their families to fall into the hands of the mutineers." Shortly after the mutiny, the married soldiers moved out of the camp, according to Oglethorpe's letter dated 11 October 1739: "The soldiers who have wives have had lots granted them, which they have improved very much, particularly they have made a little village called Ballimavee, there is about 24 families with good hutts built, and all have cleared and planted." These huts closely resembled the earliest dwellings at Fort Frederica, which were described as "little low houses Covered with Palmettos."[5]

Barriemackie had disappeared by 1753, when Jonathan Bryan traveled to the north end of Cumberland. According to Bryan, two of the companies belonging to the regiment had settled near the north end: "A good many of the Soldiers who had Familys were settled in a Village on the Side of a Creek, which runs into the Island." This may have been Christmas Creek. Bryan wrote that although more than twenty families had been settled on the south end, no trace of their plantations remained. A guard of a corporal and six men resided at Fort William.[6]

Although Barriemackie had ceased to exist, in 1755 it was named as one of only three settled communities on the extreme southern frontier of the United States. Out-of-date European atlases said that southern Georgia had two towns, Frederica and New Inverness, and one village, "Barimake." Barriemackie had evidenced none of the attributes that make a real town—commercial opportunities, religious cohesion, or a rich agricultural hinterland—and so, when the fort was abandoned, the village collapsed. Barriemackie was said to be deserted, to live on "only in the traditions of the island."[7]

"Engaged in Small Traffic with the Spaniards": Edmund Gray's Settlement

Barriemackie's disappearance from the records does not mean, however, that it had really disappeared. People apparently continued to live near the site of Fort St. Andrews. And within a few years a settlement of seventy to eighty men and their families developed on the island under the leadership of an able Indian trader and Quaker named Edmund Gray.

Official correspondence regarding Gray's settlement is fairly voluminous, and a census of sorts exists for his group. At its peak, the settlement included more than three hundred people. Gray's followers consisted of a large number of landless men, a few of whom had served in Oglethorpe's Regiment, which disbanded in 1749. Frederica's fort was in ruins by 1755, and the town was ravaged by a terrible fire in 1758. British authorities practically deserted Frederica, and it offered no future for the few soldiers who remained. Many of them, their families, and a few mestizos banded together under Gray to become "Gray's Gang." The men became hunters, cattle drovers, and boatmen.[8]

Georgia Governor Henry Ellis described Gray as a "fellow of infinite art and finesse." Originally from Virginia, Gray had arrived in Georgia as early as 1749, bringing with him about thirty Quaker families. Since they settled near Augusta, Gray undoubtedly had learned the dynamics involved in a successful trading town. He saw opportunities in the Indian trade, although he seems to have been more principled than most traders. On 27 February 1750 he petitioned for land between the Little and Savannah Rivers in Georgia. Gray and his coreligionists apparently intended to settle as a group, a form of emigration encouraged by the trustees. Gray was elected to the Lower House of the General Assembly. After a series of run-ins with the colonial government, however, Gray fled south of the Altamaha River, where British settlement was discouraged. In 1755–56 he moved beyond the southern frontier of Georgia to the Satilla River, where he established a settlement called New Hanover. Gray and many of his followers eventually moved to Cumberland Island so that they could better trade with the Lower Creeks. Gray's community drew the ire of British colonial authorities because it lay beyond the legal British border. Ellis evidently tried to intervene, asking Secretary of State William Pitt why it was unreasonable to establish a settlement on Cumberland Island, where "we have a Fort and Garrison."[9]

Even though the settlement was legally beyond British jurisdiction, Gray's Gang agreed to self-imposed community discipline in regard to land allotments and Indian trading. On 3 February 1756 at the New Hanover settlement, Gray's followers drew up a compact setting out rules by which they would govern themselves. The covenant admitted that the settlement was not in Georgia, but the settlers declared themselves loyal subjects of the British crown. William Gray, John Williams, Samuel Mills, Robert Lucas, Robert Baille, and Joseph Goodbe were appointed commissioners to run the settlement. Every person was entitled to the same quantity of land as was allowed in Great Britain's neighboring southern colonies. Furthermore, two men were designated as surveyors who would follow the commissioners' orders in recording land allotments. The commissioners were to meet every month and, with the aid of a clerk, were to enter their proceedings and judgments regarding the settlement. These commissioners would also make the necessary arrangements to enlist men in a settlement militia. The group's Quaker roots were evident in the language and content of the compact: although the settlement's main business was trade with the Indians, one of the articles specifically prohibited sale of liquor to them.[10]

Only signers of the compact received land in the settlement, and forty inhabitants signed, nearly all of them with British or Scottish names such as Mills, Carr, Pemberton, and Woodland. A few names appear to be either Spanish or Anglicized Spanish, such as Antonio Suarez, and some men may have been mestizo or descendants of mission Indians. Others, such as William McIntosh and William M'Gregor, may have been offspring of Darien's Scottish settlers. According to Ramsey, at least eleven of the settlers at New Hanover appear in Oglethorpe's regimental musters. None of Gray's allotments were legally valid, of course, and after 1765 many of these names turn up again in petitions for land in the St. Marys Basin area.[11]

After establishing his settlement on Cumberland, Gray continued to have conflicts with British authorities. Tense relations between Britain and Spain meant that the presence of British settlers trading with the Indians was threatening; each government feared the other's success in winning Indian allegiance. Ellis's support of Gray was halfhearted, particularly after Ellis learned that Gray and his partner, Ephraim Alexander, were "engaged in small traffic with the Spaniards." Gray's Gang included hunters who brought cattle, deer hides, and hogs to the settlement, and Gray and Alexander shipped beef, pork, and produce to St. Augustine. They probably also shipped food to the settlers at Frederica, where rations were scarce after the 1749 disbanding of Oglethorpe's Regiment. Relations between what was left of the garrison on St. Simons Island and Gray's settlement were apparently routine and cordial.[12]

Gray's settlement on Cumberland Island took advantage of a pattern of coastal trading with the Spanish that had been established as a result of the lack of provisions at St. Augustine over the previous twenty years. In payment, Spanish Florida offered the settlers oranges, fish, sea turtles, tortoiseshell, and—through mercantile connections with New York—money.[13]

Furthermore, the numerous privateers cruising up and down the coast brought certain advantages. Both Frederica and St. Augustine benefited from the capture and sale of British ships and their cargoes. Vessels that went ashore as a result of pilot error or a storm at sea were, under international admiralty law, salvaged ships, and their capture was allowed even in peacetime. Such prizes were then brought into port for adjudication, and if the decision went against the shipowner, subsequent sale of the cargo was often controlled by the governor, the fort commandant, or the local authority. Gray's move to Cumberland from New Hanover may have been motivated partly by considerations of this sort. Fortunes were made from privateering, and Gray and Alexander must have noted the possibility of privateers coming in under a flag of truce to refit and get fresh water. Governor Ellis, traveling south in 1757, met Gray at New Hanover and reported that the governor of St. Augustine "has sent to invite Gray & Alexander to settle upon the River St. Johns, & establish an Indian trade under his protection, promising to furnish them amply with proper goods from New York."[14]

Ellis urged Gray to settle instead on the St. Marys River on the mainland, opposite Fort William, sweetening the offer by granting Gray a license to trade with the Indians. Ellis said that Gray seemed inclined to quit acting as a "Legislator" and anxious to return to his role as merchant: "He is a shrewd sensible fellow & affects an austerity of manners by which he has acquired a considerable influence among the people of this colony & made some impression upon the Indians."[15]

On a visit to the island the following year, Governor Ellis again met with Gray. Ellis stated that Gray was settled there with his family. The cosmopolitan governor was amused by the Quaker's decorum and austerity: "Mr. Gray . . . is a very unintelligible character shrewd, sagacious, & capable of affording the best advice to others but ridiculously absurd in every part of his own conduct."[16]

Ellis recommended that Gray's settlement, although obviously illegal, be encouraged to continue, perhaps by redefining the border or by granting Gray particular favors. The governor believed that if the community could be allowed to settle on Cumberland, it would be "serviceable to this Country in general & to our Garrison there in particular." The governor's next letter on this subject stated that he understood that as many as two hundred people had "sat down with Gray upon the Island of Cumberland." It was well known that the settlers were selling cattle to St. Augustine, delivering them both over land and by water. The governor feared that Gray's Gang was selling beef to French privateers that cruised the coast looking for harbors in which to refit.[17]

As the settlement grew, the Georgia governor became increasingly nervous. Fearing British violation of the various trade embargoes, in 1759 Ellis joined South Carolina's governor, William Henry Lyttleton, in sending two commissioners to New Hanover and Cumberland with orders for the settlers to leave their houses and fields. Although the emissaries read the proclamation aloud to the gathered people and returned to Cumberland Island to check on their departure, the commissioners reported their suspicion that the settlers had evacuated the island only for a short time and would return as soon as the commissioners left. The commissioners admitted that many of the New Hanover men simply absented themselves.[18]

Governor Ellis realized that although illegal, trade with the Spanish was lucrative. In July 1760 he suggested to his council in Savannah that supplying the
Spanish with provisions might benefit Georgia. While Great Britain feared
Spanish provisioning of the French, the British were not at that time at war
with Spain. The governor reminded his council that a newly enacted Georgia
law, designed to prevent the Spanish from receiving provisions for resale, reserved to him the power to grant licenses for provisioning the Spanish for their
own use. For the next year colonial merchants conducted a brisk trade with
Florida, an activity that may have led to a rethinking of the ruling against Gray.
Later in 1760 Sir James Wright succeeded Ellis as royal governor of Georgia and
quickly reversed the policy toward Cumberland Island. In 1761 the council recommended that Gray have his license to trade renewed, "confining the same to
Cumberland Island."[19]

European alliances affected those on Cumberland, although settlers there
did not always realize that a new war had begun. The French and Indian War
between France and Great Britain began with a pitched battle near Fort
Duquesne in western Pennsylvania in 1754. Spain remained neutral until January 1762, when it joined France against Britain, a move that Governor Wright
announced to his people on 25 May 1762.[20]

But some traders with St. Augustine did not hear of these proclamations in
a timely manner. The saga of Samuel Piles, one of Gray's followers, provides in-
sight into Gray's continued trade with the Spanish. Piles was brought before
British authorities on 27 May 1762 on suspicion of "holding Correspondence"
with the enemy at St. Augustine. He was accused of trying to arrange a peace
between the Spanish and the supposedly pro-British Creek Indians. Piles testified that he had indeed gone to St. Augustine in late March, taking with him
corn, peas, and shoats. He claimed that he learned of Spain's entry into the war
only after arriving in St. Augustine. Piles was owed about $4,000 for the live-
stock and produce he had delivered to St. Augustine. The Spanish governor assured Piles that he would get his money but said that he would have to return
with another cargo before receiving full payment. Piles returned to Frederica,
where he made "the strictest Inquiry" about whether war had been declared.
No one in Frederica could confirm the news, so Piles prepared to return to St.
Augustine with a cargo of shingles, boards, dry goods, and shoats. These trading efforts were subsequently called "treasonable." As Piles's case illustrates,
far-off European alliances affected trading patterns of tiny coastal settlements
such as Gray's on Cumberland Island.[21]

Despite such trading setbacks, Gray's settlement persisted. By 1765 nearly all the land on Cumberland Island was granted to wealthy proprietors, which forced squatters without valid claims either to move or to hire out to the new owners. Nonetheless, in 1766 Governor Wright reported that seventy or eighty men, plus women and children, still lived in Gray's old settlements.[22]

Many of Gray's followers, finding a livelihood in the St. Marys Basin area, chose to continue living there after the 1763–65 land grants. Lists of names gathered by Crown commissioners show that at least a half dozen of Gray's followers moved on to Amelia and Talbot Islands in Florida. A few tried unsuccessfully to obtain land grants on Cumberland. In March 1765 one of them, John Cain, petitioned for 500 acres on the western shore of St. Marys, opposite Cumberland Island, "where he has lived some years." In 1798 James Woodland, who had become a prominent landowner in the St. Marys Basin, stated that he had contracted in the 1770s to buy 50 acres on Cumberland belonging to Angus Mackay, an ex-soldier.[23]

No description remains of Gray's island settlement or of its location on Cumberland Island, although the two Crown commissioners referred to numerous habitations and to rye that grew on the island "in great plenty." It is likely that the dwellings lay near the low bluffs of the creeks on the western side of Cumberland, the best places for boats to pull up, with rye and maize fields further to the east. Gray's Gang may have taken advantage of the "Indian old fields," as the settlers frequently called cleared areas. Hog and cow pens would have been located far enough away from the cabins to avoid overexposure to livestock but close enough that settlers could protect the animals from predators, human or otherwise. Corn, peas, and potatoes were grown not only for use within the settlement but also for export.[24]

Private Ownership: The Grantees

In 1763 the Treaty of Paris ended the French and Indian War. As part of the general peace settlement, the Spanish province of East Florida was ceded to Great Britain, and for the first time, lands south of the Altamaha River were made available for legal British settlement. British subjects could now apply to the Crown for land grants on Cumberland Island. However, conflicts for Georgian settlers were not over, for South Carolina claimed the land as its own.

In April 1763 South Carolina's governor, Thomas Boone, issued grants of 343,000 acres of Altamaha land. A month later he issued grants for another

200,000 acres. Georgia bitterly contested and won jurisdiction over the area but was instructed by the Crown to accommodate South Carolina claims. Governor Wright received instructions to issue grants in the name of the province of Georgia. The British government was anxious to see the Altamaha lands settled. All original land grants were given in the name of the king, to be signed by the royal governor. The title of surveyor-general was bestowed on the official charged with administering grants and public land surveys.[25]

On "Land Tuesday," the first Tuesday of each month, the governor and council members met in their chamber in Savannah to receive petitions for land. Each petitioner appeared before the council to present a written statement specifying the number of persons in his family, including any indentured servants and slaves. Under this "headright" system (so named because land was allotted on a per capita basis), the head of family was entitled to 100 acres for himself and 50 additional acres for each dependent, white or black. If the council considered a person capable of cultivating more than this amount of land, the governor was authorized to sell that person up to 1,000 additional acres at a nominal price. If a petitioner's family or slaveholdings increased, additional grants could be obtained.[26]

Upon swearing to the truth of his statements, the petitioner was issued a warrant from the governor directing the surveyor-general to have the tract surveyed. The petitioner then took his warrant to the surveyor-general, who issued a precept ordering a deputy surveyor to lay out the tract. The petitioner generally accompanied the deputy to point out the exact lines for marking off boundaries and to provide chain men for the survey. After completion of the survey, a plat, or measured drawing, was certified by the surveyor-general and returned to the attorney general's office within seven months. The attorney general then prepared a fiat to acknowledge the survey's legality and sent it, along with the plat, to the colonial secretary. After a series of subsequent steps through government, the plat and warrant were recorded by the registrar of the colony. The process, designed to eliminate land disputes and fraudulent claims, was fairly time-consuming. As a result, some applicants became discouraged and failed to pick up their grants.[27]

The law specified that settlers could not let their tracts stand idle but should improve them. Clearing the land for agricultural use was the most common mode of improvement, but other improvements included cattle ranges, lumber yards, landing places, wharves, ferries, sawmills and gristmills, and charitable uses, such as churches and orphanages.[28]

Government officials in Savannah were not certain about conditions in the lower part of the province. In addition to the difficulties that arose as a result of South Carolina's claim to lands between the Altamaha and St. Marys Rivers, Georgia leaders feared that Spanish subjects might have sold some of their land holdings to British subjects. Even members of the governor's council were uncertain regarding land ownership on Cumberland. James Habersham, a member of the Royal Council, protested the passage of a massive wave of would-be settlers in haste to take up South Carolina warrants: "There have been a great Number of People from Carolina passed by both by Land and Water with Surveyors, and even armed, since [5 April 1763], and we are informed that on the said Day, Warrants were issued by the Governor of that Province to survey upwards of 340,000 Acres of Land to the Southward." Habersham particularly feared that Great and Little Cumberland had already been granted to Spanish owners.[29]

The Spanish problem that Habersham feared never materialized, and the Board of Trade's 1763 decision to frame new instructions for Wright extended Georgia's jurisdiction to the St. Marys River, thereby invalidating South Carolina's claims to grant lands in this area. Even though the problem created by the South Carolina grants plagued Georgia surveyors for a number of years, by December 1764 the land dispute between the two provinces was basically settled, and the first eager applicants for land on Cumberland appeared on Land Tuesdays in 1765. Potential settlers still faced the task of establishing plantations in an area that lacked a nearby deepwater port and of living in a region that many people found infertile and unhealthy.

In general, applicants for land on Cumberland were wealthy Georgians and South Carolinians, with a few exceptions. The majority of the grantees came from an elite group of socially and politically important Georgia planters who were anxious to acquire large tracts for rice cultivation. Many of Cumberland's grantees were related to one another. For example, Jonathan Bryan acquired much of his land on Cumberland by buying grants made to his relatives and business colleagues. In another case, it appears that a former soldier, Thomas Williams, petitioned for land intended for one of his old officers, George McIntosh.[30]

Most of the petitioners are well known in Georgia history, but a few are obscure. Some of these petitioners did not receive grants and later purchased land from Crown grantees. Some petitioners applied more than once. The appendix contains an explanation of the methodology by which the title search was carried out.

JAMES BULLOCH

The Reverend James Bulloch (d. 1780) emigrated from Scotland to Charleston about 1729. A wealthy Presbyterian clergyman and rice planter, around 1758 he moved from South Carolina to Georgia, where he married his third wife, Ann Graham, sister of Captain John Cuthbert. In February 1765 Bulloch said his family consisted of a daughter and seventy-seven slaves, so evidently he had again been widowed, and he subsequently remarried.[31] Bulloch was the first person to petition for land on Cumberland.

On New Year's Day 1765 Bulloch submitted two petitions to the governor and council, each for 2,000 acres of land on Cumberland Island "in the southern part of this province." Although it was customary to name parishes on petitions, Bulloch did not do so because no parishes yet existed south of the Altamaha River. Not until March of that year did the assembly create four new ones: St. David, St. Patrick, St. Thomas, and St. Mary. Bulloch's petition also did not name any abuttors, because there were none. The first application was granted on 5 June 1765. The second tract of land was reserved for him for twelve months, but he allowed the grant to lapse.[32]

Although no plat survives, the location of Bulloch's tract can be worked out. He received only the more northern tract, and according to James Cuthbert's grant, it shared a boundary with Cuthbert's land. Thus, Bulloch's land comprised the southern portion of what is now called Great Swamp Field, with acreage extending south to just above the present-day Greyfield. Bulloch received some of the most fertile land on the island, highly suitable for tidal rice planting. On 20 September 1768 Bulloch sold his tract to Bryan for £300.[33]

JONATHAN BRYAN

Jonathan Bryan (1708–88) ultimately owned the largest number of tracts on Great and Little Cumberland: by 1769, he owned all the land on both Cumberlands except for the tracts owned by George and Lachlan McIntosh, Angus Mackay, and Peter Vandyke. However, Bryan's claim to ownership of the two Crown reserves, Fort William and Fort St. Andrews, was dubious.

Bryan was a remarkable man. He was born at Port Royal, South Carolina, the youngest child of Joseph Bryan, an Indian trader and planter, and his wife, Janet Cochran Bryan, both English emigrants who had arrived in Carolina by 1697. Young Jonathan assisted his father in the Indian trade, and he and twenty of his slaves were said to have been among those who greeted Oglethorpe when he landed at Savannah in 1733. The enterprising young South Carolinian soon contracted with Oglethorpe to make a road from Bryan's South Carolina plantation to Savannah and the southern settlements of Darien and Frederica, and subsequently served the general as a scout and soldier.[34]

Bryan's interest in St. Simons Island originated as early as his midtwenties. With the island's potential for engaging the Indian trade through the Altamaha River, Bryan and many others must have foreseen a vital future for St. Simons in 1735, when the trustees put their seal to a grant of 10,000 acres for the "new province of Frederica."[35]

Bryan married Mary Williamson on 13 October 1737 in South Carolina. They had thirteen children, only six of whom reached maturity. A tall and imposing man, Bryan and other such land speculators saw opportunities in creating rice plantations below the Altamaha River. Foreseeing the introduction of slavery to Georgia, in 1752 he moved his family to Walnut Hill, a Savannah River rice plantation. He later owned Monmouth, Seven Oaks, Dean Forest, and Brampton Plantations, all in the vicinity of Savannah.[36]

Jonathan Bryan and his brothers took an active role in the new Georgia colony, and he became one of Oglethorpe's closest associates, serving on the Governor's Council. Bryan moved cautiously in making claims below the Altamaha. He could not request land from South Carolina's governor because it would have alienated his colleagues on the Georgia council. Instead, one of Bryan's brothers-in-law, Stephen Bull, became the first Carolinian to try to make good a South Carolina grant along the Altamaha. An agent for Bull appeared before the Georgia Governor's Council to assert his claim to 7,500 acres by a grant from Governor Boone. Bryan was absent the day of the hearing. Bull's petition was rejected, setting a precedent for the rejection of other Carolinian petitions. Bryan adjusted his interests in the area to exigencies of this tenuous situation.[37]

On the subject of southeastern Georgia, Bryan was indeed something of a visionary. His "Altamaha project" to open up the region for settlement almost immediately attracted the attention of Henry Laurens, a prominent Charleston merchant. Laurens wrote enthusiastically that he was pleased to learn that Bryan had purchased a tract of land with the intention of settling:

> Our opinions coincide exactly, upon the quality of the Lands & advantages of Navigation at Alatamaha, Turtle River, Carr's old Field, Satilla, &ca., & I am quite clear that a very extensive Trade may in a few Years be carried on from Plug point [later Brunswick, Glynn County] as a center. . . .

Shipping must be invited by all due encouragement & at Length Vessels will resort to a port as Men to a well accustomed House of Entertainment, sure of free access, good company, & civil treatment altho they may pay a little more for some particular articles. I am much mistaken if Alatamaha, Turtle River, Satilla great & little, & St. Mary, under due encouragement could not in the space of twenty Years load 300 Sail of Vessels per Annum.[38]

Cumberland Island was the first area Bryan chose for expansion after the completion of his Brampton Plantation. On 3 December 1765 he submitted a petition to the governor and council to exchange a grant for 1,500 acres along the Altamaha River for 800 acres on Cumberland, specifically to include Dungeness, a large sand spit at the southern end of the island.[39]

On 16 June 1766 the governor and council ordered that 1,600 acres be laid out for Bryan on Cumberland Island "in lieu of the like quantity heretofore ordered at a Place called Butter Milk Bluff which the said Jonathan Bryan hath this day resigned." Some high-level horse-trading was involved in the transaction: Governor Wright's brothers were also interested in acquiring the Buttermilk Bluff area. To reward Bryan for his cooperation, he received a second 1,500-acre tract at the northern end of the island. The grants were confirmed, and on 7 April 1767 Bryan received both tracts.[40]

The southern tract was bounded on the south by a tract of 200 acres reserved for the use of the Crown and described as where Fort William had formerly stood. Although the fort had recently been put out of service, historian William Ramsay suggests that the reserved land continued to function through the late 1760s as a station for pilots who were assigned to the St. Marys Bar. Since Fort William was still visible in the 1790s, it is possible that its buildings were kept in moderately good repair throughout the 1770s, at least until the outbreak of the Revolutionary War.[41]

Bryan's northern grant of 1,500 acres was described as bounded on the south by the land of Thomas Williams and on the west by a tract of 100 acres "whereon Fort St. Andrews formerly stood."[42] With the exception of this land, Bryan's tract thus included the entire High Point area almost down to the Squawtown Peninsula.

Bryan correctly surmised that the value of Georgia islands would increase dramatically in the next few years. In 1767 he increased his holdings on Cumberland Island with a 2,000-acre grant. Three hundred acres of the grant completed his freehold, and the council permitted him to purchase at minimal cost 1,000 acres for himself and 700 acres in the name of his son, Josiah.[43]

Bryan subsequently was unable to obtain any additional acreage on Cumberland from the Georgia government. Governor Wright opposed land speculation, and Bryan showed no signs of planning to settle on the island. It must have been evident that he had no intention of developing a rice plantation: placing a large slave workforce on an isolated island like Cumberland ran the risk of the slaves running away.

Although some historians are mystified by Bryan's interest in land so distant from Georgia and Florida's population centers, his plans for Cumberland make more sense when viewed in the light of changing international boundaries. While in 1763 Bryan may have thought of exporting rice and cattle, after 1767 he altered his plans, accumulating tracts to sell to investors. The newly created provinces of British East and West Florida attracted a flood of investors, including many wealthy British-born capitalists. Grantees such as Denys Rolles and the second earl of Egmont did not intend to settle in Florida, instead sending capable young English superintendents to supervise large plantations.

Bryan quickly divined that future requests for acreage on the island would be rejected and found imaginative ways to obtain more land. First, he recruited others to obtain Cumberland land for him. Another brother-in-law, John Smith, a South Carolinian, took out a survey on 15 December 1766 and received a 2,000-acre grant on 5 May 1767, which he sold about six months later to Bryan for the sum of £50. That the tract was meant for Bryan all along was made evident by the low selling price and the rapidity with which the transaction was consummated after Smith received title. Since a plat survives for Smith's grant, his tract can be identified as consisting of Rayfield Plantation area, Oyster Pond Road, and Kill Man Field, with a southern boundary corresponding somewhat to the present-day Duck House Road.[44]

Having obtained control of more than 7,000 acres on Cumberland, Bryan began to consolidate his holdings, a process that in a few years resulted in his ownership of nearly all of Great and Little Cumberland. Bryan tested the market value of Cumberland by advertising it for sale while continuing to seek the remainder of the island.

On 10 February 1768 he advertised 7,500 acres for sale, "a great part of which is very fit for corn, rice, indigo, and cotton, with a large quantity of live oak and pine for ship building; also extraordinary range for cattle, hogs, and horses." In January 1769 Bryan purchased an additional 1,500 acres belonging to James Cuthbert, another brother-in-law.[45]

On 26 July 1770 Bryan again advertised, this time including the two McIntosh tracts in his offer:

To Be Sold

The island of Cumberland, lying between the Mouth of St. Marys River and St. Andrews Sound, 22 miles in Length and three in Breadth, containing 11,750 acres; 10,700 in my own Grants, and 750 [Acres] to Messrs. Lachlan and George Mackintosh which they have also offered for Sale; 200 Acres on the South Point where the Ruins of Fort William stand, and 160 Acres near the North End, where formerly Fort St. Andrew stood, reserved by the Government for Use of Fortifications, include the Whole of this Island. . . . from the Middle to the South End, the land is very good for planting corn, Cotton, or Indigo, and great Conveniency for setting up Indigo Vats upon the many springs which vent themselves through the Island. The Navigation will admit Vessels of any Burthen from one Inlet to the other within Land; and the Island abounds with great quantities of Live-Oak, of the best kind for Ship Building.

Two wealthy Charlestonians, planter Thomas Lynch and merchant Alexander Rose, purchased all Bryan's holdings on 6 August 1770 for £1,100.[46]

By 1769 Jonathan Bryan had become an effective leader in preparing resolutions that aligned Georgia with other provinces critical of Great Britain's imperial policies, and in September of that year he was expelled from the Royal Council of Georgia. During the American Revolution the patriotic activities of Bryan and his son, James, resulted in their 1778 capture and confinement to British prison hulks off Long Island, New York, for more than two years. Despite being nearly eighty years old, Jonathan allegedly kept his health by swimming around the hulk once each day. The two men were exchanged in 1781, and Jonathan Bryan was subsequently appointed to the state's executive council. He lived out his days at Brampton Plantation, on the Savannah River.[47]

JAMES AND JOHN CUTHBERT

Although there are several James Cuthberts among the Georgia planters, the one who received land on Cumberland seems to have been Dr. James Cuthbert Jr. of South Carolina. Interlocking familial relationships and the large number of children born to Jonathan Bryan's parents resulted in marriages that connected Bryan to many South Carolina planters. In 1757 Cuthbert married Anne Bryan, half-sister of one of Jonathan Bryan's daughters-in-law. Mrs. John Smith, Mrs. Jonathan Bryan Jr., and Mrs. James Cuthbert Jr. were all kinfolk of Jonathan Bryan. On his petition, Dr. Cuthbert stated that he had a wife, four children, and sixty-four slaves. Like Bulloch, Cuthbert was a wealthy man.[48]

On the same day as Bulloch, 1 January 1765, James Cuthbert petitioned for a 1,500-acre tract on Cumberland, and John Cuthbert (probably James's son) petitioned for an adjacent tract of 550 acres described as lying about two miles south of "Hester's Bluff near the middle of the Island." John Cuthbert's petition described him as having been in Georgia for about four years and as owning nine slaves. On 5 August 1766 James Cuthbert obtained his grant, although John Cuthbert did not: the council learned that he and his family, settled in Charleston, did not intend to emigrate to Georgia.[49]

No plat survives for James Cuthbert's tract, but its location can be determined. It lay south of John Smith's tract, for which a plat does exist.[50] Cuthbert's tract comprised the northern portion of Great Swamp Field, with acreage extending north up to the present King's Bottom area. Cuthbert and Bulloch evidently intended to invest in the same fertile inland swamp area, which probably explains why both men petitioned on the same day. (Alternatively, the Cuthberts may have petitioned for land at Bulloch's behest, intending to turn it over to him.) Had all the Bulloch-Cuthbert petitions succeeded, the combine would have acquired 6,050 acres of prime rice land.

Although John Cuthbert's petition was unsuccessful, the description of his acreage helps to establish the locations of both Hester's Bluff and the land granted to a later applicant, Peter Vandyke. Cuthbert petitioned for what is now identified as the Plum Orchard area, described as "bounded on the west by a creek leading from St. Marys River." This creek was what we now call Brick Hill River, a deepwater tidal creek, which meant that the tract possessed superb potential for docking and loading rice.

LACHLAN, GEORGE, AND JOHN HOUSTOUN MCINTOSH

Lachlan (1727–1806) and George McIntosh (1739–79) were among the sons of John McIntosh Mohr, a Highlander from Inverness, Scotland, who settled with his family, followers, and servants on the Altamaha River in 1736. There was never any question in Georgia about the courage and clannishness of the McIntoshes of Darien. They had a tendency, however, to feather their own nests.[51]

Lachlan, the chief's second son, spoke Gaelic as well as English. As a boy, he lived frequently with the Indians, and he later became a cadet in Oglethorpe's Regiment. When Lachlan was twenty-one, he took his eleven-year-old brother, George, to South Carolina, where they spent the next eight years. The brothers prospered in Charleston, the younger at school, the elder making social and business connections that lasted throughout his life. On 1 January 1756 Lachlan married Sarah Threadcraft, then living with her mother and stepfather, John and Esther Cuthbert, in Williamsburg, South Carolina. John Cuthbert was constantly in debt to his son-in-law. In Charleston Lachlan began his life-long friendship with Laurens, who was strongly interested in the lower Altamaha.

When Lachlan returned to Georgia, he commenced what later became one of his consuming passions, land acquisition. In April 1763 Laurens received a warrant of survey for 3,000 acres in the disputed lower Altamaha region, near Darien, Lachlan's old home. Colonel Thomas Middleton, a South Carolinian, was competing for the same tract. Lachlan is said to have gotten Middleton's surveyor so drunk that McIntosh's man completed the survey for Laurens. By the early 1770s Lachlan was among the greatest landholders in Georgia, although he was by no means among the wealthiest. A man with many friends, he was considered remarkably astute, even cunning. Unusually competent in military affairs, during the American Revolution Lachlan became a brigadier general in the Continental Army, and he served with General George Washington at Valley Forge.

On 2 April 1765 Lachlan McIntosh applied for 200 acres on Cumberland, to the north of Cuthbert's tract. McIntosh's petition stated that he had twelve persons in his family. The tract was surveyed on 22 April 1765, and he received his land on 9 September 1766. The surviving McIntosh plat clearly shows that his grant consisted of a portion of a large peninsular extension of land on the west side of the island, now called Table Point. Since subsequent maps referred to McIntosh's grant as Table of Pines (meaning a stand of pines), it seems likely that McIntosh's grant was heavily wooded. His plat is marked "oak land."

In April 1765 George McIntosh, youngest of John McIntosh Mohr's six sons, also petitioned for land on Cumberland, asking for 100 acres on its northern end "where one Johnson family formerly lived." His grant seems to have been denied, probably because it lay within the area of Fort St. Andrews that had been reserved for Crown use. Two years later Thomas Williams sold George 450 acres on Cumberland Island, near Lachlan's land. The two McIntosh tracts were separated by only a low marsh, semiflooded at high tide and perfect for rice cultivation.

George McIntosh married Anne Priscilla "Nancy" Houstoun, from another large and propertied Georgia family. The couple had a son, John Houstoun McIntosh, on 1 May 1773. Nancy died when she was twenty-one years old, followed shortly by her second infant son. George McIntosh died intestate in 1779, and his only surviving son, six years old at the time, inherited his parents' vast holdings. The Houstoun family, one of the most powerful in Georgia, moved to take charge of the wealthy young orphan. His guardians included two maternal uncles, Sir Patrick Houstoun and George Houstoun. Upon attaining his majority, John H. McIntosh stood to inherit extensive properties from both his Houstoun and McIntosh relatives, including more than 13,000 acres in Liberty, Glynn, and Camden Counties.

In 1784 William McIntosh, one of John McIntosh's paternal uncles, successfully petitioned to revoke the letters of administration given to the Houstouns, and by the end of the decade two McIntosh uncles, Lachlan and William, were in charge of their nephew's properties. In 1793 John H. McIntosh, now twenty years old, filed a bill of complaint against Lachlan and William and freed himself from a sea of interested relatives.

The plat to John's Cumberland Island tract was evidently lost during the Revolutionary War, and in 1797 he ordered its resurvey. James M. Lindsay, Camden County surveyor, stated in his plat that he was running off the lines of the tract "formerly belonging to Thomas Williams."

ANGUS MACKAY

In the early days of the trusteeship, Captain Hugh Mackay, one of Oglethorpe's favorites, had joked with Oglethorpe that "if the colony subsists but three years there will be more Mackays in America than in the Highlands."[52] Angus Mackay may well have been a clansman of the half dozen Mackays who served under Oglethorpe. Political persecution and personal suffering among the Highland Scots led many of them to follow their ministers and clan leaders to Georgia.

There are a number of Angus Mackays recorded in early Georgia (in St. Andrews, St. Thomas, and St. Marys Parishes), and distinguishing among them is difficult. Some were indentured servants who, after their contracts ended, became troopers or boatmen for Oglethorpe's Regiment. Others, however, emigrated as young boys with their families and were never trust servants, and any one of them could have enlisted at Fort Frederica. While some soldiers were discharged in Georgia when their terms of enlistment were finished, others may have reenlisted to serve elsewhere in North America.

Under the terms of the Royal Proclamation of 1 January 1755, disbanded soldiers from Oglethorpe's Regiment were granted 50 acres of land as a bounty. After selecting the land, they were issued warrants. Some eligible ex-soldiers died, lost interest, or moved away before the process of getting a title was completed. In such cases, their warrants were advertised as expired. In January 1764 one such advertisement stated that "Angus M'Kay" had taken out a warrant on 3 July 1759 but had allowed it to lapse.[53] It is possible that he had reenlisted to fight in Canada at the time he was supposed to pick up his warrant.

Following the British triumph in the French and Indian War, a royal proclamation decreed that land in America was to be granted to "private soldiers as have been or shall be dis-banded in America and actually residing there [to each] private man, 50 acres." The bounty process for former soldiers was redefined after the Treaty of Paris. All regular troops who had fought for the Crown were entitled to a bounty. Ex-soldiers could apply for 5 acres; noncommissioned officers, 50 acres; commissioned officers, 200 acres.[54]

As a result, on 3 June 1766 Angus Mackay again petitioned Governor Wright and the council. Mackay claimed that "he had been twenty Years in the Province being one of the disbanded Soldiers of the Regiment by General Oglethorpe and was desirous to obtain a Piece of Land whereon to settle, having had none yet granted him therefore praying for Fifty Acres on Cumberland Island at a Place there called Graham's Old Field in Vertue of the Royal Proclamation." On 13 September 1768 Wright granted Mackay 50 acres in the Parish of St. Marys, "land bounded on every side by vacant land." The petition does not specify where the tract was located, but the size of the grant indicates that Mackay must have been a noncommissioned officer. In 1798 Mackay's land was put up for auction for back taxes, and in 1799 it was delineated by the county surveyor. From these events, it is known that Mackay's tract was at Half Moon Bluff, on the extreme north end of Great Cumberland.[55]

The location of his acreage—near abandoned Fort St. Andrews and possibly Mackay's Town—seems to confirm Angus's relationship to the Mackay officers who commanded in Oglethorpe's Regiment. It certainly seems likely that Angus Mackay knew Barriemackie and sought personal advantage when he petitioned for land on the island. He may have sought the landing site near the fort for trading purposes.

PATRICK MACKAY

Like Angus Mackay, Patrick was a petitioner from Oglethorpe's Regiment, but his exact identity cannot be determined. He may well be the Patrick Mackay who fled Scotland in 1738 on a felony charge—not an unusual charge against the Highlanders, who were considered adept cattle rustlers. Termed an "Arch-

Incendiary" and a "mischief-maker" by some Georgia contemporaries, this man may also have been the Captain Patrick Mackay who was reprimanded for insubordination in 1753 and was apparently discharged from further military service.[56]

In 1763 Patrick Mackay petitioned for land "formerly given by General Oglethorpe to Major Hugh Mackay of his Regiment or any other part of that Island found vacant." However, this petition was turned down along with hundreds of others because the status of all lands south of the Altamaha River was uncertain.[57]

On 5 March 1765 "Patrick Mackay, Esq." petitioned again, this time for 1,126 acres on Cumberland Island. On this occasion, he said that his previous warrant for land off the Sapelo River showed that the tract he wanted had already been surveyed for other petitioners. "He asks that his warrant be renewed for a like quantity on Cumberland Island formerly given by General Oglethorpe to Major Hugh Mackay." This warrant was allowed. On 5 August 1766 Patrick said that he had been misinformed about the land near the Sapelo River and wanted to change his warrant back.[58] Although the request was rejected, Patrick Mackay's reference to Oglethorpe's grant to Hugh Mackay opens up some interesting possibilities about other land grants made by the general. If Oglethorpe did grant land on Cumberland, such grants had no legal validity, and in any event, none have survived.

JAMES HABERSHAM

James Habersham (1712–75) was one of the most influential men in colonial Georgia. He arrived in Georgia in 1738 and shortly thereafter opened a school for destitute children at Bethesda, in Savannah. Faithfully serving the royal governors, Habersham was a staunch loyalist in the years leading up to the revolution. In 1740 he married Mary Bolton at Bethesda, with noted evangelist Rev. George Whitefield presiding over the service. The Habershams had ten children, only three of whom survived their father. Literate, astute, and socially mobile, James Habersham acquired much of his wealth through his commercial house, Harris and Habersham. To his family, Habersham left a substantial amount of property in southeast Georgia. At the end of his life Habersham owned 198 slaves and was producing about seven hundred barrels of rice each year.[59]

In 1766 Habersham petitioned for Little Cumberland Island. He stated his intention to reserve 100 acres for the Crown where "Fort St. Andrew was built."

Habersham apparently was using an inaccurate map that showed the fort on Little Cumberland, when it was actually at the north end of Great Cumberland. On 3 June 1766 Habersham received a warrant for 1,000 acres on Little Cumberland (nearly the whole island), and on 6 January 1767 he obtained 1,400 acres on the island, apparently the result of his hiring a more competent surveyor. On 24 October 1767 Habersham sold Little Cumberland to Jonathan Bryan.[60]

JOHN SMITH

John Smith was a wealthy South Carolina resident who owned fifty slaves. He applied for a grant of 2,050 acres on Great Cumberland, which was surveyed for him on 15 December 1766. His plat, which survives, shows that his tract was located at the area later called Rayfield Plantation and included Oyster Pond and Kill Man Fields, with a southern boundary that corresponds with the present Duck House Road. Smith received his grant on 5 May 1767 but sold it about six months later to Jonathan Bryan, for whom Smith may have been acting as a front. Smith was one of Bryan's brothers-in-law.[61]

THOMAS WILLIAMS

On 3 February 1767 Thomas Williams was granted 450 acres on Great Cumberland.[62] Although no plat survives, his tract abutted John Smith's property and therefore can be identified as the present-day Squawtown area, a broad stubby peninsula whose sides are cut by long outflows and overlooking a large marsh to the west.

The petition yields a few details about Thomas Williams. He had been in Georgia about two years and had a wife, Rebecca; four children; and two slaves. By 1767 standards, Williams was not a wealthy man. There is also substantial evidence that he was illiterate: he sold his tract to George McIntosh later in 1767, and after Williams made his mark on the colonial conveyance, someone else wrote in for him, "Of the Parish of St. Marys, laborer."[63]

Williams may have sold his grant to McIntosh as a result of some obligation, or Williams may have petitioned for land to cloak McIntosh's interest. It is quite possible that this man was the Thomas Williams who served during the 1750s in the Independent Regulars. When Oglethorpe's Regiment was disbanded in 1749 and posted back to Gibraltar, many soldiers who stayed behind enlisted either in the Independent Regulars or in the South Carolina Regulars. This might explain why Williams appeared to be a recent arrival in Georgia: he may have returned to South Carolina with the other regulars. Most Independent Regulars were stationed at Fort Frederica, where young George McIntosh had been in charge of the commissary of supplies, becoming well acquainted with the regiment. Williams and McIntosh may have known each other from that time.

PETER VANDYKE

Originally from South Carolina, Peter Vandyke arrived in Georgia in 1761 and settled on Skidaway Island, near Savannah. He was not a wealthy man: his petition stated that he had a wife, four children, and two slaves.[64]

In 1764 Vandyke obtained a warrant for 350 acres known as Hester's Bluff. He wanted to obtain this land in family right and to purchase an additional 150 acres. Because the council at first found this tract to have been given to John Cuthbert, Vandyke's petition failed. But when the council learned that Cuthbert was leaving Georgia, Vandyke renewed his petition.[65]

On 4 December 1764 Vandyke obtained the 350 acres at Hester's Bluff, but he still wanted the other 150 acres. In 1766 Cuthbert issued a caveat, warning Vandyke to desist. Over Cuthbert's furious opposition, on 3 February 1767 the governor and the council gave the entire 500 acres to Vandyke in two separate grants.[66]

Vandyke's two tracts correspond to the present-day Plum Orchard and Lanes Landing areas. In 1772 both Vandyke's tracts were put up for sale. John Houstoun, son-in-law of Jonathan Bryan, purchased both of them for a small sum. Vandyke's widow, Rachel, applied for letters of administration in Liberty County on 22 September 1788, so Vandyke must have died before that date.[67] It seems doubtful that Vandyke was a land speculator. That he owned only two slaves suggests that he was a small-scale planter.

JOSIAH BRYAN

On 1 March 1768 Josiah Bryan (1746–74), one of Jonathan Bryan's sons, successfully petitioned for 700 acres on Cumberland that was described as having been part of the 2,000 acres in Bulloch's second, unapproved, petition. Josiah's tract was bounded on the west by salt marshes and on the south by land belonging to his father. On the same day, Jonathan Bryan successfully applied for two tracts, one for 870 acres and the other for 300 acres. Thus, father and son received 1,870 acres, representing almost the entire balance of Bulloch's lapsed warrant. Much of this land lay south of Great Swamp Field but north of Dungeness.[68]

FOUR

Cumberland's First Plantations

Insular Estates

*M*ost of Cumberland's colonial grantees were land speculators. Although rice and indigo were probably Cumberland's first large-scale agricultural pursuits, it is doubtful that extensive rice and indigo planting on Cumberland began before 1770. With the advent of the American Revolution in 1775, vicious partisan warfare on the Georgia-Florida borderlands soon brought these profitable agricultural plans to a close.

For many years, rice had been cultivated in relatively small fields, somewhat like paddies, on mainland Georgia and particularly on freshwater islands, where lowlands were easily turned to rice production. Saltwater islands, even those that, like Cumberland, contained a supply of freshwater, were more difficult environments. A sizable portion of Cumberland Island consists of marshland that fringes the Inland Navigation. Because of the high salinity of the water, these marginal lands could not be cultivated in indigo or rice, but the luxuriant carpet of grasses and rushes served as excellent rangeland for cattle. South Carolina planters had learned how to construct tide gates and canals in the seventeenth century, but not until capitalists with extra money to invest appeared in the 1770s did Cumberland planters turn to rice. Cumberland land remained valuable primarily for hunting, growing corn, and horse and cattle ranching.

Coastal residents' core diet was corn and pork, supplemented with seafood, small animals, and gathered plant food. All island residents, including slaves, further varied their diet by raising vegetables and livestock. Subsistence technology included guns, fishing equipment, traps, and beehives made of hollow logs.[1]

In 1774 botanist William Bartram traveled to East Florida and saw so few inhabitants in the Georgia settlements and on Jekyll and Cumberland Islands in particular that he commented, the greatest part of these are as yet the property of a few wealthy planters, who having their residence on the continent, where lands . . . are of a nature and quality adapted to the growth of rice, which the planters chiefly rely upon, for obtaining ready cash, and purchasing family articles; they settle a few poor families on their insular estates, who rear stock of horned cattle, horses, swine and poultry, and protect the game for their proprietors. . . . The inhabitants of these islands also lay open to the invasion and ravages of pirates.[2]

Nonetheless, Cumberland's residents were comparatively comfortable. It was hard to go hungry on the island, because residents knew where to look for food. When Jonathan Bryan stopped at Cumberland, hunters gave him bear meat and venison. Bear, hogs, raccoons, and humans competed for sea-turtle eggs, laid on the island's Atlantic beach from early May through July.[3]

Behind the beach dunes, in the chain of narrow lagoons called sloughs, Cumberland Islanders hunted ducks. In the interior, residents set out hog traps and needed only to notch a catch's ears to claim it. Fishing in the creeks from the docks brought drum and mullet. Seining was a group activity: some families shared their nets with neighbors to pull hundreds of pounds of fish from the Atlantic beach. On the creek side, when the tide was out, old and young gathered bushels of oysters. Finally, with skiffs and hand nets, Cumberland Islanders used their knowledge of the tides and tidal creeks to bring home abundant shrimp.[4]

From the sixteenth century onward, islanders grew corn, both for their own consumption and for export. In 1787 a Spanish officer at Amelia Island wrote to Governor Vicente Emanuel de Zéspedes about obtaining corn from Cumberland to replenish St. Augustine's exhausted supplies. Cumberland was not a new source of corn for the garrison: Spanish records as far back as the 1580s indicate that the mission Indians of Cumberland were sending corn for the relief of famished St. Augustine.[5]

Cumberland's poor settlers roasted or ground corn for meal, and corn blades (the leafy part of ripening corn) served as a fodder for their livestock. Corn also attracted bears, who swam from the mainland to the Sea Islands when cornfields were ripening. Florida bears were common on Cumberland until about the 1920s, and the last one was seen at Plum Orchard in the 1930s. Quash, a young former slave, settled at Brick Hill in the 1870s. In the 1880s, Quash recalled walking down the island's main road in absolute darkness when he began to wonder if another person was walking silently behind him.

I was 'bout to turn and run when I saw it wasn't anything but a bear. He was walking just as straight as I was, and he was most as tall and a heap wider. We come to
a place in the road where de moon was shin' thru' and I saw him had his arms full
of corn. He looked at me and I looked at him, and didn't either one of us say anything. I kep' on my side of de road and he kep' on his side of de road, and we
walked along real friendly like. After awhile we were nearly to Brick Hill and he
stopped and looked straight at me. I looked at him, and he say, "Ump! Ump!
Ump!" just like he was sayin' "Good night, Quash," and I say, "Good night,
Mr. Bear."[6]

The luxuriant carpet of grasses and rushes in the Cumberland marshlands
provided excellent range for cattle and horses. As mentioned earlier, in 1597 the
Spanish gave a horse to San Pedro's cacique, Don Juan. Although ethnologists
think the island Timucuans would have found horses impractical for coastal
travel, Spanish officers surely introduced mounted transport to the islands.
Similarly, Spanish friars may have tried to bring asses, mules, or oxen, although
no archaeological evidence yet exists of their early use. Raising stock for resale,
however, was always profitable. Horse and cattle raising on Cumberland succeeded for three reasons: first, feral livestock on the Sea Islands could forage for
themselves; second, theft of horses was difficult on an island where the rustlers
were apt to be known; and third, natural increase of island livestock proceeded
with minimum interruption.[7]

In the early days of settlement, semigentled horses may have been swum to
the mainland to be sold. According to Bryan, Cumberland Island was about two
miles offshore, and records indicate that in 1866 two Cumberland Islanders
swam horses over to Camden County, to the fury of the Freedmen's Bureau
agent. Modern-day Camden County horsemen believe swimming horses to be
possible using a route starting in the marsh south of the Plum Orchard dock.
The horses would swim to the mouth of Brick Hill River, then down the eastern shore of Cumberland River, much of which is composed of shell, making a
hard bottom. Conducting the swim at low tide would result in minimal current,
making the endeavor easier on the horses. One man suggested having a small
boat alongside to hold the horses' heads up as they cross the Cumberland River.
The horses could land at a point about three hundred yards south of Cabin
Bluff.[8]

Livestock occasionally traveled to the mainland on flat boats. In 1789 a horse
catcher wrote from Cumberland to Captain John McIntosh, "I have the pleas-

ure to inform you that we have got 13 head of horses much better ones than the last, there is none of them more than 3 years old . . . but cannot get Mr. McIntosh's Flat to take them over, so beg you will meet me at Hockings Island wednesday fore noon to see about geting a boat."[9]

Although islanders rounded up feral horses primarily to sell as mounts and workhorses, horses also provided a source of food during crises. During the American Revolution, a British expeditionary force was ordered to rendezvous at Cumberland's south end. The unit's Florida commissariat failed to deliver, and the nine hundred troops were compelled to eat horseflesh.[10]

Wild cattle easily fed themselves on the rich grasses of the hard marsh (marsh solid enough to support their weight). Eighteenth-century Cumberland Islanders quickly found that they could round up other people's cows with impunity and declare them as their own. While privateers could negotiate with islanders to buy cows, when no one was around, the sailors could catch and slaughter the animals without paying for them. During the revolution, the Americans noted the quantity of free-ranging cattle between the St. Marys and the St. Johns Rivers: "The southern parts of Georgia contain vast stocks of cattle, and our most valuable rice plantations lie that way. By some computations there are said to be upwards of thirty thousand head of black cattle in the Provinces, and hogs without number."[11]

The broad salt marshes that edged the island were suited for cattle production, but the real money lay in the cultivation of rice, which became the most profitable coastal crop. Some of the Sea Islands were too small to ensure profitable rice plantations, but Cumberland Island both was sufficiently large and had an inland swamp of the kind deemed absolutely necessary for the hydraulics of planting rice.

Rice, Live Oak, and Indigo

Preparing Cumberland Island's marshlands and inland swamps for use as rice fields was a tremendous task. Clearing the swamps, building embankments, laying off ditches and fields, and setting trunks and gates required considerable engineering knowledge and capital investment, including large numbers of slaves. However, experienced and wealthy rice planters saw that the tidal hydraulics of the central third of Cumberland made growing rice potentially profitable.

The lands along the Inland Navigation were called the "rice coast." Early

sites were on inland river floodplains, but as knowledge of tidal action increased, planters established rice fields near tidal estuaries. Planters relied on
tidal dynamics to flood rice fields, an ingenious adaptation viewed by modern
agricultural experts as without parallel elsewhere on this continent. The adaptation depended on two conditions. First, the tidal range had to be from three
to seven feet to facilitate field flooding. Second, strong layering of freshwater
was needed to prevent saline water from entering the rice fields and destroying
the crop.[12]

The salt wedge was the ideal site for planting rice. During high tide, the encroaching saltwater wedge acts as a sort of dam or plug that holds up the freshwater flow, thus creating an impoundment of freshwater that can then be
tapped to flood the rice fields. When the tide ebbs, the freshwater rushes in to
cover the field. Ideal rice-growing conditions existed when freshwater stream
flow dominated the estuary. The saltwater estuary developed a pronounced layering of freshwater on top of salt water. Care was taken to ensure that extremely
high tides did not force salt water onto the rice fields. To drain the fields, the
process was reversed, allowing water to run off the fields during low tide.[13]

This system of utilizing the salt-wedge estuary was perfected in South Carolina, perhaps as early as 1690. The technique subsequently spread both north
and south along the coast as far as North Carolina and Florida. The necessity
for flooding fields with freshwater severely limited the number of suitable sites,
and the substantial requirements of time, capital, and labor made it unlikely
that farmers with small families could successfully compete with slave labor.[14]

The vagaries of coastal environments, including periodic storms, devastat-
ing high tides, and occasional freshets, meant that a substantial amount of
maintenance was needed to keep the rice fields in good order. The critical demands of tidewater plantations limited them to a few areas where certain conditions were met: the narrow intertidal zones between the muddy flats of the
marsh and the freshwater inland swamps.

Remnants of a salt-wedge estuary are found on Cumberland Island in Great
Swamp Field. Divided by a tidal creek into a northern and a southern part, this
large area and its drainage comprise almost one-third of the island. The southern portion of Great Swamp Field contains several artesian springs. For most of
the coastal plain region of Georgia, the principal source of groundwater is the
coastal plain aquifer. Prior to the nineteenth century, artesian pressure caused
water to rise to an elevation of about sixty-five feet above sea level in wells tap-
ping the aquifer in the Cumberland Island area. These wells supplied an out-

flow of freshwater north through Great Swamp Field until it was plugged by the salt water of flood tides. Although the artesian flow from these springs has generally now ceased, their presence and utility were well known in the eighteenth century.[15]

Great Swamp Field is such a perfect example of prime rice land that it is no wonder that Rev. James Bulloch and Dr. James Cuthbert Jr., the first petitioners for land on Cumberland, asked for the field's northern portion and southern portion, respectively, tracts totaling more than 6,050 acres. To begin cutting and logging in Great Swamp Field was a slow process and represented a considerable investment. Rice cultivation probably began in earnest on Cumberland Island well after 1770, when Bryan sold all his holdings on the island (including Great Swamp Field, which he had purchased) to Thomas Lynch, a wealthy and experienced rice planter from South Carolina, and Alexander Rose, Lynch's agent and factor, in Charleston.[16]

One of the most noticeable trees of Cumberland Island's native forest was the stately live oak. Cutting live oak for shipbuilding was a lucrative business throughout the seventeenth century. Transient settlers on Cumberland, especially large groups like Gray's Gang, cut live oak timber for sloops and cutters. Privateers and Spanish *guardacostas* raiding the Georgia and Carolina coasts obtained live oak from the sea islands either by purchase or by illegal cutting.[17]

Although live oak's long, curved limbs made bow stems for coastal work boats such as cutters and large dories, live oak was particularly valuable for the building of tall-masted vessels. The tree's natural curves suited shipwrights, fulfilling their requirements for a variety of shapes and permitting them to avoid the weakening effect of cross-grain cuts. With great tensile strength and resistance to rot, live oak was durable. Eighteenth-century property owners advertising land for sale in Georgia and South Carolina newspapers nearly always called attention to the availability of live oak and pine for shipbuilding. As early as 1769 the Royal Navy was examining the possibilities for live oak contracts in the southeastern Georgia parishes, finding that "Live Oak on the Salt water Creek, or Islands is far superior to those on fresh Water with less Sap & a finer grain of Wood."[18]

Although live oak was used in shipbuilding well before 1740, colonial shipyards began to look for it more eagerly just prior to the American Revolution, and a major change occurred in 1794, when the new republic found itself obliged to build a navy. Indiscriminate and illegal cutting of live oak on the Sea Islands, long a problem for landowners, became more profitable and more or-

ganized when the U.S. Navy concluded agreements with private timber contractors who had to meet government specifications.[19]

A typical live oak operation, whether illegal or authorized, involved large
gangs of white men under contract to a shipowner, often supplemented by slave
labor provided by plantation owners where the live oak was cut. Live-oakers, as
these men soon came to be known, expected the contractor to provide shelter,
provisions, grog, some medical assistance (sometimes consisting of little more
than a medicine chest), and draft animals, preferably oxen, who were strong
and docile and had cloven hooves that prevented them from getting stuck in
muddy places. The men lived in simple thatched huts and cabins, constructed
by the live-oakers themselves, with a kitchen shed or two and rudimentary
shelters for the animals.[20]

Georgia's marshes and winding creeks often forced ships carrying live-
oakers to anchor far from shore. Since all materials had to be carried from the
ship to the campsite, a bluff where the ship could tie up was preferable to a
mooring several miles away. The location of a live-oaking camp considerably
modified an island's road system—if it had one. Because green live oak is much
heavier than water, it could not be floated downstream, so live-oakers' first task
was to clear trails to the landing. As the most readily available timber was
cleared, the men began working deeper into the woods, eventually walking several miles away from camp to find suitable trees. The live-oaking trail system
thus created a spokelike system, with all trails converging on the landing place.
Low bluffs edged by deep water made good landing places and were advertised
as such.[21]

Although it is not known exactly where live-oakers' ships tied up on Cumberland, they likely used the bluffs at Linchus Creek (Beach Creek), Little Old
House Creek, Brick Hill Bluff, Plum Orchard Bluff, McIntosh Creek, and
Greyfield. Plantation owners often attempted to combine the live oak operation with cotton, as land cleared by logging could subsequently be advertised as
suitable for planting.

Lynch and Rose bought what the deed termed nine plantations, so called because they had been Crown grants, comprising 10,870 acres. Because they
bought the land as tenants in common, both men had undivided interests in
each tract. The purchasers gave a token sum of five shillings to the seller, but a
second indenture, signed by the seller and his wife within a day or two, stated
the real purchase price of £1,100.[22]

Between 1770 and 1783 Rose's undivided half interest in the land passed through several hands. In the mid-1770s it was acquired by a well-known Charleston land speculator and timber merchant, John McQueen (1751–1807), who specialized in purchasing Sea Island land. He was motivated in part by the possibilities of a contract with the French navy. On 1 August 1783 McQueen, who was heavily in debt (partly as a result of the American Revolution), transferred his interest in the two Cumberland Islands to John Banks, another Charleston merchant. Banks's equity in the land would ultimately become the property of General Nathanael Greene.[23]

Thomas Lynch may have planted indigo, which was often grown on parts of the Sea Islands that were not well suited to rice cultivation. The only record of indigo planting on Cumberland is a 1794 writ prepared by Camden County's sheriff against Peter Belin (ca. 1715–ca. 1791), a tax delinquent and an employee of Lynch: "Executed four hundred acres Land in the Indigo Fields of Cumberland Island." Cumberland's indigo fields were probably near Great Swamp Field and the Plum Orchard outflow. Great Swamp Field, south of Belin's residence, would have been eminently suitable for indigo cultivation.[24]

Indigo, a source of dye, was one of the first moneymaking crops that British plantations in the Carolinas and Georgia took up in the eighteenth century. Those parts of the Sea Islands with hammocks of live oak and hickory trees were considered particularly favorable for indigo planting. None of the Cumberland grantees were known to be large indigo planters.[25]

Making indigo dye was a difficult process. A large force of slaves was required, and their supervision and maintenance required housing, livestock, and water. Furthermore, indigo plants had to be steeped in large vats of freshwater, so nearby water sources (such as natural springs and vents or streams) were necessary. Outdoor temperature affected the steeping process. Finally, the process originally required human urine as a catalyst and was consequently rather smelly. Because of the odor, indigo operations were usually located well away from the residential areas of the plantation. With luck, prevailing winds carried away the odor. When the catalyst was added to the steeping plants, the liquid began to thicken and turn purplish. This "indigo mud" was dried and shaped into bricks, the form in which it was shipped. Although profitable, indigo preparation was a difficult and expensive process.[26]

Development of the indigo industry was stimulated by government legislation. Bounties were offered, often at the behest of Carolina merchants when rice prices were down. British clothiers and dyers encouraged Parliament to subsidize the American plantations, providing a tremendous impetus to the

American industry. However, European buyers pronounced Guatemalan and Caribbean indigo to be of better quality than dye produced in Georgia and South Carolina.[27]

Indigo production was labor intensive. The location of the island, close to east Florida in a largely underpopulated region, prevented efficient supervision of the slaves. Slaves could easily flee Cumberland to Spanish territory, where they could sometimes hide, intermingled with the Indians or enlisted by Spanish at Fort Mosa near St. Augustine. After 1763–65 the grantees may have placed slave labor on the island to clear and drain its inland swamps. The American Revolution, however, would have interrupted these arduous efforts. Once again, adequate slave supervision became impossible for indigo production and other slave-dependent labors, because under wartime frontier conditions, slaves ran away.[28]

When the American Revolution began in 1775, the European market was closed to indigo from the former colonies. England stopped the bounty paid on indigo production in America, and India began growing indigo for world markets. In 1792 Thomas Jefferson, then secretary of state of the newly founded United States, explained to Congress that Spain refused to accept American indigo and that the French intended to levy heavy taxes on foreign indigo. World prices for indigo had begun to slide, and by 1800 indigo no longer was reported as an export crop.[29]

Although in the 1780s there seems to have been something of a Lynch presence on Great Cumberland, almost nothing is known of their activities there. A 1775 French map of Cumberland shows a square labeled "Fort William Ruine" at the south end of the island. The adjacent large creek, now known as Beach Creek, was called "Crique de Linchus." This name suggests that the waterway served as a landing place for the Lynch interests.[30]

Belin's hydraulic improvements greatly interested John Bowman (1746–1807). Bowman married Sabina Lynch, Thomas Lynch's daughter. Trained in Scotland as a lawyer, he took over many of the problems of administering Lynch's estate. Lynch's will ordered the sale of his numerous properties in Georgia, South Carolina, and east Florida. Bowman acted as the Lynch attorney during the period of their tenancy in common with the Greene family (1783–1802). By the early 1790s even the most knowledgeable observers occasionally referred to Cumberland Island as belonging half "to General Green & the other to Mr. Bowman."[31]

The American Revolution probably caused the failure of any Lynch plantations on Cumberland. It is likely that they had shipped rice and perhaps indigo from Beach Creek for a few years before the outbreak of hostilities, but any shipping arrangements would have been greatly restricted by the British navy at the beginning of the revolution, and slave supervision would have become almost impossible during the hostilities. After the war, the Lynch family interests' depressed credit status may have closed down all their planting arrangements on Cumberland.

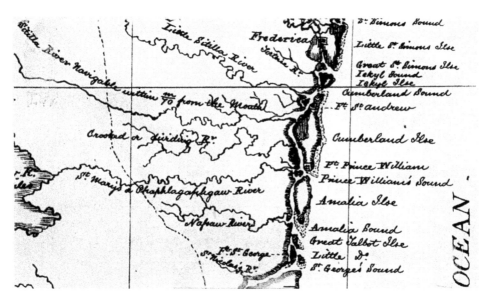

A section from Thomas Wright's 1763 map
of Georgia and Florida showing the inland navigation.
University of Georgia Libraries Special Collections, Map G 3870, 1763, W7.

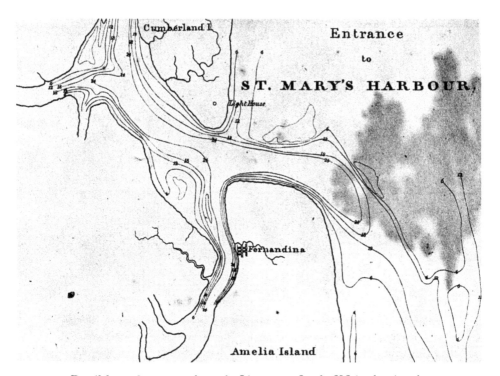

Detail from 1829 survey drawn by Lieutenant Searle, U.S.A., showing the
entrance to St. Marys Harbor and the Inland Navigation.
Peabody Museum, Salem, Mass.

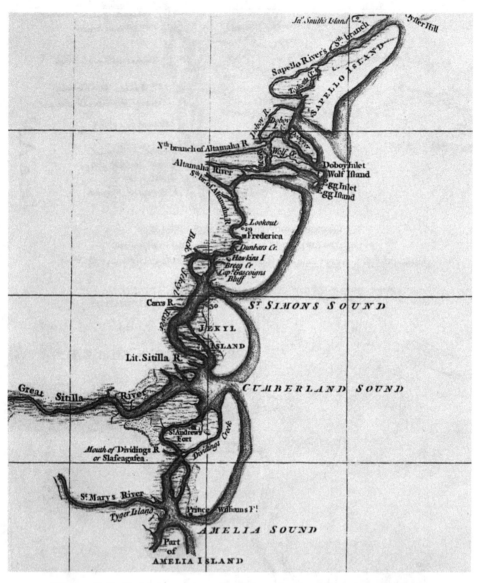

William G. De Brahm's 1757 map showing southeastern Georgia's sea islands,
marsh islands, and inlets, including "The Dividings" at Cumberland.
University of Georgia Libraries Special Collections, Map G 3910, 1757, D4.

Tidal creeks wind through the salt marshes to reach high land at Laen's Landing, Cumberland Island. Photo by Sophie Ann Rice.

Cumberland's great sand dune, called Dungeness Dune.
Photo by Roy C. Craven Jr.

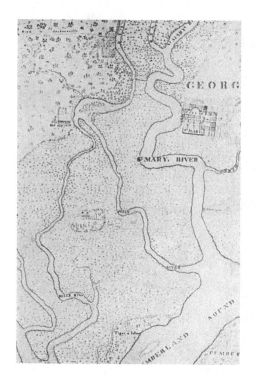

Section from Lieutenant J. W. Gunnison's 1841 survey of the inland navigation, showing waterways of St. Marys Basin. PKY 1699.

Below: Detail from a crude map drawn in 1811 by George I. F. Clarke, a Spanish subject, of the waterways of the Spanish side of St. Marys Basin. PKY 1507, East Florida Papers, Reel 87, Manuscript Division, Library of Congress.

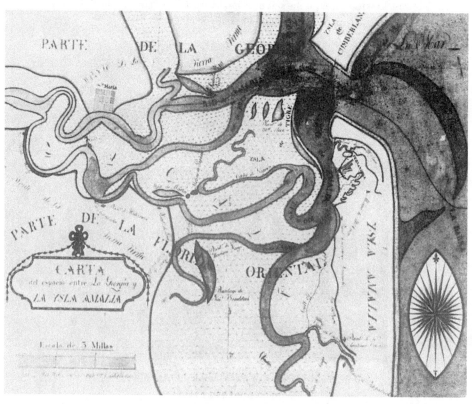

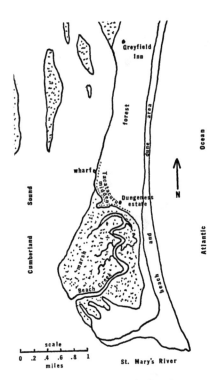

Archaeological sketch showing the location of an aboriginal shell midden at Cumberland's South End. Courtesy of Jerald Milanich.

A plan of mission Santa Catalina de Guale on Amelia Island, 1691. It would have resembled Cumberland's San Pedro de Mocama. Courtesy of España, Ministerio de Educación, Cultura y Deporte, Archivo General de Indias.

Artist's rendering of the Franciscan church at Mission San Luis de Talimali by John LoCastro. The mission San Pedro de Mocama may have looked like this. Courtesy of the Florida Division of Historical Resources.

A feral horse in Cumberland's forest. Photo by Emily Runge.

From the bottom of the bluff
where Fort St. Andrews formerly stood.
Photo by Roy C. Craven Jr.

From the bluff where Fort St. Andrews
formerly stood, looking over and down to
St. Andrews Sound and Cumberland River,
showing Jekyll Island at extreme right.
Photo by Roy C. Craven Jr.

Chief Tomochichi and nephew Tooanhowie,
from Verelst's 1743 portrait.
Courtesy of the New Georgia Encyclopedia Project.

McKinnon's 1802 map of Great and Little Cumberland Islands. Its lines of division
correspond closely with the original grants. Georgia Department of Archives and History,
box 105, folder 11-1-002.

Poling through Cumberland's slews, ca. 1924.

Low bluff, Little Old House Creek. Live oakers unloaded heavy equipment from their schooners at bluffs like this. Photo by William R. Bullard Jr.

Left: General Nathanael Greene.

Below: An oil painting
by Clement Nye Swift of a Georgia
sea coast house of the type live oakers
constructed for their visits. Courtesy of the
ESK Collection, South Dartmouth, Mass.

The Greene family cemetery on Cumberland Island. Courtesy of Cumberland Island National Seashore, National Park Service, Department of the Interior.

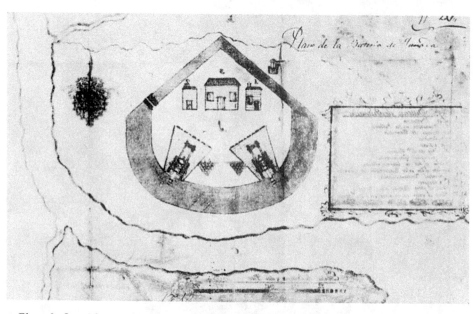

Plan of a Spanish armed battery by Lieutenant Mariano de la Roque, 1791. PKY 1912; East Florida Papers, Manuscript Division, Library of Congress.

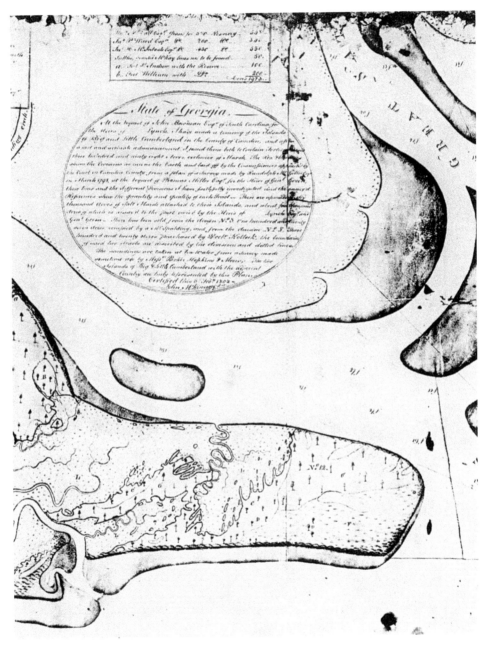

Detail from John McKinnon's 1802 map of Great and Little Cumberland Islands.

Plate 53

Plan and elevation of a house similar to the Greene family's Dungeness. No. 1, basement story
floor, (a) hall or principal entrance, (b) kitchen, (c) office, (d) library; no. 2, parlour floor,
(f) dining room, (g) parlour, (h) breakfast room, (i) pantry or china closet.
From Asher Benjamin's *The American Builder's Companion*,
6th edition (New York: Dover, 1976; reprinted from the 1826 edition).

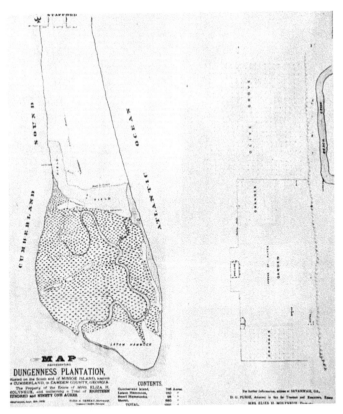

Plat of Dungeness Plantation by surveyor John Tebeau, 1878. His
measurements show standing walls six feet thick. Georgia
Department of Archives and History, box 105, folder 11-1-003.

Stereoptican view of Dungeness ruins. Courtesy of the Coastal Georgia Historical Society.

Another view of the ruins,
taken in the 1880s.

Undated stereograph captioned
"thatched cabin on Cumberland Island,"
possibly photographed in 1880.
Courtesy of the New York
Historical Society.

Monochromatic ink and sepia drawing
of the ruins by Frank Hamilton Taylor,
early 1880s.

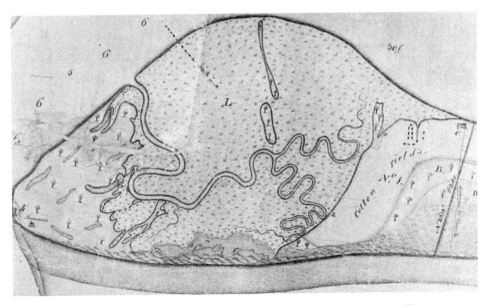

Detail from McKinnon's 1802 map, showing the location of Dungeness House, Garden Point, slave settlement, and cemetery.

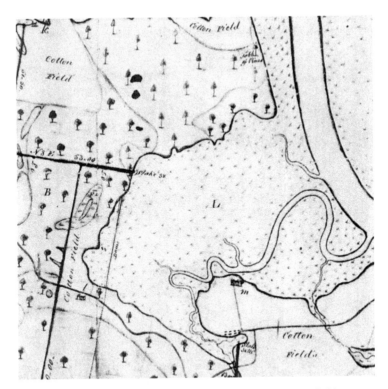

Detail from McKinnon's 1802 map, showing the Rayfield Plantation area and dam.

Left: Admiral Sir George Cockburn. National Maritime Museum, Greenwich, neg. no. 6728.
Right: Aquatint of an enlisted man in his regimentals, Fifth West Indian Regiment.
Anne S.K. Brown Military Collection, Brown University Library

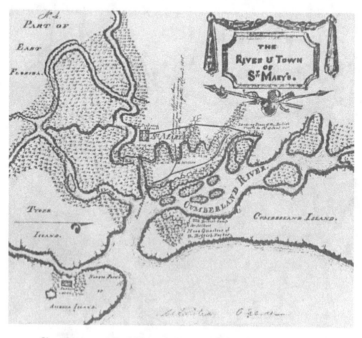

Sketch map of St. Marys and Cumberland Island showing
British headquarters and encampment, 1815. National Archives, Record
Group 77, Civil Works Map File.

FIVE

The American Revolution

"Beef from Several Large Islands": Cattle Raids

he American Revolution's great battles, France and Spain's intricate diplomatic alliances, and southern Whigs' fiery political broadsides did not particularly affect Cumberland Island. Nevertheless, the war brought great savagery to backcountry Georgia and South Carolina. Some Sea Islanders remained quietly loyal to the Crown and stayed aloof from the Georgia militia, only to finally become polarized by the Georgia Council of Safety's policies of theft and destruction.

Georgia was the weakest of the American colonies, sparsely populated and threatened by Indians to the west. In addition, British East Florida to the south offered a haven for Tory refugees and a base from which the British could launch raids into Georgia.

In the 1750s Georgia's militia, or armed volunteers, became the dominant military alternative in the absence of rangers and a substantial number of regulars. Only two small contingents from the three Independent companies, supplied by the scout boat *Prince George,* augmented the militia companies along the seacoast. In 1763, a watershed year for Georgia's military posture, a division began to appear between the royal government and armed American volunteers, and by the 1770s the governors, especially James Wright, showed disdain or even contempt for the militiamen as a viable military force. Even though the militia had provided valuable protection against the Indians during a period when no regulars came from Great Britain, the royal governors considered these troops unreliable and had reason for such beliefs.[1] On Georgia's coastal islands the question was never how to fight. Rather, Sea Islanders wondered whether the British or the Continental government could better provide protection from the militia's depredations.

The fort nearest to Cumberland Island was Wright's Fort, a simple wooden

79

stockade about twelve miles from the mouth of the St. Marys River on its northern side. Two of Governor Wright's brothers, Jermyn and Charles, were major landholders in Georgia and East Florida, and in 1773–74 Jermyn built Wright's Fort as protection against a flare-up of Indian hostilities. Wright's Fort became the strongest refuge for Loyalists within St. Marys Parish.[2]

Late in 1775 Georgia rebels began raiding Loyalist plantations on the East Florida side of the St. Marys River. The Georgia Council of Safety received a letter declaring that several vessels were loading timber "up Sapelo and other rivers to the southward," obviously intending to pursue the now forbidden West Indian and Florida trade. On 24 December the council ordered public money to pay for men to prevent "such wicked and daring attempts." Thus encouraged, armed and mounted militiamen raided outlying plantations, taking slaves, cattle, and boats.[3]

On 27 February 1776 the Continental Congress created a Southern Military Department, headed by Major General Charles Lee and consisting of regular troops and militia from Virginia, the Carolinas, and Georgia. Arrayed against them were the British forces in Florida, which consisted of the Royal Americans, an old and well-trained unit experienced in guerrilla fighting; a few naval detachments; and some Seminole Indian warriors.[4]

In 1776–77, raids and counterraids multiplied on the East Florida–Georgia frontier as southern Whigs sought to carry out their long-held belief that Georgia should annex the best lands in East Florida. Although the battles were often fought tenaciously, this type of border fighting aimed at forcing the civilian populations out of the area, and settlers scrambled to reach safer locations.[5]

The attacks also reflected the British and Scottish tradition of cattle raids. South of the Satilla River, almost as far as Payne's Prairie in Alachua, Florida, large grassy tracts served as ranges for enormous herds of feral cattle. Many south Georgia settlers were sons of Highland Scots, who had long considered cattle stealing a legitimate tool of war. Since stealing cattle was an accepted wartime objective, retaliatory raids characterized the early months of 1776. The province of East Florida announced that its troops were not to enter Georgian soil; similarly, Georgia announced that its forces were not to enter East Florida. However, unofficial punitive raids were sanctioned by the rebel Captain William McIntosh and his mounted followers. Cattle stealing had become a political statement.[6]

Both British and American strategists declared the Sea Islands valuable as sources for livestock, and each side believed that the enemy should be deprived of this resource. In May 1776 the Georgia Council of Safety took the offensive in the southern parishes, noting that some Loyalists were building "forts and fortifications." On 14 May the council ordered McIntosh and his men to reduce Wright's Fort and capture any disaffected men, black or white, and their provisions and armament. Captain McIntosh was further ordered to take any shipping in the St. Marys River. During the late spring and early summer of 1776, McIntosh, with his militia and Continentals, perhaps only three hundred strong, despoiled the East Florida frontier, pillaging exposed plantations, capturing small vessels in the St. Marys River, and appropriating cattle and slaves.[7]

With the 1776 arrival of the first Loyalist refugees in East Florida, Floridians learned of American plans to remove both cattle and slaves from the St. Marys area. Governor Patrick Tonyn requested that Colonel Augustine Prevost send a captain's guard to protect the St. Marys crossing about twenty-five miles upstream and that the colonel arm local planters and settlers.[8]

A British warship, the schooner *St. John*, was ordered to transport troops to St. Marys to protect civilians and arrest any rebels who would prevent the Loyalist settlers from rounding up cattle. Failure to comply with roundup orders carried political implications. Many settlers, after making sure their own cattle were safe, paid off old grudges by driving away cattle belonging to wealthier planters.[9]

The British forces set off from St. Augustine in early May. Bad weather prevented the troops from crossing St. Augustine Bar on schedule, and they did not reach the St. Marys area until 27 May, when they finally anchored northeast of Cumberland.[10] With their arrival, Cumberland Island met the American Revolution.

By 29 May British troops had established their camp on the south side of St. Marys River, opposite Wright's Fort, as well as set up a hospital on the north bank, near the stockade. The *St. John* anchored downstream. George Mills, an East Florida settler, was absent, participating in a raid on the Wilkinson plantation in East Florida. The *St. John* seized Mills's armed sloop, which was tied up in the river, and took it to Cumberland, where it was used to carry wood, water, and fresh beef to feed the British on the mainland.[11]

On 5 July the Council of Safety received a communication from Jonathan Bryan, John Houstoun, and Colonel Lachlan McIntosh, reporting, "Not one of the thirteen United Colonies is so weak within, or so much exposed from without [as Georgia]. To the east the inhabitants suffer the ravages of British cruisers, their negroes are daily inveigled and carried away. . . . British fleets may be supplied with beef from several large islands well stocked with cattle, which line their coasts and around which large ships may sail."[12]

In late July 1776 the Wrights and their slaves left the fort to camp on Cumberland. In early August, the British learned that the Americans were preparing to attack the *St. John*, Wright's Fort, and Amelia Island and adjacent plantations.[13]

The expedition began on 5 August. Three American ships launched a strong attack. After hiding in Cumberland's woods to escape patriot landing parties, sometime around 6 August the Wrights and their slaves fled to safer quarters on Amelia. The *St. John* moved from the mouth of the St. Marys to the northern end of Amelia.[14]

On the morning of 7 August, the *St. John* saw several rebel boats round Cumberland and sail unopposed into Amelia's North River. That evening, the *St. John* set sail for St. Augustine, reaching it ten days later after again encountering bad weather. The Wright brothers fled with their slaves from Amelia to the St. Johns River. More than sixty years old, Charles Wright and twenty-four of his slaves died of exposure and malnutrition.[15] The British had withdrawn from Georgia.

This success in attacking the Wright plantations led General Lee to ask Georgia's Council of Safety on 19 August 1776 how next to proceed. The council recommended that Lee make every effort to drive the border population away from northern Florida and southeastern Georgia and into St. Augustine, where overcrowding would create severe shortages. Lee's 1776 campaign marked the first American invasion of East Florida. Dissension and shortages of basic military supplies, however, plagued his Continental troops, and by mid-September the invasion collapsed, although the soldiers inflicted considerable damage on both Loyalist and rebel property.[16]

Lee was recalled to the northern theater of operations in late August, and North Carolina's Robert Howe assumed command of the rebel forces in Georgia. While in Georgia, however, Lee had gauged the area's importance to the Continental cause and had formulated ideas about how to reduce the region's weakness. At the urging of both Lee and Howe, on 29 August the Georgia Council of Safety ordered owners of cattle on the Sea Islands to remove all livestock to the mainland by 1 November, thereby discouraging the British from occupying or raiding the islands. Any remaining cattle would be destroyed, and owners would receive no compensation. Judging from numerous British and American references throughout the revolutionary period, cattle removal from the islands on such a scale turned out to be impossible.[17] These orders caused much suffering for the poorer Cumberland residents, who, in effect, were ordered to deprive themselves of their most salable commodities, beef and hides.

In late October the British launched a raid into southern Georgia but quickly retreated into East Florida. Both sides launched counterraids during the rest of 1776 and into 1777, and persistent and well-founded fears for their safety caused increasing numbers of Georgians to become refugees, heading north or south according to their political persuasions.[18]

The second American attempt to invade East Florida began on 28 April 1777. Georgia Whigs, rejoicing after Washington's triumphs at Trenton and Princeton, resolved to invade East Florida and advance to St. Augustine. Capturing East Florida and disbanding Colonel Thomas Brown's Rangers were the best ways to protect Georgia and to intimidate incipient Georgia Loyalists. General Lachlan McIntosh and the radical Button Gwinnett organized this second Florida invasion, hoping to annex East Florida. The 1777 invasion of East Florida ultimately failed, however, and McIntosh and Gwinnett's troops only reached the St. Marys River. As a result of insufficient provisioning and the exigencies of the climate, American troops began to desert. The Americans crossed the river with difficulty and once again ravaged Amelia Island, carrying off slaves and cattle. During May Florida-based British troops continuously harassed rebel armies and thus saved East Florida. The American invasion of 1777 also was marred by intense factionalism among the Georgia troops and hostility between Lachlan McIntosh and Gwinnett. The two men fought a duel, and McIntosh was wounded and Gwinnett killed.[19] East Florida and southern Georgia remained relatively quiet for the balance of 1777. St. Augustine–based privateers raided any remaining Whig plantations on the Sea Islands and liberated Loyalists. Regardless of political principles, settlers sometimes found it simpler to leave for St. Augustine than to face the continuing raids.[20]

Some letters from Cumberland Island offer glimpses of coastal warfare during the American Revolution. On 30 May 1777 Colonel Samuel Elbert of the Continental Army, stationed on Cumberland, reported to Colonel James Habersham that four men had deserted to the enemy. Consequently, Elbert decided to lose no time in retreating from Cumberland to the Satilla River "as the Enemy will from them be informed of our Strength and what is worse, of our having nothing but Rice to Eat for five days past." The next day, Elbert wrote that British Major James Mark Prevost had sent an envoy under a flag of truce, demanding Elbert's surrender as well as fulfillment of the articles of capitulation made at Fort McIntosh, a stockade on the Satilla River that the British had captured the previous February. Elbert reproached Prevost for British-allied Indians' butchering of captured Americans at Fort McIntosh, but despite this brave response, Elbert immediately departed Cumberland. His next report was dated 1 June 1777 and was written from Old Town, at Satilla, where his men became "very Clamorous for want of Provisions." Hot, sick, hungry, and unpaid, Elbert's men differed from other Georgia Continentals only in their willingness to follow their colonel. Even so, their loyalty snapped when they ran out of food. Elbert did not get the necessary provisions, and many more soldiers deserted. Looking back at his wartime experiences, General William Moultrie referred often to the problem of Continental desertion to the British East Florida forces. Desertion in the province of Georgia became notorious.[21]

Orders to remove or kill cattle rather than allow them to fall into the enemy's hands devastated settlers. In the name of patriotism, cattle thieves committed atrocities that roused partisan feelings as never before and resulted in small-scale farmers defecting to British authorities.[22]

Mary Clubb, living at the south end of St. Simons, sold cows to Colonel Elbert on 15 May 1777. Although Clubb and a few other islanders apparently saw remaining on St. Simons as an opportunity to sell cattle, the men in her family fled to East Florida. The Clubb family thus typifies the Sea Island farmers whose political allegiances were divided as a result of the revolution.[23]

Elbert left Cumberland the following day, crossing over to Amelia's north end, where he immediately dispatched a party to secure all the inhabitants of Amelia. He subsequently tried to sail farther south but, like generations of coastal boatmen before him, was unable to make any progress through the Amelia Dividings.[24]

The Georgia Sea Islands provided both the British and the Americans with bases from which to harass each other as well as with small amounts of food and rudimentary shelter. Because the islands were so thinly settled, however, there was never enough food. While the Inland Waterway provided a transportation route, neither side had enough warships in the south to control it, and it was always easier to sail out to sea than to attempt to conquer the tortuous windings and strong tides of the inland route. Nevertheless, the islands' large herds of cattle became a focus of military activity. As a result, cattle stealing and its attendant savagery forced many settlers from their homes. Most of the Clubbs probably remained loyal to the British Crown because American militiamen stole livestock.

By 1778 the British had a new war strategy based on two principal ideas: first, the war could be carried from the south to the north; second, there were enough loyal Americans to conquer the rebels in New York and Pennsylvania. Governor Tonyn felt that British forces were strong enough to control the Inland Waterway. On 20 October General Henry Clinton in New York notified Brigadier General Augustine Prevost in St. Augustine that a British expedition would be sent down to Savannah. The expedition would consist of a fleet and transport of three thousand men under the command of Lieutenant Colonel Archibald Campbell. Campbell's forces landed unopposed near Savannah on 29 December. Confusion and dissension prevailed among the Georgia forces, and the Redcoats quickly took the city.[25]

The British also planned to have forces from St. Augustine attack Georgia. General Prevost sent both land and sea expeditions into the lower part of the state in late November. Troops under the command of Lieutenant Colonel Lewis V. Fuser reached Sunbury and attempted to force the surrender of Fort Morris. But the second British expedition, under the command of Lieutenant Colonel Mark Prevost, met American troops, burned buildings at Midway, and then returned to Florida.[26]

Learning that Prevost's men could not reach Sunbury, Fuser fell back first to Sapelo Island and then to Jekyll. When all his craft had passed the Altamaha River, Fuser crossed St. Andrew Sound. At the Cumberland Dividings he received orders to wait at Cumberland's south end, where he was to be joined by Brigadier General Augustine Prevost and all the garrison troops of St. Augustine. It is interesting that General Prevost's force expected to unite with Fuser and his detachments at the south end of Cumberland. Its usefulness as a harbor and the availability of freshwater at Dungeness probably dictated the choice of location. Because Fort William was still standing, it served as a gathering point of sorts.[27]

This plan was a logistical nightmare: the commissariat necessary to feed such a large force on the march rarely caught up with it. The total British force moving up the coast by way of the Inland Waterway numbered about nine hundred officers and men, of whom more than four hundred belonged to General Prevost's regiment. Such a large group would probably have required the whole Dungeness area as an encampment. Supplies for the army were conveyed along the coast in boats, which were often compelled to make wide detours to avoid the armed American vessels. Consequently, British troops experienced severe food shortages and were sometimes reduced to subsisting on oysters found in ocean inlets and on a scanty rice supply.[28]

Savannah, with all its stores and munitions of war, was now under British control. On 4 March 1779 civil government under British rule was reestablished in Georgia, with James Mark Prevost as lieutenant governor. On 14 July Governor Wright returned to Savannah, and a week later he resumed the royal governor's office. The British victory in the South was complete.[29]

Although the Georgia Sea Islands' military role in the American Revolution may appear negligible, they nevertheless played an important part in providing beef supplies. Guerrilla warfare, the stealing of cattle and slaves within the Georgia settlements, and the orders of Georgia's Council of Safety brought misery to many Sea Islanders and caused many of them to flee.

Nathanael Greene

When Nathanael Greene (1742–86), a brilliant military strategist from Rhode Island, joined the Continental Army's Southern Department, within two years the fortunes of war reversed. By December 1781 Greene's military campaigns brought him to Charleston, whose evacuation by the British signaled the beginning of war's end. Savannah, Georgia's capital, capitulated to the Americans on 11 July 1782, once again becoming Georgia's seat of government. The definitive treaty between the United States and Great Britain ending hostilities was signed on 3 September 1783 and was ratified by Congress in 1784. General Greene became a citizen of Georgia.[30]

Although the general's connection with Cumberland Island has long been known, his business affairs have been little understood. Greene lacked the knowledge and the capital necessary to enter the rice market, and he did not particularly favor slavery, but he nevertheless almost accidentally acquired an equity in the Cumberlands.

Nathanael, the fourth son in a family of eight boys, was born into a strict Quaker family. The Greenes operated a large forge and mill near Warwick, Rhode Island, where ship anchors and other heavy ironwares were made. A natural outgrowth of the prosperous Warwick manufactory was the Greenes' ironworks at Coventry, Rhode Island, which grew so big that in 1770 Nathanael's father chose the twenty-nine-year-old as resident superintendent at

Greeneville, a mill town where more than a hundred families lived in the vicinity of the forge. Although the senior Greenes tended to refer to themselves as blacksmiths, they were actually quite rich. Well read in spite of his family's conservative Quaker precepts, Nathanael was a clever and industrious student with a special interest in mathematics. In 1774 he married Catharine Littlefield of Block Island and Newport. As a commander, Greene was a strict disciplinarian, but he was always solicitous of the welfare of his men and ready to share their dangers.[31]

Joining the groundswell of mounting colonial opposition to British imperial policies, Greene helped organize a Rhode Island militia company. He rose rapidly through the ranks of the Continental Army and in 1776 became a major general. George Washington became Greene's friend, a relationship cemented by the shared hardships of winter in Valley Forge. Greene was a stupendously talented organizer. When in 1778 the Continental Congress began to appreciate his competence, it made him quartermaster general, with congressional permission to reorganize the department, long plagued by accusations of embezzlement and dishonesty. Some of these accusations continued throughout the war, and even Greene's record was tainted by whispers of corruption and bribery.[32]

By December 1781 the British had been cleared out of South Carolina, with the exception of Charleston. Greene's army besieged it for more than a year, but the British did not evacuate until 14 December 1782. As Loyalist merchants and their families fled Charleston for the safety of British warships anchored in its harbor, Greene's ragged troops marched into the city and began plundering food shops and warehouses. The general and his officers feared mutiny and looting if their men were not soon clothed, shod, and fed, and Greene made every effort to provide for his soldiers. The South Carolina legislature, meeting for the first time in years, voted Greene a princely appreciation of ten thousand guineas, but he benefited little from this gift, dedicating most of it to his army.[33]

The British government permitted only certain Loyalist merchants to remain in Charleston, and few of them were anxious to sell supplies to the general because of skepticism about the Continental treasury. Only John Banks, a young merchant, offered the American general services as a broker. Banks said he could arrange for the Americans to purchase supplies from the large inventories abandoned by departing British merchants. Although Greene thought the prices Banks offered were exorbitant, no other merchants offered competitive bids. The American troops were becoming increasingly mutinous, so the general felt compelled to accept Banks's services.[34]

In early 1783 Greene, Banks, and Ichabod Burnet personally guaranteed a loan of one thousand guineas, payable in English money, to John McQueen of Charleston, a well-known speculator in coastal and inland Georgia timberland who had been a major purchaser of land confiscated from Loyalists. The loan was to be used to purchase supplies for American troops. The bonds of Mc-Queen and his partner, Patrick Carnes, became part of Banks's assets, and Banks and Burnet secured the loan by putting up assets that included Mc-Queen's one-half undivided interest in Great and Little Cumberland Islands.[35]

Soon after contracting to supply Greene's army with food and clothing, Banks began speculating in other directions and could not comply with his contract. Merchants agreed to furnish further credit only if the general would guarantee Banks's debts, and Greene signed notes guaranteeing payment to Banks's creditors. Many people saw this action as undeniable proof that Greene was a silent partner in Banks's speculative ventures.[36]

Greene acquired his undivided half-interest in nine tracts on the two Cumberlands in August 1783 from Banks and Burnet. The indenture came in two parts, as was customary: a deed of lease and a deed of release. In the deed of lease, dated 11 August 1783, Banks and Burnet sold an undivided interest in nine tracts on the Cumberland Islands to Greene for five shillings, a token consideration. In the deed of release, dated 12 August, Banks and Burnet bound themselves to pay Greene one thousand guineas—the real consideration. Greene probably acquired the land on Cumberland, with its huge quantities of live oak, intending to speculate in the timber industry.[37]

Banks failed as a merchant, and his creditors set after Greene for payment of outstanding debts. Soon after the end of the war, Greene learned that he and his family faced a debt of £30,000. Although Greene had bitter enemies who criticized his role in the Banks affair, his actions were later publicly reviewed, and he was exonerated by Congress and the secretary of the treasury. Because of his involvement in Banks's bankruptcy, Greene found himself almost penniless. In recognition of all he had done for Georgia in the Revolutionary War, a grateful legislature presented Greene with Mulberry Grove, a Savannah River plantation, and Greene moved to Georgia.[38]

Greene and many of his military contemporaries believed that the federal government should reimburse him for wartime army expenses. Congress remained strangely silent in regard to the general's desperate financial situation, although it did pass an appropriation that enabled Greene to hire a personal secretary, a recent Yale graduate named Phineas Miller, to help untangle his financial and legal affairs.[39]

Aware that he had acquired a "valuable isle," Greene began searching for business partners. He would certainly have heard of the well-known and patriotic Lynch family, and he soon met John Bowman, who represented the Lynch interests. In September 1784 Greene and Bowman jointly complained to Georgia Governor John Houstoun about unauthorized persons cutting live oak on Cumberland. Georgia's Executive Council decided to communicate with Vicente Emanuel de Zéspedes, the new Spanish governor of East Florida, as well as the departing British governor, Patrick Tonyn, requesting their intervention on the matter of illegal cutting. Zéspedes replied there was little he could do to control British residents on the St. Marys River until British evacuation plans were completed.[40]

In late March 1785 Greene set out for St. Augustine, traveling with Benjamin Hawkins, a congressman from North Carolina. Greene visited his property on Cumberland Island both on his way to Florida and on his return and was delighted with what he saw:

> We visited all the Islands particularly Cumberland in which I am interested. I find it a very valuable property and had I funds to improve it to advantage it might be made one of the first commercial objects on the Continent. The Island is twenty odd miles long and great part of it excellent for Indigo. The situation is favorable for trade, the place healthy and the prospects delightful. On the seaside there is a beach Eighteen Miles long as level as a floor and as hard as a Rock. It is the pleasantest Ride I ever saw.[41]

On his second visit to Cumberland, Greene noted that there were at least twenty British transports in the mouth of the St. Marys River, evacuating the inhabitants of East Florida to Nova Scotia and the Bahamas. Most of these people were Loyalist refugees from Georgia and South Carolina, but others were English residents unwilling to face the future Spanish administration in Florida. Greene spent four days on Cumberland, escorted by local residents, including Alexander Semple, who kept a store at Cumberland's North End, and Henry Osborne.[42]

After returning to Charleston, Greene commented about how valuable the Cumberland property would be if he had the money to develop its potential in live-oaking. Furthermore, he stood to lose the great profits because unauthorized persons continued to cut live oak illegally and ship it away on foreign vessels.[43]

Greene pleaded with his friends to invest in Cumberland Island. He wrote to Jeremiah Wadsworth,

> it is one of the best stands for trade in the Country. A Capt. Sample of Philadelphia has opened a store on the Island and sells . . . goods for great profit and all cash. . . . I am confident you may increase your own fortune and . . . your friends in taking a concern. We can supply all the Northern States with live oak and ship a great deal to Europe. But besides selling timber a large [stroke?] of ship building can be drove at the place and lumber of all sorts may be got in any quantity and it is constantly a cash article.[44]

The general died unexpectedly and prematurely on 19 June 1786 at Mulberry Grove. His death was believed to have been caused by nervous strain as a result of his complex tangle of debts, possibly abetted by sunstroke. The general's heirs included his wife, Catharine, and five unmarried children. His executors were his widow and Wadsworth. In 1786 the general's family, then residing at Mulberry Grove, was both unable and unwilling to move to Cumberland Island. One of the first acts of the two executors was to grant power of attorney to someone in Camden County who could protect the general's Cumberland property.[45]

The initial entries in Camden County's first deed books deal with these powers. The first entry lacks a date and has only a few legible words, which are highly significant: *last will and testa-, -niel Greene, City of Hartford,* and *late of Mulberry.* In the second entry, dated 31 October 1786, Greene's executors gave power of attorney to Captain William Littlefield, Catharine Greene's brother, who sailed frequently from Rhode Island to Georgia. Since neither a town nor a court existed in Camden County in 1786, it was important to bestow power of attorney as quickly as possible to someone such as Littlefield who could get to St. Marys from Savannah if necessary. In the third entry, dated 1788, Littlefield appointed James Seagrove and Jacob Weed of Camden County as his "lawful substitutes" because of the "trespasses and other injuries" on Cumberland.[46]

The "injuries" were caused by itinerant woodcutters looking for live oak. The Lynches were suffering from the same depredations. In Charleston on 6 December 1788, Bowman gave power of attorney to Peter Belin, ordering him to protect Lynch property from transient settlers, "to prevent the removal of Horses, Cows, Hogs, or any other useful animal from the Islands of Cumberland by any persons whatever . . . likewise to prevent the felling or removal of any sort of timber from said Islands of Cumberland."[47]

Miller, Greene's secretary, had become a friend of the Greene family members, and he tried to help with their financial problems after the general's death. They, in turn, were devoted to him. Miller had worked diligently to clarify the mountain of claims presented by Banks's creditors. Catharine Greene and Miller soon formed a closer bond and contemplated marriage as early as 1791. On 27 April 1792 Congress passed an act providing £8,600 for Catharine Greene. Four years later, on 23 May 1796, partial financial relief finally arrived: Congress approved Catharine Greene's claims and paid her £11,000. A week later, on 31 May 1796, Catharine Greene married Phineas Miller in a quiet family wedding. Miller continued to advise his new wife in her financial affairs, and his guidance probably led them to live on Cumberland Island. On 1 June 1796 Congress passed a second act reimbursing General Greene's estate for £11,297, and on 7 June Congress voted to reimburse his widow £7,000 of the Banks-Burnet debts.[48]

SIX

Legacy of War

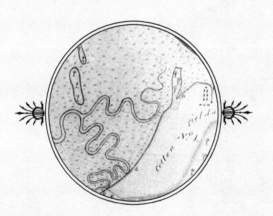

Cotton Plantations on Cumberland

Georgia's postrevolutionary boom was followed by a lengthy period of economic depression from the 1790s to 1815. It became increasingly difficult for the Greenes to meet expenses. Individual members of the Greene family, as well as the groups called the "Estate of General Greene" and the "Heirs of Lynch," began to appear regularly on the tax rolls as delinquents. The Lynches were posted as tax defaulters in 1796 and again in 1797. When fresh financial difficulties arose in 1798 for all private landowners in the United States, the Greenes clearly faced a new imperative to sell property from the general's estate.[1]

In 1798 Congress passed the Evaluation Act (better known as the Window Tax), which levied a direct tax on landholdings, houses, and slaves. This direct tax was the first of its kind and one of only a few such levies imposed prior to the twentieth century. The measure was an experiment aimed at obtaining revenue from property owners. Although the tax was politically unpopular, it passed in part because of the Federalists' need to prop up American defenses during the quasi-war with France. Because of the tax on slaves, southern agrarian landowners felt the heaviest burden. The Lynch family had vast holdings in South Carolina, Georgia, and Florida, and as a result, such a property tax hit them with special force. In an agricultural economy where land was the source of credit, a well-known, long-prosperous family such as the Lynches presumably had ample credit resources, even in an economically depressed period. Credit was essential for the southern agricultural economy, because planters borrowed money to plant next year's crop. Even though the Greenes were hardly in the same financial bracket as the Lynch family, the direct tax hit Catharine Miller with equal force. If she were to continue plantation life in the South, she needed to improve her credit standing.[2]

The Greene family first attempted to sell Mulberry Grove, advertising it in 1798. Miller despairingly referred to it in a letter to Eli Whitney: "Your pecuniary difficulties I shall have in my power to relieve, if we can obtain a good sale for this Plantation which we now offer on reasonable terms, & indeed shall sell on almost any terms." Mulberry Grove did not sell until 1800, when Major Edward Harden purchased it at public auction. The same year, the Greenes lost almost all of the general's property by order of the federal marshal.[3]

Cooperation between the Greenes and the Lynches evidently continued during the 1790s, and some evidence shows that the two family units may have decided to join forces. In 1799–1800 the U.S. Navy signed contracts with Phineas Miller of Cumberland Island, Georgia, and Colonel Thomas Shubrick of Bulls Island, South Carolina, to supply frames for two seventy-four-gun warships. Shubrick was a relative of the wife of Thomas Lynch Jr., Elizabeth Shubrick Lynch. Miller and Shubrick apparently knew one another fairly well, for Miller wrote to Shubrick that completing the naval contract was far more troublesome than had been foreseen, an opinion Shubrick strongly reciprocated.[4]

Phineas and Catharine Miller must have realized that a legal division of the Cumberland property between the Estate of General Greene and the Heirs of Lynch would be necessary if the land were to be sold. In the early spring of 1798 Camden County court officers ordered a division of the Cumberland Islands. Sometime during the same year, Phineas Miller, representing the interests of General Greene's estate, intervened in this court-ordered sale. Such writs usually were prepared in response to a petition presented by the interested parties. The county records do not give the date for the writ, but Miller probably petitioned for a court-ordered partition, for which a survey was needed. The result was a beautiful map providing a comprehensive view of Cumberland in the eighteenth century. The map shows the division of land via a series of parallel east-west lines that mark off twelve tracts, identified as belonging to Lynch or Greene. The surveyors, Randolph McGillis, J. M. Lindsay, and Patrick Tegard, attested that to the best of their ability, they had tried to conform to the intention of the partitioners, named as the Estate of General Greene and the Estate of Thomas Lynch.[5]

On 26 March 1798, four days after the survey was finished, McGillis, who also served as tax collector for Camden County, advertised the sale of land on Cumberland Island. The notice was addressed to proprietors, agents, and trustees for land in Camden County "said to belong to non-residents of Georgia," called the Heirs of Lynch, tax defaulters for the years 1796 and 1797. This public sale, scheduled for 1 October, never took place. Miller was actively seeking contracts with the U.S. Navy Department, and a public sale of the Lynches' equity would jeopardize the Greenes' ability to cut and haul live oak. It is also possible that the Greenes' claim to ownership was questioned: in April 1799 the Camden County Superior Court recorded a long series of documents relating to the Greene title, apparently at Miller's instigation.[6]

On 9 October 1799 the interrupted partition process was resumed:

> Upon the petition of Phineas Miller ... stating that the Heirs of ... Nathanael
> Greene together with the Heirs of Thomas Lynch, ... hold divers tracts and
> parcels of Land on the Island of Great and Little Cumberland ... as tenants in
> common, and that it was the Intent & desire of the Heirs of ... Nathanael Greene
> that the same should be divided as the Statute in such cases direct; ... It is there-
> fore ordered that a Writ of Partition of the said Lands as Issue in Usual Form.[7]

The 1798 survey was finally recorded on 7 December 1799, and on 17 January 1800 James Lindsay, county surveyor, began tracing a series of plats of Cumberland for the county records. Lindsay's drawings show that the Estate of General Greene was to receive tracts 1 (the Dungeness area), 3, 5, 8, 9, and 12 (Little Cumberland), while the Lynches were to receive tracts 2, 4, 6, 7, 10, and 11.[8]

Lindsay finished his task on 23 January 1800. He had not yet completed it when Phineas Miller, who obviously thought the division was now legal and complete, advertised the sale of tracts 8 and 9.

COTTON LANDS FOR SALE

Jan. 14, 1800

To be sold on good terms with indisputable title, if application be made immediately ... two tracts together containing about 2000 acres adjoining the plantation of John H. McIntosh Esq., lying on Cumberland Island. Application may be made to the subscriber on Cumberland Island or to William Belcher at Savannah.[9]

Miller's advertisement was premature, however, and on 18 February the Lynches advertised their intention to stop any public sale until the partition was acceptable to them.

NOTICE

The heirs and devisees, of the late Thomas Linch ... being equally concerned with the estate of the late Major-General Green, in an undivided property, comprehending Little Cumberland and most of Great Cumberland Islands ... do

hereby forbid the sale of any part thereof, as *divided* and advertised. . . . The said
heirs . . . not acquiescing in a late partition and division said to be made of the said
property, and the same not yet being finally and legally confirmed by the Superior Court of the County of Camden objections and an appeal will be interposed
by them.[10]

As a result, the federal marshal postponed the sales on Great Cumberland.
Throughout 1800, however, properties that indisputably belonged to the
Greene estate were sold, including Mulberry Grove on Savannah River, the
general's 2,000-acre tract on Crooked River, and certain tracts on Cumberland
on which the Lynches and Greenes evidently agreed.[11]

Phineas and Catharine Miller visited Cumberland in April 1799, presumably
to examine the island, talk with the county court officers, supervise and pay off
the live-oaking crews, and meet the other residents. The Millers may also have
discussed a possible house site. On 3 May 1800 one of Nathanael and Catharine's daughters, Cornelia, wrote to a friend that she was then residing on Cumberland, and on 6 August Cornelia wrote that her mother and stepfather had
gone to Dungeness, "a place so called at the South End of the Isle," where her
mother was building a house. The Lynches and Phineas Miller apparently had
reached an agreement about tract allocation in general and about tract 1 in particular. On 10 October Cornelia wrote, "Mama is on the point of moving to her
place at Dungeness where we have put up a small *temporary* house to reside in
until she builds one that is to last her lifetime."[12]

When the federal marshal ordered the sale of all the Greenes' Georgia properties, Dr. Lemuel Kollock of Savannah bought tract 1 and immediately presented it to Catharine Miller, his friend and client. At Kollock's request the
transaction was not entered in the county records until 1806, when Catharine
Miller repaid her friend for his great kindness.[13]

Judging from the fact that in 1800 the Lynches and Greenes had agreed on
nearly all the tract allocations on Great Cumberland, it seems clear that the
Lynches were protesting Lindsay's map, which was not completely accurate, especially in its depiction of the northern portion of the island. Tract 10, allotted
to the Lynches, was drawn too small. The Lynches wanted a resurvey, and in
1800 John Bowman found them a more accomplished surveyor, a Savannah
man named John McKinnon who completed his task in 1802. In that year the
Lynch-Greene holdings were divided by court decree into a series of twelve
parallel tracts that formed the basis for all land transactions on Cumberland

Island during the nineteenth century. McKinnon's survey included references to 1800–1801 sales of Greene tracts. McKinnon also provided considerable information about landowners, residents, settlements, land quality, and manmade features, such as roads, an impounded water area with a dam, and houses, including the completed Dungeness mansion.[14]

Dungeness House

Dungeness mansion, the Millers' house at the southern end of Cumberland, was an extraordinary building. Information combined from different sources and dates provides a fascinating glimpse into the way this New England family lived on the Sea Islands. The house was unique, the only four-story tabby house ever reported in the United States. Never converted, changed, or enlarged, Dungeness stood for many decades almost literally as a coastal beacon. Its enormous height made the mansion a point of reference for navigators at sea and in the Inland Waterway. An 1821 pilots' guide said that nearing the inlet, sailors should look for Dungeness, a "large flat-roofed house on Cumberland Island." Traveling on a steamer from Savannah to St. Marys in 1866, William McAdoo was astonished to see "a very large brick house, and the roof and upper story lift themselves abruptly and unexpectedly above the green of a dense live oak grove."[15]

The architects for the new house are unknown. Nineteenth-century journalistic literature often referred to Phineas Miller as an Englishman who built his wife a stately mansion, calling it Dungeness "after a place he had inherited in the old country." McAdoo was told that General Greene's widow married the "architect of Dungeness" and that her marriage was "beneath her." In 1798 Ray Sands, a brother-in-law of Catharine Miller who later managed many of her business affairs, had moved from Rhode Island to Cumberland. Miller and Sands probably collaborated on the new house, which was completed in 1802 or 1803.[16]

Among architecture's important cultural determinants are technological skills, available tools, cultural traditions and preferences, cost and availability of suitable building materials, and perceived function. By 1799 Miller and Sands knew coastal Georgia well enough to note an architectural tradition beneficial to their purpose: the use of tabby, a concretelike conglomerate of shell and lime, as a building material. The most important consideration facing the Greene family was Catharine's personal financial situation. As executrix for her late husband, she inherited heavy liabilities against his estate that mandated a permanent yet inexpensive solution to the question of her residence. Among the technological skills and available tools present were her personal slave force and the numerous sawmills springing up in Camden County. In addition to supporting agricultural labor, Catharine's social situation dictated generous hospitality. Astute New Englanders, Miller and Sands would have used pattern books, architectural handbooks popular at the time. Either man could have sent for *The Country Builder's Assistant*, a wildly successful pattern book published in 1797 by Asher Benjamin, a clever carpenter from Greenfield, Massachusetts. Miller and Sands probably adroitly used this guide to design a house plan suitable for Catharine's needs.[17]

There are no pictures of Dungeness House while it was standing, although there are photographs of the ruined building as well as a detailed plat of the property. According to an 1878 survey, the building measured sixty-three feet by forty-five feet, eight inches.[18] The mansion was built on a symmetrical rectangular plan, with a main elevation of five bays and a side elevation of four bays. It had three stories over a high basement and was topped by an attic. The basement would ordinarily have been used for servants and services. The first-floor rooms were grand and lofty, as demonstrated by the very tall windows, and were generally thought of as public rooms. The second floor contained living rooms for the family. The third floor had bedrooms (called chambers), which took their names from their location over rooms on the second floor. Thus, for example, a bedroom over the drawing room would have been called the Drawing Room Chamber.[19] A kitchen, detached from the house because of the summer heat, a common southern feature, might have been added later. Judging from the small windows at ground level in some photographs, in addition to the traditional above-ground basement there was a sub-basement known as a cellar.

The facade seems square. The window openings were four feet wide, and thus the space between the windows was about eight feet. It appears that the mansion was about sixty-eight feet high from terrace to eaves. The house had a low hip roof, sheathed in copper. After a particularly destructive 1813 hurricane, a St. Marys resident wrote that Dungeness, "though covered with copper, has been unroofed in the gale!"[20]

The most fascinating aspect of the house was its enormous height. To support the towering mass, Dungeness had very thick walls—according to Frederick Ober, six feet thick at the base of the house, narrowing slightly above ground to four feet. Like many coastal families, the Millers feared flooding from hurricanes and may have intended Dungeness House to serve as a refuge for island residents. Ober stated that the house was built atop "a large shell mound," so estimating the full height of Dungeness requires conjecture about the shell mound's height. Modern architects think the house and its base towered about seventy-six feet above ground level. The high land on which Dungeness stood is approximately twenty feet above sea level, so the top of the house may have reached ninety-six feet above sea level. The Dungeness mound almost certainly originated when Spanish soldiers, working with Indian laborers, constructed a platform to serve as the base for San Pedro de Mocamo.[21]

The mansion evidently faced north onto a terrace that contained a broad flight of steps, probably made from hewn granite, leading from the ground to the mansion's main entrance, which was quite formal. The facade was decorated with full-height Doric pilasters running from a molded belt course at first-floor level to the cornice. Photographs seem to show four pilasters, although a nineteenth-century visitor wrote that there were six stone pilasters rising to the eaves. Close study of the photographs of the ruined Dungeness reveals vestiges of elaborate architectural trim around the front door and possibly over the first-floor windows. The entrance was faced with hewn granite. An approach road clearly went to the front entrance. The 1878 survey shows five openings on the north side, four windows and the front door. The south side has only four windows overlooking the gardens.[22]

Twenty rooms existed on the upstairs floors. The room in the southeast corner of the third story was the Shaw-Nightingale drawing room. Immediately behind it, in the northeast corner, was the dining room. Frederick Ober said that a wide hall ran through the center of the third story. Nothing suggests the presence of porches at Dungeness House, even after the Nightingale occupancy had ended, so the central hall may have served as a summer living room. A spacious and lofty through hall was a breezy spot in summer. Families resorted to the hall as soon as the cold season was over, transforming it into the summer sitting room, dining room, game room, and music room. These wide central passages were often furnished with extra chairs and even with pictures and plants to make a summer parlor. On the opposite side of the wide central hall, in the northwest and southwest corners, were a schoolroom and sewing room, respectively. To judge from the inventory of Phineas Miller's estate, one room must have housed his personal library and surveying tools.[23]

There were four brick chimneys, two in each end wall, and sixteen fireplaces. The mansion's exterior bearing walls were made of tabby blocks in a mode called post and tabby. The finished exterior building surface was stuccoed, but, according to an 1878 observer, only above the first floor. Dungeness's interior was heavy timber frame with wood and a crude plaster finish. Several observers commented on the house's unfinished interior walls, with some 1818 visitors finding the effect ludicrous. Seated in an elegant dining room with fine furniture, they were astonished to see oyster shells sticking out of the walls. Their hosts reported that the thick walls had taken so long to make that the Millers became impatient and failed to plaster the interior of the house. George Washington Greene, grandson of the general, remembered the large room in which General Henry Lee died and "its unfinished walls of tabby-work." Subsequent inhabitants, the Nightingales, evidently also left the interior walls unplastered.[24]

While a number of outbuildings appear on the 1878 plat, few are visible on the McKinnon survey. These outbuildings represent additions made over the nearly sixty years that Dungeness was inhabited. The outbuildings included a three-story building that housed a cotton gin; carpenters' and blacksmiths' shops; and stables. Near the Dungeness dock stood a slave settlement that probably had a small hospital and a slave driver's cabin. Outhouses also do not appear on any of the surveys of Dungeness, although they undoubtedly existed.[25]

Perhaps as early as 1800, Louisa Greene Shaw, an accomplished horticulturist, established hothouses for propagating oranges. Her mother might have brought to Dungeness a Scottish gardener, who was still living there during the Civil War. Pharmacists sold crystallized citric acid to emigrants in covered wagons and to naval surgeons as a preventive against scurvy. Early-nineteenth-century surveys of Dungeness show a mysterious round building adjacent to the mansion that may have been the main propagation building, or orangery. Advertising Dungeness for rent on one occasion, Shaw stated that her "orangeway" was included.[26]

Conflating several maps from different times in the nineteenth century shows vestiges of formal gardens, drives, and a terrace. Ober said that a high masonry wall separated a 12-acre garden of specimen plants from fields surrounding the mansion. This wall joined two or three small houses to Dungeness House and undoubtedly discouraged deer from feeding in the gardens.[27]

In an 1862 letter to his wife, Union admiral Samuel Francis DuPont described some vandalism at Dungeness but noted that "there was, however, no desecration of the house, and the grounds were uninjured. The garden was beautiful with flowers of every kind, and flowering shrubs of rare beauty, among them one or two mimosas, almost trees; one of an umbrella shape was covered with a pink flower like the 'bottle washer,' which I had not seen before." In 1865 another Union officer, Cornelius H. Longstreet, described his amazement:

> when we got up into the creek opposite Dunginess, as we were ahead of the tide, we stopped to visit that famous old place. . . . The house is built of concrete and is an immense structure of *five* stories. Many of the huge rooms were never finished. The grounds were beautifully laid out and contained almost every variety of tree, shrub and flower. Some of the finest magnolias that I have seen in the South are here, with groves of olive trees, oranges and peaches in the lower part of the garden. I saw on either side of the walk a small cluster of tall reed-shaped bamboo, and a little further on was a little thicket of *cane,* such as are used for walking sticks, fishing rods, etc. Here are also some huge specimens of the *century* plant, and several fine *date palm* trees with their long lance-shaped leaves ranged on either side of the immense long stem. . . . The appearance of these grounds is intensely tropical. I have not seen anything like it before. The view from the top of the house must, on a clear day, be indescribably beautiful. I found on a heap of stones, the first, by the way, that I have seen in Georgia, a fine large specimen of a peculiar coral formation.[28]

Although privateering had peaked during the American and French Revolutions, in the early 1800s many potentially dangerous vessels continued to sail through the inlet. With the appearance of South American pirates in American waters between 1805 and 1820 came a real need to identify vessels entering Fernandina and St. Marys. Dungeness House had an observation platform, possibly covered by a cupola, from which its occupants could view the harbor. In 1818 visiting naturalists enthusiastically reported that from the top of the house they could see Amelia Island, the sea, and the mainland, "a magnificent view." On an 1834 visit to Dungeness, mainland planter Charles Rinaldo Floyd "went to the top of the house, and had a fine view by moonlight." Residents at Dungeness could use telescopes to identify boats entering the inlet, and the house may have sported some light guns. The Springs Plantation, where Catharine Miller's son-in-law, John Nightingale, lived, was fronted by six cannon, possibly taken from Nightingale's ships.[29]

Cotton Cultivation

Catharine and Phineas Miller were the first major cotton planters on Cumberland. Although poorer residents may have grown some cotton for their own accounts, the Millers' efforts to make money from selling Sea Island cotton were driven by their wish to create a new life at Dungeness. Miller's partnership with Eli Whitney, inventor with Catharine Greene of the cotton gin, was a factor in the Greene efforts to plant cotton.

Sea Island long-strand cotton was famous for its tensile strength, with filaments that were longer, more elastic, stronger, and silkier than the short-strand variety. Spinning mills preferred Sea Island cotton because the filaments did not break under the pressure of mechanical looms. When buyers graded Sea Island cotton as "fine," they were identifying the staple that their clients— America's expanding textile mills—wanted for high-volume production. Many twentieth-century historians persist in thinking that long-strand cotton was valued chiefly for lace making or fine dress material, but the list of products for which Sea Island cotton was especially desirable includes army and navy uniforms, sail canvas, tents, umbrellas, and, most valuable of all, thread for a splendid new invention that soon revolutionized home manufacture of clothing, the sewing machine.[30]

Phineas Miller was a keen investor. Always interested in machinery, he sought out local businessmen whose enterprises would draw support. First he turned his attention to sawmills. St. Marys' booming timber industry sent shingles, planking, and spars to eager buyers in Europe and the Caribbean. St. Marys Basin attracted many small-scale sawmill operators. Some of its marsh islands, like Martins Island, where David Garvin's *molino* (mill) was located, utilized the force of the tides to operate sawmills. In 1798 Claud Borel, a Frenchman, commissioned two Pennsylvania builders to come to St. Marys to build a wooden tidal mill on his land: "Said mill was to work eight saws and to be completely finished with its mill house, canals, and locks." Hydraulic sawmills were essential if St. Marys was to ship out timber products, and many small sawmills were replaced in 1803 by a bigger and better mill, the Steam Saw Mill of Camden County. Apparently the creation of Frenchman John Chevalier, it was sold to nine local investors, four of whom belonged to the Greene-Miller family: Phineas Miller, John C. Nightingale, Peyton Skipwith Jr., and William Pitt Sands.[31] Cotton planting was financially worthwhile.

Little information exists about how or when cotton agriculture began on

Cumberland. In 1802 there apparently were six cotton fields on the island, some of them quite small—50 or 100 acres. Tract 1 in McKinnon's map shows that Dungeness had a large cotton field of about 150 acres, stretching almost to Cumberland's beach, with nearby slave cabins and an overseer's house. This suggests that before 1802 either the Lynches or the Greenes, or perhaps both families in collaboration, supported cotton cultivation and paid wages to an overseer. In tract 3 the Isham Spaldings planted a small field of about 50 acres. Two more fields of perhaps 75 acres each were planted at Table Point, owned by descendants of General Lachlan McIntosh.[32]

After the division between the Greenes and the Lynches, Littlefield Plantation, a unit of about 150 acres within tract 5, became the Greenes' largest cotton field. According to McKinnon's map, Littlefield had a resident overseer named Bell. A cotton field of perhaps 200 acres is shown at the present-day Squawtown. It remained in McIntosh hands under the name of Cotton Bluff.[33]

The Greene family hoped that Littlefield Plantation would bring wealth. Although only two family members are known to have been shareholders (Nathanael and Catharine's daughter, Cornelia, had lot 8, and her sister, Louisa, had lot 2), others seem also to have invested, and it would not be surprising if Miller was the first investor and his wife, the second. Peyton Skipwith of Virginia, who married Cornelia, is said to have invested in land on Cumberland as a planting partner of Phineas Miller and John Nightingale, Martha Greene's husband. Catharine's brother, Captain William Littlefield, may also have been an early investor, for his ships frequently sailed from Rhode Island to Georgia, and shipping raw cotton back to the burgeoning mills of Rhode Island and southeastern Massachusetts made for lucrative voyages. In exchange for raw cotton from the island planters, New England manufactories sent articles still hard to obtain on this part of the coast: nails, granite, salt, anchors, rope, iron bars, and other necessary hardware. Captain Littlefield's son, Ned, who later married his first cousin, Cornelia Greene Skipwith, after her first husband's death, may have been another early investor.[34]

Sea Island cotton grew prolifically on the sandy pine-barren soil. Even though high-quality Sea Island cotton cost about twice as much to produce as short-staple cotton, after the invention of the mechanical gin, Sea Island planters found an ever-enlarging market for their crop. At the beginning, they planted on old indigo fields, and by the 1830s they sometimes planted in rotation with rice to reduce the grasses and weeds peculiar to each type of culture.[35] Since only the Lynches had planted before the American Revolution, their superior knowledge of the soil may well have prompted Miller to encourage a Greene-Lynch joint venture, especially in the old indigo fields of tract 5.

The best and silkiest fibers were produced in conditions found only on the Sea Islands, where moisture-laden sea breezes allegedly made the staple longer and glossier. Planters believed that the best fields had an ocean exposure. Slaves using hoes or occasionally plows "ridged" the fields where cotton was to be planted. These ridges made the task of dressing cotton plants much easier. Slaves walked the furrows between the ridges to cut away lateral roots. Seeds were planted beginning in mid-March. As planters' experience grew, a second planting nearly always took place immediately after the first growth broke through the soil. Any young plants destroyed by frost or strong wind would be replaced by sprouts from this second planting.[36]

Soon after the young plants appeared, slave hands moved into the field with hoes, removing grass and replacing eroded soil to support the stalks of the growing plant. Most planters and their slave drivers believed that thinning cotton plants so that they never touched each other was essential to healthy production. Female field hands often performed the thinning process.[37]

In July the plants began to blossom. The flower changed from a strong yellow color to red to a rich chocolate brown. After the blossom dropped, only the pod was left. It took from three to six weeks to mature. Around 1 August, the bolls began to open. At that point the field hands began the first of ten to twelve successive pickings, which continued until the first frosts began to kill the plants, generally in early January. Lint, the fibrous portion, was separated from the seed by roller gins, a process that continued into the first part of the new year.[38]

Since the cotton bolls had to be stored before the ginning process began, curing (drying) them was very important to the planter. To avoid spontaneous combustion in the cotton house, the bolls had first to be dried. If they became too dry, however, their filaments lost their prized elasticity. While still in the fields, hands carried the bolls, in panniers on their backs or in carts, to a drying area, where they could be spread on a drying rack under cover.[39]

Preparing Sea Island cotton for market required still more slaves, who sorted the cotton by hand, ginned it to separate the fiber from the seed, and carefully moted (cleaned) the cotton of cracked seeds and foreign particles. Slaves then separated the cotton according to grade. Moting and grading demanded skillful workers, and planters often believed that women were better moters than men. Much of the cotton's market value depended on the skill of the slave moters. Fifteen hundred pounds of unginned cotton generally made one three-hundred-pound bale. One bale required the labor of fifty-three people: a dryer, thirty sorters, twelve ginners, seven moters, two packers, and an overseer.[40]

Cotton planters faced numerous hazards. The principal agricultural danger was insect infestation. Another danger was weather: rain and hail caused irreversible damage to young cotton plants. The only favorable comment planters could make about coastal Georgia's violent storms was that their torrential rains apparently killed off the caterpillars.[41]

The other danger was erratic prices. Sea Island cotton planters learned to store their bales against the possibility of low prices at the next season's sales. Planters were extremely vulnerable to any fluctuation in world prices. To reduce dependence on long-staple cotton, coastal planters soon learned to diversify their agricultural output. Although there are almost no records regarding rice planting on Cumberland, relict banks in tract 5 make it likely, as do some modern botanical analyses of seeds and grasses in today's Swamp Field. The planters also found it expedient to grow food as well as cotton.[42]

After Phineas Miller's death in 1803, Ray Sands took over administration of Catharine's island plantations. With the assistance of Louisa Greene, Sands successfully supervised their cultivation and marketing. In doing so, Sands removed a great burden from Catharine, who happily declared in 1811 that she was "ignorant of the amount of the Crops for the last seven years. I have only seen by accident one Sail of one Lott of Cotton—amount 15,000 dollars." In November 1805 frost greatly damaged mainland crops, but Cumberland's cotton fields were unharmed. Catharine Miller was able to gather "12 or 1400 w[eight] a day—which may last until the 1st of January." In August, when cotton picking season usually began, she had already gathered 3,000 weight and expected to make a large crop: "The planters are all alive with hopes." By 1810 traveler John Melish commented admiringly about "sea-board cotton," noting that the "principal islands where it is raised are St. Symons and Cumberland." Cumberland may not have been the first island on which cotton was extensively planted, but it may well have been the second.[43]

Cultivation of Sea Island cotton was labor-intensive, requiring numerous slaves, who had to be purchased, clothed, fed, and administered by overseers, who in turn required payment and housing. In the beginning of the nineteenth century, many island owners lacked the capital to invest heavily in slave labor. Although Catharine Miller had little money, she was rich in slave labor. In 1810 she owned 196 slaves, nearly all of them on Cumberland. At her death on 2 September 1814 the Greene family apparently administered more than 210 slaves on the island.[44]

By 1815 the Greene family was administering three successful Cumberland plantations, Rayfield, Littlefield, and Dungeness, each with its own cotton house. Dungeness had the largest cotton house, three stories high, and that year it held two years' worth of crops—seventy bales, only partly ginned and bagged and estimated to be worth between $7,000 and $8,000. The cotton had not been sent to market because of the illness of James Shaw, Louisa Greene's husband. At Rayfield, the cotton house held twenty bales of cotton, ginned and packed, ready for market.[45]

By the mid-1830s a few cotton sales were recorded, giving some information about Cumberland's cotton planters. Major planters included Louisa Shaw, in charge of Dungeness and Rayfield; Robert Stafford, the owner of Littlefield; and the Estate of Peter Bernardey, centered at Plum Orchard. All reported cotton sales valued between $3,000 and $3,500. Robert Deloney, whose Longwood Plantation would soon be sold to the Downes family, reported 1833 sales of $1,024.[46]

The South Point Community

Cornelia Greene wrote that she had "never expected to find anything extraordinary & never saw any thing very pleasing" about residing on Cumberland Island.[47] Her pessimism was based on its bad reputation.

As early as November 1770, only a few months after their joint purchase, Thomas Lynch and Alexander Rose complained that "loose and disorderly Persons" were living on the island's public land and destroying livestock. After the American Revolution, much of the savagery of partisan warfare drifted down to touch the St. Marys area. One of Georgia Governor Samuel Elbert's first orders, issued in 1785, was "to secure the villains who are at this time assembled between the St. Illa and St. Marys Rivers; with a number of negroes, horses, and other property, supposed to have been stolen from the citizens of this State." At the end of the revolution, it was said that Camden and Glynn Counties sheltered "only wild beasts and outlaws."[48]

Cumberland was home to many of these so-called outlaws, who usually were desperate men made homeless by guerrilla warfare. Some were murderers; nearly all had witnessed atrocities committed by Georgia militiamen. In 1789 Frederick Barrons, a Flemish man who had resided for three years on Cumberland, begged Spanish authorities to let him emigrate to East Florida because he wished "to live among Christians." The examining officer wrote that Barrons was a desirable immigrant: "Carado de que es católico" (fortunately he is Catholic).[49]

A large settlement of these men congregated on public land at South Point, the former site of Fort William. The community contained both lawless and law-abiding people who were united as refugees. The walls of the ruined fort, which were still standing in 1785, served as a visible reminder that military reservations were public lands. Even before the end of the Revolutionary War, Georgia's legislature had passed a law discouraging transient squatters of any sort: "persons building huts and not cultivating land . . . to be declared vagrants." Nevertheless, many refugees continued to believe that moving to public land was legal, in the same way that earlier settlers fled to the nearest fort when facing Indian raids. Many were ex-Loyalists who dared neither return to the United States nor emigrate to the West Indies or Great Britain. Fear and desperation drove them to the St. Marys Basin and to South Point.[50]

In 1785 the legislature passed an act aimed at validating land transfers made during the troubled times of the revolution. "To render easy the mode of conveying land," the act sought to legitimize deeds that were "deficient in point of form." Georgians wanted to ensure the validity of wartime land transactions that had been improperly measured, witnessed, and/or recorded. A justice of the peace could approve such a deed, and the clerk of the county court could then register it.[51]

In September 1785 Elbert was surprised to learn that petitioners were acquiring public lands in Camden County. Captain Robert Montfort, surveyor for Glynn and Camden Counties, informed Elbert that the three Crown reserves in Camden—Wright's Fort near St. Marys and Fort William and Fort St. Andrews on Cumberland—had already been surveyed for private conveyance. In the governor's opinion, these grants were surreptitiously obtained. He declared that "care will be taken that the works [fortifications] shall not pass into a grant before the [next] meeting of the Legislature."[52]

Nevertheless, nearly all the public land at South Point did pass permanently into private ownership. Henry Osborne acquired it by headright on a warrant dated 6 June 1785. Osborne, an ambitious Irish lawyer intent on feathering his nest in Georgia, had moved to the St. Marys area, where he befriended merchant Alexander Semple. At his store in the Crown reserve of Fort St. Andrews, Semple had for several years conducted a booming trade in contraband, even attracting Spanish officers from St. Augustine. By usage he acquired trading rights in Cumberland's two Crown reserves. Both Osborne and Semple sought to ingratiate themselves with General Nathanael Greene when he visited Cumberland in 1785, and Osborne even traveled with the general to St. Augustine. Many unsavory men were moving to southeastern Georgia, wrote Osborne, and he recommended Semple to Governor Elbert "to deter the unworthy": "Many characters are attempting to settle themselv's near St. Marys who, I humbly apprehend are very exceptionable some of whom are charged with capital offences lately committed and whose present conduct indicates no kind of reform."[53]

In consequence, the governor appointed Semple "Magistrate of the Southern Counties." Semple then appointed Osborne a justice of the peace. Osborne submitted his land application to Semple, a fellow justice of the peace, who, unsurprisingly, approved it. Osborne had been using his South Point land since at least 1785, probably as a store and pilots' station and possibly in partnership with Semple. Within the 200-acre tract was a 6-acre reserve that both the state of Georgia and the federal government eventually claimed.[54]

In the mid-1780s many difficulties and disappointments faced persons moving into the St. Marys Basin. First, the 1783 British evacuation of East Florida caused the exodus of hundreds of English families over the next two years. Second, the eruption of the Oconee Wars brought—or threatened to bring—the horrors of Indian warfare once again to frontier settlers. Third, the already-existing tension between Spanish and American administrations was exacerbated by unscrupulous French, Spanish, and British spies and negotiators for their own purposes.[55]

In 1788 a traveling Frenchman saw many *habitations* (little houses) on Cumberland, built, he said, by refugees from the depredations of Creek Indians. The refugees put up thatched-roofed huts, much like those erected by the British troops at Barriemackie. In the early 1790s the South Point community was increased by mainland residents who fled Camden County to escape the Oconee Wars, intermittent Indian raids down the St. Marys River that peaked in 1794. The Indian troubles were incited by Edmond Genêt, the envoy from the new French republican government to the United States. He arrived in 1791 and in a short time was engaged in intrigues designed to attract support for French objectives. Among his ardent supporters was American General Elijah Clarke, who received from Genêt a commission, a salary of $10,000, and covert diplomatic support.[56]

In 1794 Clarke, who was popular with land-hungry Georgians, led many Georgian supporters across the Oconee River, thereby stirring up angry countermeasures from the Creek nation. Among the results were continual Creek raids down the St. Marys, Satilla, and Altamaha Rivers.[57]

Spanish authorities were anxious to learn what American settlers planned to do. In 1786 a Spanish subject named Henry O'Neill wrote to his superiors that the Americans wanted arms to protect themselves:

> Yesterday I was on Cumberland Island where all the inhabitants of the State of Georgia is assembled that live Contiguous to the Island—they had made that place their Sanctuary at present to escape the dangers of the threatened war by the Indians. . . . [Colonel Pengree, late of East Florida,] had formed a petition to Governor de Zéspedes praying for 4 or 6 cannon, 12 muskets and banots one hundred weight gunpowder and with Salt [petre?]—which would be Returned or Paid for by him or by the State. . . . I have given orders to the people not to Irritate the Indians on any pretence that [it is?] on their own Defence.[58]

Some county responsibilities were held at South Point. Because there was not yet a county seat on the mainland, the sheriff held Camden County's public auctions on the island. Nathaniel Ashley was the county sheriff as well as tax collector. The Ashleys were a tough bunch, accustomed to taking charge. Since O'Neill was a Spanish-appointed magistrate, some jurisdictional dispute may have caused Sheriff Ashley unsuccessfully to warn O'Neill away. Ashley went into the "house of James Cashen on the South Point of Cumberland Island," where he shot O'Neill with buckshot. O'Neill lingered from 24 April until 1 May 1788, when he died, leaving the sheriff to face murder charges. Another reminder of the temporary importance of South Point to Camden County was that Ashley was one of the twenty signers of the 28 November 1787 Articles of Agreement establishing the town of St. Marys. The articles were drawn up on Cumberland, probably at South Point.[59]

The Spanish government mistrusted General Greene's motives when he visited St. Augustine in March 1785, believing that he intended to invite British families to reside on Cumberland, "which up to the present has been uninhabited." At the time of Greene's visit, twenty British transports were anchored in St. Marys Harbor, still taking aboard evacuees from East Florida. Many refugees dismantled their houses and abandoned the framing on the beach. William Maxwell, a former British officer now in the Spanish service, accompanied General Greene on his return trip. When Greene was invited to dine aboard the Spanish brig, Maxwell took the opportunity to make an unautho-rized reconnaissance to South Point. "Upon the point of this Island facing the North point of Amelia is the foundation of the old fort. . . . it has been built with Bricks and with Arches, but all of these are Ruined and in Many places the foundation seam to be Dig up and the Bricks taken away."[60]

The federal government did not condone Clarke's activities. In St. Marys James Seagrove, superintendent of Indian affairs as well as intendant of the city of St. Marys, was responsible for advising the U.S. secretary of state on devel-opments in regard to the terrifying Indian raids and the ominous possibilities of their collusion with French and Spanish forces. Although military stations were built at Coleraine and Burnt Fort, providing food and forage for the Cam-den County militia proved almost impossible. A militia lieutenant wrote de-spairingly in 1794, "The last Vessell that arrived from Savannah, Brought on a few Barrels of Beef, no flour nor corn, I spoke to [militia captain William John-ston], he tells me it's impossible for him to supply us if he is not supported by Mr. Public." Local planters warned the military commanders at Savannah that unless supplies were forthcoming, they would "go on Cumberland Island."[61]

Privateering

Most coastal residents were shipowners, shipbuilders, pilots, officers, or sea-men. Many hired out as crewmen for vessels owned by wealthier neighbors. Privateering was legal, and nearly everyone was familiar with the laws of sal-vage permitting the capture of "wrecks" or "abandoned ships," which then could be brought to vice-admiralty courts and claimed (along with their car-goes) as prizes. Ordinary citizens claimed the right to salvage: Wreckers Road, on Cumberland Island, allegedly got its name from the fact that when word reached residents that a vessel was stranded, they hurried down to the beach over this trail.[62]

Ships and islanders did not always help vessels in distress, sometimes profit-ing from the wreck instead. Residents who were afraid of being caught turned the salvage over to the courts. From time to time, islanders did both. In 1764 the crew of the sloop *Molly* was wrecked on Cumberland on its way from Kingston, Jamaica, to Savannah. The captain and crewmen arrived in Savannah in an open boat, having saved only their sails, rigging, and part of their cargo. Any-thing of the *Molly*'s that washed up on Cumberland's beach was quickly picked up by islanders. The schooner *Princess Mary*, bound from Tobago to Savannah and loaded with rum and molasses, ran aground on 10 March 1775 on a bank near Cumberland. The schooner was entirely lost, but the people and most of the cargo were saved. The ship's spars and rigging would still have provided valuable salvage, as would the rum. In 1796 a stranded vessel apparently lost its commander, possibly by murder:

> Yesterday a discovery was made on the island of Cumberland of 10 or 12 Brigand Negroes, who, on examination before Judge Pendleton, appear to be a part of those people employed by the Spaniards in St. Domingo against the French republicans; they are part of the villanous murderers at Port Dauphin, and were under the command of the black General John François, now in St. Augustine. . . . it appears that they had a white Captain but . . . I think there is not a doubt of their having killed him. His name appears to have been Peter Aspenall, a native of Virginia; the vessel in which they were, was stranded a few days past on Cumberland Island. It was a schooner, about 15 tons; they had several trunks and boxes on board, chiefly valuable female clothing, apparently plundered from the unfortunate French planters of St. Domingo. . . . A great part of the goods on board have been plundered by some worthless wretches on Cumberland, and parties are sent after them.[63]

In 1809 the *Pizarro*, carrying rice and naval stores from New York to Amelia Island, went ashore within the St. Marys Bar. The ship drifted onto Cumberland's South End, where it bilged. As dangerous as the two great bars that marked the entrance to St. Marys Inlet were the shoals lying off the beach at Cumberland's midpoint. As late as 1898, Superintendent William E. Page mentioned the loss of the schooner *Lizzie Heyer* on Stafford Shoals.[64]

Privateering was always a threat to Cumberland Islanders. In 1799 Henrique, a notorious pirate, menaced the entire southeastern coast. Robert Mackay wrote to his wife, "Mr. Phineas Miller came up a day or two ago & brings an account of the capture and destruction of the Spanish post & Galley at Amelia by two Providence privateers who were in search of Henrique's Ship & Cargo—fortunately for [Miller] however a contrary wind had forced him into Tybee, & he is now here."[65]

Privateers had commissions permitting them to capture on the high seas. Whether the Inland Navigation was legally beyond their reach was debatable. In 1783 an American committee sought further clarification, and in a letter to federal authorities, the officers cited a recent example in which a Spanish vice-admiralty court had condemned some American slaves as prizes. The committee said that the slaves "were taken in a Small row Boat, while Left high & dry upon a Sand Bank by the Tide as they were removing from one plantation to another."[66]

In 1782 General Lachlan McIntosh reported that depredations in the St. Marys Basin and southeastern coastal islands of Georgia were being committed by South Carolinian raiders who came by both the Inland Waterway and the open sea. McIntosh wrote that Andrew DeVeaux, late of South Carolina, was believed to have received a commission from the governor of that state and had fitted out some "Armed Boats" in Charleston. Captain DeVeaux "came inland from East Florida, plundering plantations in his way." Sailing through the Inland Navigation, he raided coastal Georgia settlements as far north as twelve miles south of Savannah.[67]

The Greene family was aware of the dangers of privateering and had hesitated in moving to Cumberland because residence there was perilous. Although in 1797 they considered visiting the island to escape the hot summer, Phineas Miller wrote that the family's plans would be greatly influenced by European diplomatic developments resulting from post–French revolutionary struggles: "We shall make our decampment for the summer—but the place where we shall . . . pitch our tents still remains [to be determined?] by the opinion of the French Directory, whose decisions respecting the molestation of our sea coast we have not yet learned."[68]

When privateers threatened the islands, coastal planters warned each other. Miller wrote to John McQueen on Fort George Island,

> A Mr. Piles belonging to the Island of St. Simon has just arrived upon this Island and gives us the unpleasant information that a privateer schooner is just fitting out at the Bahamas for the express purpose of carrying off a number of your negroes—She is to take with her two flat-bottomed Batteaux for the purpose of enabling the pirates to ascend a small creek, or go over [in] flats if necessary—My particular interest for your individual character, as well as consideration for the good neighborliness which subsists between the citizens of an unjust Government induce me not to delay for a moment giving you this unpleasant intelligence, that you may make instant preparation to avoid the impending danger.[69]

With the Oconee Wars still fresh in their memories, some settlers continued to fear Indian attacks. But coastal slave owners saw strange vessels as a greater threat, fearing that organized landing parties would carry off slave property. French republicans declared their detestation of American slavery, but French

sea marauders often captured humans for resale. Both privateers and real pirates separated their prisoners by race. Mulatto sailors were usually recorded as
free seamen, but those seamen who were recorded as having the "blood of Negroes" could be condemned as cargo and sold at prize auctions. In one case, a
French-speaking carpenter who had shipped out from the Caribbean was imprisoned as a prize in New York until a man from St. Domingo wrote to testify
that the carpenter was freeborn.[70]

Some coastal planters armed themselves against privateers. John Nightingale loaned a cannon to some settlers on Amelia so that they could install it on
a new blockhouse they were hastily building at the Amelia Narrows. He offered
to lend more cannons to McQueen, but McQueen advised Nightingale to contact the governor before offering to arm Florida citizens.[71] The U.S. government
could provide only minimal protection. In 1798 the U.S. Navy commissioned a
galley named *St. Marys* to be built by a shipyard in the river. Armed with one
24-pounder cannon and five howitzers, it was constructed for coastal defense
during the quasi war with France. The *St. Marys* cruised off the Georgia coast
from 1798 to 1801 to protect coastal settlements from armed French vessels. Because galleys depended on oar more than sail, the cruising range was necessarily limited to Inland Navigation and St. Marys Inlet.[72]

As prices for cotton and slaves escalated, so did the danger from privateers
cruising the Georgia coast. Furthermore, the U.S. government sought to avoid
any entanglements with European alliances that might cause war. By demonstrating American neutrality, the Embargo Acts were supposed to protect U.S.
ships from capture. While the Embargo Acts more or less achieved this goal,
they interfered mightily with conventional American trading and shipping
arrangements. One of the results was an enormous increase in smuggling, especially in the secluded waterways of the St. Marys Basin. Smuggled cargoes
included cotton, slaves, lumber, naval stores, and agricultural products. Cumberland was ideally placed to serve smugglers, and some very respectable citizens soon joined their ranks. Merchants saw no reason why the Embargo Acts
should affect their activities, and many businessmen intended to trade with the
enemy. One citizen wrote to the local newspaper under the pseudonym "Republica," "We expect a large English armed vessel to load by force. If she does
we shall have warm work. The day before yesterday sixty-four barrels of provisions were taken out a-flote on Cumberland Island, belonging to Josiah Smith,
and carried to St. Marys."[73]

The English ship was violating the Embargo Acts, and so was Smith, who was anxious to sell provisions. Although most coastal planters thought the Embargo Acts foolish, Smith was punished anyway. An anonymous person wrote from St. Marys,

> A day or two ago all the property, all the provisions for sale, belonging to Josiah Smith of Savannah, was seized by the collector of St. Marys and the officers of the gun-boat, I believe, on suspicion of his being a smuggler—he has before been detected in thus violating the laws of our country. It is truly distressing to reflect on the sufferings of the people of Florida. I am told they are absolutely starving, without a grain of corn or morsel of bread of any kind. A man, a few days since, obtained permission from the collector, to carry some corn to Cumberland, with the hope of getting it over to Amelia at night. In attempting it, however, he was discovered by the gun boat and brought back.[74]

In 1809 a special Savannah vice-admiralty court ruled in *United States v. Three Bales of Cotton*, a case regarding contraband brought from St. Simons to Cumberland. John Calder, owner of the cotton, could not defend himself against the charge that he transported the cotton in question for resale to foreign customers. Judge William Stephens asked sarcastically, "Is it possible that the great cotton market, the town on St. Simons, should be inferior to a hidden point of Cumberland Island? An old house there for the deposit of two bales, and the hiding of a third behind a garden fence near the same place, are irresistable proofs that there was no doubt the intention was to seek a market in Amelia Island, a foreign port." The judge ruled that the three bales were forfeited and must be sold at auction in St. Marys.[75]

Prize schooners and their cargoes sometimes drifted onto Cumberland. Captured vessels were usually escorted by a prize master, customarily an officer ordered by the captain of the privateer that made the capture to sail the prize to port. Local magistrates often viewed these unexpected arrivals with justifiable suspicion. In 1818 several people whose vessel had been seized arrived in Charleston from Cumberland Island, claiming that the schooner from which they hailed (a prize) was loaded with dry goods and sunk in four fathoms of water. At the same time, another prize schooner was drifting around Cumberland. Its crew had mutinied, but its prize master had escaped and was at St. Marys. The crew had locked up the prize master but was unable to navigate the ship, so he was released with orders to bring the ship to Cumberland's North End. The cargo, consisting of silks, powder, and brandy, was brought to the island. However, the crew had unshipped the schooner's masts and set it adrift. The

crew was armed and appeared determined to defend its property. It turned out
that privateers had captured a neutral ship that was breaking up on the Florida
coast, saving the lives of many of its crew but keeping the cargo. Anxious to hide
the evidence, the privateers were trying to scuttle their boat. It drifted and
beached in the marshes, where officers from the U.S. gunboat stationed at St.
Marys Inlet went to examine it.[76]

One authentic privateer resided on Cumberland, although he later became
respectable. John McKinnon's 1802 map shows a house site at South Point that
was occupied by "Thomason." It was a curious site for a house or settlement, located on the southern beach side of the island, about where the present North
Jetty extends out to the sea, marking the entrance of St. Marys Inlet. Thomason was a pilot, and one of his stations was St. Marys Bar. In 1793 Americans in
St. Marys enlisted the aid of "Pedro Thomasson" to go to a Catalan vessel prey-
ing on French ships. In 1794 "Pedro Thompson," described as the Cumberland
Island pilot, carried letters and information to the Spanish governor of East
Florida, Juan de N. Quesada. Throughout 1794–95 Spanish authorities viewed
French privateers with increasing apprehension, fearing the aims of revolutionary France. As Spanish opinion of Napoleon dropped, so did Quesada's
opinion of Thompson. Captain Carlos Howard, an Irish officer in the Spanish
service and a resident of East Florida, wrote scornfully, "His name is really
Tomasini." Howard and the governor agreed to keep an eye on the man, however, and in 1795 the captain reported that Thompson had gone to Savannah to
purchase "una balandrita de quince toneladas" (a little sloop of fifteen tons).
Thompson denied that he had spent the previous year privateering, but Captain Howard wrote, "I think we can say that Thompson took a Campechan
named *José María*." Although Thomason's place of origin remains unknown,
he was undoubtedly a French speaker, possibly from the Mediterranean. By
1825 he had become the French vice-consul in Savannah under the name Paul-
Pierre Thomasson.[77]

Tidal Mills

Another Frenchman who lived on Cumberland was Brittany-born Thomas
François LeRoi (1766–1816). On McKinnon's map, tract 8 contains a dotted
straight line labeled "dam" that crosses a marshy bottomland cove separating
Table of Pines Point from the present-day Squawtown Peninsula. In 1801, the
presumed date of McKinnon's surveying, McIntosh descendants still owned

that land. In 1809, however, friends of the Greene family who had acquired part of tract 8 at public auction sold their purchase to "Francis Le Roy." The area is still called Kings Bottom and probably takes its name from "LeRoi's Bottom Land."[78]

On an 1870 map, what McKinnon had identified as a "dam" is labeled a "dike," and an 1898 map calls it an "old levee." Traces of this feature can still be seen in aerial photos. McKinnon correctly understood its function: it was a dam built to impound water. LeRoi had invested in a tidal sawmill, possibly at the instigation of the McIntosh family, which controlled timber areas at either side of the bottomland. McIntosh Creek, with its strong tidal pull, was within their jurisdiction. It does not look from McKinnon's map as though the mill house stood on the dam.[79]

Well understood by Europeans in general and by Bretons in particular, tidal mills run on power generated by tides rather than by the current of a river. In Georgia, dikes were built near the early tide mills, but each locality had its own devices for gathering and releasing power. Millers were assured of power for two to three hours twice a day and thus had irregular but predictable workdays. According to Marion Nicoll Rawson, slaves would sometimes leave the cotton fields to work in mills. LeRoi owned ten slaves, who would have been adequate to operate his mill.[80]

After the abandonment of the mill, the causeway acted as a levee against the incoming tide, a not-uncommon method of reclaiming marshland. By building up new bottom land, LeRoi's old mill pond became known as "Kings Bottom." Reclamation of salt marshes for cotton planting was often discussed, and sometimes practiced, by Georgia's planters. Land of this sort, situated at the head of saltwater creeks, was commonly called "coves." Banking a cove was extremely laborious, and furthermore, the bank generally broke under high tides. If, however, the reclaimed land survived inundation, the cotton from it was apt to be remarkably luxuriant and tall.[81]

The War of 1812

When an invader finally landed in force on Cumberland Island, it was neither pirates nor privateers; rather, it was the British.

In late 1814 a British squadron under the command of Rear Admiral Sir George Cockburn was ordered to the St. Marys area from Chesapeake Bay. He arrived offshore with orders to attack the port, destroy its guns, and retreat to

Cumberland Island, where the squadron would await further developments. Although the War of 1812 had ended with the British defeat in the December 1814 Battle of New Orleans, the attacking squadron did not yet know that the war was over. At daybreak on 10 January 1815 the British forces attacked St. Marys, encountering little opposition. After two weeks of raiding warehouses and stores, the attackers evacuated the city in favor of Cumberland Island, with the admiral choosing Dungeness as his headquarters and raising the British flag there on 25 January. The island was occupied territory. During the approximately eight weeks that Cumberland was occupied, British ships took aboard 1,483 slaves to carry them to Bermuda, Trinidad, or Halifax, Nova Scotia, where they could settle as free persons.[82]

No other Sea Island has ever been so completely occupied by the British. During the American Revolution the barrier islands were far from the theater of war, and control of the Inland Navigation was never completely in British hands. During the War of 1812, however, there were strategic reasons for the squadron to occupy Cumberland Island: the British government believed that the Royal Navy could cut the Inland Navigation and consequently American communication. The government thought that thousands of warriors would aid in the capture of Mobile and New Orleans, thereby forever expelling the Americans from Louisiana. In addition, the British forces were running low on water and food. The large house on Cumberland Island exactly suited the admiral's purposes.[83]

Above and beyond strategic considerations lay a cunning political policy. London politicians believed that disaffected American residents would be happy to defect to the British. A British proclamation read in part, "all those who may be disposed to emigrate from the United States, will with their families be received on board his Majesty's Ships or Vessels of War . . . near the Coast of the United States, when they will have their choice, of either entering into His Majesty's Sea or Land forces, or being sent as Free Settlers to the British possessions in North America or the West Indies." The government hoped to attract slaves, and the proclamation legitimized British policy.[84]

Most vessels in the squadron anchored a quarter to half a mile southwest of Dungeness. Cumberland Harbor, as it was called, provided good anchorage in two to seven fathoms of water, had a good mud and sand bottom, and was capacious enough to allow ships to swing around when the wind changed. While the sailors remained with their ships, the three West Indian regiments accompanying the squadron camped on the island itself, within Dungeness's orange groves. The Third West Indian Regiment consisted of former slaves from the Chesapeake area. The British sick and wounded were placed inside the first floor of Dungeness House. Louisa Shaw, her family, and their guests were ordered upstairs. From his Dungeness headquarters, Cockburn ordered three vessels immediately to sail north to attack St. Simons and Jekyll Islands, seizing any valuable merchandise, capturing ships, taking American citizens prisoner, stealing livestock, and bringing back any blacks who were willing to join the British.[85]

In addition to running Dungeness and Littlefield Plantations, Shaw was administering the slaves on Rayfield Plantation, a tract on Cumberland that had gone to her brother, Nathaniel Ray Greene, after their mother's death. Shaw's 149 slaves were the first to be freed by Admiral Cockburn, who had them taken aboard the *Devastation*. By going to British territory or going aboard a British ship, enslaved blacks became free. Because Admiral Cockburn declared Cumberland Island occupied territory, all slaves who reached it would automatically become free persons under British law. The British correctly believed that many slaves would enlist with freedom as a reward.[86]

Cockburn was somewhat surprised to find so many slaves flocking to Cumberland Island. He had barely enough vessels to ship them to Bermuda. He encouraged his officers to go to Jekyll and St. Simons Islands to solicit plantation hands. Many slaves left Georgia and Florida plantations after hearing that the West Indian regiments were composed of free black men.[87]

Slaves seeking emancipation came from all parts of the southeastern coast. Only the limited duration of the British occupation cut short the flood. Although many blacks came from the Spanish side of the St. Marys River, the most determined group to reach Cumberland Island was the "Florida refugees," sixty-six slaves who arrived by dugout canoe from John Forbes's plantation about twenty-three miles up the St. Johns River. Forbes, a prominent Indian trader and wealthy planter, was a British subject who resided in Florida. When the Spanish governor protested British recruitment of Spanish property, Cockburn firmly answered that the British were unable to prevent the property's desertion from Spanish territory. On 11 February Cockburn informed his superiors at Bermuda that he had captured St. Simons Island, writing, "The Numbers of Refugees who have joined him has induced him to prolong his stay."[88]

A mounting chorus of protest from coastal planters only made the admiral dig in his heels. In addition, Cockburn had an ace up his sleeve. Although many

Americans remained unaware of the British defeat at New Orleans, Cockburn read the news on 10 February in a European newspaper found on a captured Swedish vessel. Both Great Britain and the United States had already signed the Treaty of Ghent. Although only Parliament had ratified the treaty, Cockburn knew that peace would take effect when Congress ratified it. The admiral studied the treaty's first article, which stated that all slaves captured during the recent war would be returned to their owners.[89]

But the wily admiral intended to follow the verdict of the Somersett case, a British matter in which a former slave avoided recapture and enslavement by virtue of having enlisted in the Royal Navy. To be aboard a British vessel was in effect to be on British soil, and "British soil knows naught of slavery." In February 1815 Cockburn sought instructions from his commander-in-chief, Vice Admiral Sir Alexander Cochrane, stationed at Bermuda, about how to handle property rights when American and Spanish slave property had escaped to independence on British territory—Cumberland Island and British ships.[90]

While Admiral Cockburn awaited instructions, he continued to receive refugees. Every time he could detach a vessel, he shipped former slaves away from Cumberland Island. Finally, on 5 March, two American commissioners, Thomas Spalding of Sapelo Island and Captain Thomas M. Newall of the U.S. Sea Fencibles, called on Cockburn with a copy of the *National Intelligencer*, an American journal, announcing the ratification of the Treaty of Ghent and the commencement of peace on 17 February. Cockburn at first refused to acknowledge the validity of the newspaper; when the commissioners returned two days later, Cockburn declared that he must await instructions. The flagship with his commander-in-chief aboard swept into Cumberland Harbor that evening, and Cochrane wasted no time in initialing each page of Cockburn's letter, thereby authorizing him to carry away all refugees who were on British soil as of 17 February.[91]

Spalding and Newall had no chance to argue for the return of slave property. Bad weather prevented them from coming aboard the flagship, and when the squadron sailed out of Cumberland Harbor on 10–11 March, Spalding and Newall could see that every ship was loaded with refugees. Cockburn did, however, notify the American commissioners of his intention to leave behind property and slaves "originally captured on Cumberland Island and which appear to have remained on it at 11 P.M. of February 17, 1815." His list consisted of eighty-one named slaves, a few bales of cotton, and some horses and cattle. About seventy-five of the returned slaves had come from Louisa Shaw's three plantations, and malicious local gossips wondered what she had done that so pleased the admiral.[92]

The majority of the freed slaves went to Bermuda or Trinidad. The Florida refugees went to Bermuda, where they were isolated pending Forbes's arrival. He never appeared, however, preferring to institute legal proceedings from afar. Forbes's pleadings were fruitless, and his slaves were freed. Many of the slaves who reached Bermuda were transshipped to Halifax, Nova Scotia, where their descendants live today.[93]

The British flag was struck at Dungeness on 13 March and was immediately replaced by the American flag. The American gentlemen assembled for the occasion quickly agreed that a U.S. Army captain with a detachment of twenty-five men should be ordered to come to Cumberland Island to catch any remaining fugitive slaves. Some refugees were still attempting to board British ships. One British vessel had trouble crossing the bar, and the *Albion*, Cockburn's ship, remained behind to help. On 18 March the admiral took aboard one last refugee and departed amid a storm of American criticism for stealing slaves.[94]

The occupation was hard on Cumberland Island's residents. Food and water ran short. All able-bodied white men were placed under house arrest, and British troops were stationed at each plantation house. The island's North End was guarded by two schooners and a shore detachment. There were some lighter aspects to the situation, however. At Dungeness House, naval officers relented enough to ask the Shaws and their guests to come downstairs for dinner. The British men had caught sight of the pretty young ladies who had been invited to share the Shaws' Christmas holidays. Two couples, Lieutenant John Fraser of the Royal Marines and Anne Sarah Couper from St. Simons Island and Susannah Stafford and Lieutenant George Drew Hawkins, met during the occupation and subsequently married.[95]

SEVEN

Slavery, Freedom, and Interdependence

The Greene Children and Cumberland Island

Nathanael and Catharine Greene had five children: George Washington (1775–1793), Martha Washington (1777–1839), Cornelia Lott (1779–1865), Nathaniel Ray (1780–1859), and Louisa Catharine (1784–1831). The eldest died in a boating accident on the Savannah River at the age of eighteen years. In 1795 Martha married John Clark Nightingale of Providence, Rhode Island, at Mulberry Grove. The Nightingales moved with Catharine Miller to Cumberland Island in the early 1800s, building a home in tract 3, which they called the Springs. They had four children, the youngest of whom was Phineas Miller Nightingale. John Nightingale died unexpectedly in 1806 at the Springs (site of the present-day Greyfield, where his grave lies). Four years later, his widow married Dr. Henry Edward Turner of Rhode Island and moved with him there. Seeking a wider medical practice, the Turners moved back to Savannah in 1822. In 1802 Cornelia Greene married Peyton Skipwith, son of a prominent Virginian planter family. Their marriage was performed at Dungeness by Phineas Miller in his capacity as justice of the peace. Skipwith bought land in Camden County on Crooked River, very close to Cumberland Island, intending to plant rice. He died unexpectedly in 1808, however, and in 1810 his widow shocked society by making a runaway marriage with her first cousin, Edwin Brinley Littlefield (ca. 1786–1836), considerably younger than she. The eldest son of Captain William Littlefield, Catharine Greene's brother, Ned had moved in 1809 to St. Marys to practice law.

Ned Littlefield and Henry Turner began pushing their wives to demand their shares of the property belonging to the Estate of General Greene, which was still a legal entity. As late as 1815 its initials, E.G.G., were stamped on the cotton sacking used for bagging cotton. Property division was becoming a family issue. In a family division drawn up on 24 April 1810, Catharine Miller's children signed a "voluntary agreement" to allow their mother to hold their "negro property . . . until every debt agreement against said Estate be paid." Catharine received seventy slaves, Martha received thirty-two, Cornelia received twenty-nine, Nat received thirty-five, and Louisa received thirty. They also divided the land. Catharine Miller received two tracts, "the one known as Dungeness" as well as tract 8. Martha received the tract called the Springs. Cornelia was to receive "Lot no. 5" at Littlefield. Nat, who already had inherited his father's holdings on the mainland, near Crooked River, received part of his mother's tract 8. Louisa received "Lot no. 2" at Littlefield. While Catharine's authority to administer the plantation was unchallenged, two of her children, Martha Nightingale and Cornelia Skipwith, desired greater autonomy over their share of land and slave property. Often sick with undiagnosed nervous complaints, Catharine Miller resented their demands, and when Littlefield and Turner insisted on dividing the general's military honors and library, she lost her temper and dismissed them from her presence.

The two allotments "at Littlefield" pose a bit of a mystery. They are perhaps demystified by remembering that the enumerated tracts of the Lynch-Greene division were merely legal entities; they were not plantations. From later property transactions we learn that "Littlefield" is, in fact, tract 5. Lots 5 and 2 "at Littlefield," therefore, refer to the creation of an investment unit that would establish a cotton plantation within tract 5, the principal investors of which were Phineas Miller, Captain William Littlefield, John C. Nightingale, Peyton Skipwith, and Ray Sands, another Rhode Island relative of Catharine's. Similarly, cleared land in tract 8 (later known as Rayfield Plantation) had not reached plantation status.

In 1813 Ned and Cornelia secretly planned to emigrate from Savannah to Tennessee, taking with them the requisite plantation equipment and furniture and, in violation of the 1810 agreement, Cornelia's share of slaves from the Estate of General Greene. Catharine Miller happened unexpectedly to pass through Savannah, where she saw certain slaves from Dungeness. Realizing what was happening, she called the sheriff and had her daughter arrested. Before going any further with their plan, the Littlefields were required to sign bonds guaranteeing payment for the slaves, whom they had handpicked for relocation in Tennessee. In 1815, when Catharine Miller's will was read, it was discovered that Martha and Cornelia received only one dollar each. To rid herself of her Georgia property, Cornelia leased tract 5 to Robert Stafford. Stafford also leased those slaves left behind when the Littlefields emigrated to Tennessee.

Regarding land and slave property, Catharine Miller's relationship with her son was difficult but less stormy. Nat had principled reservations about owning slaves. He did not wish to own property that required slave labor, nor would he consent to owning slaves himself. He did not wish, however, to condemn slave-holding friends and relatives. He transferred his equity in the Dungeness slaves back to his mother in 1813. When she revised her will for the last time, she devised tract 8, now called Rayfield Plantation, and its slaves to Nat's children. Although Nat and his Rhode Island wife resided at Dungeness from about 1808 to 1815, Louisa administered Rayfield Plantation, with Nat's full permission. At the end of the British incursion in 1815, Nat returned to take up residence permanently in Rhode Island. Still unwilling to jeopardize his children's inheritance, he leased Rayfield for twelve years to his father-in-law, Ethan Clarke of Rhode Island. Clarke took up part-time residence on Cumberland Island to administer what was becoming a thriving cotton plantation. After Nat's children had reached their majority and with their permission and authorization, he sold Rayfield Plantation and its slaves to Robert Stafford.[1]

Orange Cultivation at Dungeness

Phineas Miller Nightingale, the second son of Martha Greene and John C. Nightingale, was born on Cumberland Island in 1803. Phineas was three years old when his father died at the Springs Plantation (the present-day Greyfield). He was close to his aunt, Louisa Shaw, and as a boy he divided his time between Cumberland and Rhode Island, where his mother remarried.[2]

Early in February 1818 Phineas, then fifteen years old, watched a schooner nearing Dungeness's dock. Sailors carried a feeble old man from the vessel. General Henry "Light-Horse Harry" Lee, Revolutionary War hero, now dying of cancer, had asked the ship's captain to put him ashore. When Lee learned that Phineas was General Greene's grandson, the old man threw his arms around the boy and said, "Tell Mrs. Shaw I am come purposely to die in the house and in the arms of the daughter of my old friend and compatriot." General Lee died two months later and was buried at the little family cemetery at Dungeness. In 1832 the general's eldest son, Major Robert E. Lee, sent a headstone to mark the grave through the good offices of General James Hamilton of South Carolina, who had married into the Lynch family.[3]

After the War of 1812 American property owners who had suffered losses from British depredations submitted requests for compensation. These "spoli-

ation claims" dragged on until 1828, when international arbitration finally recognized most of the American claims as valid. Louisa Shaw, who hired a skillful and aggressive lawyer, John McPherson Berrien, to represent her, was ultimately awarded almost all she claimed. Although she lost fewer slaves than had
other coastal Georgia planters, she suffered greater real property damage. Because Dungeness served as Admiral George Cockburn's headquarters, Shaw
had lost substantial amounts of corn, cotton, cattle, and live oak. In addition,
her entire cotton house and machinery were destroyed by fire allegedly caused
by sparks from the pipe of a careless British Marine. She received $20,883, only
$1,385 less than she had claimed. Previously well-off, Shaw now became rich.[4]

Like his aunt, Nightingale was a careful horticulturist. In the early 1820s he
took up full-time residency at Dungeness, paying his poll tax for the first time
in 1827. Cotton prices were very low in 1827, and the Georgia legislature's Joint
Committee on Agriculture and Internal Improvements urged planters to diversify their farm products. Suggestions included production of silk, olives,
wine, and white poppies for processing into opium and the raising of grasses,
indigo, tobacco, and sugarcane.[5]

Louisa Shaw had learned how to propagate oranges from seed, and by 1825
Dungeness Plantation had an orange grove with two thousand trees. Nightingale responded to the committee's plea for diversification by improving and en-
larging the orange groves and by marketing oranges and olives as well as cotton. In November 1827 Savannah newspapers announced the arrival of thirty
thousand oranges from Dungeness. In December Nightingale advertised the
sale of two hundred thousand sweet oranges "now on the trees at Dungeness
plantation." He believed that orange cultivation could be commercially successful.[6]

Citriculture was becoming a boon to physicians. In the late eighteenth century a Scottish naval surgeon named James Lind had shown that scurvy could
be cured and prevented by drinking the juice of oranges, lemons, or limes. By
the early nineteenth century both American and British navies had accepted
the need for providing their personnel on long cruises with citric crystals or
syrups that could be diluted with water. Pharmacists also provided essence of
citrus for the medicine chests of emigrants to California and Oregon, of lumber
and turpentine camps, and of backcountry farms and plantations. Citrus distilling could have taken place at Dungeness. Shaw may have been especially attracted to this kind of commercial activity. Her will prohibited the sale or removal of her slaves from Dungeness: such restrictions, in tandem with her slave

labor force's predictable natural increase, would sooner or later create a su-
perfluity of slaves.[7] Distilling crystals from oranges might well have been Shaw
and Nightingale's answer to the problem of finding a labor-intensive home industry.

Shaw was in bad health and died on 24 April 1831. She had revised her will
in 1829, leaving generous legacies to many relatives, partly as the result of her
large award. Phineas Nightingale inherited Dungeness and Oakland, a Cumberland Island plantation once owned by James Shaw, her late husband, as well
as her slaves. Louisa Shaw's will ordered Nightingale to provide annuities and
other monetary gifts to a long list of beneficiaries, nearly all of them Greene or
Shaw relatives. By inheriting her land and slave property, Nightingale became
one of the principal men on Cumberland Island.[8]

Nightingale planned to continue citriculture, and he clearly wanted to acquire tract 2, which would round out the acreage devoted to the orange groves.
He took out a mortgage and in May 1831, little more than a month after Shaw's
death, bought all the Lynch property on Great Cumberland Island—tracts 2,
4, 6, 7, and 11. Nightingale immediately put up all the Lynch tracts except tract
2 for sale or lease, and they were soon snapped up by small-scale planters.[9]

Nightingale had chosen to be a southern planter, but his wife was Mary Ray
King, a high-minded northerner who favored abolition. Although he carefully
followed Georgia's black codes, which defined and regulated interracial relations, he inherited numerous scruples about slavery from his Greene forebears.
Although Phineas and Mary Nightingale realized that their personal fortunes
depended on slave labor, they attempted to ameliorate certain aspects of the peculiar institution.[10]

From Maine to Louisiana the winter of 1834–35 was unusually harsh in
both intensity and duration. Charleston, South Carolina, saw snow on 3 January 1835. Charles Rinaldo Floyd, owner of Bellevue Plantation in Camden
County, said of the "big freeze" that on 8 February his thermometer stood several degrees below zero. Eggs and oranges were frozen solid, and pitchers were
broken apart because the water in them had turned to ice. The devastation was
widespread. A young man stationed in St. Augustine wrote to his mother, "The
people [in Florida] all lament the loss of their orange trees, they must have
added very much to its beauty and something to its revenues. The crop was
about four millions of oranges annually. As far as I can judge the trees are as
thoroughly destroyed as about Savannah."[11]

It took two to three years before general interest in orange growing revived.

In 1837, however, another enemy to orange cultivation appeared, and it was even more deadly than the freeze: brown or purple scale, an insect infestation. A. J. Downing, a prominent horticulturist, wrote in the early 1840s that the orange plantations of Florida had suffered "very severely within a few years, from the attacks of the scale insect (Coccus Hisperidum), which, in some cases, has spread over whole plantations and gradually destroyed all the trees.... All efforts to subdue it in Florida have been nearly unavailing." No horticulturist of the period knew how to kill the infestation except by syringing each tree, and Nightingale's resources may not have been adequate for this process. It is likely that the freeze of 1835 weakened rather than killed the Dungeness grove, but Nightingale lost his chief cash crop to the purple mite. More than twenty years later, in January 1862, no less a personage than General Robert E. Lee commented on the loss of the Dungeness orange groves. While touring coastal defenses, Lee visited his father's grave on Cumberland and noted, "The orange trees were small, and the orange grove which, in Mrs. Shaw's lifetime, during my tour of duty in Savannah in early life, was so productive, has been destroyed by an insect that has proved fatal to the orange on the coast of Georgia and Florida."[12]

Before the freeze, Nightingale was the most distinguished landowner on the island and certainly the wealthiest. A genial gentleman, his contemporaries described him as smiling and cheerful, wealthy and well-educated, a father and husband who was moral and pious. Nightingale went broke in 1839. Louisa Shaw's will, with its obligations to pay lifetime annuities to various relatives, became a heavy burden, and he had overextended his credit when he took out the mortgage to buy the Lynch tracts. In 1840, beset by lawsuits, Nightingale advertised the sale of his Cumberland property.[13] In 1848 Nightingale's increasingly complicated finances drove him to ask his father-in-law, New York Governor John Alsop King, for help with his financial situation. Although King's response did not indicate whether he planned to loan Nightingale money, the governor remarked that he and his wife regretted learning that Nightingale might be forced to sell Dungeness.[14]

Intervention by both Phineas and Mary Nightingale's relatives prevented his complete bankruptcy, but by 1850 he abandoned full-time residence at Dungeness. He moved to Baker County in western Georgia, where he represented his father-in-law's interests in a new railroad line. Before the beginning of the Civil War, Nightingale returned to coastal Georgia as a rice planter on Cambers Island, a fertile river island in McIntosh County. Although Nightingale never sold the Dungeness property, more than once he came perilously close to losing title to it.[15]

Dungeness ceased to be a productive plantation as early as 1841, by which time the house was described as "abandoned." Another observer described it as "formerly a fine house on the estate, but . . . now going to ruin." The Nightingales subsequently used the plantation as a summer and autumn residence where they and their large family could escape inland Georgia in favor of cooling ocean breezes.[16]

Land Use at Midcentury

In 1898 an aging man named Cray Pratt fondly remembered who was living on the island when he was young:

> My first trip to Cumberland was in 1837. I remained there two years and at that time there were a good many families on the island. I will name families to show how the population has gone down since that time. The first family at the Point was Mrs. Holder—the next Mrs. Downes, the third Mrs. Bunkley, the fourth Mrs. ———, fifth at the Inlet Mr. I. Spalding, sixth Capt. Thompson, seventh Mrs. Church. To the west from there—Brick Hill, Mr. Hawkins, Eighth.—Mr. Holzendorf, Ninth, [and] Ray Field, Mr. Hart. These place[s] owned by Mr. Stafford.—Tenth, To the West, Capt. Laen. Eleventh, Mrs. Bernardey at Plum Orchard. At the Bluff Mr. Lassier had a shop. To the south of that Stafford had a church for his colored people on the north of the bridge, twelfth:—and on the east side of the swamp in Pine Woods Mr. J. Clubb, thirteenth—Two miles to the South was Mr. Stafford, fourteenth. Three miles from that was Mr. Gray. 2 miles from Grays, Mr. Nightingale. And at [that] time the Light House was kept on South Point by Mr. Lathorm. At that [time] there must have been about 500 persons on the Island.[17]

Pratt, formerly the mail carrier on Cumberland, had a good memory. His account correlates very well with the 1840 U.S. Census for Cumberland, which listed seventeen free white persons—three of them women—as heads of households: Phineas M. Nightingale, John W. Gray, John Hart, Winifred Downes, Charlotte Holder, David Thompson, James A. Clubb, Thomas Bunkley, Thomas Goodbread, Robert Church, Thomas Drew Hawkins, Alexander Holzendorf, Henry Hart, William Laen, Margaret (Marguerite) Bernardey, James McDonald, and Robert Stafford.[18]

By 1840 Cumberland had five main centers of white settlement, each sur-rounded by cotton and cane fields, vegetable gardens, and slave villages. Some of these communities were called plantations, while others more resembled clusters of farm buildings. Some smaller settlements were interspersed among them.

At the South End stood Dungeness House, which still belonged to Greene descendants, although they now came only to escape the summer heat of main-land Georgia. At the opposite end of the island, called the North End or High Point, lay a more dispersed settlement consisting of five or six small farms clus-tered around the single docking area. Members of the Clubb family, the oldest white family on Cumberland, originally owned 4 acres. John Clubb, an Eng-lishman, served in General Oglethorpe's regiment, first as a private and later as a noncommissioned officer. As a reward for his military service, he received a land allotment on St. Simons Island in 1765. His son, William, left St. Simons in 1807 and purchased two lots of land (8 acres) on Cumberland at the site where Fort St. Andrews "had formerly stood." William may have thought he was purchasing land in the hopefully named town of St. Andrews, but the spec-ulation failed, and he lived the quiet life of yeoman farmer, stockman, and sailor at the North End with his wife, Celia; their two sons, James A. and William Jr.; and numerous daughters. In 1816 one of them, Rebecca, married Thomas Pitt Bunkley, who thereby became head of household for her acre. In 1825 Bunkley and Isham Spalding Jr., husband of another Clubb daughter, Martha, had purchased 80 acres near High Point. When Nightingale offered tract 11 for sale in 1832, the purchasers from High Point included James A. Clubb, Bunkley, and Winifred Downes from Spanish East Florida, who had in-herited 112 acres at High Point from her deceased husband, William. Winifred Downes, her daughter, Charlotte Holder; Captain David Thompson (second husband of Celia Clubb); James A. Clubb; Bunkley; and Robert Church (hus-band of Rachel Clubb) were all closely related.[19]

Since the land that the High Pointers purchased from Nightingale was not especially good for planting Sea Island cotton, they seem to have grown a little cotton, a little cane, and some rice, probably for home consumption; tended their vegetable patches; looked after their livestock; and engaged in some log-ging. Basically, however, they turned to the sea for their livelihood and became fishermen, sailors, boatbuilders, smugglers, lighthouse keepers, or pilots of St. Andrews Bar. Other North End residents included Isham Spalding Jr.'s family and descendants, transient lighthouse keepers and pilots, and a few others. The

"Lassier" to whom Pratt referred was probably either George or Joseph Lasserre, and his "shop" was probably a smithy. "Mr. Lathorm" was Amos Latham, who succeeded Robert Church as lighthouse keeper at South Point from 1829 to 1838. Latham was an old-timer who had been a friend of the senior Staffords, and he subsequently moved to Fernandina, Florida, where he died and was buried in 1842. All High Point families possessed slaves, usually as a result of family legacies. In 1837 most High Pointers owned only two to four slaves, and none owned more than six.[20]

In the middle of the island stood Robert Stafford's home, Planters House, with its wharves extending to the Cumberland River. For nearly forty years Stafford administered a highly successful and efficient cotton plantation from this simple frame structure. Stafford was the chief source of credit for nearly all his island neighbors. In 1837–40 three white island residents worked either directly or indirectly for Stafford. Two were tenant farmers: Thomas Drew Hawkins, Stafford's nephew; and Alexander Holzendorf, who was married to Jane Spalding, Stafford's half-sister. The third was John Hart, the overseer at the Stafford plantation, Rayfield. Hart was followed by James McDonald, who remained in the position for more than a decade. After Hart's death, his son, Henry, became a carpenter for Stafford.[21]

Robert Stafford's father, Thomas, had once worked for the Greenes. Thomas and his brother, also named Robert, were poor Englishmen who emigrated from Spanish East Florida to Georgia in 1784, becoming U.S. citizens by 1788. The brothers jointly owned a small sloop, the *Camden Packet,* that carried rice from Charleston to Spanish East Florida, where it picked up cotton bales for shipment to Savannah. Florida Governor Juan de N. Quesada referred to "los hermanos Staffordes en la Ysla de Cumberlan" (the Stafford brothers of Cumberland Island) in his correspondence, especially in connection with paying what the Spanish government owed them for food supplies.[22]

Young Robert came from a respectable, hardworking family just beginning to accumulate property. When he was about eighteen, he began to buy finished products from American manufactories in exchange for raw cotton grown on Cumberland. On 15 April 1813 his family bought Cumberland's tract 5, a productive 600-acre cotton field, from Cornelia Greene Littlefield. Over the next four decades, Stafford became the largest landholder on Cumberland. Although his first purchase took place with the cooperation of his mother and two sisters, subsequent purchases were his own. By the outbreak of the Civil War he owned 8,125 acres, almost one-third of Great Cumberland. Had not the Civil

War intervened, Stafford would have undoubtedly acquired 3,300 acres more, property of Cumberland resident James H. Downes, who was heavily in debt to Stafford.[23]

Stafford died in 1877 at the age of eighty-seven. He is buried with his mother and his sister, Susannah, in the small graveyard near their Cumberland Island home. Because his will made no mention of any Georgia property, that state ruled that he died intestate, and his Cumberland Island property went to his nearest kin—that is, his white nephews and nieces, Thomas D. Hawkins, Susannah's son; and Robert, John, and Lucy Tompkins, children of Mary Stafford Tompkins.[24]

Plum Orchard Plantation lay immediately north of Stafford's land. A family of French origin named Bernardey had purchased the land in the mid-1820s and was firmly committed to growing cotton and living on the plantation. Peter (Pierre) Bernardey died in 1827, and his widow, Catharine, subsequently married Captain William Laen. They continued to live on Cumberland at what is still called Laen's Landing. The Bernardey slaves were the property of two women, Catharine Laen and her mother-in-law, Marguerite Bernardey.[25]

In 1825 the Nightingale tract, property of the widowed Martha before her return to Rhode Island, passed into the hands of John W. Gray. Like Bernardey, Gray came to Cumberland from Jekyll Island, where both had been tenant farmers of the DuBignon family. Gray and Bernardey had brought slaves from Jekyll. Both of these men had been itinerant planters, a class of antebellum agriculturalist particularly favored by ambitious young men. Would-be planters who lacked land but possessed slaves could enter the planters' world by hiring themselves out, moving from farm to farm with their labor squads and occasionally specializing in a particular crop. Such tenant farmers sometimes made a profit by contracting with the landowner to plant and sell "on their own account"—that is, the tenant would keep a share of the crop for himself. In 1825, when he had amassed enough money from his employment with the DuBignons, Gray bought a 500-acre Cumberland Island tract, the Springs Plantation, which lay immediately south of Stafford's land. To become a landed proprietor was to move socially upward, although Gray's tax reports show that he continued to work as an overseer for various neighbors.[26]

By the late 1840s a few free persons of color resided at Stafford's plantations. One of them, Thomas Delany, gave his occupation as "mechanic." Under the same roof but in her own room lived Esther Low, and in a separate cabin lived Samuel Joseph. They undoubtedly made their living through specialized contributions such as blacksmithing, shoemaking, leather tanning, and boat repair. Low may have been a midwife. On a small land unit such as Cumberland, these free blacks probably worked for any landowner who paid for their services.[27]

The Peculiar Institution

The slave system in the southern United States was peculiar to the region's agricultural needs. The southeastern United States had relatively few cities and vast plantation areas. Under the plantation system, home was a unit in which the resident persons owed obedience to or depended on its head. On Cumberland Island in 1837, there were seventeen to twenty households, and each white head of household lived with between three and twelve people, usually kinfolk. A typical nuclear white family unit included eight people, so Cumberland's white residential population numbered approximately 160 people. Pratt's account is therefore startling, because he said that in 1837, "there must have been about 500 persons on the Island." The slave population made up the balance. Each plantation and dispersed white settlement was surrounded by a slave village.

Pratt's estimate was right on target. In 1815 Cumberland's slave population had been about 225, but according to poll tax records, in 1837–40 seventeen Cumberland slave owners controlled 360 slaves, a ratio of more than twenty to one. As of 24 October 1846 the island's population comprised "thirteen white men, eight white boys, seven girls, eight women, and [of] negroes four hundred."[28]

As plantation and farm units became the norm, their residents formed part of the "peculiar institution." Work collaboration between master and slave was central to the success of southern life. So dependent did white property owners become on their slaves' exertions that every sort of menial task was assumed to be the natural duty of slaves. Slave owners regularly interacted with their slaves. From such daily contacts came countless varieties of human reactions. Over four decades, Robert Stafford acquired a large number of slaves to tend agricultural areas, mend dikes and ditches, clean and gin cotton, handle and mend the boats and flats needed for island transport, store and cook food for plantation personnel, cut wood, police slave health and sanitation, and fill all self-supporting plantation functions. In 1850 he owned 348 slaves, placing him among the very small percentage of Georgians who owned more than one hundred slaves. Stafford, like many of his wealthy neighbors, rented his slaves out to various mainland companies, chiefly Georgia's burgeoning railway and canal construction ventures, whose investors hoped to profit from the state's internal improvement program.[29]

Between 1830 and 1860 Cumberland's acreage was consolidated into the hands of fewer landowners. Whereas in 1837 there had been seventeen households, in 1860 there were only nine. Acreage consolidation caused some residents to move away. This also resulted in fewer resident slaves, a temporary deficit more than compensated by the rate of slave natural increase. A few landowners found that their acreage was too small to make slave ownership profitable, and for some landowners, overpopulation by slaves was a problem. The number of slaves resident on Cumberland between 1815 and 1860 appears to have doubled, from roughly 225 in 1820 to more than 400 in 1861. Certain slave owners (Stafford and Nightingale) were now leasing their extra hands to mainland entrepreneurs. By 1860 only six persons reported ownership of slaves living on Cumberland: Stafford, who owned 110; Nightingale, who owned 63; Margaret Downes, who owned 40; James A. Clubb, who owned 15; Thomas P. Bunkley, who owned 12; and Rachel Church, who owned 6. Almost all the slaves were black, although Stafford owned 11 mulattos (all of them probably his children and their mothers) and Clubb reported owning a mulatto infant. The records do not indicate clearly whether the landowners owned slaves in other counties.

By 1860 the census had redefined its definition of "plantation" and "farm." By that date only Downes, Stafford, and Nightingale reported themselves as planters; all other Cumberland landowners—Thomas P. Bunkley and his son, William R. Bunkley; Church; Isham Spalding and his son, Edmund; and James A. Clubb—reported themselves as farmers.[30]

Slave dwellings were commonly laid out in units of eight, four to six people per house. In more informal settlements, such as High Point, slave cabins were less regularly laid out. Nightingale had eight slave cabins, seemingly not enough for all his slaves, but many of his hands lived off-island. Stafford reported ownership of twenty-four slave cabins. Downes reported eight slave cabins for her forty slaves. Church owned no slave houses: her slaves lived in and around her home and perhaps on land owned by other High Pointers.[31]

A few generalities may be made about Cumberland's slaves. First, the bulk of the slave population came after 1785. Second, because island living conditions were generally healthful, the slave population tended to grow through natural increase. And, finally, like Georgia's other Sea Islands, Cumberland slaves developed somewhat separatist communities.[32] Many of their members spoke Gullah, an English-based creole that developed from the necessity for the New World plantation owners to accommodate different African languages.[33] Although there is reason to believe that by the beginning of the nineteenth century Cumberland slaves had embraced Baptist preaching, most Sea Island blacks either participated in or witnessed their own communities' clandestine quasi-religious customs, such as the ring shout, hand clapping and drumming, and ecstatic preaching.

Personal Accommodations to Slavery

Obtaining detailed information about individual slaves is difficult. Written records contain little information about slaves because they did not participate in white civil life. They did not register to vote, pay poll taxes, appear in state or federal censuses, or serve in the military. For slaves, even the most basic of vital statistics—births and deaths—were not recorded. Slaves were property, not persons. Finding information about specific slaves requires looking at testamentary provisions, mortgages, and sales. Changes of ownership can be very revealing, because the transfer to another owner often radically changed a slave's life. Here are some specific slaves of Cumberland Island. Some found freedom.

WILLIAM DOWNES AND MELINDA

In 1822 William Downes purchased a half interest in property at High Point identified as formerly the site of Fort St. Andrews. Here he lived on a high and breezy bluff with his wife, Winifred; his mother-in-law, Ann Griffiths, from Spanish East Florida; and his five children, Robert, James, Sarah, Ann Eliza, and Charlotte.

In 1818 Downes appeared as defendant in a civil suit regarding a forty-two-year-old slave named Melinda who had belonged to Winifred before her marriage to Downes. Melinda had run away from her current owner, Joseph F. Gants, fleeing to the Downeses' home in Camden County. Gants wanted his property returned. Downes declared that Melinda "did come to him of her own accord" and stated that he would not give her up unless compelled to do so by due course of law. The case apparently ended when, against Gants's opposition, Downes purchased Melinda back again.[34] Downes seems to have realized that his family had made a mistake in selling Melinda to Gants and rectified the error.

ROBERT STAFFORD AND ELIZABETH BERNARDEY

Plantation administration called for resident owners' active participation in cooperation with their wives, mothers, or sisters. In 1836 Stafford's mother and sister died within weeks of one another. Regardless of his personal grief, their deaths presented Stafford, who was unmarried, with the immediate task of re- placement. Problems regarding slave health and sanitation required constant vigilance. Not only were physicians scarce in Camden County, but Cumberland residents always felt vulnerable because of the island's isolation. Partly because it was hard to get a doctor, and partly because of local sensitivities, examination of pregnant or sick slave women was usually carried out by the plantation mis- tress. To look after his sick slaves, Stafford purchased Elizabeth, a young mu- latto woman, from one of his island neighbors.[35]

Stafford and Elizabeth subsequently had six children. The first, Mary Eliza- beth, was born in 1841, followed by Robert, Armand, Ellen, Adelaide Clarisse, and Medora. All except Medora were born on Cumberland. Stafford went north each summer to visit Connecticut, Massachusetts, Rhode Island, and New York in search of business opportunities. Each of the first five children eventually boarded with a family in Connecticut, attending a private academy. In 1853 Stafford built a large house in Groton, Connecticut, for himself and his family, which he visited each summer. The civil status of the seven mulatto persons in the Groton household remained secure as long as Stafford remained solvent. Busy making plans for their financial future, Stafford returned each year to Cumberland to supervise his plantation affairs. Although Stafford eventually became the wealthiest planter on the island, Phineas Nightingale did not for- get the other man's origins. Toward the end of Stafford's life, he wrote bitterly to Nightingale, "You never ever said kindly to me."[36]

When Stafford died, he left a Connecticut estate of more than $345,000, all of which was bequeathed to his surviving daughters and their children. He had also established a trust fund for Elizabeth. After the war, Elizabeth returned to Cumberland Island, where the 1870 census lists her as Elizabeth Bernardey, a fifty-five-year-old mulatto who was looking after Maria Bernardey, age thirty- five, black, and a deaf-mute. Northerners bought Stafford Place in 1882, and sometime between 1883 and 1884 an elderly black woman scolded Thomas M. Carnegie Jr., a small boy playing near Stafford House, because he was throwing stones at a cat. When Carnegie later asked who the woman was, his parents told him that she was Elizabeth Bernardey. She later moved to the North End. In the late 1880s a small cemetery was established at the northern end of the island, and Elizabeth may be buried in it, although if so, her grave is unmarked.[37]

NED SIMMONS

Some Cumberland Island slaves found freedom long before the Emancipation Act. Ned Simmons was a slave who attained freedom in 1815, only to find it taken away. Ned Simmons's life and death would be unknown today were it not for a northern journalist who wrote in 1864 from occupied Fernandina,

> Ned Simons, an old negro belonging to the Dungeness estate of Gen. Nathan Greene, on Cumberland Island, and who was left by the rebel inheritor, Nightingale, on his evacuation of the place, died here last week, at the home of the lady teachers, who have kindly cared for him since their arrival here. Ned was over one hundred years old, and remembered Gen. Washington well, and was one of the number who assisted in carrying him through the streets of Savannah on his last visit to that place.[38]

In 1808 the Greene children began to quarrel with their mother's continued administration of the family property on Cumberland, and in 1810 the family agreed to divide the estate, including the general's medals and ribbons. Simmons and thirty-two other slaves went to Nathanael and Catharine's son, Nat. In 1813 Nat conveyed back to his mother thirty of the slaves he had received in the 1810 distribution, possibly in an attempt to show his willingness to cooperate with her in the aftermath of the dispute. However, Nat also knew as early as 1813 that he was unwilling to be a slave owner.[39]

Royal Navy logbooks show that a "Ned Simmonds" voluntarily left Cumberland to join the Third Battalion of Royal and Colonial Marines in 1815, during the short period when the British controlled the island. He remained on so-called British territory as of eleven o'clock on the night of 17 February. On 10 March Simmonds was stripped of his British uniform, arms, and insignia and was returned immediately to Cumberland and to his slave status.[40]

In 1834 Nat and his adult children sold Rayfield Plantation and its slaves to Robert Stafford, who had been renting the land as a tenant farmer. Simmons evidently remained on Cumberland until the occupation of Fernandina in 1862.[41]

In the twentieth century the remains of a slave settlement at Rayfield Plantation were the subject of an archaeological examination. Among the excavated artifacts was a military button from an 1808 uniform. The British squadron had carried old uniforms to the southeastern Atlantic coast as part of a program to induce male refugees to enlist with the Royal and Colonial Marines. Simmons may have retained this military button as a precious talisman marking his brief career as an enlisted man. Furthermore, only one chimney remained standing in the little Rayfield settlement. It is possible that as a result of residing on Cumberland longer than most other slaves, Simmons maintained his cabin longer than did others.[42]

POLYDORE

In the winter of 1815 three slaves, Polydore, Jerry, and Alick, furtively departed William McNish's Satilla River plantation. They fled to Cumberland, where their stay was short. Nevertheless, it changed Polydore's life, for on 15 February he enlisted in the British Corps of Colonial Marines stationed at High Point under the command of Captain Sir Thomas Cochrane. In 1816 he went with others from the corps to Trinidad, where they were disbanded on 16 August and where Polydore settled.[43]

The former Marines received land grants and created a series of settlements called Company Villages, named after the Colonial Marine companies. In each village a former sergeant of the company was charged with maintaining civil order. During the nineteenth century the residents of Company Villages acquired a reputation for skill and hard work. Always isolated, the community became self-contained and independent, active Baptists in a country predominantly Roman Catholic or nativist. Its settlers were long known as the "Merikin Baptists," although few scholars recognized the origin of "Merikin." They retain a powerful apocalyptic form of religious worship, and their strict moral code is supposed to have helped them keep their identity.[44]

LOUISA SHAW AND ABU

Catharine Greene Miller owned a slave woman named Abu, whom Miller bequeathed to her daughter, Louisa Shaw, along with thirty-seven other slaves. Since Abu's name appears to be African or Muslim, she may have been purchased by someone in the Greene family from Thomas Spalding at Sapelo Island or John Couper on St. Simons Island, both of whom owned Muslim slaves. Spalding's head man, Bu-Ali, had many children, including a daughter with the Muslim name Yaruba. Her name had a variant spelling, Yarrabuh, that resembles Abu.[45] The Shaws and the Coupers were intimate friends. Catharine may have offered some special enticement to obtain Abu, such as promising to

let her travel freely between her old home and Cumberland. Catharine Miller
may have sought Abu for special training in nursing.

Abu first appeared in the written record in Louisa Shaw's will. Shaw left all
her slaves to her nephew, Phineas Nightingale, with an important restriction:

> I positively forbid any sale Exchange or alienation of my negroes whatever. It be-
> ing my will that they should as far as possible be all kept together and descend to
> my future heirs . . . and as in this last solemn act of my life I feel it a very pecu-
> liar and binding duty to guard the happiness and comforts of those poor people
> in every way in my powers I hereby positively prohibit my said negroes from be-
> ing removed to any place over Fifty miles from Cumberland Island, unless . . .
> some circumstance which menaces their safety should in the opinion of my Heirs
> and Executors render such a measure necessary . . . and that they are to be re-
> turned to their homes in Camden County.

Shaw had a special problem in providing for Abu:

> As there is no part of this Instrument of writing that has caused me half the Em-
> barrassment and perplexity I have felt . . . [for my] affectionate and long tried ser-
> vant Aboo I trust that my dear nephew and . . . friend Henry Sadler Esq. will par-
> don the liberty I thereby take of naming them for Trustees to . . . Aboo and her
> infant child Emily.—It is my will that my said Servant Aboo should go where and
> reside where she pleases having full liberty to follow her own inclinations in all
> matters and things connected with the future mode of life of herself and her child
> Emily.[46]

Shaw required Nightingale to build a house for Abu's use as long as she lived.
In addition, he was to pay Abu $100 annually for the rest of her life, provide her
with twenty-five bushels of corn and fifty pounds of bacon each year, and furnish the house with chairs, a bedstead, china crockery (including a teapot),
sheets, and blankets.[47]

In December 1856, almost a quarter of a century later, a Connecticut woman,
Mrs. C. A. Taft, wrote to William Mackay, a Savannah attorney, on behalf of
"Maum Abbou," who resided in Hartford and worked as an assistant to Taft's
husband, a doctor. Abu wanted to come south to see her children and needed
money. Mrs. Taft wrote, "Abbo's health has been failing for some time, and she
is quite unfit to remain at service. . . . Maum Abbo *needs* the money now as much
as she ever can, for unless she has something to support her during the coming
winter, she will have to be dependent upon her children, and she feels they are

not able to afford it." Nightingale directed Mackay to send $50 to Abu, explaining that this sum was an advance of the interest payable to her on 1 July 1857.[48]

SANCHO PANZA

According to Nightingale family tradition, all of Louisa Shaw's slaves remained loyal to her, with one exception: the British "offered the slaves their freedom, but such was their devotion and attachment to the place and to their masters that but one availed himself of the opportunity to escape." After the War of 1812, Shaw claimed restitution for the loss of one slave, a fifty-five-year-old man named Sancho Panza. Panza appeared as a "refugee man" (the Royal Navy's category for slaves taken aboard in response to the proclamation) on the register of the HMS *Albion*, Cockburn's flagship, on 18 March 1815, the day before the admiral left Georgia. Despite Cockburn's strict interpretation of what property he would return to Cumberland, Panza evidently was taken aboard just before the admiral's departure, long after the 17 February deadline.[49]

Panza's Spanish name may indicate that he had come from Spanish East Florida; furthermore, the presence of a surname (unusual for a slave) might mean that he had been a free man. It is possible that when Panza reached the *Albion*, he was able to convey to the British that he was not a slave but a subject of Spain, thereby leading Cockburn to offer special treatment to Panza.

Under Spanish administration, Florida had a large class of free blacks, many of whom were runaway slaves from the American colonies who had managed to acquire papers of some sort. The province was home also to many dark-skinned free persons. Because of the unsettled conditions in the St. Marys Basin area, American Patriots were able to raid outlying Florida farms with impunity, kidnapping blacks and mulattoes and selling them in Georgia as slaves, although this form of slave importation was a felony under U.S. law. Slave stealing became a political issue on both sides of the border. In 1814 advertisements for the return of stolen slaves from St. Augustine and Amelia Island were common, with blame going to a group called Georgia Patriots. Between 1803 and 1821, no free person of color in the St. Marys Basin area—including Cuban soldiers serving as part of the Spanish military presence on Amelia Island and the lower St. Johns River—was safe from the Patriots' depredations.[50]

BINA

In 1810 Robert Mackay of Savannah, a friend of the Greene family, was actively engaged in smuggling slaves from Florida to Georgia. Mackay wrote to his wife that Catharine Greene Miller and her daughter, Louisa, had cooperated in receiving and taking care of his smuggled slaves, who were the property of his late father-in-law, John McQueen. Despite the fact that McQueen's slaves had become legally his daughter's property, Mackay was breaking American law by importing them into the United States. Many of Mackay's trips to Dungeness, where he unloaded his slave cargoes, took place under cover of darkness. Dungeness Plantation apparently served as a way station for the slaves until Mackay could find adequate transportation to mainland Georgia.[51]

Bina, an African-born woman, specifically mentioned the Nightingale family in a story repeated by one of her descendants: "[Bina] get heah on a big boat and she lan down theah on Cumberland Ilun on a big dock in the time of Mr. Nightingale an she say they put em in a lill pick house to keep em safe an the chimbley of that same lill house is standin about two hundud yahds out in the rivuh off Cumberland today."[52] There is some evidence for an unrecorded small settlement on South Point, just across Beach Creek from Dungeness. Louisa Shaw may have operated a private lazaretto at the site, holding Bina and other slaves in quarantine until Mackay found a suitable vessel in which to smuggle them to Savannah.

JOHN PARKER AND SOPHY

Selling slaves represented the ultimate betrayal of any human relationship that might have grown up between owners and slaves. A public slave auction was disgraceful and was often viewed as such, even by slave owners. Family units were disrupted—children torn from their parents' arms, wives separated from husbands, and young women removed from protective family units. Some slave owners in poor financial shape reached the shameful and pitiful realization that their estate debts could be paid only by auctioning faithful servants. Freeing slaves by last will and testament was not permitted under Georgia law.

John Parker was a tenant farmer from Charleston living at Cotton Bluff Plantation (present-day Squawtown). Like John Gray and Pierre Bernardey, Parker was an itinerant planter. His father, Isaac, had evidently lent him money to buy slaves. When Isaac died in 1818, his will stated that the unpaid bond should be returned to his son. Cotton Bluff's owner, Henry McIntosh, son of John Houstoun McIntosh, did not reside at Cotton Bluff, and John Parker effectively was becoming the plantation's superintendent. Parker's will said that if he died before the end of 1819, his executors were to find a person "whose humanity can be relied upon to superintend the completing of his crops, so that a sale of the same can be accomplished, so his debts in *Georgia* can be met." Parker's six slaves were to be sold only at private sale and only to residents of Camden County. He required that slave woman Sophy's family not be broken up. Parker died about 1827, and it is not known whether his wishes were carried out. Since he appeared on Camden County's insolvent list, however, it is likely that his property had to be sold at public auction to meet his debts.[53]

JOHNNY

Johnny appeared in a runaway slave advertisement in the *Savannah Daily Georgian* on 4 January 1828. Acting as agent for his aunt, Phineas Nightingale offered a reward of $50 for the capture and jailing of the slave, $100 for his return to Cumberland. Failure to punish such a breach of plantation discipline would set a bad example. Johnny was described as five feet, nine inches tall, thickset, with one broken tooth and a bright black complexion. When last seen, he was wearing clothes made of satinet. He had "a downcast look" and could "seldom look a person in the face when speaking." Because his wife lived at Captain Stockton's plantation on Turtle River, Johnny might be "lurking" in the neighborhood of Darien.[54] In this case Nightingale was obeying the law as well as doing what sensible slave owners had to do to prevent the system from self-destructing.

LEWIS JACKSON

Charles Jackson, a Greene family friend and New England lawyer who died on 25 October 1801 at Dungeness, purchased Member Norris for the purpose of freeing her during a short time (roughly 1800–1817) when Georgia law permitted personal manumission of slaves. In 1823, at age fifty, she was living in St. Marys with a very young boy.[55] That boy was probably Lewis Jackson.

According to an obituary in the *Darien Timber Gazette*, Lewis Jackson died in McIntosh County on 14 August 1886. Born 24 November 1820 to slave parents on Cumberland Island, Jackson entered the world as "property of Nightingale," who was said to have "instilled thoughtful and religious habits" in Jackson. At nine years old, Jackson was apprenticed as carpenter to True and Webb of Savannah, where he learned to read and write. "This knowledge [Jackson] turned to good account when in 1868 he was elected" a judge in McIntosh County's inferior court, serving two four-year terms.[56] In this position, Jackson showed courage and steadfastness in quelling the mob at the time of Tunis G. Campbell. It is likely that Phineas Nightingale was responsible for obtaining the apprenticeship for Jackson, and Nightingale probably wrote this obituary.

Nightingale almost surely was responsible for sending young Lewis to Savannah to be apprenticed. Nightingale protected the boy as best he could despite Georgia's laws, which by 1822 required either registration or expulsion of "free persons of color."

PENNY CLUBB

Interracial liaisons were common throughout the South, generally involving white men and black women. Since it was illegal for such couples to marry, it was rare for such relationships to last over the long term. As a result of the lack of legal or civil sanction, records about interracial families are scarce.

Among William Clubb's children was William Jr., who in 1815 intended to permanently depart Cumberland Island: a list of "distressed inhabitants" who boarded the British frigate *Surprize* on 10 February includes him; his wife, Alice; and his three unmarried sisters, Rachel, Rebecca, and Martha. All were described as white. Accompanying them were Nanny, a black woman, and two children, Penny and Clarice Clubb. The group returned to Cumberland on 12 March for reasons that remain unknown.[57] Although the naval register described Penny and Clarice as "white children," there is some evidence that they were mulatto and that Nan and her children were part of the Clubb family.

When William Jr. took Nan and her two mulatto daughters, he was taking his parents' property. But he may also have been taking his two children. Because the British described Nan's children as white, it is reasonable to assume that their father was white. Since the young Clubbs were emigrating together, they must have felt they could do better living elsewhere. Penny (b. 21 April 1807) was the first named slave entered in the Clubb family Bible, which also contains considerable information about her descendants. One likely explanation for these inscriptions is that she was the child of William Clubb Jr., although there is no further evidence to support this theory.[58]

Penny later passed into the possession of Thomas P. Bunkley, a neighbor who married one of the Clubb daughters. Penny eventually married another Bunkley slave and had two children, Jack (b. 1824) and Sally (b. 1827). Sally's children are all carefully recorded in the Clubb Bible.

CLARISSA, JACK, AND CLARISSA

Because slaves were personal property, they were frequently put up as security for loans and mortgages. In 1837 Charles H. Frohock, Sarah Clubb's husband, put up a "Negro girl," Clarissa, as security for two promissory notes he owed Robert Stafford. In 1838 Robert and Rachel (Clubb) Church put up two slaves—Jack, who was about fifty years old, and another Clarissa, about seventeen years old—as security for a loan from Stafford. In both examples, the slaves belonged to the women, not to their husbands. As heads of household, however, the husbands could use their wives' property as security. Because such transfers were common on Cumberland, slaves frequently moved among the island's plantations, and it is impossible to trace these movements. The sale price of the slave property had to be precisely calculated. A breeding woman fetched a high price; similarly, a young female slave with one or two babies could enable a man to get a good-sized loan. Prices generally followed the most recently publicized slave auctions.[59]

SARAH DOWNES MILLER AND NELLY

Once Sarah Downes Miller put up her slave, Nelly, as security for a small loan from Stafford, which she was unable to repay. After losing her slave, Miller apparently was overcome by remorse, and Stafford returned Nelly to her former mistress as a gift on the condition that Nelly was to "remain and be with the said Sarah Miller."[60]

PHINEAS MILLER

Miller seems generally not to have owned slaves. Although references to his slave property appeared from time to time, the slaves in question probably actually belonged to Catharine Greene Miller. Camden County records show Miller to have owned only two slaves, identified as a "Negro boy" and a "Negro girl" on the inventory of Miller's estate at the time of his death. Both children were listed as valueless and "without feet." Miller probably acquired them to protect them.[61]

PRIMUS MITCHELL

Among the diverse reactions to slavery was the development of religious impulse. Songs provided an antidote to the numbing monotony of the daily agricultural schedule, and Sea Island religious music included chants and shouts that enlivened the slaves' days and nights, even though nighttime congregations were illegal. Preaching, traditionally an outlet for religious enthusiasm, attracted those who wanted to carry a spiritual message to their fellow slaves. For male and female slaves unable to become preachers, testifying and song leading assumed religious functions.

The 1834 slave inventory for Rayfield Plantation contains a listing for a slave named Judy, with "Prime"—probably her son—listed on the following line. Prime, age nine, was one of fifty-three slaves Nat Greene was selling to Robert Stafford.[62]

Primus Mitchell almost certainly abandoned Stafford's plantation when Union forces occupied Fernandina in 1862. By 1864 disease and squalor prevailed in that overcrowded seaport, and Mitchell may have been among those who heeded the advice of Fernandina Bureau of Refugees, Freedmen, and Abandoned Lands agent Ansel E. Kinne to move back to the island. In late 1866 Phineas Nightingale ordered all freedmen illegally residing at Dungeness to leave, but in 1868 a freedman at Brunswick brought a claim against "Primas Mitchell," then residing at "Dungeon S" on Cumberland.[63]

Although Mitchell paid a Camden County tax assessment in 1878, he does not appear on the 1870 census for Cumberland. He may not have wanted to work for his former owner, a common reaction among freedmen, and could not be persuaded to live at Stafford's plantation until after Stafford's death in 1877. Stafford's heirs may have sought out Mitchell to look after the untenanted farm, which they were unable to sell until 1882.

Mitchell first appeared on the U.S. Census for Cumberland Island in 1880, when he was a fifty-five-year-old farm laborer with a wife, Amanda, and seven children. (The family subsequently added another child.)[64]

In 1882 Primus met the Carnegies, the Pittsburgh family that had purchased the Stafford tracts. He told them that he had been a slave of Robert Stafford, whom he described as a good master who had only once, on impulse, struck a slave: "Never knew 'm to hit but one man; e gave him a lick alongside e head, and e never hear good afterwards." Mitchell identified the double-chimneyed cabin at Stafford's slave quarters as the slave hospital. He moved to High Point after black farmers purchased land there in 1892. In 1894 he was one of four trustees, two of whom were his sons-in-law, who purchased land for the construction and use of the "(Old) Baptist Church of Cumberland." At the end of the nineteenth century, Primus Mitchell lived in a rickety house located close to the canal at the northern end of Old Swamp Field, north of the bridge on the old Main Road. His house probably also served as a substitute black church.

Mitchell died about 1915 and is buried at High Point Cemetery on Cumberland. The Carnegies subsequently remembered him as remarkable and charismatic.[65]

Primus Mitchell's physical presence encouraged freedmen from the mainland to emigrate to Cumberland, where they both followed his advice about dealing with specific island whites and married into his family. The exact nature of Mitchell's role as a preacher is not known, although his accommodation to slavery may have been as an exhorter, a position within the Methodist and Baptist denominations created shortly after the Civil War. According to historian Eugene Genovese, slaves and free blacks heard not only black denominational ministers but also exhorters—class leaders, assistants, or prayer leaders who did most of the effective preaching, sometimes without any training. Every plantation had its exhorter. According to Genovese, "The great pity is that so little is known about [the exhorter's] relationship to the black preachers who passed through and so little about the relationship between both and the plantation conjurers. It would not be surprising if some black preachers were all three at once. On the Georgia coast as late as the 1930s black Baptist and Methodist preachers openly shared their congregations' retention of African beliefs in ghosts and witches." Furthermore, Amanda Mitchell was known on Cumberland as a witch, and island blacks were terrified by her.[66]

EIGHT

The Civil War
and Its Aftermath

Cumberland and the War

*A*t the outbreak of the Civil War, Georgia's Sea Islands found themselves in a relatively defenseless position. On 19 April 1861, five days after the evacuation of Fort Sumter, President Lincoln proclaimed a blockade of the seceding states. On 29 January 1861, before the war broke out, Phineas Nightingale had written to Georgia Governor Joseph Brown to ask what plans were being considered for the defense of the coast: "We have on this Island five white men, and about four hundred slaves. I reside on the south end of the Island, and probably there is no man on the coast more exposed to marauders than myself." Adjutant General Henry C. Wayne answered on 7 February that although he did not believe the Confederate efforts to be perfectly adequate for coastal defense, he could say that two regiments of regular troops were being organized.[1]

In 1860 Nightingale had sixty-three slaves on his two coastal properties, ten or twelve of them at Dungeness and the rest at a rice plantation on Cambers Island in McIntosh County. The remainder of the Cumberland slaves to which he referred were the property of other planters, mostly Robert Stafford.[2]

Most white Camden County residents feared slave insurrection. In 1861 St. Marys population numbered about 550, approximately half white and half black. Outside the little seaport, however, whites were greatly outnumbered by the county's 4,000 slaves. The major exports were cotton, naval stores, cattle and cattle-related products, and timber, much of which was finished in several great steam sawmills found upriver in Camden County and in Nassau County, Florida. Much of Camden County's exports went to Cuba and the Bahamas.[3]

With an eye to safeguarding themselves, leading property owners wrote to Confederate President Jefferson Davis on 25 April 1861. If the enemy should land and "arouse the slaves to hostilities," St. Marys could not defend itself. Remembering very clearly the events of 1815, Cumberland Islanders reminded Davis "that in the war of 1812 the British made this place a place of attack and a basis of operations, on account of the facility of landing troops and munitions of war."[4]

The situation soon worsened. Fearing a Union attack, Savannah strengthened its fortifications in November 1861 by pulling Confederate troops from the Camden County area. Fear of imminent Union attack caused the planter population to evacuate St. Simons Island in December. In February 1862 the Confederate War Department ordered its forces to abandon East Florida to reinforce troops in Tennessee. By March all troops were withdrawn from the Florida coast, including those stationed at Fernandina, which was the Atlantic terminus for Florida's railway system. East Florida felt completely abandoned. By the end of May three thousand of the four thousand troops defending East and Central Florida had left the state. As a result, the islands, even less protected than the mainland, lay almost completely exposed to naval invasion.[5]

Cumberland Island, unable to do anything but wait, saw the inevitable realized in March. The federal expedition for the occupation of East Florida sailed from Port Royal, South Carolina, to Fernandina, a distance of less than 150 miles. The Union fleet consisted of about twenty-four steamships and eight sailing vessels. Eighteen of the steamers were gunboats. The fleet commander was Commodore Samuel Francis DuPont. One brigade of infantry, the Ninety-seventh Pennsylvania and the Fourth New Hampshire Infantry, was aboard, commanded by General Horatio Wright. The squadron entered St. Andrew Sound to come down the Cumberland River behind the guns of Fort Clinch. The occupation of Fernandina on 2 March, wrote a *New York Times* journalist, took place on a clear, starlit night. As the warships entered St. Andrew Sound, the reporter rhapsodized, "The fleet glided majestically around the point of [Cumberland Island] while from the light-house, which stood near the point, floated the Stars and Stripes, placed there by some of the active little gunboats which had preceded us." The Union flotilla, wending its way slowly down the difficult Cumberland River, paused for the first night "abreast of a large, splendid mansion with quarters and factories lying around it. The owner, a Mr. Stafford, had said he would not leave it."[6] The fleet anchored in St. Andrew Sound, thus commencing the official occupation of Cumberland Island.

The next day DuPont learned from Louis Napoleon, a slave picked up at sea, as well as from a few residents on Cumberland's North End, that Fernandina's defenses were being abandoned. Napoleon had received permission from his owners to go to Fernandina and had slipped out over the bar in hopes of meeting one of the Union vessels and informing its crew that the guns at Fernandina were being dismantled. Napoleon also told the U.S. troops that the fort at the southern end of Cumberland Island had been evacuated.[7]

Napoleon's information was confirmed by the lighthouse keeper on Little Cumberland Island, James A. Clubb, reported to be a "Union man." Clubb carefully took down the lighthouse lens and came to DuPont's flagship on 2 March. Although descended from a long line of southerners, Clubb was a Coast Guard appointee with an obligation to the seamen who relied on his services, and he saw the safety of the lens as his duty. The commodore reported, "The lighthouse keeper . . . has impressed me very favorably by his spirit and loyalty."[8]

When DuPont learned that Fernandina's guns and munitions were being carried away, he ordered his forces to push forward through the sound. Navigation down the sound was described as "quite intricate," and nearly all the vessels taking the Inland Passage grounded on a falling tide three miles from Fort Clinch. Only three ships sailed south of the "flats at the dividing line between tides that meet in the sound from the north and south." Nevertheless, most of the squadron eventually reached Fernandina through the Inland Passage.[9]

On 3 March an advance squadron entered Fernandina Harbor. As the first gunboats approached, the last train left, crowded with fugitives and piled high with household goods. The Florida press reported that fourteen gunboats and seven frigates attacked Fernandina. All the Confederate guns were dismounted, and "we had to beat a hasty retreat. We lost all our guns and every scrap of provisions."[10]

St. Marys was occupied at midnight on 2 March. While the panic in Fernandina was great, St. Marys remained fairly calm. By 11 March Union naval officers were reporting, "St. Marys perfectly quiet, not a white left." The occupation of St. Simons Island took place on 9 March, and Brunswick and Jekyll Island were occupied the next day.[11]

On 13 March Commodore DuPont officially reported the occupation of St. Augustine. He had arranged with Brigadier General Wright for a joint U.S. Army-Navy occupation of the Florida and Georgia coasts, "including protection from injury to the mansion and grounds of Dungeness, on Cumberland Island, originally the property of the revolutionary hero and patriot, Gen. Greene, and still owned by his descendants."[12]

At the start of the Union coastal occupation, most slaves remained at their settlements. One slave told Union officers that he believed that the Yankees had come to buy or steal cotton from the Confederates as well as to kidnap slaves and send them for sale in Cuba. Consequently, he had seen no reason to go over to the Union side. Generally speaking, Sea Island slaves remained silent, suspicious, or only moderately helpful to the invaders. The insurrection Nightingale feared failed to materialize. After the fall of Fernandina, however, the slaves began slowly to move. By the late spring of 1862 Union officers had escorted most of Stafford's slaves from Cumberland to Fernandina, using the excuse that it was for their own safety.[15]

Slave movement on the mainland as well as on the islands created problems for the occupying forces. Legally, the slaves were still property, and, as such, Union armies had no right to move them. Union officers could neither give slaves orders nor enlist them. As a result, General David Hunter decreed slave emancipation in Georgia, Florida, and South Carolina on 9 May 1862, an order clearly reflecting the Union forces' initial success in subduing the southeastern coast. President Lincoln and Congress considered Hunter's order premature, however, and Union officers continued to consider slaves fugitive property. When such slaves entered Union lines, they were referred to as contraband.[14]

Pilotage was a major concern and frequently served to bond whites and blacks. DuPont had great respect for contraband pilots, and white pilots were generally mentioned as being accompanied by contrabands. In May 1862 DuPont wrote that there were few domestics among the incoming contraband, "the intelligent and likely ones being boatmen, pilots and watermen." Elsewhere he wrote of a superior class among the slaves "of pilots and watermen who have had their own time, paying their masters for it a certain sum."[15]

Contraband watermen could accompany naval detachments setting out buoys to mark the confusing and intricate coastal waterways as well as provide boats, either their own or planters'. The Union occupying forces were ordered to retrieve sylvan products such as turpentine, live oak frames, and sawmill lumber and to seize cotton, salt, and beef. But many Union vessels could not navigate the narrow St. Marys River. The products the U.S. forces wished to take generally had to be towed, and naval schooners and barks could not do this. In other cases Union naval officers saw small Confederate ships under construction in coastal shipyards, but taking these vessels required towing. Contraband watermen assisted Union forces with these tasks in spite of the constant danger caused by snipers.[16]

Contraband pilots also played a major role in providing information about the location of Confederate settlements. When fuel for the Union steamers ran low, armed boats were sent to the inlets to obtain firewood. Commander S. W. Godun noted in June 1862 that he had hired men from the large settlement of contrabands at St. Simons Island to cut wood for the steamer *Darlington*. Contraband and white watermen even joined together in refugee settlements, one of the largest of which was Pilots Town on the St. Johns River. Residents at this locale gave information on the whereabouts of docks and small vessels, which the invaders destroyed systematically in an effort to hinder Confederate raiding and foraging activities. With the exception of the boatmen, however, Union officers tended to view slaves with pity, derision, or mistrust, a feeling that many blacks reciprocated.[17]

Other concerns weighed more heavily on Union officials than did fugitive slaves. Planters feared that Union vessels would be unable to protect cotton from destruction by Confederate sympathizers. One Union commander requested the immediate return of the *Darlington* from Port Royal, saying that with it "the communications inland from Brunswick to Jacksonville may be kept open, at present this entire distance which is more than fifty miles is entirely under the control of the enemy, who from the continued absence of our flag must gradually recover confidence. Mr. Stafford fears they will come from the Main and burn his buildings, which I am helpless to prevent."[18]

During the Civil War Cumberland was almost completely abandoned by its white landholders, with the exception of Stafford at Planters House and Rachel Church at High Point. Stafford's determination to remain on his land remained unshaken throughout the war, although one particular episode frightened him so much that he departed for a short time. In September 1862 Stafford was threatened by the unexpected appearance from Amelia Island of some of his own slaves with a number of strange blacks. Quartering themselves on his plantation, they refused to submit to any control and killed his cattle. When, armed with guns and clubs, they overran his private residence, Stafford feared for his life and sent a message to Union naval officers stationed at Fernandina. Reminding them that he had much valuable property, Stafford told them he was afraid to remain any longer without a guard. An armed detachment sent from the USS *Alabama* arrested the worst of the mutineers. Stafford was sick and in a state of great anxiety, and one of his own boats brought him to Fernandina, where he remained for a few days.[19]

One reason for Stafford's eagerness to remain on Cumberland was that he wanted to safeguard the valuable commodities in his possession, food and Sea Island cotton. From the beginning of hostilities, getting cotton to British markets was a primary consideration for both the Confederate and Union governments. The winter of 1860–61 saw almost uninterrupted commerce between Savannah and the St. Johns River, with the continuous appearance of steamers crossing St. Marys Bar. In December 1861, before the arrival of Union forces in Fernandina, a large detachment from the Wayne County Rangers was ordered to proceed by steamer to Cumberland for the purpose of removing Stafford's crop because it was believed that he intended to "place it in the hands of the enemy." Confederate authorities doubted Stafford's loyalty and took steps to confiscate whatever he had to sell—peas, corn, potatoes, and cotton.[20]

After the fall of Fernandina in March 1862, the situation changed. Georgia Sea Island planters now had the option of selling their cotton to the Union. Federal shipping proceeded unchecked among New York; Port Royal, South Carolina; and Fernandina. Buyers representing New England textile factories began to appear in Fernandina as early as 9 May. Some of the greatest cotton mills in America were in Rhode Island, and the state's governor, William Sprague, was married to a daughter of Secretary of the Treasury Salmon P. Chase. Many people believed that the governor exploited his father-in-law's position to further his cotton mills' interests. In 1862 Sprague wrote to Chase in defense of the purchase of Confederate cotton, "Our policy is to get out as much cotton as we can, paying as little as possible for it. The cotton is of more value to us than money to the enemy." Sprague's activities became a profound political embarrassment to his father-in-law, and the ensuing scandal played a major role in transferring the power to confiscate Confederate property from the Treasury to the War Department.[21]

As competition grew between the British and New England textile industries, cotton purchasing became intertwined with U.S.-British diplomatic relations. In spite of more than forty years of opposition to the extension of slavery and the slave trade, British commercial interests soon became overtly hostile to President Lincoln and Union policies. Cotton became an extremely valuable commodity, and Sea Island cotton was among the products traded illegally during the Civil War.

Union officers considered Stafford a Confederate. He lived within Confederate lines, and he had owned many slaves. Nevertheless, he may have sold cotton to the Union with the connivance of army officers from Fernandina. The U.S. Treasury sent agents, some of them handpicked by Secretary Chase, to collect cotton. On 3 December 1861 General Thomas W. Sherman appointed special army officers to collect and store cotton found on deserted plantations.

Planting cotton soon became a responsibility of the Union Quartermaster Corps and, to a lesser extent, of the Provost Marshal Department. These departments were soon also charged with maintaining discipline among various civilian groups, including blacks residing on abandoned plantations.[22]

The legal method of exporting cotton from Confederate territory was through confiscation. Stafford's cotton could legitimately be confiscated even if he remained on his plantation. When cotton was confiscated, it was usually seized in the name of the United States. If the cotton was privately owned, the owner received a receipt; after the war, receipt holders would be compensated after proving their loyalty. The United States passed several confiscation acts. Property taken under the authority of the Second Confiscation Act (passed on 17 July 1862) was expected to come into the Treasury, whose agents were ordered to buy cotton. Chase appointed a special body of agents to collect and sell such property.[23]

The Treasury agent system led to many abuses. In Confederate territory, cotton was worth about ten cents in specie; on its way to the North or to Europe, however, cotton was worth seventy cents or more. Collection of cotton by Treasury agents was transferred to the War Department on 28 June 1862. As early as midsummer 1862 the sale to the Union of cotton from Fernandina became physically possible and enormously profitable. Sea Island cotton was well known to have been among the commodities Treasury agents bought during the Civil War.[24]

In 1860 Stafford, who reported a total of forty thousand pounds of ginned cotton on hand, owned one hundred slaves to work his principal cotton fields. In the 1863 Camden County poll tax records, however, Stafford had only seventeen slaves on Cumberland, and he was owed a total of $31,815. By 1866, the date of his next tax report, these outstanding debts had been paid up, but Stafford reported only two remaining former slaves.[25]

Nearly all the $31,815 owed to him in 1863 and paid before 1866 may have represented payment for a sale of cotton to officers illegally acting under War Department jurisdiction between late June 1862 and April 1863. Although no records have been found regarding Stafford's cotton sales during the war, Stafford may have sold his stored 1861 cotton crop to one of the Rhode Island cotton buyers flocking to Fernandina. With military assistance, Cumberland cotton could have been lightered from Stafford's dock to vessels anchored at Fernandina.

Stafford may have sold his 1862 crop in April 1863 with the connivance of a

Union army officer, Lieutenant Colonel George F. Gardiner of the Seventh Connecticut Regiment. Under the command of Colonel Joseph R. Hawley, the Seventh Connecticut embarked on 13 January 1863 from Hilton Head for Fernandina, where the unit was stationed for about two months. Hawley evidently was acquainted with Stafford in Connecticut, writing to friends in New London that detachments from his regiment were stationed briefly at Stafford's plantation.[26]

On 1 April the colonel was ordered to return to Hilton Head, taking five companies with him and leaving Lieutenant Colonel Gardiner in command of the regiment's remaining units. After Hawley's departure, Stafford or a Treasury agent acting at Stafford's request may have bribed Gardiner to help in exporting cotton. Union officers stationed at Fernandina referred contemptuously to the Seventh Connecticut as collaborators, and in May 1863 Gardiner was forced to resign his commission because of his "complicity with the Connecticut Copperheads."[27]

Stafford may also have bought his Cumberland neighbors' cotton for sale to Treasury agents and may have rounded up some of his absent neighbors' livestock to sell to the Union. In 1860 Stafford had declared that he owned 30 horses, 75 milk cows, 225 other cattle, and 250 hogs. It appears, however, that in 1863 he sold 800 cattle at $50 a head and 150 horses at $75 a head. His livestock supply had increased greatly. After the war, Stafford, declaring himself to have been a consistent Union supporter, produced records showing his sales to Union quartermasters of cattle, horses, hogs, beef, bacon, yellow pine, boats and flats, corn, and potatoes.[28]

Later in 1863 Stafford lost much, if not all, of his stored cotton to arson. Mainlanders saw dense, oily, black clouds of smoke over Cumberland and whispered to one another that cotton was burning on the island.[29] Only Stafford would have had enough cotton to store in his cotton houses, and only Confederate sympathizers would have set it afire. If Stafford succeeded in selling his 1862 crop to the Yankees, his Confederate neighbors would have seen to it that his 1863 crop was torched.

In the spring of 1865 the Confederate world crumbled, then fell. In April General Robert E. Lee surrendered to General Ulysses S. Grant at Appomattox Courthouse in Virginia. A day later Lee's troops stacked arms, weeping until Union regiments, drawn up to attend the surrender, honored the Confederates by presenting arms. President Lincoln was assassinated. On 23 May a somber Grand Review of the Army of the Potomac and William Tecumseh Sherman's

Army of Georgia marched two hundred thousand strong down Pennsylvania Avenue. And on 22 May Stafford went to Fernandina, where he swore allegiance to the United States of America. A Union list of "Refugees who came into our lines since May 15th 1865," described him as a refugee from Georgia, light complexioned with mixed gray hair and gray eyes, and six feet, two inches tall.[30]

The Sea-Island Circular

Islanders identify with their sea-bound homes, regardless of what nation or administration is in charge. Islanders resent change. Complex human feelings entered the Cumberland picture when landless freedmen claimed some of the land they had cultivated as slaves. Some former slaves shared the intense attachments that Stafford and other white residents felt to this island as their home. Cumberland was the only home that some blacks knew. Northern officers noted the slaves' strong feelings toward their Sea Island homes. Commodore DuPont wrote to his wife on 5 June 1863, "One thing I feel convinced of, that the Southern planters would make more by hiring and paying the Negroes than they do now, and the latter would be contented, for their local attachments are wonderful—if free, you would never see one of them go North."[31]

In January 1865 William Tecumseh Sherman's "Sea-Island Circular," also known as Special Orders 15, struck dumb all white landowners on the South Carolina, Georgia, and Florida coasts. The order declared that the islands from Charleston south, the abandoned rice fields along the rivers for thirty miles from the sea, and the Florida country bordering the St. Johns River were to be set apart for the settlement of the Negroes who were now freed by acts of war and by the proclamation of the U.S. president. The reserved area was soon called the Sherman Reservation. By July 1865 another set of orders known as Circular 13, issued by the Bureau of Refugees, Freedmen, and Abandoned Lands (known as the Freedmen's Bureau), ordered distribution of land within the Sherman Reservation. Sherman's original order forbade whites from entering the territory without proper authorization. Some hopeful black homesteaders interpreted this clause literally, and on some Sea Islands determined freedmen ran off whites.[32]

Between 1865 and 1866 Union agents obviously informed Stafford that his island property had been confiscated. The Sea-Island Circular assumed that all white landowners living within the defined coastal zone had abandoned their plantations. Despite Stafford's protestations that he had never abandoned his property, his plantation was on a Sea Island defined as part of the reservation and was therefore eligible for resettlement.

Stafford was among the first landowners within the Sherman Reservation to declare that he had never abandoned his land. Although his claim cannot have been unique, it was certainly unusual. At the outbreak of the war, some landowners, such as the Arnold brothers of Providence, Rhode Island, and New Bedford, Massachusetts, had abandoned their southern seacoast plantations to return to New England, where they could sit out the war. Some plantation owners left behind managers such as A. G. Bass on Sapelo Island, hoping thereby to placate Union invaders and to handle any problems with insubordinate slaves. A few Georgian landowners with European connections, such as the Molyneux family of Savannah, went to England or France. Most male Sea Island landowners either joined the Confederate forces or moved to the mainland, where they organized blockade-running, set up saltworks, or drove cattle for Confederate quartermasters. However, many Sea Island plantation owners left their plantations simply out of fear.[33]

In March 1862 Phineas M. Nightingale allegedly burned thirty thousand bushels of his rice crop and moved inland to live in a log cabin at Tebeauville (now Waycross), Georgia: "his winter plantation on the Altamaha is accessible to the Yankees & has been vacated; while his splendid summer place on Cumberland Island—which he has spent a lifetime in beautifying—is now in the possession of the enemy. And yet this patriotic planter is perfectly cheerful." Stafford's neighbor to his north, the widowed Margaret E. Downes, fled Cumberland Island in favor of the Woodstock Steam Saw Mill at Kings Ferry, Florida, a community far inland, where she and her children sought safety from Union invaders on the coast.[34]

Island living, never secure in the best of times because of vulnerability to storm, disease, and isolation, offered even worse conditions in wartime. Moreover, the structure of the plantation system was threatened by the absence of white males. Unlike many of his island neighbors, Stafford evidently believed that he could fend for himself on his island and that unless threatened by arson or physical attack, he could live off the natural resources with the aid of a few slaves who preferred, like him, to remain on the island. Similarly, Rachel Clubb Church remained constantly at her Cumberland home throughout the war until old age forced her to retire to Brunswick. Her slaves never left her.[35]

Like Stafford and Church, a few small enclaves of freedmen preferred to remain isolated on Cumberland during the war, trusting neither their former masters nor the Union officers in Fernandina. Ned Simmons was apparently still living by himself at Rayfield in 1863, consenting to go over to Fernandina only at a very advanced age. While on the island, he may have feared attacks from the mainland. In October 1862 Captain John Readdick, an officer in the Camden Chasseurs, led a "descent upon Cumberland Island and captured some dozen negroes this is one of many bold descents on the Islands by our brave coast guard." Old Jack, "from Africa," is thought to have remained on Cumberland throughout the war, ostensibly to protect the property of his owner, Margaret Downes. Such elderly slaves found abundant food resources on Cumberland, and its isolation shielded and protected them.[36]

Land Redistribution

Since many coastal landowners had fled inland for safety, white abandonment of whole islands was not unusual. Whites' return spelled difficulties for the Freedmen's Bureau, which was supposed to administer land allotments for the new class of black yeoman farmers.

In May 1865 President Andrew Johnson issued an amnesty proclamation, pardoning most southerners and restoring their property rights. Southern planters rejoiced, but freedmen mourned. The European and American press widely criticized Johnson's proclamation, declaring that it revoked the 1863 Emancipation Proclamation. The newly established Freedmen's Bureau, under the direction of General Oliver Otis Howard, similarly interpreted the amnesty proclamation, realizing that landless Negro agriculturists would be forced into the position of either leaving the land or becoming wage slaves of the southern plantation owners.[37]

By 4 June 1865 General Rufus Saxton reported to General Howard the settlement of about forty thousand freedmen on the Sherman Reservation. On 28 July 1865 Howard issued his Circular 13, which ordered land distribution in 40-acre lots within the Sherman Reservation. There was nothing ambiguous about Circular 13's language or purpose. In 1860 Stafford owned 8,125 acres on Cumberland. Circular 13 would have meant the loss of some of his most valuable land. If two hundred freedmen each received the right to purchase 40 acres, Stafford would retain only 125 acres for his own use.[38]

During the autumn and winter of 1865 divisions sharpened in Congress and in the War Department, which administered the Freedmen's Bureau. The bureau despaired over the intense feelings generated by the issue of whether to restore land to former Confederate sympathizers. The Sea Islands appeared to be the only area where the bureau had some chance of acquiring title to abandoned land, and division into lots for qualifying freedmen began as early as mid-January 1865.[39]

In August 1865 a bureau agent, William F. Eaton, was ordered to report on abandoned lands within the Sherman Reservation. Working from St. Simons, Eaton hired a boat and went to Cumberland to inventory its plantations: "On Cumberland Id. I believe there are thirteen plantations, all of which have been abandoned except Robert Stafford's and Mrs. Church's. . . . Very few persons live upon this island, probably not a hundred black and white. On Little Cumberland are three plantations. The owners I do not know but will ascertain."[40]

Eaton's next report, probably written in late August 1865, listed all the "abandoned lands" on Cumberland. First on his list was Dungeness, which he said had been abandoned since the commencement of the war. He reported that Stafford had never abandoned his land, residing there since the commencement of the war "with the exception of a few days." Eaton reported that the land north of Stafford's boundary was divided into small lots owned by five farmers: William R. Bunkley, George W. Stockwell, James A. Clubb, Thomas Bunkley, and Margaret Downes, all of whom had abandoned their lands.[41]

The absence of Stafford, Church, and Edmund Spalding's names on Eaton's report is notable. Rachel Church, like Stafford a hardy islander, had never quit her home at the North End. Spalding had voluntarily assisted Union naval detachments, partly as a form of retaliation against his Confederate tormentors for holding hostage his wife and children. Spalding's small tract may have been omitted from Eaton's list because Spalding had abandoned his land involuntarily.[42]

Stafford's relationships with freedmen evidently were unsatisfactory, for he soon attracted bureau attention and disciplinary measures. The Freedmen's Bureau called on three Sea Island landowners to account for misdemeanors and threats committed against freedmen trying to farm on St. Simons, Sapelo, and Cumberland. In February 1866 Eaton was ordered to supervise the "return" to certain "former owners" of their island land. The return of such land was subject, however, to restrictions contained in General Davis Tillson's Special Field Orders 3. Copies were sent to General Howard, Eaton, Mallory P. King (a major planter on St. Simons Island), Bass (superintendent on Sapelo Island), and Stafford. In the spring of 1866, King, Bass, and Stafford were still "former owners" and were forbidden to threaten former slaves, use violence, or do anything to disturb the peace. Grants of land made in compliance with Sherman's Special Field Orders 15 were still valid, but Eaton received the right to set the lands apart and consolidate them contiguous to each other. He was ordered to place them "in such manner as to give the freedpeople a part possessing acreage, fertility and other advantages and at the same time place no unnecessary obstacles in the way of the owners occupying and cultivating the remaining portion of the plantation."[43]

On 27 February 1866, only two weeks later, General Tillson returned Dungeness to Nightingale. Nightingale was no longer a Cumberland Island agriculturalist, and his interest in Dungeness lay in keeping the ancestral Greene mansion and its magnificent gardens in his possession. Nightingale may have personally informed Tillson that he sought to cooperate fully with the bureau, thereby assuring the return of his mansion.[44]

A presidential veto, however, overturned the Sherman Reservation. President Johnson stated in March 1866 that among his many objections to the Sherman Reservation was that it violated the white owners' constitutional rights to their property. The veto came to the Senate, where the measure had originated. Thirty of the forty-eight senators voted to override, falling short of the two-thirds required to overturn Johnson's veto.[45]

In July 1866 Congress adopted another amendment to the Freedmen's Bureau Act. This time Congress surrendered completely to the idea that Sherman Reservation land should be returned to its previous owners, all of whom were, of course, white. The new amendment provided that Sherman Reservation "title holders" still physically on the lands could not be ousted until they had harvested their current crops as well as been compensated for any improvements they made. By 1867 the new policies were in effect, and Cumberland's freedmen discovered that they were not going to receive island land grants. Reconstruction policies that were more favorable toward white ownership restored Stafford's claims to all his land. The bureau's agents soon saw that freedmen did not intend to work for Stafford on his terms, however. Although deeply reluctant to order the eviction of former slaves, the bureau realized that the law was on Stafford's side. By 1868 all lands on Cumberland had been returned to their former owners.[46]

Sometime after 23 April 1866 Dungeness House caught fire and burned almost to the ground. Only the tall tabby walls and brick chimneys remained. In the 1940s Tecumsah Commodore shared her memories of the fire with Lucy R. Ferguson: "I vas livin at Dungeness wen e burn. Oh my! Yankee sojers station in de Big House. All kine of bad tings goin on. Drinkin, carousin, whorin. No place for a young gal. Day and night. Yes mam. I saw de Big House on fiah." In 1870 General Robert E. Lee visited Cumberland with one of his daughters to decorate his father's grave, writing, "The cemetery is unharmed and the graves in good condition, but the house at Dungeness has been burned and the island devastated."[47]

By 1868 Stafford was worried about the amount of money (possibly as much as $10,000 to $15,000) owed to him by Nightingale, and Stafford wrote that he wished to call in his loan. He suggested that Nightingale turn over the abandoned Dungeness House, since the ruins were too much for him to repair. Instead, sometime in 1869 Nightingale apparently repaid Stafford by transferring tract 2 (about 600 acres) to him.[48]

Nightingale was in debt to a number of other people as well. In January 1870 Nightingale signed a document acknowledging his indebtedness to the estate of Edmond Molyneux of England, which possessed six of Nightingale's seven bonds. Another major creditor was William H. M. Sanger, a New York rice broker, who suggested in the summer of 1870 that Nightingale declare bankruptcy. Nightingale protested that doing so would not be sufficient to repay his debts to Sanger: "Mrs. Molyneux and Mr. Spalding who hold the first lien in the [Dungeness] property will absorb every dollar that the whole place can bring under a forced sale at this time when everything is unsettled and depressed." Nightingale sent a statement of his financial condition to Sanger and asked if he would be willing to take half of a Cambers Island rice plantation to settle the debt:

> It is the best thing I can do for you. The property is really worth what I value it at (the whole place $150,000) and will I have no doubt when things are established and labor properly regulated, sell for that amount. My indebtedness now is greater than I can manage under the existing circumstances, and I am determined to relieve myself by a compromise with my creditors if I can, if not by going at once into Bkruptcy, and taking a fresh start at 67 years of age—Mrs. Molyneux who is my largest creditor has consented to take my Dungeness place and relieve me in full provided I can arrange with you and others.[49]

In an effort to satisfy his creditors, Nightingale sought to interest investors in building a hotel at Dungeness, enlisting the aid of a New York firm founded by his wife's uncle, James Gore King, a prominent Manhattan banker. In 1869 the firm published its "Plan for the Organization of the Dungeness Hotel Company," a prospectus to attract investors. The plan proposed purchasing Dungeness Plantation, rebuilding the mansion, erecting all requisite additions, and repairing the premises, with a view to the comfortable accommodation of families "who may desire to escape a northern winter, or during the summer, may wish to pass the warm months in the enjoyment of refreshing sea-breezes." There were 4,000 acres for sale, as well as the 10 acres that included the mansion, gardens, and groves. The prospectus glowingly described what investors would get for their money and thus offers a good picture of Dungeness in 1869: "Adjacent to the dwelling house is a garden of ten acres, containing a choice variety of flowers. There are five hundred bearing olive trees and a grove of more than two thousand sweet orange trees. . . . Golden dates, guava plants, limes, lemons, citrons, peaches, figs and other fruits abound. . . . The adjacent sea, sound and streams are replete with choicest fishes, oysters, clams and crabs. The island is alive with deer, quail and other game . . . snipe, turkeys, ducks."[50]

The prospectus said that a line of "very comfortable steamers" ran semiweekly between Dungeness and Savannah, and by mid-July 1869 the Brunswick Railway would be completed, providing daily service between Brunswick and Savannah. The organization would be incorporated under the laws of New York, and capital stock would consist of $500,000, to be divided into five thousand shares of $100 each. Article IV stipulated that $100,000 of the capital stock was to be expended in the purchase of the plantation, and article V said that the balance of the capital was to be spent in constructing a hotel, purchasing furniture, and generally improving the grounds. Any holder of at least fifty shares of capital stock had the right to have an acre of ground in the vicinity of the hotel on which to erect a cottage for personal use. Although unstated by the brochure, another advantage of the project was that Nightingale would retain access to his family's acreage. "If you could only get the Cumberland Island scheme through you would be all right," wrote Sanger.[51]

The hotel scheme did not succeed, and in 1870 Dungeness became Molyneux property. In early April 1873, worn out by illness and financial distress, Nightingale died at his home in Brunswick. The Sangers sued Nightingale and later his heirs to recover $51,250 that he had owed Sanger. In 1879 Katie Sanger brought a suit against Nightingale's executor—his son, William—who was seeking to make the Nightingale-Molyneux transaction invalid and to recover Dungeness. But the Molyneux family retained Dungeness.[52]

Freedmen's Settlements

For more than six months in 1865, freedmen who resided within the Sherman Reservation believed they had a legal right to tracts within that zone, and two freedmen's settlements arose on Cumberland, although later events deprived the settlers of these lands.

During Fernandina's 1862–65 military occupation, numerous opportunities existed for former slaves to find employment. Because of the effectiveness of the blockade, a market for lumber and turpentine continued to prosper, and freedmen worked in the numerous sawmills and turpentine camps of northeastern Florida and southeastern Georgia. Contrabands also found work in pilotage, stevedoring, and loading lumber for Union forces. Among the Yankee philanthropic institutions created during this period were several black orphanages, a hospital for freedmen, and a number of schools, all requiring cooks, laundresses, and yardmen. Fernandina attracted hundreds of hungry, ragged former slaves, who roamed the streets looking for employment.

Overcrowding in Fernandina increased disease and vice in the old seaport, and Union officers and the Freedmen's Bureau urged blacks there to go to Cumberland to engage in food production. In late 1864, at the advice of Fernandina Freedmen's Bureau agent Ansel E. Kinne, a large settlement of freedmen established themselves in Dungeness's abandoned slave quarters and outbuildings, where Kinne sent them supplies. By the autumn of 1865 sixty freedmen resided there, most of them strangers to Nightingale. Union officers, the War Department, and Treasury officers believed that this new black settlement could be kept in line by the small detachment of Union soldiers that had been stationed at the empty mansion since 1863 to guard it from vandalism and arson. Two boys from the mainland stole a boat and crept down to Cumberland to see the settlement. One of the boys, William Penniman, later wrote that because "we had learned there was a number camped at Dungeness, we pulled out for that point. We arrived about eleven o'clock [at night], I should judge, and finding a big tabby wall surrounding what seemed to be a kind of corral, we crept up to it and there we saw quantities of run-away negroes, horses and Yankees."[55]

In the fall of 1865 the Freedmen's Bureau ordered Stafford to consolidate acreage within his tracts to provide suitable land for a second freedmen's settlement, and in early 1866 Eaton informed Stafford of the possibility that none of his land would be returned unless he complied. Stafford may have seen the order as being to his benefit, because the freedmen would become tenants, thereby providing him with a labor pool. But he would have insisted that things be done his way, while the freedmen would have seen the land as theirs and consequently believed that there was no need to obey Stafford's orders. The situation was clearly a recipe for failure. Although Stafford may have acquiesced in the placement of this settlement, the Freedmen's Bureau compelled him to do so. Stafford was long remembered in Camden County for threatening insubordinate freedmen and was widely quoted as having said, "If you don't work for me, I'll burn down your cabins." Former slaves who would not work on his terms would have to move elsewhere.[54]

The consolidated acreage Eaton suggested for a freedmen's settlement was probably at the high bluff lying between Little Old House Creek and Gray Field landing. Stafford may even have recommended using Gray's slave cabins. The area would have been highly suitable for a freedmen's settlement because it lay within Stafford's jurisdiction, provided access to navigable streams and natural springs, and was some distance away from Stafford's home, an important consideration for the freedmen. There is no archaeological or substantial written evidence, however, to pinpoint the exact site of Stafford's freedmen's settlement.

Camden County's 1870 tax records show Stafford owning only 8,000 acres, a decrease of 125 acres from 1866 that is probably accounted for by the creation of the freedmen's settlement. Furthermore, Stafford reported that his property was woodland, which suggests that his fields had become overgrown. After 1874 he once again reported holding his original 8,125 acres.[55]

Antebellum plantation settlement had usually followed a pattern that ensured maximum slave surveillance, with the houses of the planter and the overseer located near the linearly arranged slave quarters. With formal emancipation, this spatial pattern changed. The houses of former slaves, now small farmers, became dispersed throughout the plantation lands as the freedmen sought better access to boat landings, timber stands, freshwater sources, more productive soil, or whatever other combination of natural resources appeared desirable.[56]

When returning to the land on which they had been slaves, Camden County freedmen divided themselves into semiautonomous groups of peer workers, generally composed of extended families and each trying to occupy its own settlement cluster close to its fields. Although such dispersed settlements existed on Cumberland, they were greatly modified by the application of Special

Orders 15. This settlement pattern generally represented a transition from civil slavery to wage slavery. Many freedmen had no choice but to pursue agriculture, the only livelihood for which they were trained, and to hire themselves out for a pittance. Many former slaves became tenant farmers on their former owners' land. This drift toward tenancy was interrupted by the arrival of the Carnegies, who were almost completely uninterested in agricultural production on Cumberland.[57]

Two more freedmen's enclaves appeared. A freedmen's settlement grew up at Downes's Landing on Brick Hill River, part of Longwood, Margaret Downes's plantation. Poor and isolated as the Brick Hill farming community was, it became a magnet for a few freedmen seeking peace and isolation. During the war, Downes, her sister-in-law, and their female slaves had fled to Woodstock Mills, a Florida lumber settlement owned by Edwin Alberti, leaving behind one old male slave to guard her property. When she returned, she found a settlement of strangers in addition to a few slaves who had originally come from Cumberland. Respectfully greeted by the ones who knew her from before the war, Downes ventured to criticize the settlement's pretensions to landownership. When she assumed that the settlers were her tenants, she met stormy opposition. Quash Germain, one of the strangers, warned Downes away, telling her to wait until she got her land back before attempting to drive off the freedmen.[58]

Germain and a former slave named Rodgers Alberty probably migrated to the island from Edwin Alberti's mainland properties. Alberty and Germain married two sisters, Chaney and Ellen, who are known to have been slaves of island residents, the Bunkleys. The women would have been familiar with Bunkley-Downes relationships and with James H. Downes's death just before the war and may have presented the alluring possibility that the Bunkley and Downes families would welcome the former slaves and their husbands at the Downes homestead.[59]

In 1863 thirteen blacks were living at Brick Hill. Two years later, the number had grown to sixteen, and in 1866 twenty-six former slaves resided there. The 1870 census shows ten family units containing a total of thirty-one people, including Alberty, Isaac Brown, Abram Trimmings, John Hubbard, Deneris Williams, and Henry Commodore. They grew Indian corn and sweet potatoes; only one settler reported owning livestock. The settlement seems much smaller on the 1880 census, although other evidence indicates that some forty people were living there. The reason is probably that the census enumerator recorded only those settlers who reported a certain dollar valuation for their farm production. Furthermore, only tilled land was reported, so a free black man who subsisted on his crops but sold honey from beehives, for example, would go unrecorded.[60]

A fourth small community of former slaves lived on Stafford's land. Unlike many postbellum Sea Island plantation owners, Stafford, who had an excellent credit rating at both his Connecticut and New York banks, could afford to pay his hands. Crop failures in 1867 and 1868 as well as difficulties with contract labor forced Stafford and many other coastal planters to abandon any further hope of growing cotton, but Stafford could hire a few hands for limited farm activities such as vegetable gardening, caring for stock, clearing land, gathering wood, and repairing boats. This community consisted of Stafford's five paid black servants, including a cook named Catharine Williams, a young stableman and gardener named Henry Commodore, and a young maidservant named Tecumsah Cooper, who later married Commodore.[61]

Before the war, field hands were organized into work gangs directed by slave drivers. Immediately after the Civil War, most planters tried to revive the centralized plantation system using gang labor. To this end the Freedmen's Bureau recommended creation of signed contracts between landowner and laborers. Although labor contracts are extant for Nightingale's Glynn County rice operations, no Cumberland contracts have been found. Because of the familial connections among Cumberland residents, white and black, it seems likely that Stafford tried to create a new workforce composed of family squads that would work the land in shares, a form of tenancy with which Stafford was already familiar since it was how he himself had begun. The freedmen on Cumberland Island decided where they would work. In 1882 a journalist wrote from Cumberland's Seaside Hotel, "The chief or head man makes the contracts, and . . . certain members come to do the work. But the negroes on Cumberland work but little for anybody." There was little work on the island in the 1870s and 1880s.[62]

Monochromatic ink and sepia drawing of Dungeness cemetery
by Frank Hamilton Taylor, early 1880s.

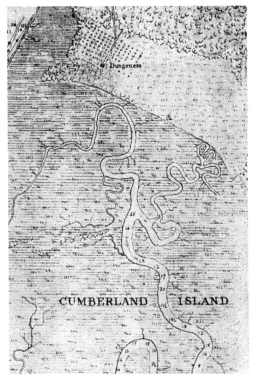

Detail from Captain John Mackay's 1843 map
of Cumberland Sound and Amelia Bar,
showing the location of Dungeness house, gardens,
orange grove, and cemetery. PKY 1547;
National Archives, Record Group 77, N93-1.

Cemetery of Robert Stafford, his mother, and his sister.

Standing chimneys from Stafford's slave settlement. Photo by Roy C. Craven Jr.

Primus Mitchell and his wife Amanda, ca. 1888.

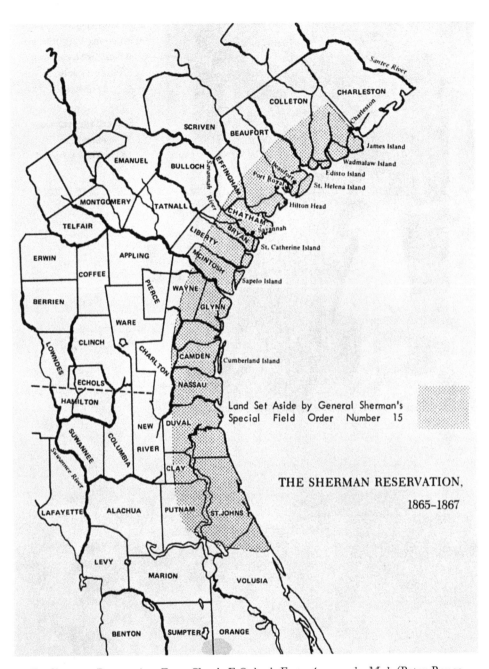

The Sherman Reservation. From Claude F. Oubre's *Forty Acres and a Mule* (Baton Rouge: Louisiana State University Press, 1978).

Left: Cumsie Commodore with young Ferguson girl at Greyfield, ca. 1939. Photo by John H. Ricketson.

Below: Standing slave chimneys, Greyfield (1890).

Above left: Charlie Trimmins, 1940s. Photo by
Joseph C. Graves Sr.

Above right: His wife, Liz Trimmins, 1940s.
Photo by Joseph C. Graves Sr.

Left: Rodgers Alberty, son of a Brick Hill
freedman of the same name,
taken in the 1940s.
Courtesy of Muriel Williams.

Right: Nelson Merrow. Photo by Davis Pratt.

Andrew Carnegie and his brother,
Tom, about 1853.

Above: Thomas M. Carnegie Jr.'s family and
William E. Page on the Dungeness
verandah, 1894 or 1895.
From left: William E. Page, manager;
Bertha S. Carnegie and her husband,
Andrew Carnegie II; seated at their feet, his
sisters Nancy T. and Florence N. Carnegie;
Will C. Carnegie; Lucy C. Carnegie;
Will's wife, Martha Gertrude Carnegie;
(standing) Thomas M. Carnegie Jr. and
(seated) his wife, Virginia B. Carnegie;
unknown woman; (standing) butler,
probably Eliphez Bird;
(in hammock) Sally G. Ricketson and
George L. Carnegie and his wife,
Margaret T. Carnegie; (standing) waiter
Willie Robinson; F. Graham Blandy;
Frank Carnegie; Oliver G. Ricketson's wife,
Margaret C. Ricketson, or Retta;
and (sitting on floor, from left)
two unknown young boys;
Coleman Carnegie; and
Oliver G. Ricketson.

Above left: Studio portrait of
Thomas M. Carnegie at thirty-one years
of age, 1875.

Above right: Studio portrait of
Lucy C. Carnegie,
ca. 1882.

Right: General William George
Mackay Davis, 1861.
State Photographic Archives,
Strozier Library, Florida State University.

An architectural rendering for a proposed Dungeness Cottage.

A house at Dungeness, built before 1881, perhaps by General Davis.

Looking east from the Dungeness water tower toward the Atlantic Ocean, 1905.

Looking west from the Dungeness water tower toward the mainland and Cumberland River, 1905.

Dungeness House during its 1905 renovations

Western facade of the "Casino" (Swimming Pool House), ca. 1905.
Courtesy of Dollie Whitby McLaren.

Christmas dinner party at Dungeness, ca. 1900.

The Cottage.

The Grange.

Rules and Regulations

GOVERNING

EMPLOYMENT

ON THE PROPERTY OF

Mrs. Lucy C. Carnegie

ON

CUMBERLAND ISLAND.

1901
THE H. & W. B. DREW COMPANY
JACKSONVILLE FLA.

Above left: Catherine Rikart,
in house for white female help.
From the Nancy C. Rockefeller Collection.

Above right: After hours in the workmen's
quarters at Dungeness.

Left: Booklet of rules and regulations
governing employment
at Dungeness.

James Foreman, butler at Greyfield, ca. 1910.

Sam Green, coachman at Dungeness, ca. 1888. From the Nancy C. Rockefeller Collection.

Beach scene, ca. 1905.

Hunting scene, Hickory Hill on Cumberland, ca. 1895.

The sand boat.

Mamzelle watches an uncertain passenger at Greyfield.

The main street, St. Marys, ca. 1895. Courtesy of Eloise Bailey and Dorsey Harris.

Church, St. Marys, ca. 1895.
Courtesy of the Georgia Department of Archives and History, VG CAM-355.

NINE

The Beginning
of Visitors
on Cumberland

Sea Island Tourism

he Sea Islands' breezy beaches had long attracted Georgians in search of a healthier alternative to the summer weather on coastal Georgia's swamp and tidal plantations. One of the earliest advertisements hoping to lure summer visitors to the islands appeared in 1819:

SUMMER RETREAT

The undersigned informs the ladies and gentlemen of the low country of Georgia that he will be prepared to receive genteel persons at his residence on Sapelo Island during the summer and fall months, and that no exertions on his part will be wanting to render their situation convenient and agreeable. His house is large, and the apartments well furnished and numerous, all open to the ocean. Shell and scale fish and venison are plenty in the neighborhood, and shall be at times furnished. Carriages, chairs and horses to run on the beach he will likewise supply.

Louisa Shaw also tried to rent Dungeness and its orchard for the summer in 1825, when she would be absent from Georgia.[1]

The first hotels built on Cumberland were small institutions erected at the North End around 1870. Boats sailing north-south along the Inland Waterway often stopped at the island for food, water, and rest. In contrast to Phineas Nightingale's plan for an opulent Hotel Dungeness, the High Point hotels sought the patronage of those who could afford to go to a beach but had less to spend. In true democratic fashion, High Point hotel managers sought attendance from societies, fraternities, lodges, and other associations. To find this public, hotel operators had to overcome the difficulty of being on an island.[2]

The development of popular summer resorts on Cumberland Island resulted from a boom of railroad building in conjunction with a revival of interest in steamboat traffic on the Inland Waterway. Jacksonville, Florida, was rapidly developing as a commercial shipping center when Henry B. Plant returned to Florida after the Civil War. During the 1880s he bought up several narrow-gauge railroads operating from Savannah to Jacksonville. Henry Flagler, a competing railway tycoon, began his moves toward controlling eastern Florida traffic in about 1884. By 1885–86, after Flagler built a number of large coal and lumber docks in Jacksonville, the city became a major port for the transshipment of products originating in central Georgia and Florida. Recognizing the growing importance of transportation in the region, steamboat shippers created the "Cumberland Route" from Brunswick, Georgia, to Fernandina, Florida, to give water access to Florida.

Steamers traveling through the Cumberland Route primarily carried passengers: the ships' large engines and huge stores of firewood left little room for freight. Most boats had two decks, with the lower deck carrying freight and wood to produce steam and offering cabin space for black passengers. A typical boat left Brunswick at 8:00 A.M., arrived at Cumberland's High Point around 10:00 A.M., and reached Fernandina at noon. At 2:00 P.M. the steamer began its return voyage to Brunswick, again stopping at High Point on the way. Freight for Jekyll Island, Cabin Bluff, or Dungeness could be dropped off when necessary, but those stops were unscheduled. The morning passengers had time at each stop to see a little of the place where the boat discharged passengers and cargo.

The trip itself soon began to attract some passengers. When in the 1870s steamboats began selling tickets with stopover privileges, Cumberland's two boardinghouse-type inns began to enlarge to small hotels. The *Collyer*'s rates for its run to High Point included a ride to the beach and a midday meal at the Hotel Cumberland.

For outings, special-interest groups chartered steamers along the Cumberland Route. Allie Brown Carmichael, a Camden County girl, recalled such trips between 1890 and 1903:

> I remember the yearly boat excursions to Cumberland and St. Simons. The boat started at Owens Ferry and picked up passengers all the way down the river. Our river boat had two decks. The top deck was cleared for dancing. Captain White always had our coloured band on board. . . . The waltz was the most popular with everyone, with the square dance next.
>
> It was on Cumberland Island that I saw my first mule-drawn street car. The is-

land's beaches were beautiful and everyone carried their own bathing suits, which had long full skirts with bloomers that buttoned below the knee, stockings and some kind of slipper for the feet. Big hats were worn which tied under the chin, as one must not get sunburned in those days.

Carmichael remembered how choppy St. Andrew Sound could be. The crossing was often wet and turbulent, but it was pleasant to return to the calm of the river as the little steamer dropped off its weary and happy passengers.[3]

The name *Cumberland Route* also appeared in advertisements for railroad projects billing the route as the best method of getting passengers and freight to Jacksonville. In 1896 a group of Brunswick businessmen bought the majority stock in the large steamboat *City of Brunswick* and some other vessels to create the Georgia and Florida Steamboat Company. A typical advertisement offered, "Cheap rates to Jacksonville via the Cumberland Route. $3 to Jacksonville, $2 to Fernandina." The Georgia and Florida Steamboat Company also made a regular run up the Satilla River to pick up lumber and naval stores. The company's steamboats, *Hildegarde* and *Atlantic,* carried barrels of rosin into Brunswick for transshipment abroad and to the North. Even the little steamer *Grace,* which traveled semiweekly from Brunswick to Fernandina, Florida, and back with mail, was part of the "steamboat navy" that plied the Cumberland Route.[4]

One of Cumberland's first inns was the Oriental House, which ran advertisements in Brunswick newspapers by 1870, when James A. Clubb Jr. was proprietor. James subsequently left Cumberland to live near Brunswick, and his brother, Elias, became innkeeper. The Clubb brothers, their wives, and their widowed mother helped run the hotel, but little else is known about it, and no pictures of it seem to exist.[5]

In July 1880 Elias Clubb became pilot of the Brunswick bar, and he and his family moved from the island. Mason T. Burbank, a Fernandina builder and contractor who had come to Florida from New York state in about 1870, bought the Clubb property. One of Burbank's daughters died during an 1874 yellow fever epidemic, and Burbank and his family moved to High Point on Cumberland Island, seeking a healthier climate. Burbank operated a small post office and a general store in connection with the Bunkleys' sawmill, and he changed the name of the Clubbs' hotel to High Point House.[6]

By 1883 Burbank was doing such a lucrative business that he considered building a tram railroad across the marsh to Little Cumberland Island, where he would build a deepwater dock to accommodate larger boats that could bring prospective guests more quickly from Brunswick. Announcing that he would soon have stock for sale, he estimated the cost at $3,000. In 1885 a Brunswick newspaper announced that the tramway was two-thirds financed. Nothing more appeared on this topic in the local press, however, and this tramway apparently never was built.

Either the hotel was not prospering, or Burbank needed more capital. He sold some of the High Point property he had purchased from Elias Clubb to George W. Benson of Marietta, Georgia, and Greenwich, Connecticut. Benson's purchase lay along the west side of High Point, overlooking the Cumberland River. Benson wished to build a semireligious retreat for a colony composed mostly of Marietta residents. He constructed a large, three-story house for himself and his family. Benson lived on Cumberland Island for a time, but neither he nor his colony became a permanent part of island life.[7] Although other tenants subsequently occupied the Benson house, it gradually deteriorated, and today its only remains lie near a still-flowing artesian well.

In 1890 Burbank sold another portion of his land for $75,000 to the newly created Cumberland Island Company, established by William R. Bunkley and his partners. By 1896 the Benson house served as a hunting lodge operated by Charles A. Miller. It was apparently a great success. In 1902 Miller took over the management of the Cumberland Island Hotel. With that move, his hunting lodge venture ended.[8]

The most successful of the High Point innkeepers were the Bunkleys. William R. Bunkley's wife, Isabelle Miller Bunkley, had taken boarders in St. Marys while he was serving in the Confederate Army. When the war ended, the Bunkleys returned to Cumberland Island, and after the federal government restored their land in 1867, William opened a sawmill. Sometime between 1870 and 1875 Bunkley built a small inn. In 1881 Bunkley leased his hotel property to Edgar Ross of Macon for a period of five years.[9]

Ross and his family arrived in May 1881, with servants, numerous livestock, and house and farm equipment. Ross's daughter, Hermione, wrote, "The hotel is really just an old eight-room house, but we live in the new wing over the big dining room." The number of cottages around the hotel is unclear, but during the family's first season, she wrote, "Cottages began to fill up. People sleeping four in a room, men put cots out and slept under the trees." Ross made improvements such as bathhouses and a round outdoor pavilion, designed by his wife. Its roof was thatched with palmetto, a feature she copied from the black settlement at Downes's Landing.[10]

In 1883 Ross gave up his lease and returned to Macon. Like the Clubbs and Phineas M. Nightingale, Bunkley viewed hotel keeping less as an investment than as a method of keeping his land. He again confronted the problem of finding an innkeeper and apparently settled on his son. In April 1883 Brunswick newspapers stated that Bunkley House was being readied for the summer season with William H. Bunkley as the new proprietor. A new wharf was being built, and a tramway was under construction. Until it was finished, carriages were provided for guests' transportation from the wharf to the hotel. The advertisement continued, "This Seaside House is not as splendid as some on the Northern seashore, but solid comfort and a Georgia welcome awaits every one. Not far from the main house is arranged a row of new cottages." During the summer of 1884 the North End was dubbed Bunkley, Georgia. In 1906 the North End was given the name *Cumberland* and was described as a "post-hamlet of Camden County [with] a money order post office and . . . a trading center for the neighborhood. The nearest railroad station is Woodbine, on the . . . Seaboard Air Line."[11]

The hotel expanded its services under the management of William H. Bunkley, assisted by his wife, Carrie; his younger brother, Tommie; and his father, William R. Bunkley. Whereas in early years the hotel carpenter had played the fiddle for hotel dances, in early 1885 Bunkley announced that he had retained an Italian band to play for the season. The hotel had purchased an elegant Estey upright piano and placed it in the parlor. In 1888 more cottages were being built, a larger pavilion was under construction, and a shipment of iron rails was expected for the new tramway running from the dock to the beach. Benson owned the dock and the land on which the tramway was built. In 1883 the Bunkleys received Benson's permission to build a single-track horse-drawn railroad from the dock to his hotel. Even more important, William H. Bunkley announced that his hotel would be open all winter, mostly for hunters and fishermen. The Rosses had closed the hotel during the winter months, partly in response to the fact that steamships ceased plying the Cumberland Route.[12]

Despite the hotel's success in attracting visitors, the Bunkleys were not making money, and by July 1890 rumors began to spread that the business might be sold. Although William R. Bunkley's personal and business interests had fo-

cused on St. Marys, his son was more oriented toward Glynn County. In the
1890s Brunswick was viewed as a growing city, while many people saw St.
Marys as withering.[13]

William R. Bunkley had purchased from his sisters the Cumberland acreage
they had inherited from their father, Thomas Pitt Bunkley, and by 1890
William was in a position to negotiate the sale of the entire Bunkley tract to a
purchaser, if one could be found. He began talks with the Macon Company, of
Macon, Georgia, for the sale of some 1,000 acres of highland and 600 acres of
marshland. At the time of this sale, the Macon Company also concluded an
agreement with Benson to continue using the railroad. The Macon Company
was allowed to make improvements to the dock and on the bluff overlooking it.[14]

The Macon Company agreed to pay William R. Bunkley $75,000 for the
land, the hotel cottages, and other buildings. Half the money would be paid in
cash, and a 6 percent mortgage would be given for the remainder, with ten annual payments of $2,500. Bunkley reserved 30 acres: each of his four children,
William H. Bunkley, Robert Lee Bunkley, Thomas P. Bunkley, and Madena
Bunkley Tompkins, received 7.25 acres; and 1 acre, located on the railroad track
that ran from the dock to the hotel, for services but occasionally as a school-
house for white children.[15]

The Macon Company operated the Cumberland Island Hotel with Lee
Shackleford as manager between the late spring of 1891 and 1901, a generally
successful tenure. The company showed itself willing and able to invest in expanding hotel facilities, increasing the number of guests who could be accommodated from 350 to 500.[16]

Many organizations held summer meetings at the hotel, among them the
Georgia Teachers Association, although it is not known when it began doing so.
The teachers' conventions brought to the island as many as 750 people, including prominent Georgians such as Governor Samuel C. Atkinson and Macon attorney Walter Barnard Hill as well as national figures such as U.S. Secretary of
the Interior Hoke Smith and Nicholas Murray Butler, a prominent historian
and later president of Columbia University. Another educators' organization,
the Educational Association of Georgia, held at least two conventions (in 1900
and 1903) at the Cumberland Island Hotel. At these conventions, lectures
mingled with recreational outings—driving, riding, fishing, picnicking, swimming, listening to music, and spending evenings by the firelight. When the
Macon Volunteers, a militia group, arrived for "summer maneuvers," local wits

said that the volunteers' rifles would be useless and that they would be better off trying white duck pants and gold braid.[17]

Had Dungeness Hotel taken off along the lines elaborated by Phineas Nightingale's 1869 prospectus, the southern part of the island might have become a wealthy, elitist association, a precursor to the Jekyll Island Club.[18] With the conspicuous success of the Cumberland Island Hotel at the North End, there would have been two resorts on Cumberland, each catering to the increasingly prosperous American middle class. But with the creation of a direct railway line from Brunswick to Florida, the Cumberland Route began to lose some of its profitable freight and passenger trade to Cumberland Island. For a little while longer, resorts at High Point and on St. Simons Island remained attractive, but the steamers from Brunswick to Fernandina began to reduce the number of trips per week. When the *Emmaline* abandoned as unprofitable its run to High Point in the beginning of the twentieth century, North End resort life, once open to an egalitarian public, began to draw to a close.[19]

A Refuge from Pittsburgh

At the time that Tom Carnegie purchased Dungeness, the Carnegie industrial interests were already well known in most of America. Oblivious to the world of steel, however, a Camden County resident wrote placidly of the new arrivals, "They were from England and had come to the USA to live."[20]

The Carnegie family had not come from England, however. Thomas Morrison Carnegie, born at Dunfermline, Fifeshire, Scotland, on 2 October 1843, was not yet five years old when he came to America in 1848 with his parents, William and Margaret, and older brother, Andrew. William had been a linen weaver, a proud profession in Dunfermline. The Carnegies settled in Pittsburgh, where William not only worked in a cotton mill but also tried to sell his fine damask linen from door to door. Margaret Morrison Carnegie cobbled shoes for Henry Phipps Sr., often finishing her work by candlelight at home in their tenement. After his father's death on 2 October 1855, Andy went to work. Tom was spared some of the poverty of his brother's early childhood. Tom stopped attending school at about sixteen, when he began to work as a telegrapher for the Pennsylvania Railroad Company, where his brother had secured him a job.[21]

Around 1864 Tom became interested in Lucy Ackerman Coleman, the daughter of a wealthy Pittsburgh industrialist, William Coleman, whose family had long known the Carnegies. The couple married in June 1866 and left for a short wedding trip to Europe. Tom then plunged once more into the cares of his busy job managing the Upper and Lower Union Iron Mills. In 1867 William Coleman traveled to Europe, where he learned how to make coke. Shortly thereafter, in cooperation with the Carnegie brothers and their cousin, George Lauder, he established a factory that later formed the nucleus of the Edgar Thomson Steel Works. In 1867 Andy and his mother moved to New York City, closer to the financial heart of America. Tom and Lucy received Andy's large house, Fairfield, located in Homewood, Pennsylvania, a residential suburb of Pittsburgh where her parents also lived.[22]

In 1880 Tom was the very picture of a successful Victorian husband and father, head of a large household. At the age of thirty-six, he and his wife had seven living children and another one on the way. With them lived Lucy's widowed mother; Lucy's sister, Florence; and Lucy's brother, William, who was going blind. Seven female servants looked after the household. Tom was devoted to his wife, whom he called Lu or Lulu, and she to him. He was more interested in being with his family than in traveling on business. The family eventually grew to include nine children: William Coleman Carnegie (1867–1944), Frank Morrison Carnegie (1868–1917), Andrew Carnegie II (1870–1947), Margaret Carnegie (1872–1927), Thomas Morrison Carnegie Jr. (1874–1944), George Lauder Carnegie (1876–1921), Florence Nightingale Carnegie (1879–1962), Coleman Carnegie (1880–1911), and Nancy Trovillo Carnegie (1881–1954).[23]

After the 1881 consolidation of the Thomson Steel Works, the two Union Iron Mills, and a variety of other iron- and steel-related businesses, a new and powerful firm called Carnegie Brothers and Company, Limited, appeared. Tom's appointment as chairman of its board was announced April 1, 1881, but the choice had been made a year earlier. Tom held the chairmanship until his death in 1886. In January 1886 Tom and Andy held the chief interests in two limited partnerships, Carnegie Brothers and Company and Carnegie, Phipps, and Company, that were consolidations of other holdings. The two companies were capitalized at $5 million and made $2 million during the first year. Tom's holdings in the two firms were valued at $878,096.58.[24]

The partnership's profits were plowed back into plant improvement and expansion. Tom and the other partners in the associations were somewhat disgruntled that Andy permitted them to receive little in the way of dividends. The debate over cash dividends versus capital investment was vigorously argued each year, but Andy, who held a 54 percent interest in the company, always won.[25]

When Tom became chairman of the company, he received a much larger salary. By 1880 Pittsburgh had become an extremely smoky and dirty city. Numerous furnaces, fired by bituminous coal, illuminated its perpetually darkened sky. Even the suburbs were blighted by the unhealthy air. Also, labor problems in Pittsburgh were becoming increasingly intractable. Tom and Lucy may have sought a healthier climate for their growing family. Florida boosters touted the advantages of Florida weather and its real estate opportunities. European immigrants and the increasingly mobile industrial classes alike fell under the spell of the Florida land boomers. Carnegie bought Dungeness Plantation, of which he had never before heard, in Georgia, where he had no connections, from a former Confederate general whom Carnegie had never met.[26]

In 1880 *Lippincott's Magazine* published a thrilling article about Dungeness Plantation written by a Massachusetts freelance writer named Frederick A. Ober. Ober visited Cumberland three times—in November, April, and August—probably in 1879–80, and was probably shown the property by a guide familiar with its history. Ober's preparation for his article is what drew the Carnegies' attention to Dungeness. In later life Lucy Carnegie had offprints of his article bound and presented to each of her children, inscribed, "The following article first attracted Mrs. Carnegie's attention to Cumberland Island, which in 1880 became her property." Transactions between Tom Carnegie and Dungeness's then-owner, General William George Mackay Davis, did indeed begin in 1880. It seems very probable that in 1879 the Carnegies and Ober met as fellow guests at either the Egmont or the Strathmore, Fernandina's two good hotels, and that Ober's enthusiastic account led the Carnegies to investigate the property. Another contemporary description offers a good idea of what the Carnegies may have seen: "Dungenness Castle is today a crumbling ruin. When I saw it in midwinter last it only suggested barren desolation. The chambers where the guests were wont to meet a quarter of a century ago . . . were untenanted and deserted. The walls were mouldy and decaying, and the great rafters supporting the upper tiers and the roof almost tumbling in."[27]

Based on the accuracy of the architectural data about the house that Ober provides, National Park Service historian Louis Torres believes that someone who knew the ruined Dungeness very well guided Ober through the house and grounds. His guide may have been an agent for the estate of Eliza H. Molyneux or a relation of Nightingale who showed Dungeness to visitors and prospective purchasers. In the early 1870s a "Mr. Johnston took charge of Cumberland Island for the Nightingales, hoping to sell it for them." The Johnstons, who may have been relatives of Nightingale's, were said to have lived at Dungeness until about 1876.[28]

Confederate General William George Mackay Davis (1812–1900), a friend and distant cousin of President Jefferson Davis, was the current owner of Dungeness. He had signed a contract on 21 November 1879 to purchase Dungeness from Molyneux's heirs. A shrewd Florida lawyer before the war, Davis subsequently moved his practice to Washington, D.C., where corporations, especially railroad companies, eagerly sought his services. Upon his retirement, Davis moved back to Florida, where he had numerous corporate connections in Jacksonville. Although familiar with the plantation system, Davis was not a professional agriculturist. Dungeness Plantation was conveniently located at the entrance to Fernandina, its port and inlet in need only of further dredging to make it one of the finest seaports of the southeastern coast. Furthermore, with improved steamship passage would come immigration of invalids, tourists, and potential land investors. Hotel-oriented entrepreneurs had already approached Davis, and he had been interested in building a hotel at Dungeness. In March 1880, just three months after agreeing to the purchase from the Molyneux estate, his plans were interrupted by a personal tragedy:

> A terrible accident occurred yesterday at Dungeness. Mr. B. M. Davis, son of General W. G. M. Davis, the recent purchaser, had the misfortune to shoot and kill his eldest son, a bright little fellow of five years of age. The family had just moved over from Fernandina the day before, to take possession of their new home. . . . It has spread a cloud of horror over our little community, and all tender to the bereaved parents their heartfelt sympathy. It is needless to add that the parents are almost crazed by this terrible, heartrending disaster.[29]

On 25 August 1880 Tom Carnegie wrote to J. C. Greeley, president of the Florida Savings Bank and Real Estate Exchange in Jacksonville, expressing an interest in acquiring Dungeness. Greeley replied that he would undertake to get "at the Dungeness" for Carnegie, but it could not be done in a hurry: "General Davis (a man with great expectations) is on the place but I am under the impression that Genl. Jackson has purchased a portion of it. I can get at the facts, and if it can be purchased, I can get at the price. Will report progress." Greeley evidently encouraged Carnegie to contact General Davis, which Carnegie did, offering $25,000 for the property. On 26 September 1880 Davis sent a postcard to Carnegie, rejecting his offer: "Letter received. I have not the remotest idea of selling at any such price. Have received many enquiries— same reply. I send for your information map of place." Greeley also tried to persuade Davis to sell but received the same response. Greeley wrote to Carnegie on 2 October 1880 that Davis "seems quite stiff at $40,000.00."[30]

In December 1880, the general's son, Bernard M. Davis, who had accidentally shot his own son nine months earlier, himself died, compounding the family tragedy. Word was evidently passed along to friends in Fernandina and Jacksonville that the Davis family would like to leave Dungeness. Soon after Bernard's burial in the Greene-Miller cemetery on Cumberland, the general lowered his asking price. On 6 May 1881 Davis wrote to Carnegie that he would consider $35,000 for the tract. Even at that lowered amount, Davis was still asking for more than double what he had contracted to pay only three years earlier. Davis's final payment would be due on 6 June 1881, at which time he would become legal owner. But before the sale became final, one of the legatees died, throwing the matter into the British Court of Chancery, which had to give permission for the sale of the Molyneux family's "vast holdings" in Georgia.[31]

Davis subsequently wrote to Carnegie that there had been many offers to purchase Dungeness but that he was reluctant to sell because his son and grandson were buried there. Davis wanted to reserve the cemetery to assure its future maintenance and his right to visit it, and he felt sure that any gentleman would grant him that privilege.[32]

On 17 May 1881 the broken-hearted old soldier described Dungeness to Carnegie:

There are several hundred orange trees which have been in bearing for a long time. They will not bear this year owing to the loss of their leaves by the freeze of 29 December. They will it is said, bear larger crops next year than ever before, because of the rest and new growth.

There are about six hundred old olive trees which will bear this year. They only do so in alternating years. I propose to make oil from the olives. Some I must pickle as is done in France. The yield is very great. The olives grow close together on the branches. My gardener, a Frenchman, estimated the oil products at 3000 gallons. I am not able to form any estimate.

I have planted this year fifteen thousand cuttings to form a nursery. The trees that are produced will be fit to sell when two years [old?]. They will bear two bushels each on the sixth year say 1887. Each year fresh cuttings can be put out. The demand for the trees is great. There is no supply, short of Europe.

There are many quince, pear, peach, apricot & plum trees of good variety planted by myself, also some Japan plums.

There are about thirty fig trees of fine quality and bearing large crops—A great many [tung?] trees—Some grape vines—banana plants etc. There are a great many ornamental shrubs, freesia & clematis, some large and valuable.

The water on the place is very fine. The well is thirty feet deep—temperature below 70 degrees in summer.

One hundred and fifty horned cattle and fifty horses can be pastured. They will not need shelter nor other feed than the natural grasses. My cows are not fed, yet they keep fat and give rich milk. The butter is good.

There are good deer in the forest. I have not allowed any to be shot. Hogs can be raised in the forest. . . .

PS I forgot to say that I caused the walls of the old building to be examined by a mason who says they are strong & stout. They will answer to be built on. I have a plan & estimate for rebuilding. The cost is put out at less than six thousand dollars. There is one house with four rooms with new roof, neatly plastered. . . .

There is a large new wooden building, neatly made, painted, with glass windows intended for carriage house and stable.[33]

General Davis did not exaggerate about the Dungeness groves. The old trees were still productive. The Davis family sold oranges and olives from Dungeness, and in 1881 a small boatload of Dungeness oranges arrived in Fernandina and were sold at the wharf at two cents each. According to an article in the *Fernandina Florida Mirror,* "Gen. Davis, the owner of the beautiful olive groves of Dungeness, has sent to France and Italy for practical methods of olive culture and oil making, and intends to prove that olive growing is just as profitable an investment within the limits of our State as is orange growing." When olive growing in Florida was commended, local observers referred to "some fine trees at Dungeness, or Cumberland Island, and probably in other places in Georgia and Florida."[34]

On 22 May 1881 Carnegie telegraphed to Davis, "Letter . . . received I accept your offer." On the following day Davis telegraphed back, "Dispatch recd Will make satisfactory conveyance and give perfect title." On 23 May Lucy Carnegie telegraphed to her husband, "Florence and I are delighted Hardly realize it All well." On 24 May Carnegie wrote to Davis, "Dear Sir: I telegraphed you yesterday accepting your offer for $35,000.00 and am in receipt of your telegraphic reply this morning confirming sale. Please make deed to my wife, Mrs. Lucy C. Carnegie. Your wishes in regard to the Cemetery are in accordance with mine, and of course will be respected. I hope to have the pleasure of seeing you frequently at Dungeness after the old house has been rebuilt. . . . Should . . . any one of your family wish to occupy the premises I would be glad to have them do so."[35]

The sale was not final until 17 November 1881, but on 11 June the local newspaper announced, "We have learned that Gen. Davis has sold Dungeness to parties from the North, who will erect a large hotel on the property and otherwise improve it."[56] Carnegie, however, was not building a hotel. He was purchasing a country place for his wife and children.

Some Camden County residents hoped that Tom Carnegie would renovate the once magnificent Dungeness mansion: "This old castellated structure . . . and the estate has recently, we understand, passed into the hands of a gentleman from Pittsburgh, Pa., who (rumor says) intends restoring it to something of its pristine splendor. Let us hope that he may not mar or destroy the spirit of the old place by any mansard roof or ultra-modern 'improvements.'" However, Carnegie evidently abandoned any idea of rebuilding the ruined house: twenty years of neglect had hastened the deterioration of the imposing ruin. The burned-out shell must have seemed impossible to restore. Between November 1881 and February 1882 Carnegie and Andrew Peebles, a well-known Pittsburgh architect whose specialty was designing large industrial and civic structures, found a way to demolish the Greene-Miller mansion. They may have taken advantage of the proximity of government contractors working on the north and south jetties under construction at St. Marys Inlet, which had begun by the summer of 1881. The presence of the Army Corps of Engineers, civilian contractors, and schooners with block and tackle for unloading stone probably led Carnegie to seek their services in the demolition of Dungeness. He may even have sold them blocks of tabby from the old house to use in jetty construction. The mansion's more friable remains went to island road building: "The old and picturesque house . . . was accidentally burnt a few years ago, and its wall being converted into lime by the fire, had to be pulled down, and their materials are now used as a top-dressing for the roads."[57]

The "cottage" that Peebles designed for the Carnegie family was of the sort later called Queen Anne Gothic. New England and the Atlantic coast resorts are still studded with these enormous wood-and-stone houses, wrapped by ample verandas, cooled by high ceilings, decorated wherever possible by turrets and little porches, and furnished with elaborate window treatments. Shortly after the *Florida Mirror* saw Peebles's drawings, it printed two columns of advice entitled "Florida Dwellings" in which the anonymous author warned specifically against building "Swiss Chalets" and "Gothic Cottages" in the South because these designs were "unfit for our hot and sultry clime."[38]

On 25 March 1882 Carnegie, his wife, one child, and a maid registered at the Egmont Hotel in Fernandina. He and several male friends almost immediately visited St. Marys. On 6 April Carnegie and his cousin, Leander M. Morris, jointly bought the Stafford properties on Cumberland from Robert Stafford's nephews, with Carnegie lending Morris the money for his purchase. Carnegie and Morris put $20,000 down on the property and took out a mortgage for an additional $20,000, payable in five equal annual installments at 7 percent interest.[39]

Both Stafford's nephews and former slaves who remembered antebellum plantations identified acreage called the "Gray Tract" within the Stafford properties. Although the fact was little known, Nightingale had conveyed part of his tract 2 to Stafford to cover debts. Because Nightingale's indebtedness to Stafford had never been legally recorded, most local observers were unable to explain how Stafford came to possess tract 2 and assumed the discrepancy in acreage resulted from faulty surveying.[40]

In 1882 Stafford Place contained a steamboat valued at $400 and bailed wire, ponies, and cattle valued at $6,000. The Bunkleys at High Point claimed as theirs some of the livestock roaming on Cumberland's open range, and in April 1883 the Bunkleys received $4,000 for their property. The identification of Bunkley cows was to plague the Carnegie family in later years.[41]

The first building constructed was the Carnegies' Dungeness. On 26 February 1884 the cornerstone of the new mansion was laid amid formal ceremonies. According to the house plans, the structure would measure 120 feet by 56 feet and would be two stories high with an attic. A tower 100 feet high would grace its east end. The exposed portions of the outer walls would be faced with light-colored granite, while the main roof, the dormer windows, and the pyramid of the belvedere were to be covered with Vermont slate. The combs of the higher portions of the main roof were to be topped with ornamental iron crestings.[42] The main entrance to the building was to be on its north side, opening into the vestibule of 10 feet by 11 feet with a marble floor with ornamental borders. To the left of the vestibule would be a grand hall, 21 feet wide, extending nearly the entire width of the building. The parlor and dining room were on the south side of the building. The parlor, on the east side of the grand hall, was to be 18 by 24 feet, with bay windows opening onto a broad veranda, which extended around the entire east and south sides of the structure. Opposite the parlor was to be a large dining room, 18 by 24 feet, that was connected to the pantry and china closets. At the north end of the grand hall was a small gun room with a lavatory. Next to the gun room and accessible from the hall was to be a large bedroom with an attached bathroom. A 6-foot-wide corridor led from the grand hall to the kitchen and scullery. The second story was to contain the family's living apartments, guest rooms, a library, and reading rooms, while the attic was to have six bedchambers. "The windows of the first two stories of the main building will be of the best quality of polished plate glass, while the window of the main stairs and grand hall will be of ornamental cathedral glass." The building would be completed by 1 January 1885. A lodging at the Dungeness landing was also under consideration, for the accommodation of Captain Baker of the Carnegies' steam yacht, *Missoe*.[43]

While the new Dungeness House was under construction, Tom and Lucy evidently lived in a small cottage that had been built either by Nightingale or by the Dungeness Hotel Association. The Carnegie boys stayed in the carriage house since the cottage could not have held them all.[44]

Upon the completion of Dungeness, the local press was invited to come see it. Their detailed reports show that few changes were made to Peebles's original design. The total cost of constructing and furnishing Dungeness House was approximately $285,000. The *Florida Mirror*'s article was in such demand that it had to be reprinted. The reporters' first glimpse was of the "quaint roofs and crested gables of the main building" soaring above the trees. Two roads ran from the boat landing to the house: one was a short route that wound through groves of oranges, bananas, plums, olives, and sago palms; the second road, which was for more general use, ran due east for more than a mile, straight to the beach. When visitors neared the front facade, they saw for the first time a great avenue of live oak on either side of a fifty-foot-wide road that ran north-south for about three miles.[45] This avenue led to the limit of the original Dungeness tract.

As the reporters stood in front of the house, they saw on their extreme right the main tower and beneath it the main entrance, with massive doors of polished Georgia pine. Passing through the doors, the visitors entered a square vestibule paved with blocks of blue Bordillio marble, bordered by black marble. By day, light entered the vestibule through plate glass windows with borders of colored glass; at night it was illuminated by an Eastlake lantern, "composed of rich ruby glass" with brass mountings.[46]

From the vestibule the sightseers entered the great hall, "a scene of real beauty." One reporter commented enthusiastically that it combined the highest artistic skill with solid domestic comfort. Octagonal in shape, the great hall was twenty-five feet wide and fifty-five feet long and ranged in height from sixteen feet where the great fireplace stood to twenty-six feet over the music gallery and grand staircase. The ceilings were paneled in polished pine, and the walls were similarly wainscoted. An oak fireplace and mantelpiece bore the carved legend, "The Hearth our Altar; Its Flame our Sacred Fire." The great hall featured three ten-foot-high panels of stained glass windows filled with flowers, fruit, and foliage surrounded by Japanese tracery, with examples of medieval jeweled glass at the base. The design also included a single large Scottish thistle. The stairway to the second floor featured two smaller stained glass windows with tropical birds and fruit. On the second floor were six principal bedrooms, two bathrooms, and linen closets. From this floor a small stairway led to another half floor with six more bedrooms and a bathroom. On this floor was also a "most original schoolroom for the little folks" with gaily colored windows placed high up to avoid distractions from the outside world. Some New York hotels had apartments fitted with mahogany and oak doors that slid into the walls, so that when the doors were open the rooms flowed into one another. Dungeness House had at least one set of such "pocket doors."[47]

From the third floor a flight of stairs, again with stained glass windows, led to the tower. From this room, which had conveniently arranged settees, visitors could enjoy the panoramic view. From the belvedere could be seen the Atlantic Ocean pounding on the beach, the Cumberland River winding north, and Fernandina's roadstead and harbor.[48]

In the basement were the servants' apartments, a cellar, a strong room, and a laundry. The laundry had enameled iron fittings and hot and cold running water. Dumbwaiters connected all floors. There was a hot-air system for heating the house, and electric lights and a system for ringing bells to summon servants were powered by gas manufactured on the premises.[49]

The house had broad, projecting eaves that protected the first-floor rooms from the driving rains of hurricane season. Wide, illuminated verandas around two sides of the house served as shady outdoor living rooms. The outer walls were of New Hampshire granite, ashlar treated and lined with brick or wood.[50]

At the end of April 1885 Lucy Carnegie wrote, "The new house will be finished in about a week—enough to furnish, we hope." The items listed as "furnishings" in the accounts for the house included an American flag, telephone rentals, a sectional boat, ironwork, hounds, a range and scullery tools, poultry, rugs, window glass, carpets, a refrigerator, a roller mangle for the laundry, cocoa matting, madras cotton material, mantelpieces, a sewing machine, and subscriptions to magazines and some technical publications.[51]

Paying for Privacy

General Davis had always permitted visitors to come from the mainland to view the ruined mansion, although he may have charged a fee for doing so. In the late 1870s tours to the site were numerous. Davis may not have intended to reside at Dungeness very long: as he wrote, possibilities existed for a hotel, and if so, Dungeness as a tourist attraction needed publicity, not obscurity.

Shortly after Carnegie's purchase, Davis advertised in the local newspaper that tourists were no longer welcome to visit the ruins of Dungeness mansion. While the Carnegies' house was under construction, they permitted visitors to walk through the newly cleared grounds kept "in perfect order by the new owners" in preparation for the new house. In 1884 between thirty and fifty people from Fernandina hotels visited Dungeness every week. Shortly after laying the foundation stone, however, Carnegie put forth a notice that excursionists would no longer be permitted to come ashore without special permission. Tourists interfered with construction.[52]

Later visitors interfered with the Carnegies' privacy. On one occasion in the early 1890s, a steamboat decanted fifty passengers at the Dungeness dock. When the superintendent was called for assistance, they had walked through the house and were taking their ease on its porches. Usually, however, privacy was accepted as a prerogative of ownership. The fact that Cumberland's visitors had to arrive by boat was a form of controlling access.

After the completion of the house in 1885, Tom Carnegie apparently intended to join his family there from November to mid-January each year, although it is doubtful that he planned to live there for long periods. At Christmas 1885 his wife noted in her diary that her husband and the boys had hung around the house all day complaining that there was nothing to do. Tom had said, "You couldn't hunt all the time."[53]

By October 1886 the family had been visiting Dungeness irregularly for over a year, taking a private railroad car from Pittsburgh. In Pittsburgh, most of the Carnegie children received tutoring at home and at local day schools. While on Cumberland, however, the children apparently did not attend school, although George and Coleman had a tutor who traveled with them. The Carnegie and Coleman families were proponents of the cult of the self-made man, which held that formal education was apt to harm rather than help young men. William Coleman had arrived in Pittsburgh at age fifteen with $5 in his pocket and immediately went to work as a bricklayer by day and a baker's assistant at night. Tom Carnegie ended his education at sixteen. Andrew Carnegie attracted national attention by giving speeches that condemned the value of a classical education.[54]

In the autumn of 1886 Tom was growing increasingly despondent over his lack of control of company affairs. He caught a cold that seemed not to respond to treatment; in the opinion of some of his friends, he appeared to lack the will to live. He died unexpectedly of pneumonia at his house in Homewood on 19 October 1886, one day before his forty-fourth birthday. Neither his mother nor his brother was present at his death. Margaret was seriously ill at the same time and died at Andy's Cresson, Pennsylvania, home on 10 November, just three weeks after Tom. Andy, also in Cresson, was so weak from typhoid fever that his nurses dared not tell him immediately of his brother's death. When he was finally informed, Andy suffered a serious relapse and remained for six more weeks in a darkened room. All of Tom's children except Margaret (known as Retta) were present at their father's death. Retta, a boarding student at New York's Ogontz School, made her way home in time to attend the funeral. At the time, the children ranged in age from nineteen to five.[55]

Lucy Carnegie was her husband's sole legatee in a will dated 14 June 1871. She was to have exclusive guardianship of their children, and she was his sole executrix. Although Tom's will requested that Lucy consult with her brother-in-law and her father, the request was stated "not to be binding" on her. When Tom prepared his 1871 will, he was familiar with his brother's practice of keeping the companies' property valuations down, seriously underestimating earning capacity or market worth. Thus, the companies' stock value was much lower than the real value, which is why Tom wished Lucy to take advice from her father as well as Andy. In 1876 Lucy's father had been forced out as one of Andy's partners. William Coleman had been one of Andy's early heroes in Pittsburgh. Always devoted to Andy's interests, Coleman had given wide support to Carnegie's efforts to obtain credit in his early days, and Coleman's forced departure from the company was widely criticized in conservative Pittsburgh.[56] William Coleman died two years later. Lucy was in an anomalous position regarding her brother-in-law and the company partners.

Andy and another partner, Henry Phipps Jr., immediately advised Lucy regarding the disposition of her husband's shares. The two men were primarily concerned with returning Tom's shares to the companies. Their advice could hardly fail to be self-interested. On 1 November 1886 Lucy Carnegie as ex-

ecutrix sold to Carnegie Brothers and Company most of her late husband's interests in the two companies at their book value, retaining only a 1.5 percent interest that she may have intended as a reserve toward buying a partnership for
her eldest son, Will. She sold her stock for as little as one-fifth of its real value,
with the approval of both Phipps and Andy Carnegie.[57]

Lucy Carnegie lost a large amount of money in the settlement, but by agreeing to what the partners wanted, she retained their goodwill. For at least two
decades afterward she maintained good relationships with these tough Pittsburgh businessmen, especially with her brother-in-law. If Lucy had refused to
sell the stock back to the company, she would appear to have been insisting that
she become a partner in the firm. This course would have been unacceptable
both to the partners and to Lucy—recently widowed and with nine children,
her personal income precluded any thought of participating in future recapi-
talization schemes. Although some female owners of steel mills did exist, managing foundries with the approval of boards of directors, every social and financial imperative of conservative Pittsburgh would have inhibited Lucy from
participating further in the company. She lacked the money and the training
to continue as an active partner. Foreseeing that his widow's interests would
conflict with his brother's aims, Tom Carnegie had almost surely discussed the
implications of such a conflict with his wife.

Despite selling the company stock for less than its full value, Lucy was far
from impoverished, with assets including not only property inherited from her
father but also her husband's house in Pittsburgh and its furnishings and the
Georgia real estate—the Dungeness tract had been Tom's gift to her. She also
inherited from her husband a half interest in Stafford Plantation, which at the
time consisted of little more than a dilapidated frame house, some livestock,
and overgrown acreage. Her luxury items were the steam yacht *Missoe*, valued
at $10,000, and the completed house at Dungeness. Andy gave her promissory
notes to be drawn on the company that gave her a settled income for the next
six years.[58]

After her husband's death, Lucy worried about her oldest son, Will. Captain
W. R. "Bill" Jones was the superintendent of one of the Carnegie steel mills and
a family friend, serving as one of Tom's pallbearers. Jones offered Will Carnegie
a job, and on 29 October 1886 Lucy wrote,

I am deeply grateful for the kind words and good advice you gave my son Will,
and think the place you suggest the best of all places for him. I would like very

much to have him go to work *at once* by Monday at farthest—time hangs heavy on his hands and it troubles me to see him unsettled. You understand of course I am anxious he should be made to *work*—just as hard as any stranger would have to; and no favors shown just because he is my son; if any let it be for his youth and inexperience. If he ever needs a word of advice or warning, I will take it as a personal kindness to both his Father's memory and myself. . . . Some time when passing, I would be glad to have a talk to you about my boy.

My husband had great respect and esteem for you.

Jones died on 28 September 1889 of injuries suffered in an explosion of a blast furnace at the Edgar Thomson Steel Mill. Greatly moved by his death, Will Carnegie gave up any further thought of working in the mills.[59]

In November 1886 Lucy left Pittsburgh for Dungeness, her first winter there as a widow. Two of her sisters, Nan Bradley and Florence Coleman, came to make a long visit with her. Convalescing from his bout with typhoid, Andy Carnegie also spent a large part of the winter at Dungeness, arriving in mid-December. The Florida press noted approvingly that the area's "beautiful climate" seemed to agree with him. Lucy was described as "petite, dark, pretty and surprisingly young looking," considering that she had borne nine children.[60]

In 1891 and 1892 important changes in Pittsburgh affected Lucy Carnegie and her administration of Cumberland Island. The annual payments of promissory notes by the company would terminate in 1892, and she needed a full-time manager to handle her Cumberland real estate. In the spring of 1891 she made William E. Page, the tutor for her youngest sons, manager of Dungeness.[61]

Soon after Page assumed his new responsibilities, the Dungeness estate began to take on an increased grandeur. Visitors were treated with intimidating courtesy, laborers received better living conditions, stricter accounting techniques appeared, and indecorous subjects were avoided.

Page was not at first expected to handle Lucy's income since Carnegie Brothers and Company served as a "family office" for her. Lucy held an open account at the company, which kept track of her personal affairs: monitoring dividends and income, verifying and paying bills, updating insurance, balancing the books, and the like. Company accountants would have viewed as impertinent or indiscreet any interruption of this work by the young former tutor. He would handle only administrative tasks.

On 1 July 1892 Carnegie Brothers and Carnegie, Phipps were consolidated with Henry C. Frick's coke company into Carnegie Steel. Andrew Carnegie

held a 55.33 percent interest; Frick and Phipps each held an 11 percent interest; and nineteen other partners, including Lucy, each held a 1 percent interest,
with the remaining 3.67 percent held in trust to be divided "among deserving
young men." On the advice of her lawyer, Willis F. McCook, who also served as
counsel to Carnegie Steel, Lucy bought six lots on Pittsburgh's Fifth Avenue
from the Union Land Company, an entity that included Frick and Andrew W.
Mellon. The newspapers reported that an eight-story office block would be
built on the acreage and that the building had "already been leased to allied
Carnegie manufacturing interests for one hundred years." The lease terms
were described as "peculiar" but very liberal to Lucy Carnegie: Carnegie Steel
would pay an annual rent equal to 5 percent of the building's cost. Just before
10 June 1892 McCook sent her the lease contract, although the reorganization
into Carnegie Steel had not yet been formally announced, writing that Frick
was so anxious to get the office building started that he had already begun to
evict the tenants in the present structure on the site.[62]

Construction started on the fifteen-story steel headquarters in 1893 and was
completed in 1894. The steel frame of the new Carnegie Office Building was
allowed to stand unfinished for one year to demonstrate the use of steel as a construction material, and Carnegie Steel did not move into the building until
1895. Carnegie Steel's lease on the land was intended to provide a source of income for Lucy, her children, and her grandchildren and to serve as a financial
umbrella for her Cumberland Island property.[63]

In 1895 Lucy began an overhaul of the administration of her Cumberland
Island properties, worried that she was spending too much money on them. She
evidently asked James C. Campbell, her auditor at the Carnegie Company, how
much money she had to invest. With the 1 January 1896 maturity of her eight
H. C. Frick bonds, $8,000 had been deposited with Carnegie Steel at 6 percent
interest, and her credit balance was now $709,672. In addition, she held com-
pany notes totaling $600,000. Lucy considered withdrawing money to pur-
chase mortgages, but Campbell warned that she not only would be disappointed in the interest rates but also would have to pay a state tax.[64]

Lucy wrote to McCook, expressing anxiety over her island building expenses. Lucy felt that each member of her family should assume a fair share of
household expenses on the island. Between 1896 and 1902 Page worked out an
accounting system by which Lucy's children could not only build their own
homes on Cumberland but also live in them without adding to Dungeness expenses. By 1902 Page had perfected bookkeeping methods to accommodate

family needs. At the same time, entries on the Carnegie Company books would reflect Lucy's true expenditures for all her properties, of which Dungeness was only one. Page wrote to an auditor, Robert A. Franks, "A word about our book-keeping method here. We have many open accounts with the family and the employees, and numberless petty cash transactions, all of which I keep in my own books. Pay Rolls, and such petty cash items as are chargeable to Mrs. Carnegie, I pay to myself by check on Mrs. Carnegie's account with the Fernandina Bank at the close of every month. All payments whatever for Mrs. Carnegie are therefore made by check and voucher."[65]

Franks and Lucy Carnegie viewed the Dungeness Estate as an investment. Page possessed not only a clear head for figures but also a strict sense of fairness in distribution of costs. Four of Lucy Carnegie's children built houses on Cumberland, often living in them for lengthy periods. Each residence maintained a small permanent staff. Lucy Carnegie and Page expected family members residing on the island to share the estate bills, and each house was charged for the benefits it received from the estate. By following Lucy's instructions as well as plans sent to him by various offspring and their architects, Page became in rapid succession Cumberland Island's clerk of the works, chief personnel officer, harbormaster, superintendent of farming operations, commissary agent, banker, surveyor, cartographer, and bookkeeper par excellence. Page's accomplishments eventually combined to make him the prime mover of the Dungeness estate (the name for all the Carnegie properties on Cumberland Island). Page was Lucy Carnegie's single most important employee, and improvements to Dungeness were largely his work.

For efficiency, Page purchased supplies and materials in wholesale lots, and this bulk buying became increasingly cost-effective. As Plum Orchard, Greyfield, the Cottage, and Stafford were constructed, they began to fill up with their various occupants and their children, staff, and guests. The Carnegie family discussed the possibilities of opening their commissary to the public. Page sought the opinion of Samuel C. Atkinson, Lucy's Georgia lawyer, on certain legal points:

We have been talking over the feasibility of establishing a Company Store. . . . Our object in establishing such a store would be to purchase at trade prices for the benefit of the family, and to furnish supplies at reasonable prices to our employees, the latter not being a charitable undertaking but an effort to make our laborers content with their wages. One plan I have suggested is to organize a corporation to conduct a general mercantile business under some such name as 'The Cumberland Supply Company.' The stockholders would be members of the Carnegie family. . . . Such a concern, so far as I can see, would be able to purchase goods at trade prices.[66]

Atkinson replied that although he saw no legal difficulty with the plan, he foresaw some disappointment in St. Marys, which received a great deal of trade from estate employees. He suggested that entering into competition with St. Marys merchants might generate a feeling of retaliation resulting in efforts to raise Lucy Carnegie's tax bills: "I have heretofore insisted while representing you in tax matters that there was no income-yielding enterprise at Dungeness, but on the contrary, everything was an outlay and contributed largely to the support of the local trade in the county." Page responded that the Carnegies would drop the idea for the present.[67] Atkinson's warning was regrettably effective. At this time, High Point, with its general store and its post office, was becoming a prosperous small community. The Carnegie venture would have helped to create a marketplace, one of the basics of permanent community living. A town might have developed at Dungeness. Instead, it remained resolutely noncommercial.

The U.S. Steel Bonds

By 1889 Andy Carnegie had decided to retire from active business. He made various offers to syndicates that might be interested in buying the company. Over the next ten years, however, there was no one who could afford to buy Carnegie Steel Company. In the interim Andy, as chief partner, and all junior partners worked toward cutting product costs, streamlining transportation, and undercutting other companies' prices. The result was a mighty organization that resembled, in the words of the contemporary press, nothing so much as an independent government within the United States of America. The 1892 Homestead Strike, in which thirteen men died and many more were injured, focused the astonished world's attention on the Carnegie partners, and the company began to come under closer scrutiny. Andrew Carnegie was called the "archsnake of the age."[68]

Henry Phipps and Henry Frick's efforts at making the great steel company more efficient resulted in increased tension between Frick and Carnegie, which all the partners knew would reach an ugly climax. Frick resigned from the steel company on 5 December 1899, placing the other partners in a difficult situation regarding their personal loyalties. Frick subsequently sued Carnegie, drawing international attention as the truth about the company's real capitalization was revealed. Both litigants were bitter and abusive. According to John K. Winkler, "Belaboring each other like enraged washerwomen, the great leaders of industry furnished an edifying spectacle. The quarrel and its consequent revelation of the stupendous profits of the Carnegie Company, hitherto suspected but never proven, attracted world attention. Here was the responsible manager of the firm swearing that the value of its assets as of 31 December 1899, was no less than a quarter of a billion dollars—ten times its capitalization."[69]

When Carnegie finally capitulated in 1900, public discussion was at its peak in editorials and sermons on both sides of the Atlantic. Carnegie Steel Company and Frick Coke Company were amalgamated into the new Carnegie Company, with a total capitalization of $320 million. Andrew Carnegie received stocks and bonds worth nearly $175 million, Phipps received almost $35 million, and Frick received more than $31 million. Lucy Carnegie's allotment had a value of just under $5 million.[70]

In the wake of the furious quarrel, Andrew Carnegie decided to sell his interest and to devote the rest of his life to philanthropy, which had always figured prominently in his personal credo. No single person could afford to buy out Carnegie, but J. P. Morgan formed a syndicate that did so in late January 1901, creating the U.S. Steel Corporation. The momentous transaction was announced to the board of Carnegie Steel by 4 February. The deal included an important stipulation on which Carnegie had insisted: "For his own personal holdings in the company and those of George Lauder and of his sister-in-law ... only first mortgage, 5 percent bonds would be accepted. Carnegie had no intention of becoming the major shareholder in the new corporation." Lucy received nearly $6.2 million. In March 1901 Campbell wrote to Page, "I congratulate Mrs. Carnegie on the consummation of the deal which will be so advantageous to her."[71]

This sudden influx of money to Lucy's account had important effects for her island economy. Much more money was available with which to build. One of the first signs of change was that Lucy was asked to move her account with Carnegie Steel. In 1899 Page had been promoted to become the general business manager for all of Lucy Carnegie's properties. Lucy's business affairs were interwoven with her house-building program and her Cumberland Island improvements, which, in turn, correlated with the interests of some of her children. Auditing these accounts taxed Campbell's professional capabilities, and he had begun to urge Page to consider consolidating Lucy's affairs. From Campbell's point of view, Page was more than able to handle the books for Lucy Carnegie's properties. Page finally agreed to pay all her bills except for those relating to the Homewood house. In July 1899 Campbell wrote that he felt it more practical to pay Lucy's bills from Dungeness, where "she spends most of her time," suggesting that she was beginning to consider Cumberland Island her home, whereas Dungeness previously had been merely one property among many.[72]

After 1 April 1901 Lucy Carnegie's account was handled by the Hudson Trust Company in Hoboken, New Jersey. Page sent quarterly statements to the holding company and took on the added responsibility of explaining Lucy's income to her. In 1901 her monthly average income was $33,958.35, not all of which was spent on Dungeness.[73]

A resident of Pennsylvania who owned property (including the Carnegie Office Building) there as well as in Georgia, Florida, and New York, Lucy's complicated accounts were audited by carefully chosen professionals, to whom Page originally had reported, rather than them reporting to him. In 1913 a new auditor was selected, and the accounting system was revised. Page would now keep the accounts, and the auditor would prepare financial reports, sending copies to the Hudson Trust Company, Lucy Carnegie, and Page. Part of Page's bookkeeping involved making certain that the Dungeness account showed no income receipts that could be interpreted as profits. In 1912 more than $5,000 a month was needed to support the estate and all its houses and roads.[74]

TEN

The Canon
of Domesticity

Home and Family Values

*B*y the 1850s the crusade for the ideal family home had become a central feature of what historians have come to call the American Victorian outlook. Abolitionists, temperance advocates, religious leaders, family reformers, and housing promoters argued that society was evolving to a higher level of civilization and that the American family home was the key instrument of progress. A new image of the middle-class American family home projected a cult of domesticity in which the household should serve as a refuge from the outside world, a fortress designed to protect, nurture, and strengthen the individuals within it. Religious tracts and magazine articles promoted this glorified image of the sacred home.

Advice manuals pictured women as morally superior to men, biologically suited to counteract the disruptions caused by the expanding and transient American economy in which people moved frequently. Advocates of the canon of domesticity most often pictured the house in a protected rural or small-town setting, nestled in a grove of trees, with children playing, unattended, in the front yard. Whereas the eighteenth-century middle-class family had been tied together by common needs and economic necessity, the nineteenth-century family ideally was bound by feelings of warmth and intimacy.

The Carnegies fully supported this doctrine. Andrew and Tom Carnegie and their mother, Margaret, were fiercely loyal to one another and upheld the values of home and family. When Andrew Peebles, the architect who designed the new Dungeness mansion, ventured to suggest that perhaps the carved legend "The Hearth our Altar; Its Flame our Sacred Fire" was too long for the fireplace, Andy Carnegie emotionally warned Peebles to shorten it only at his peril.[1]

The domestic ideal encouraged specialization of gender roles. Women were expected to dominate at home. While paying careful attention to the moral and educational needs of the children, mothers were to become masters of the household. The domestic obligations to bear and rear children, sew, cook, clean the house, wash, preserve food, and nurse the children remained. The new domestic ideal had considerable appeal for middle-class women because it elevated them in status over working-class women who had to labor outside the home. The mid-nineteenth-century home was considered the center of power in society. Mothers were respected authority figures and arbitrators in the middle-class family.

How much of the new domestic ideal was believed? Generally speaking, behavior fell short of the mark. Lucy Carnegie, however, took the idea of home very seriously. She gave $10,000 to each child upon his or her marriage. Although the amount was generous, her gift was somewhat qualified: the money was supposed to help the son or daughter prepare for the serious responsibilities of married life—specifically, to build a house. Victorians identified the construction of a house almost literally with home, children, and family. Lucy apparently viewed the money as an advance on her children's inheritances, a common philosophy among Pittsburgh families of the Carnegies' acquaintance. For example, when Will married, he was required to repay the money plus 10 percent interest. She may have intended to forgive the loans if they were not repaid, but some sort of formality accompanied each "gift." These gifts figured significantly in the shape of things to come on Cumberland Island.[2]

The canon of domesticity tended to view both the industrial world and unfettered nature as inimical. Nature was to be regulated into paths, schedules, fences, and comfort-serving devices.[3] The differences between the Greenes' and the Carnegies' points of view are illustrated by the two great Dungeness Houses. Both were designed for family living, and both families planned to entertain others. Both had observation towers. From the Greene-Miller mansion, occupants could view St. Marys Inlet, through which sailed vessels that could endanger the Greenes' safety. From the tower of the new Dungeness, however, the Carnegies could sit and gaze at a panoramic view. With privateers and smugglers, the Millers faced a menacing environment; the Victorians saw the same coastal features as a spectacle designed to give them pleasure. It became their duty to reorganize the natural landscape.

With the 1901 creation of U.S. Steel, Lucy Carnegie had become a very rich woman. Unlike others among "Carnegie's millionaires," as they were called, her lifestyle did not change greatly, and she generally continued to live and travel much as she had before, except that she now had a great deal more money. Lucy began to spend all her winters at Dungeness but departed the South in late April or early May. By 1892 this pattern became an accepted one. She would spend her summers renting private seaside homes in Manchester, Massachusetts, or on Long Island, New York. She also stepped up some aspects of her Cumberland construction program, building houses, roads, and sports facilities. Finally, she increased her children's allowances. Prior to his December 1890 marriage, Will's allowance had been $75 per month. Now, however, each of her sons would receive $15,000 a year, a very large sum by the standards of the time.[4]

Lucy's program of "Dungeness Improvements" first applied to Dungeness House, then to its immediate grounds and support systems, and much later to upgrading the game preserve. Not all the new buildings were separate homes; some buildings were called "Additions." In 1896 William E. Page wrote a long letter to James C. Campbell, explaining two items to be added to the Dungeness account: the house would receive a two-story Addition measuring forty feet by fifty feet, and more extensive porches would replace the present porch. Both new porches and the Addition were to be of shell concrete, "commonly used in this region." Furthermore, balconies would be added to the second story, and alterations were to be made to the roof and third story. Page wrote that all of these changes, with the exception of replacing the present wooden porch, which was rotting, were additions and improvements to the property. The dining room in the Addition featured a parquet floor made from wood from Dungeness's century-old olive trees, signaling the demise of the olive groves.[5]

In May 1896 a swimming pool building was added to the main Dungeness grounds. In addition to the pool itself, which was for use by men and women of the "family," the building was to contain a gymnasium, dressing rooms, a billiard room, a small gun room, card rooms, and four sleeping rooms: "The designation swimming pool therefore hardly suggests the extent of the work." This building was soon called the Casino, not entirely facetiously. It served as an informal residence for Lucy's unmarried sons and their bachelor guests as well as for physicians on duty at Dungeness.[6]

Lucy Carnegie was a good businesswoman. The construction of the Addition and the Pool House clearly indicated that she considered the Dungeness Estate a capital investment.[7] In 1896 she was adding recreational and service capabilities to Dungeness, seemingly for her children but with an eye to the property's future sale. She not only added considerably to the dimensions of the house itself but also constructed separate support facilities of every conceivable nature in the area around the house, hiring Peabody and Stearns of Boston, one of the country's most prominent architecture firms, to supervise the work. The firm had begun to adopt the Italian Renaissance style made fashionable by novelist Edith Wharton, who taught new American millionaires to admire European antiquity in her 1904 best-seller, *Italian Villas and Their Gardens*. The Palladian Italianate style came to dominate American gardens and parks. Peabody and Stearns not only redesigned Dungeness and its surrounding gardens but also in later years submitted Italianate designs for Dungeness's cemetery vaults and crypts, dairy buildings, and stables.[8]

In December 1890 Will Carnegie married petite, vivacious Martha Gertrude Ely of Cleveland at a large and fashionable society wedding in Cincinnati. Will and his bride began to visit the island more frequently. Sometime between their marriage in 1890 and their 1891 decision to live at Stafford Plantation, Will and Martha must have chosen the quiet life of a cotton planter, a decision that pleased his mother. Will and Martha Carnegie moved into the existing Stafford House, which they remodeled with some of the money provided by his mother. Will became Stafford's manager on 1 May 1892.[9]

The first Cumberland Island residence to be constructed by one of Lucy's children was Plum Orchard, which appeared in the accounts in 1898. George Carnegie was about to marry fashionable and wealthy Margaret Thaw of Pittsburgh. As his wedding present, his mother intended to assist him with a home on Cumberland Island. Lucy told Peabody and Stearns that she proposed building a "simple house on this island, on a site about eight miles from here," with a cost limit of $10,000. On 1 December 1898 Page described the project as "fairly launched."[10]

At the beginning of 1899 Page asked Peabody and Stearns if the firm wished to submit drawings for a "simple" cottage to be built at the opposite end of the pergola at Dungeness. By "simple," Page explained that he meant a house that would cost between $5,000 and $6,000. Thomas Morrison Carnegie Jr. (known as Morris) had married Virginia Beggs of New York in 1898. They were considering a cottage. In July Page wrote to Morris that work on his new house could not begin before August because scheduling problems had arisen from construction already in the works at both Plum Orchard and at Stafford, where an addition was to be built. Work so progressed on Plum Orchard during 1899, however, that in August Page wrote to George, "The portico of your house is the finest thing in Georgia. After work hours the men gather in front to drink in its beauty, and their manners are noticeably improving."[11]

During 1900 the fourth residence (and third new construction) was planned at the site known as Gray's Fields. Designed by MacClure and Spahr of Pittsburgh, this was a house for Lucy's daughter, Margaret (Retta), and her husband, Oliver Ricketson Sr., who had married on 19 November 1891 in Pittsburgh. He had suggested that they look for a deepwater landing on Cumberland where he could tie up his seventy-foot schooner. In the records, Greyfield, as it soon came to be called, was almost always referred to as Oliver Ricketson's place, and he may have paid for its construction. Greyfield was the first Carnegie house on Cumberland Island to utilize a Georgia vernacular. It was a long, narrow two-story frame house with double galleries, simple and well ventilated, very much in the spirit of Robert Stafford's house. Page told the architects that the Ricketsons wanted "the absolute simplicity and farm house aspect of your original sketch."[12]

Greyfield's construction evidently had already begun when Stafford House and its new addition caught fire and burned to the ground in January 1901. Will and his wife moved temporarily into a four-room tabby structure that stood directly behind the old Stafford house. Page, who was in charge of coordinating the various building programs, wrote to Will later in the year that Lucy Carnegie had directed that the Ricketsons' house should have precedence over the reconstruction of Stafford Place. In this case and probably in many others, mother and manager worked together to create a harmonious building schedule so that there would be no quarreling within her family, another example of the Victorian belief that families ought to be happy.[13]

Lucy did not require all of her children to build homes on the island. Andrew Carnegie II married but never built a house on Cumberland. While his mother was alive, he and his family stayed at Dungeness House when visiting the island.[14] Two sons, Frank and Coleman, neither married nor built homes on the island. They and their friends had access to the Casino.

William Page and the Grange

William Enoch Page was born on 7 August 1862, at South Danvers, Massachusetts, the son of Enoch Paige and Ruth Devoll Paige. Somewhere around 1888 Page became a teacher in Chicago for a year, and by 1890 the Carnegie family employed him as a tutor for the youngest boys. In the spring of 1891 Lucy Carnegie made him manager of Dungeness. Self-disciplined and well-educated, with degrees from Haverford College and Harvard University, he was the perfect choice to execute her views on domestic harmony. The reference books Page kept at Dungeness indicate that he was an unusually intelligent, resourceful, and well-read man with a background in law, the ministry, and accounting. For many years he served as a member of the Board of Managers of the First National Bank in Fernandina, a position that gave him a responsible footing in commercial life on the Florida mainland. Page found a home with the Carnegie family, and they in turn respected and admired him in spite of his formality. One of Florence Carnegie Perkins's sons, Coleman, remembered Page as "the one who parted his hair in the middle and spent Grandmother's money for her."[15]

Beginning in 1891 Page lived on the first floor of Dungeness House in the large bedroom with its own bathroom, next to the gun room. In 1901 Page received a legacy from his half-sister, Julia, who had died a year earlier. He had long been engaged to Eleanor Tucker Bickford, a Chicago journalist, and informed Lucy Carnegie of his intention to marry whenever he could promise his fiancée a home. On 20 September 1901 Lucy loaned him $12,500, secured by stock in the Fernandina Dock and Realty Company. Construction on the Grange, the last large house built on the Dungeness Estate, began in 1902 and was completed by the end of 1903, by which time a total of $25,483 had been spent on the house. On 23 November 1903 Page and Bickford married in Waukegan, Illinois, and she joined her new husband on Cumberland Island. William Page lived in the Grange for the rest of his life.[16]

Estate Staffing

It is not known how many people were employed in building the new Dungeness, and it is not known how many employees the Dungeness Estate had in 1886. General Davis managed his Dungeness property himself with the aid of his gardener. At that time a gardener meant a specialist whose responsibilities were similar to those of a modern landscape designer. Hiring someone who was familiar with the property was a priority of Tom Carnegie. He wrote Davis that he would like to retain Davis's gardener, a Frenchman. Davis was obliged to tell him that unfortunately his man had fallen very ill, and it was feared that he would not live.[17]

When the Carnegies first arrived from Pittsburgh, they lived rather simply, although they probably brought some nursemaids to help with the children and laundry. The names of any such staffers have not survived, however, and

Dungeness's first recorded employee (as opposed to a day or seasonal laborer) was A. Marcou, who went "on wages" on 11 November 1886, shortly after Tom Carnegie's funeral. Marcou may have previously served as General W. G. M. Davis's gardener and been promoted by Lucy to act as a temporary superintendent.[18]

Tom Carnegie had set up local banking arrangements long before his death. Because the family got off the train in Florida, banking and credit arrangements were conducted more efficiently in Fernandina. H. E. Dotterer, a shipping agent who worked for the railroad, became Carnegie's local banker. Carnegie Brothers sent sight drafts to Dotterer, and Dotterer paid small bills and kept accounts, sending them to the business in Pittsburgh. Tom paid larger bills himself. When Dungeness's manager needed to meet a payroll, he drew on Dotterer, and Marcou's bills were rendered to Dotterer.[19]

When Marcou disappeared from Dotterer's accounts, he was replaced by Leopold Beugnet, who became Dungeness's first manager on 4 March 1887 and remained for four and a half years. Born in Belgium, he was about forty years old when he began work on Cumberland Island. Newspapers described Beugnet as a florist "in charge of the work" at Dungeness. Beugnet had previously acted as a contractor in clearing the grounds and in road building around Dungeness House and the beach. One of his first duties as manager was to draw up a contract with O. H. Wade, a well-drilling contractor from Jacksonville. Dotterer gave funds to Beugnet for salaries and food, so he must have lived on the island, overseeing labor. By February 1891 Beugnet's work for Lucy Carnegie was drawing to a close. Sums paid to Beugnet indicate that specific projects were being completed. His departure is significant because it marked the beginning of a new administrative era overseen by Page.[20]

Management of the Dungeness Estate in the 1880s differed considerably from the plantation administration that immediately preceded it. Whereas plantations sent agricultural products and livestock to market, the Dungeness Estate was not intended to make a profit. Estate administration called for a hierarchy of employees, of which the most important was the manager, a paid specialist. The manager recommended contractors, engineers, captains and other seamen, stablemen, lumber specialists, and unskilled general labor. In rural communities the manager was apt to hire his relatives and friends, which gave him considerable power. Plantations rarely give such freedom to their superintendents. Typically, plantation owners gave their superintendents and overseers all the necessary orders but retained hiring and firing duties.[21]

In the 1880s Fernandina contained a substantial group of French and Alsatian immigrants who, anxious to leave Europe after the Franco-Prussian war, responded eagerly to advertisements of emigrant societies at that date boosting northern Florida. Often the Europeans tended to hire their compatriots.[22] Apparently Marcou, the first superintendent of Dungeness Estate, and then Beugnet, the second one, hired Frenchmen from Fernandina.

At the Dungeness Estate the manager was responsible for hiring a labor force that would ensure self-sufficiency. On islands, a ferry and a responsible captain are very important, so immediately below the manager in the hierarchy of Dungeness Estate's administration was the captain of the Carnegies' steam yacht, *Missoe.* The first captain was William Thompson, who first appears in the records on 12 January 1887. He was replaced in 1888 by Captain George W. Yates, an Englishman. Yates hired (subject to the manager's approval) mates, crew, and stokers when necessary. For Lucy's ocean-going steam yacht, *Dungeness,* which required the services of seventeen men, a Japanese man served as cook and steward.[23]

Directly under the jurisdiction of the manager was the workforce for building roads and bridges, clearing forest and brush, carpentry, and building. The Dungeness Estate's high standards made labor hard to obtain. On 4 July 1901 Page wrote that he could not find enough skilled carpenters in St. Marys, Fernandina, Brunswick, and Jacksonville and would have to go as far afield as Savannah, Atlanta, Chattanooga, and Cincinnati to find workers. Prior to 1901 Page repeatedly placed advertisements in those cities' newspapers, and he specifically recruited black labor in the Brunswick and Savannah areas.

Hiring responsible workers was a problem. Not all were mentally stable. Dungeness employed a night watchman, who was authorized to carry a revolver. On 28 June 1902 Levin Dougherty, the night watchman, shot and killed Preston Davis, a kitchen assistant, for substituting salt for sugar in Dougherty's coffee. Dougherty was described as white, age twenty-eight, swarthy, and with bright eyes of "an odd staring appearance." He had often complained of a roaring or buzzing on the left side of his head and had been heard to curse and threaten blacks on the estate. Dougherty fled to Florida, and the estate offered a $500 reward for information leading to his arrest. He later returned to Camden County, turned himself in, and was tried in 1903 and convicted of the murder.[24]

After the first of various homes and farm outbuildings were constructed, their superintendents were responsible to the manager. Each of the homes the

Carnegie children built on Cumberland had its own superintendent who lived year-round in a separate dwelling near the main house. Family men were often sought and were accompanied by their wives and children. At Stafford Place and Plum Orchard, the first manager was E. B. Powers, who served from roughly 1887 to 1889. Powers was succeeded by Captain John Dilworth, a Civil War veteran and native of Camden County. A gentleman, Dilworth had earned the Carnegie boys' respect and awe. To them he represented the best in rural southern values, contrasting favorably with the vulgarity and materialism of American political and business life, which had become identified with the city. Dilworth became a good friend to the young Carnegies, teaching them how to ride and hunt. Will Carnegie succeeded Dilworth as the manager of Stafford Place.[25]

Another Camden County man, Natty Pratt, served as acting superintendent at Stafford Place prior to 1916. He was described as being capable of doing fairly good work as a carpenter but very lazy. Pratt was succeeded as Stafford's caretaker by Henry Miller and his wife, Bridget Finnegan Miller. Finnegan had emigrated from Ireland to the United States, where she obtained several good positions as a cook. Lucy Carnegie invited Finnegan to come to Cumberland Island, where she met and married Miller, a local man. Bridget evidently first worked at Dungeness House, for she later described to her sons the routines involved in getting the large kitchen organized to accommodate the meal schedules of its various guests.[26]

Greyfield's caretaker was Joseph C. Whitby, who moved with his family from Philadelphia after losing his arm in a sawmill accident. With his financial compensation, Whitby purchased an orange grove near Sanford, Florida, which was lost in the big freeze of 1894–95. In 1900 or 1901 Whitby became caretaker at Greyfield and worked there until his death five or six years later. His wife remained until around 1920 as a housekeeper-cum-manager, overseeing the day-to-day administration of the house and grounds. Greyfield also had about ten black male workers, who boarded at Dungeness Black Quarters.[27]

Victorians were troubled by the implications of hiring someone to look after family duties. The triumph of domesticity, which equated the family hearthstone with the center of the universe, found it troubling to employ a stranger "to sweep up the hearth's ashes." For a family such as the Carnegies, who strongly valued home and hearth, hiring domestics was a serious matter. From the beginning of their domestic life at Dungeness, Lucy and Tom Carnegie believed that they were creating an estate with its own special qualities as a legacy for their children. Andrew Carnegie had congratulated his brother and sister-in-law on establishing a "house," by which he meant a family dynasty that would reign calmly and beneficently over its lands for many decades. Lucy, a middle-class woman, would have expected to do her own housekeeping, which she did early in her married life.[28]

In 1886 the Carnegies hired a housekeeper, Catharine Rikart. Beugnet may have suggested hiring Rikart, a French national who was born at Mulhouse, Alsace, in 1831. She appeared on almost the very first payrolls and remained at Dungeness until her death in 1911. As housekeeper, Rikart would have been charged with keeping household accounts and supervising the female household employees, and she may have shared cooking duties with Lucy. Not knowing anyone on the mainland, Lucy depended greatly on the advice of her sister, Florence; Rikart; and Beugnet.[29]

In the 1890s Lucy Carnegie employed only white women for service within Dungeness House, using New York employment agencies to find suitable servants and paying for their transportation from New York to Georgia. Many of these women were French or Irish; some were German or Scandinavian. Female European immigrants often entered domestic service in U.S. cities, partly because it was considered excellent training for farm girls and partly because the new arrivals usually lacked other skills needed in the United States at that time. In some cases, prospective employees contacted the Carnegies. For example, on 11 September 1912 Edward Carr of Newport, Rhode Island, applied for a chauffeur's position, explaining that he would be out of work when his present employers went south for the winter. Seasonal employment was common among domestic workers as wealthy families migrated among large houses.[30]

In 1913 Dungeness's house staff totaled thirteen: three laundresses, one seamstress, one butler, three cooks, three chambermaids, and two waitresses. Nearly all were from New York or New Jersey, and although race was not given, their names and places of origin indicate that all were probably white. The laundresses were Margaret McCabe, Marguerite Connors, and Jennie Anderson. The three cooks were female: Augusta Seiffert, first cook; Clothilde Gratianette, second cook; and Mary Lyons, third cook. Although the rank of first cook nearly equaled that of chef, there were important distinctions. Chefs were men and demanded much higher salaries, a small staff of assistants, and regular days off. Dungeness would have been unable to cope with a chef's requirements, but female cooks were more willing to oblige. The head cook would have met with Lucy to discuss the availability of certain foods and to plan menus. Assistant cooks would have handled special needs, such as meals for children or for elderly guests or breakfasts for young men leaving before sunrise to hunt. All three cooks were expected to help with dinner parties. Dungeness House hired two women for the dining room in 1913. First waitress Delia Carslan served each guest individually from hot serving dishes. Second waitress Lydia Herterych usually worked behind a screen in the dining room, quietly giving instructions to the pantry to ensure a constant supply of hot food. Carslan cleared between courses, while Herterych sorted plates, glasses, and silver before passing them through the pantry for washing. Nothing in the household accounts indicates that the domestic staffers received days off, although they occasionally had access to a carriage for transportation to the beach for swimming. The white female servants lived together in the old Davis cottage, with Catharine Rikart acting as a general housekeeper.[31]

On one occasion, Lucy's daughter, Nancy, who had married James L. Hever in 1903 and had four children, was billed for a separate three-person staff consisting of a nanny, an assistant nursemaid, and a personal maid.[32]

At Dungeness House, probably around 1911, a man named Thomas Hall served as the steward for the gymnasium and the pool, which were more frequently used by men than by women. Another male household employee was Albert Domingue, a butler, who earned $75.00 per month. Lucy Carnegie did not customarily employ a butler, and Domingue may have been employed for a special reason, perhaps for a long winter house party. John Beatty earned $50.00 each month, although the records do not specify his job. His relatively high pay indicated that he held some sort of specialized position, perhaps serving as a combination footman and valet. Visitors generally did not bring personal servants with them, and the arrival of a "gentleman's gentleman" would have been awkward. However, since all cleaning, pressing, and mending of men's clothes necessarily had to be done at Dungeness, some sort of valet service would have been required.[33]

For about three years starting sometime in 1901, Joseph Brock served as a game warden, known locally as a "woods-runner." The woods-runner rode or walked the estate boundaries to note changes in the habits of wildlife or signs of human invasion. Brock's duties included watching for trespassers and poachers who violated the posted hunting preserve or Georgia game laws. Brock and his family lived at Brick Hill in a one-and-a-half-story house with a big porch.[34]

Page made Gilbert Roberts foreman of the "colored hands" for the entire estate. Page probably did so after receiving advice from local whites that black laborers would work better for a black foreman, an antebellum concept. However, Page was apparently unwilling to categorize employees by color. Under his administration, employee lists were racially undifferentiated.[35]

For some, working at Dungeness was an education in urban technologies and estate management and served as a springboard to better employment. English-born Richard Bealey served as head superintendent at Dungeness prior to about 1901. When he died, the position passed to his son, Sam, whose duties included overseeing the dairy, the poultry yards, and the vegetable gardens. He gave orders about what to slaughter and cook. In addition, he ordered supplies for the commissary. Because part of his job was to improve the quality of the livestock, he once attended the St. Louis Exposition to purchase good dairy cows. Sam's brother, Will, was in charge of the power plant at Dungeness. After 1916 Will Bealey was in charge of a new power plant in St. Marys, and Sam Bealey took a position of responsibility at the Jekyll Island Club.[36]

As was the custom for superintendents at the time, Page posted work regulations. Accepting the necessity for some men to work their own acreage on the mainland, he expected them to request permission for absences. In 1901 Page posted a notice in the men's dining room that stated that absenteeism would not be tolerated: "The only 'reasonable' excuses for absence without permission are: Arrest; Summons of court after leaving the Island; Disabling illness of self; Dangerous illness in family." Unreasonable excuses were: "'The boat left me,' 'Business,' 'Had to work on my place,' or 'Sickness' of self (or others) falsely alleged." Another notice read, "Our employees have no choice of a boarding-house and must be assured peace and quietness at their meals in this room. No person is wanted here whose conduct is offensive to his neighbors. Quarreling is offensive. Profane language is offensive. Loud abuse of food and service is offensive. Proper criticism of food and service, to W. Bealey or at the Office. 'Chronic kickers,' who cannot help it, must find employment elsewhere."[37]

Occasionally there was a death, and then it was left to Page to pick up the pieces of a life dissolved. In 1911 one Rose McMahon died while in service on Cumberland. On 8 May Page received property of hers "left at Dungeness." It consisted of an Emigrant Industrial Savings Bank Book, $102.01 in cash, and miscellaneous jewelry. Rose's sister and administratrix, Bridget McMahon, wrote to the Carnegies, "I could not thank the Family all for how nice the[y] have been Paying all the expences[.] It was more than I expected any strangers to do."[38]

Considerable social segregation existed among island employees. Working for the Dungeness Estate had serious drawbacks, such as social isolation. All lo-

cal workers, black and white, took the Dungeness workboat back to the mainland every Friday afternoon and returned to the island each Monday morning.
Male workers lived in racially segregated dormitories. Wives and children were
permitted to visit the island only in the summer, when the Carnegies were
away. During these two- or three-week visits, white family members stayed in
the White Quarters. The wives and children walked or rode to the beach, where
they swam, fished, went seining, or hunted for shells.[39]

Employees were not expected to use the land in the same way or at the same
time as the Carnegies and their guests. In 1916 Page was obliged to reprimand
Captain Yates for his son's behavior. Willie Yates had used his father's car without permission, hunting on the estate with friends from the mainland. Captain
Yates broke down and cried, admitting his inability to control his son. But Page
understood that Cumberland's pleasures were too much for an adolescent boy
to resist—unused land, absent owners, the opportunity to show off to one's
friends: if hunting and fishing were so invigorating for the young Carnegie
men, why blame Willie for showing off?

Social segregation was not totally rigid. The white staff had use of a small
recreation hall in which dances were held and visiting evangelical preachers
sometimes spoke. Emma Roberts, working as a nursemaid for the children of
Greyfield's caretaker, met Sam Bealey, her future husband, at a Christmas
dance held in the hall. In 1975 an elderly woman who had worked as a waitress
at Dungeness in 1905, shortly after immigrating from Sweden, reminisced
about a grand Christmas party, with music and dancing. Everyone danced with
everyone, and she had danced with Andrew Carnegie.[40]

At the beginning of his tenure, Beugnet treated the whole estate as one unit
for payroll purposes. His salary was the highest, at $100.00 monthly, followed
by Max Rival, a contract carpenter, at $74.25 per month and Eugene Barratt,
among Beugnet's assistants, at $29.00 per month. Three years later, Beugnet
had divided the payroll account into two separate groups, estate and house. In
1890 Dungeness employed twenty-three men and women, and in July of that
year Beugnet was responsible for a total monthly payroll of $307.57. Eighteen
of the employees were paid from the estate account, and five were paid from
the house account. The five house employees and their monthly wages were:
Virginia Packard (possibly the laundress), $10.71; Rikart, $15.00; Camel
Gowan, $4.50; Chance Johnson (possibly the coachman), $15.00; and Page
(then the children's tutor), $30.00. In 1891, after Page had become manager,
both Johnson and Packard received raises, Johnson to $20.00, Packard to

$12.00. Johnson was black, as was Packard, judging from the pay scale. Although no race was designated, the eighteen people on the estate payroll who earned considerably less money were probably black.[41]

By August 1896 Page had instituted a new accounting system, with three payroll accounts: the house account had seven employees earning a total of $130.00 per month; the farm account paid fifty-three employees a total of $665.37 each month; and the Addition account included seven employees who received $505.60 per month.[42]

Taxes

Working as he did for Lucy Carnegie's interests, Page danced a delicate quadrille with Camden County's tax assessors. Regarding "undeveloped land," he could not see eye to eye with them. Even though roads and outbuildings were being constructed, he believed that lands classified during Reconstruction as wild land were still undeveloped. In Page's opinion, building roads and a new house for the game warden and cutting trails did not constitute improvements, and he failed to see why the land should be assessed at a higher rate. Page did not deny that Dungeness Estate had received many improvements, but he saw no reason to advertise them to the Camden County assessors. County officials, however, saw that Dungeness's "wild land" use was not that of impoverished agriculturists and acted accordingly.[43]

Page reacted with genuine dismay when he received a notification of new assessments from A. B. Godley on 16 April 1897. Godley informed Page that a grand jury had raised the assessment for Lucy Carnegie's properties to more than double the 1896 assessment. Page sought the advice of attorney Samuel Atkinson, who settled the matter by having a little chat with the chairman of the grand jury.[44]

The problem reappeared in 1906, and Page wrote to Harry Dunwody, Atkinson's partner, that when Dungeness made improvements, the estate was doing Camden County a favor: "Our neighbors on the mainland feel that Mrs. Carnegie should pay increased taxes as she increases or improves her property. Mr. Atkinson [in 1897] successfully took the ground that the property is not used for money-making purposes, and a tax upon improvement would be a discouragement of the same, and would diminish her employment of the people of the county."[45]

Mechanization and Hydraulics

Getting sufficient water was the Carnegies' first need. An 1882 newspaper article said that household water came from rainfall caught in immense cisterns. A second source of water was the river, near which a Rider's compression engine pumped a continuous stream of salt water to the house. Both freshwater and salt water were forced through the house by an Ericson hot-air engine. These resources evidently were not enough, because a deep artesian well was drilled in 1887. The Carnegie well became one of the finest on the coast, 680 feet deep and 6 inches across, with a daily flow estimated at eight hundred thousand gallons. Water rose 51 feet above ground. The local press stated that the well cost $2,200, although the estate accounts indicate that the actual amount was considerably less.[46]

Beugnet's enthusiasm for the new well was expressed in the following letter to Mrs. Carnegie:

Madame

Enclosed I forward contract on account of Artesian Well up to date as requested. The well is flowing at the rate of 500 gallons a minute or 720,000 gallons in twenty-four hours. The quantity of water is all that is wanted and greatly sufficient for all actual [sic] or future use. Only the pression [sic] is not strong enough to elevate the water in the building or for proper distribution on the grounds. . . . I have commenced work on a fountain in circle fronting the mansion. House, [illegible], and livestock should have the benefit of the water—also the grounds and groves.[47]

Most of Cumberland Island's groundwater comes either from a deep-lying limestone aquifer known as the principal artesian aquifer (Coastal Plain aquifer) or from a shallow water-table aquifer. The Carnegie well apparently was the first to tap the Coastal Plain aquifer. In 1889 and 1890 High Point neighbors drilled two more wells and had nearly as much success as did Lucy Carnegie. Both new wells were bored for the use of the New Cumberland Island Company's resort hotel and cottages, and water rose 12 feet above the surface for both wells.[48]

In 1897 Page inquired of a Pittsburgh manufacturer about water filters: "We use rain water collected from roofs (shingled) of buildings to supply bath rooms, laundry, etc. . . . When our rain water supply gives out we use water from surface wells. This water is clean enough for general washing purposes but . . .

gives clothes a reddish tint from the presence in the water of very finely divided sand [which] contains tannin from palmetto roots." Stone filters were apparently installed, because in August 1898 Page wrote that after five months of use at a pressure of forty pounds, the "filter stone" had become thoroughly impregnated with silt, and he ordered new "cylinders of stone." Page's orders show that new 4- or 6-inch surface wells were dug from time to time, although their locations are not always clear.[49]

Page began searching for technologies to support a mansion that could accommodate large numbers of guests. In May 1900 Page received a water purification plant from New York's Industrial Water Company. Page wrote enthusiastically of its performance,

> Our plant is the smallest yet made, having a capacity of 1000 gallons an hour. The cost of operating the plant is between 3¼ and 3¾ cents per 1000 gallons. The plant requires the attention of one man a few minutes only every day, and for one or two hours once in every four or five weeks. . . . We operate two electric power plant boilers with the purified water and find it works perfectly. There is absolutely no scale, and the only deposit is one of soft chalky material in very small quantities, which is easily blown out.[50]

In 1901 the water purification system began to give trouble. Page's analysis of the problem and suggestions for its solution show considerable hydraulic and chemical knowledge. In a subsequent letter to a chemist testing water at Dungeness, Page explained that he had arranged for the boring of a second artesian well and that it was a potential source of power: "We may deepen the artesian well to get power enough for [an] elevator and other purposes, or we may have to put in a balanced hand car. Although our pressure is small the supply of water is so great we had hoped [to find] some way of running a small car by it." Page subsequently consulted with J. J. Ball, a Jacksonville steamfitter who was working on the Pool House, and the two men devised a better solution:

> Since writing you in June we have decided to put up a water-tower which will materially change the conditions for running our proposed elevator. The tank will hold about 10,000 gallons and the foot of it will be at least ninety feet above the elevator valve. Water will be brought to [the] valve through a four inch pipe about 400 feet long, and straight except for the bend at [the] foot of tower. This pipe will also supply water for house, but the drain at any one time will be slight. The exact rise of car will be 23′6″. A car 3′ × 6″ will be large enough. Its running

should be as noiseless as possible. One outside door will swing, and we want an automatic sliding door. We prefer to have a car frame of wood or iron to be paneled here.

By September 1896 Page had accepted the elevator proposal of Boston's Whittier Machine Company. There would be landings in the basement; on the first floor, nine feet above the basement; and the second floor, twenty-three feet, six inches above the basement.[51]

In 1896 Page wrote to W. E. Caldwell and Company of Louisville, Kentucky, soliciting a bid on an all-iron water tower and tank. He also asked for a statement on the cost differential between iron and cypress tanks. Caldwell's proposal for a steel tank was accepted on 6 October 1896, but in 1901 Page had the tank replaced with a cypress tank, stating that the steel had rusted excessively.[52]

Dungeness House had a telephone system. In the autumn of 1896 Page ordered fifty dry batteries and fifty pounds of pure sal ammoniac for charging batteries, supplies needed for the telephone system. The mansion was rewired in the summer of 1897, and electric fixtures were installed at that time. Page wrote that an electric plant was going to be installed during the following year.[53]

On 6 June 1898 Page wrote to the Niagara Falls Acetylene Gas Machine Company that he would like to try a small "ten light machine" in preparation for installing a large machine to replace the "gasoline gas outfit" presently in use at Dungeness. On 7 July 1898 Page ordered one "40 light" machine with thirty-six special carbide burners, "enough for one month."[54]

The decision to install an electric plant was made sometime in April or May 1899. Page decided that the new building for the electric plant would be located about one hundred yards northeast of the stables. In June 1899 Page inquired about a pump large enough to fill a ten-thousand-gallon tank one hundred feet high in four to five hours. The pump was to operate while the lighting plant was at work and would be placed in an engine room with a feeder pump and a heater. By 30 November 1899 Page referred to the lighting plant as "installed and working," with a marble switchboard in place. The General Electric Company of Atlanta furnished the electric plant as well as a steam plant installed at about the same time. The electrical system generated power for three to five hundred lights, had two circuits, illuminated all buildings at Dungeness, and provided a storage battery. General Electric was also asked to provide lighting plants for two other houses on Cumberland Island. Since construction on Greyfield had not yet started, Stafford and Plum Orchard are the likely candidates.[55]

Preservation of food is as vital as growing it. At the beginning of the Carnegie administration, coastal schooners delivered ice from Maine to Dungeness's landing. This was an old practice, common to many coastal Georgia communities. Other methods of preserving foodstuffs included salting, drying, pickling, and smoking. With some successful technologies in place by 1900, Page became ready to try a refrigeration plant. He wrote to the Remington Machine Company in Wilmington, Delaware, asking about prices for "an Ice-making and Refrigerating Plant for a private place, to be delivered within two months after order . . . to be set up on Cumberland Island and started under your supervision. . . . We have in our employment a mechanic thoroughly competent to set up the plant."[56]

The manager was responsible for safety and fire prevention training. The water and electrical system provided a sophisticated means of fighting fires. In the event of a blaze, a general alarm would sound, "repeated short blasts of the power house whistle." The engineer was to report immediately to man pumps at the power house, while the assistant engineer was to run to the hydrants nearest the fire. The foreman of laborers was to detail men to assist at hydrants, to fetch ladders and buckets, and to get the reserve hose. If the fire started in any of Dungeness's dwellings, the labor force was ordered to call all occupants, to close all doors and windows, and to use extinguishers. Fire cocks—water pumps—were to be used only when the extinguishers were exhausted. Page's regulations reminded workers, "Use no more pressure and no more water than necessary. Remember that water does more damage than a small fire." If fire started in the stables, everyone was expected to lead the horses out after covering their heads with coats or sacks: "Tie horses to fences or trees, or put them in closed lots. Remember, a loose horse runs back to the burning stable." When fire was beyond control in a building, Page instructed the men to waste no water on it until the adjoining buildings were protected. His directions concluded with orders to "Shut off all artesian valves." Engineers and foremen were required to learn the position and uses of all Dungeness fire equipment and to teach their men how to open and close valves, connect and disconnect hoses, use spanners and fire extinguishers, raise ladders, and train hoses on particular spots as directed. Chiefs and foremen were held responsible for transmission of Page's orders to laborers, some of whom were almost certainly illiterate. In effect, Page had created an autonomous fire department.[57]

Social Life

According to Henry James, the novelist who carefully delineated Gilded Age American society, neither hotel nor retreat was secure from the new million-aires and their desire for "conspicuous privacy." Most of them had an insatiable itch to flaunt their belongings.[58] When young, the Carnegie children showed off the island to their friends.

Friends joined the Carnegies on fishing expeditions in nearby waters or the Caribbean, using the yacht. The yacht also transported the Carnegies and their associates to special events, such as parties at the Jekyll Island Club: Lucy arrived there on 16 March 1889 with a group of fourteen people, and during a 1903 visit to Dungeness, Andrew Carnegie accompanied her to the club for a reception and dinner.[59]

The Carnegies' favorite form of entertaining, however, was the house party. Guests were invited to make long visits and included casual friends as well as family intimates. When a party of young people was invited, it was assumed that courtship might result. Sharp eyes in Pittsburgh, New York, Cincinnati, and Cleveland noticed—and gossiped—about who was going with whom. For large house parties, formal evening dinners were normal. Although mothers and aunts gave teas and receptions for their young female relatives in Pitts-burgh, debutantes and their affectations were frowned upon at Dungeness. For many friends of the younger Carnegies, however, Dungeness's charm lay in its informality. Picnics and beach exploration remained the most popular activities.

Because houses on the island were far apart, even the simplest visit called for a ride through the woods. Picnics were a major project. Male guests might ride ahead on horseback, while the women and children would ride in carriages to meet the men at a set place. These journeys provided the happiest memories for out-of-town guests, who had never seen domestic doings on such a grand scale. At almost any time, organized games and sports such as golf, badminton, cro-quet, and tennis were available, and lazier guests were welcomed as spectators. Carnegie family albums contain countless photographs of children riding in carts harnessed to ponies, goats, large dogs, and even other children.[60]

On a darker note, young bachelor visitors sometimes hired a private railway car to stop at Yulee and take them to Jacksonville, where they visited hotels and bars. They may also have visited a famous madam, Cora Howorth, whose girls accommodated well-heeled young men. Her house was one of the best-run in

Jacksonville, and her customers could be certain that nothing would happen to attract police attention.[61]

By 1900–1901 Lucy had become very fat and moved unwieldily. She took up fishing. Her married children having moved away from Pittsburgh, she invited them to visit her during the summers and occasionally visited them. In the winters, her children, grandchildren, and their out-of-state friends came to Dungeness for weeks at a time. An unidentified young woman who was visiting Will Carnegie's wife, Martha, at Stafford in 1898 wrote,

Stafford, Friday, April 1, 1898
Here I am in the sunny south and so enthusiastic over it I can hardly know where to begin.... There was some mistake so the yacht was not there to meet us, but we came over in a large ferry effect which stopped especially for us at the Island.... if you could close your eyes and imagine yourself in fairy land, or perhaps better—at your castle in Spain, you might get some idea of [Dungeness House]. A long lane of white oyster shells leads up to the house. The palm trees with hanging moss meet over this lane.

The house is like a large hotel of white stone with a huge white stone porch in front and palms and lilies and great chairs scattered around. Inside it is superb: winding halls and heavy staircases.... I met Mrs. C. and found her to be a fat motherly kind of woman. Then we had lunch. I nearly went wild when I saw the huge bowl of sweet peas on the table. Isn't it perfect: sweet peas in March! Then Nancy took us around to see the sights. Back of the house is a cottage ... which is used for billiards and with [the] back part a swimming pool. It is larger than the Natatorium in St. Louis, all tiled and large palms sitting around the sides. A regular gymnasium is in the room too and adjoining it a room for the guns etc. for they shoot all the time.... After meeting the family we went to watch them shoot pigeons just in front of the house.

There are about seven Carnegie men and a few visitors and a tutor from the senior class of Harvard who drove us over [to Stafford Place]. He is the tutor for the youngest Carnegie age 19 and these two are the only men I have talked to. Thank heavens all the men leave for a yachting trip on Saturday for I can't talk to men and it makes me feel like a stick.... I am crazy over the place and everything as you can probably see.... It is warm although they say it is cooler than usual.... We are going driving this morning and will pick flowers—just think! The roses around the house are perfect, also pansies and wild violets. How you would love it here.

They have a yacht, a launch, any number of horses, etc.—there has been a regular house party at the Carnegies [at Dungeness] but the people left the day before we got here. I would have written yesterday but no mail left the Island so it was useless. Don't worry if you don't hear from me for it is hard to get letters off of the Island. I am breathing in the most perfect balmy air—and oh if you could have seen the sunset across the water, and through the palms![62]

Camden County and Dungeness

The Carnegies rarely visited St. Marys: Camden County was almost a foreign country. Pittsburgh and Camden could hardly have been more different. In 1890 Camden County had a population of 6,748. St. Marys, the county seat from 1872 to 1922, had a population of 529. In 1890 the various plants of the Carnegie Steel Company in Allegheny County, Pennsylvania, employed in seasons of prosperity more than 23,000 men. In 1907 the company employed men from twenty-six countries and forty ethnic divisions. In one steel plant, notices and announcements were posted in seven languages: English, German, French, Russian, Serbian, Polish, and Romanian.[63]

In 1898 most Camden County residents were still living a rural life. St. Marys, a once prosperous seaport, was stagnating because it was unable to berth larger ships. Its harbor needed dredging. According to F. Graham Blandy, a friend of Frank Carnegie,

It is a deserted place now; but once a stream of life flowed backward and forward along what are now beautiful grass-grown streets. . . . Many of the houses were falling in ruins, and one I noticed was thatched and moss-grown. Large village pumps stood in the center of the streets and old live oaks clustered about the wells. A few whites, but a majority of negroes, greeted us at the wharf and stood looking at me with staring eyes as I took a photograph of them. The warehouse at the dock had long since been deserted. . . . The whole scene was wild and everything was in keeping: the gray moss which hung in profusion from the trees was a fitting shroud for the old city of the dead.[64]

Although St. Marys's vitality was at a low ebb at the end of the nineteenth century, the town certainly did not deserve to be called a "city of the dead." St. Marys in the early 1900s was very poor, and it was still reeling from the Panic of 1893 when it experienced another recession. Although the end of the Civil War had brought renewed vigor to turpentine milling and logging, sawmilling had been St. Marys's most profitable land-based industry for a century. No other industry existed in Camden County. In 1892 a visiting railroad engineer wrote that St. Marys was almost deserted, "with houses and fences tumbling down, with no evidence of the recent use of a saw or hammer, with no industries of any kind, except Dungeness."[65]

ELEVEN

Conflicts in
Land Usage

Cotton Planting Revived

he Carnegies used their island land for commercial purposes in only one instance. Despite predictions that long-staple cotton would never reach its antebellum prosperity, Will Carnegie briefly succeeded in planting and marketing Sea Island cotton.

As early as May 1866 most Georgia Sea Islands were "under the control of the northern men," who tended to give General Davis Tillson high marks for quietly helping Yankees get a foothold on the Georgia coast. New Englanders envisioned a day when "it will become the fashion to take a winter trip to St. Simons for a deer hunt, rather than a summer tour to the Adirondacks or Moosehead Lake." Many Sea Islands, notably Jekyll and St. Simons, did indeed become resorts for northern wealth. In 1866 Senator William Sprague of Rhode Island told the U.S. Senate that he feared the country had lost the great cotton interest forever and that in two years "cotton would only be produced in some gentlemen's gardens." True, output of most southern agricultural commodities—including cotton—did not reach prewar levels until the late 1870s, but by 1880 southern cotton producers were regaining their share of the world market. Consumption was as high or higher than ever before. Between 1891 and 1894, Georgia's production of Sea Island cotton rose steadily, far surpassing that of Florida and South Carolina. The total U.S. Sea Island cotton crop in 1893–94 was 61,052 bales, of which slightly under half went to American spinners and the rest went to manufactories in Great Britain and on the European continent. Between 1894 and 1895 the price of a pound of cotton increased from forty-two to ninety-one cents, a jump of more than 100 percent.[1]

These years coincide with Will Carnegie's tenure as Stafford Farm's salaried superintendent. He began planting Sea Island cotton in 1890, at a time when high prices coincided with his desire to live on the island year-round. Even at the time of his purchase, Tom Carnegie had viewed Robert Stafford's old cotton fields as cleared farmland, with an "aggregate acreage of about three hundred acres [which was] used as pasture for stock, game and fisheries." Tom and his cousin, Leander Morris, fenced the tract's northern boundary, intending to plant the old fields.[2]

Before Will moved there, Planters House served primarily as a sort of hunting lodge. Little money was spent on the property, although its adjacent fields were kept cleared. Some photographic evidence indicates that Frank Carnegie lived there when his parents were building at Dungeness, using it as a hunting camp. Stafford House subsequently remained empty for many years. Leander Morris sold his share in the Stafford property to Walton Ferguson of Pittsburgh, who is not known to have visited the house. Mr. Powers, a Stafford superintendent, pointed out to Lucy Carnegie the Stafford property's value as a farm, recommending putting in more livestock. Robert Stafford's home remained in good enough shape that the Carnegies were able to use it. A new veranda and entrance steps may have been put up at this time.

Shortly after his December 1890 wedding, Will decided to use some of his $10,000 wedding gift from his mother to fix up Stafford as a residence for himself and his wife, Martha. A new kitchen addition may have been built at this time. Will and Martha moved into Stafford House in the early spring of 1893, for his mother wrote in their guest book: "Lucy C. Carnegie. April 13, 1893. First meal and night—at Stafford."[3]

By 1895 Stafford Farm cotton was being exhibited at state expositions: "W. C. Carnegie of Cumberland Island won 1st premium of $25.00 for the best Sea Island cotton display at the Atlanta Exposition of 1895. . . . The Manufacturers' Records says that one of the enthusiastic cotton planters of the south is Mrs. Carnegie who owns a large estate on Cumberland Island, and has made a specialty of raising Sea Island cotton. She has been so successful that at the Atlanta Exposition she took one of the premiums for the excellence of her exhibit."[4]

In 1897 Will ordered a Doig cotton gin. William Page asked its manufacturer for instructions for setting it up, saying, "We expect to use it on the finest grade of Island cotton." On 12 May 1898 Page wrote that the cotton gin was running nicely. Americans soon found themselves undercut by foreign cotton producers, however, and in 1901, cotton prices fell from seventy-nine cents a pound to forty-four cents. Word may have gotten around that the Stafford gin was not being used as much as anticipated, because Page wrote to a Kingsland man that Will Carnegie's "long staple cotton gin was not for sale." New priorities were overtaking old ones. Cotton planting on Cumberland was abandoned for the final time. Will Carnegie was very fond of golf. In 1901 Stafford Farm purchased a steamroller to create a golf links. Page specifically mentioned that the "old fields" at Stafford were to be rolled with the new steamroller.[5]

Open-Range Grazing

After the Civil War, Cumberland natives used most of the arable land primarily for grazing. Old South herders grazed their livestock on the open range without paying for the privilege, a practice that began during the colonial period and was protected by state laws until well after the Civil War. A 1759 Georgia act set guidelines that endured throughout the antebellum period: if animals broke into a farmer's field, his fencing had to meet certain standards for him to collect damages.[6]

The Carnegies were by no means the first to restrict hunting on Cumberland. While ownership of fishing rights and oyster beds had been discussed by the state legislature as early as the 1870s, in 1874 the Georgia legislature passed two special acts, "An Act to prohibit hunting on the lands of another in the counties of Quitman and Camden, and for other purposes," and "An Act for the preservation of game on Cumberland Island, Camden Co., Georgia." The preservation act's preamble declared that Cumberland Island landowners were anxious to preserve its game. Hunting Cumberland's deer, duck, curlew, quail, or other game with dogs or traps would become unlawful.[7]

When the Carnegies arrived, the concept of enclosing livestock remained foreign to Cumberland's cattle herders. Cattle and hogs ran wild, making it difficult if not impossible to improve the breeds. Most cattle were small and scrawny, and hogs were lanky and lean. Nevertheless, mainland and island farmers resisted laws that would require them to fence their livestock. The question of fencing became a lively political issue in many communities in the 1870s and 1880s, and in 1872 Georgia enacted a law permitting county elections on the issue. A degree of class conflict was involved: poorer people who owned no land but had a few head of livestock wanted to let their animals roam at large. When this issue was debated at an 1878 meeting of the Georgia Agricultural Society, an opponent of fence laws asked, "Shall we pass a law that will press upon nine-tenths of the people for the sake of a few nabobs of the country?" Another Georgian declared that a fence law would "oppress the poor and induce the planting of more cotton." Hunting and fishing were important means of subsistence in the Old South, although woods and streams frequently ran through privately owned land. Public access to unimproved land was sanctioned by custom and law: "The right to hunt wild animals is held by the great body of the people, whether landholders or otherwise, as one of their franchises," antebellum South Carolina planter William Elliott wrote ruefully.[8]

Riding

Cumberland horses, called marsh tackies, were small and strong. Stafford may have imported foreign stock in the 1850s, and General W. G. M. Davis was also interested in improving the island horses' bloodlines. Page and various members of the Carnegie family periodically interested themselves in restocking horses and cattle. In 1888 the Jekyll Island Club, which wanted to reduce its herds of cattle and horses, sold some to the Thomas Carnegie family on Cumberland. The Carnegies were passionately interested in horseback riding, which they considered a necessary adjunct to social living, and began to experiment with improving the stock. In addition, two large silos were built at Stafford Place to hold fodder. In 1896 the Carnegies purchased a white stallion that came from the Imperial Stud farms of the Russian czar. On 17 November 1921 Oliver Ricketson Jr., who had been driving horses in the southwestern United States, telegraphed Page from Fort Apache, Arizona, "Please advise Mother at earliest opportunity can buy fine American bred three and four year old mares unbroken for twenty dollars will bring East and break on island." These mustangs arrived on the island in late 1921, and Ricketson took his horse to Greyfield, where, to the applause of admiring relatives and employees, he rode it up the front steps and into the front hall.[9]

Horses required special services. In 1898 Page wrote that he needed a good horseshoer to look after twenty-five horses and mules. The man should be unmarried, able to handle rough iron welding, and able to give his attention to a "small mill containing farm machinery." For these services, he would receive $40 a month plus free board and lodging.[10]

Recreational and Subsistence Hunting

The Carnegies quickly learned a great deal about Cumberland, its weather, and its animal habitats. They fished, seined, went clamming and oyster picking, shot game birds, and hunted. In early 1894 a newspaper article praised the Dungeness estate's beauty, recreational facilities, and large and valuable hunting area:

> Mrs. Carnegie is an enthusiast on most outdoor sports, and has on her island home one of the finest game preserves in the country. . . .
>
> . . . Mrs. Carnegie's game preserve covers the 13 southern miles of the island, which is in some places nearly five miles in width. Most of this land is covered with forest, and the woods abound in deer, bear, wildcat, raccoons and other furred game.
>
> There are thousands of quail about the place, and Mrs. Carnegie has had the place stocked with English pheasants. . . . Few of her guests are able to bring down better bags of game than she, and her daughter and some of the young ladies from Pittsburgh who are occasional guests at Dungeness have attained considerable proficiency with the shotgun, as well as the rifle.[11]

Two native Georgians, John Dilworth and Cray Pratt, introduced the young Carnegie boys and their relatives to overnight camping and deer hunting on Cumberland. Dilworth had been a member of the Camden Hunting Club in the days of Robert Stafford, Phineas M. Nightingale, and General John Floyd. Dilworth now familiarized the Carnegie youngsters with the club's codes. Men who hunted should meet regularly and at appointed places. Any hunter who fired at a deer less than forty yards distant should be fined or reprimanded. No deer was considered hit unless it was killed or blood was seen. Guns must be carefully guarded and cared for because hunters who failed to take proper care of their guns jeopardized the safety of their fellows. Furthermore, some person should always be responsible for examining the guns. If disputes arose over shooting, a method of adjusting the dispute must be found, a role once taken by the club. Hunters should never go out in the woods alone. Proper game to hunt were deer, bears, hogs, feral cows and bulls, wildcats, and turkeys.[12]

The Carnegies hunted by driving the deer, as practiced by the Camden Hunting Club. Humans rode horseback, and dogs were used to run down deer. F. Graham Blandy, a friend of Frank and Andrew Carnegie, wrote around 1898,

> Arriving at Stafford, Mr. Dilworth, the overseer, met us with a most sincere Southern welcome. The dogs came yelping about our heels as eager as we for the hunt. There were about a dozen, some brown and white, others a slate color, and as pretty a pack as ever my eye rested on. Out the gate we went and turning to the

left went on toward the pasture, one side of which bordered a thick woods. Along this Mr. Dilworth rode whistling the dogs in, while we remained out on the road so as to gallop ahead to stands.[13]

Not all guests were expected to hunt. A lady might join, provided she was a good rider. Although the open fields and stone fences of the English fox hunt were absent, grassy spaces and cleared land existed on Cumberland. Children and women who were not good riders could travel in carriages or jaunting carts for an elaborate picnic lunch with the hunters. In season, duck hunting became the sport of choice, and the Duck House was built to facilitate meeting near the sloughs, from which the duck hunters emerged, hot and thirsty, in late morning.

Like many other prosperous young men of the time, the Carnegie boys were passionate about hunting and stalking, viewing them as the real sports. American sociologist Thorstein Veblen, a contemporary critic, believed that the "addiction" to such sports marked "an arrested development of the man's moral nature. This peculiar boyishness of temperament in sporting men immediately becomes apparent when attention is directed to the large element of make-believe that is present in all sporting activity. . . . These huntsmen are also prone to a histrionic, prancing gait and to an elaborate exaggeration of the motions, whether of stealth or of onslaught, involved in their deeds of exploit."[14] The young Carnegie men, however, believed that hunting brought forth the outdoorsman's chief virtues: resourcefulness, independence, patience, and respect for the quarry and its habitat. Seeking to be hunters as a form of preparation for life, they were largely unaware of outdoorsmen who hunted for necessity. Hunting not only was exciting but could transform them into brave and self-reliant men.

The Carnegies hunted on their land, which was posted. To protect their game supply, they prevented others from hunting on their land. On the island, surveyed boundaries were supposed to mark limits of privacy, but neither streams nor surveyed boundaries meant anything to livestock and beasts of prey. Owning enough land that it can be restricted is a sign of exclusivity. Hunting was an old and valuable adjunct to Sea Island life. Cumberland's natives resented restrictions. Furthermore, the existence of game provided an extension of southern antebellum values. "Blooding" (dabbing with blood) a young man who had just killed his first deer was an old social rite and a generational signpost as well as part of "hunter's law." Unauthorized hunting became a problem.[15]

Indigenous prey included deer, raccoon, poisonous snakes, and bears. In 1881 William Bunkley of High Point allegedly killed a six-foot otter. George Nimmick, a houseguest at Dungeness, killed what may have been the last of the bobcats: "1885—March 1st—5 A.M.—Wild cat killed 31 inches long. 19 in. high." Bears were not uncommon, often swimming from the mainland in the late summer in search of food. Frank Carnegie shot a bear in the winter of 1886, and during the 1890s the High Point community occasionally found bears examining the garbage. In 1933 what may have been the last bear on Cumberland got into the chicken house at Plum Orchard and could not be ejected. Observers thought that the bear, a large one, seemed either sick or drunk, perhaps as a result of eating chinquapin berries, which can intoxicate.[16]

In 1898 naturalist Outram Bangs noted the remarkable rapidity with which Florida was being opened up and stated that the railroads running in all directions over the state had played havoc with Florida's deer. He was happy to learn that there was a "tremendous herd of deer on Cumberland Island, about all the island can support, and of course, they are carefully protected."[17]

The Carnegies also imported a number of exotic animals to Cumberland. In 1898 Stafford houseguests Howard Eaton and Edward Lewis Lyon of Medora, North Dakota, brought by rail thirteen elk, three antelope, and one mule deer. Other nonnative species introduced to Cumberland included pheasants, which were a gift from Thomas Sherlock, brother of Bertha Sherlock Carnegie, Andrew Carnegie II's wife; six Adirondack bucks; and live pigeons specially brought for trapshooting, which was first mentioned as a sport in 1898. In 1903 Samuel C. Atkinson sent a pair of male black fox squirrels to Page, adding that a female would soon follow. In 1898 Page ordered two peacocks, four peahens, and a pair of white guinea hens, all intended for decoration rather than for shooting.[18]

Page's responsibilities regarding the game preserve included introducing new stock, restocking existing species, and eliminating competing species. A good deal of his time was devoted to giving or denying permission to hunt on Carnegie land. On 2 July 1896 he denied permission to J. W. Shinholser of the Hotel Cumberland to let parties land at Dungeness from the steamboat *City of Brunswick*, with only a few exceptions. On the same day Page also denied the hotel's Lee T. Shackelford permission to hunt, reminding him that Carnegie employees were forbidden to sell anything or perform any services for visitors. Page did, however, grant Shackelford permission to seine on the beach. Heyward Ravenel of U.S. Customs, Fernandina, received permission to shoot "south of Beach Creek" in 1901 but was asked to mention the matter to no one. Restricting unauthorized hunting and fishing on the Carnegies' behalf led Page into conflict with local custom.[19]

Probably no point caused as much trouble for the Carnegies and the Bunkleys as did the stray cattle belonging to High Point residents. When Carnegie and Morris purchased the Stafford properties in 1882, they paid $9,400 for an unspecified number of cattle, horses, and hogs and some farm implements. Carnegie and Morris thought they were purchasing range stock associated with Stafford's plantation. In 1901 Page wrote to Leopold Beugnet in Fernandina for information on a hunting agreement allegedly drawn up between Tom Carnegie and the Bunkleys in 1882. It was no longer clear to anyone whether the island's free-ranging cattle were descendants of Stafford or Bunkley animals. Page admitted that there had been some attrition of Bunkley cattle: he had given orders to shoot any and all Bunkley cattle found within posted Carnegie land. Page offered to authorize payment of restitution at about $7 a head, but William H. Bunkley's widow, Carrie, would have to sign a release against future losses. She refused to do so, saying that she did not know the exact number of Bunkley cattle ranging south of the High Point–Fordham tract line. A solution was finally found when Carrie Bunkley signed a receipt for the "lost cows" with the proviso that she would be permitted to gather her stock. Page had ordered the installation of a "high fence" between the two properties, and he persuaded Bunkley to approve an insert to the receipt that said that after the construction of the fence, any remaining Bunkley cattle would be shot, with compensation paid. Atkinson subsequently advised that because bad feeling persisted, Bunkley should present an account of and identify any of her cattle that remained on the Carnegie side of the fence: "She can then have her cattle hunted out at once, and there will be no more complaints."[20]

Page was encountering a culture different than his own. In Georgia, fences were erected only to prevent free-ranging cattle from destroying gardens and crops. Planted areas rather than livestock were fenced in. The Bunkleys' representations about their cattle were statements not only about their land but also about their social status, a point of view that Page did not understand.

High Point thieves occasionally shot Carnegie cattle and sold the meat. In such instances, blacks were blamed, and the Bunkleys and the Carnegies drew together to decry the crime and catch the miscreants. Witnesses were generally hard to find. In one case, an anonymous note identified the thief as a white man named Adams from High Point who occasionally worked at Dungeness and who had successfully placed the blame on neighboring blacks. Another case involved the slaughter of a bull belonging to Dungeness. Page learned that the butchered beef had been sold in Brunswick, and Adams was again identified as the culprit. Although a warrant was sworn for Adams's arrest, Atkinson advised Page that the best solution would be to fire the man.[21] Increased competition for game and livestock was leading to violations of the peace.

Fishing, Shrimping, Crabbing, and Oystering

Public access to Georgia's marshes was becoming an increasingly pressing commercial matter. Harvesting Cumberland's fish, crab, shrimp, and oysters had long been an issue between island landowners and off-island poachers. In 1896 the Georgia legislature passed a bill, probably at the request of the proprietors of the Hotel Cumberland, which boasted not only of its deer hunting but also of its very fine oysters and fish. This act sought "to protect the fish, oysters, clams, shrimps, terrapins, crabs, prawns, and other food products in the waters of Christmas Creek and the creeks and inlets tributary . . . and in the marshes contiguous [and] situated between Great . . . and Little Cumberland Island." Henceforth it would be unlawful to catch, drag, or seine for these animals or "to use explosives or poisons for the purpose of killing or catching [them] without first obtaining a written permit." The permit was to be signed by owners of land abutting Christmas Creek. Owners and guests of the Hotel Cumberland were excepted from these restrictions. The High Point settlement evidently wanted to exclude trespassers from its territorial waters.[22]

The Fordham-Shepard Tract

Before his death in 1886 Tom Carnegie had enquired of Silas Fordham what the price would be for his land on Cumberland Island. At that time Fordham answered that he would sell him some land south of Horse Pen Hammock at one hundred dollars an acre. Under cross-questioning on a related land problem in 1892, Fordham described the exchange.

Q. And he would not give it?
A. Well, he said that he was going to have the whole island, and he died very soon after he asked me the price.
Q. Did that kill him, when you asked him?

A. No, sir, I guess not. No, I think if Mr. Carnegie had lived, he would have owned the whole island before this.[23]

In 1870 Silas Fordham and Joseph Shepard bought all of the Cumberland property belonging to Margaret Bernardey Downes and her children, about 3,000 acres known as the Longwood, Fairmont, and High Point Plantations. Fordham and Shepard were Yankee carpetbaggers. In 1869 Fordham, of Trojan County, New York, had arrived in St. Marys accompanied by his wife, Mary; his brother-in-law, Colonel Joseph Shepard; and Shepard's sister, Lettie E. Shepard. Fordham, a substantial investor in real estate, intended to buy up acreage wherever he could. Fordham's local contact was Major Eliaphalet McWhorter, whose wife was a niece of Mary Fordham. In 1871 Joseph Shepard was elected mayor of St. Marys, and he served as the town's customs collector from 1873 to 1881 and again from 1883 to 1887. Major McWhorter succeeded in that post, retaining it until 1891.[24]

In 1876 Shepard sold his undivided half interest in land on Cumberland to his sister, Lettie Shepard, as repayment of a debt to her. She subsequently transferred her interest to J. M. Hunter. In 1890 Silas Fordham and Hunter decided to develop the land, envisioning a hotel surrounded by 125 house lots measuring at least fifty feet by fifty feet and with 2,000 acres for a hunting preserve to be open only to "those investing at High Point . . . Boating, Fishing, and Pleasure unsurpassed." Fordham and Hunter named their venture the High Point Cumberland Island Company and called their proposed preserve a "game and hunting park." The park would begin south of the site of Fort St. Andrews and extend south to include the land they had purchased from Margaret Downes. The high bluff where Oglethorpe's Highlanders and Rangers had once looked over a grassy savannah to the lands of the Spanish dominions was to become Crescent Bluff, with a street called High Point Avenue running along it. To the east were approximately fourteen blocks of house lots. The hotel would be built on the site of the former fort. The residential community would terminate at the site of Abram's Point, and to the south, down to McIntosh Creek, would be the game and hunting preserve. In February 1891 Fordham and Hunter began a process of subdivision. At the beginning of March they advertised lots for sale, and in July the plan was recorded. Hunter and Fordham spent more than $2,500 clearing the land to get it ready for sale. The game and hunting park was an inducement for prospective investors. Had the venture succeeded, the park might have undergone further subdivision and sale.[25]

Greatly surprised by and displeased with the potential appearance of a rival hotel, the Bunkleys challenged Fordham's ownership in 1891, contending that High Point Plantation had not fully been James Downes's property at the time of his death in 1859, and, therefore, he could not have devised it to his wife and children. Fordham and Hunter took the offensive and hired Walter B. Hill, a lawyer with the Macon firm of Hill, Harris, and Birch, to sue the Bunkleys for compromising the success of the scheduled sale. The Bunkleys had known for more than thirty years that they had an interest in High Point Plantation but had failed to speak up until they saw the financial opportunities created by the High Point Cumberland Island Company. Consequently, Hill argued, the Bunkleys were guilty of fraud.[26]

Atkinson represented the Bunkleys. In 1892 the two parties settled, but Fordham remained owner of High Point Plantation. Although he sold a few lots, his company failed. Fordham had testified that he lacked sufficient capital to build a hotel, and the Panic of 1893 scared away future investors.[27] Both the Carnegie and Bunkley families felt threatened by Fordham's development plans.

The Brick Hill Community

The Brick Hill community of black farmers had lived since the 1860s within the tract at Downes's Landing facing Brick Hill River. A few Brick Hill residents had moved to High Point, where there was domestic and service employment at the hotel. Relations between the Brick Hill community and High Point were harmonious, and the two settlements helped one another in emergencies. One Christmas night the Ross family lighted a bonfire. Hermione wrote:

> [Papa] had gathered a great pile of lightwood knots, and when he touched a match to it, it blazed furiously—it lighted up the whole place, the white cottages and hotel reflecting the light. Soon many negroes from Brick Hill came running up the road and joined the hotel servants.
>
> "Lord sabe us, sho' tink de hotel a-burnin. We run so fast us fall down ober one annarrer, but now we here."
>
> From somewhere they brought cotton, made it into balls, and dipped them into kerosene. These they lighted and a thrillng mock battle ensued. We had never seen fire balls used before. It was better than fireworks at home.[28]

Soon two groups were ambuscading one another, one headed by Ross, the other by a hotel guest. Finally drinks were served to the men who had run so fast to help the hotel: "then there *was* hilarity." The distance between the High Point and Brick Hill settlement was about three miles.

The Fordham-Shepard development plans affected the Brick Hill settlement. Silas Fordham knew that the blacks lived there but testified in court that he had very little dealings with them. The Dungeness estate was aware of the settlement but had little contact with it other than hiring some of its men for roadwork and land clearing. Concerned with the possible purchase of the Fordham-Shepard tract, Atkinson wrote to Page that he suspected a need for some fencing around "the small piece of land next to Brick Kiln."[29]

After the Civil War, Margaret Downes and her children resided in St. Marys. She was coming to view her island properties from the perspective of a real estate speculator. Her claim to title depended on the federal government returning the land to her, and she may have been told that accepting a freedmen's settlement at Brick Hill would make it easier for her to sell the rest of the land. Her 1870 deed of sale to Fordham and Shepard specifically exempted an 8-acre parcel lying between Downes Creek and the highland.[30]

In 1890, when Fordham decided to exploit his tract, conditions had changed. Squatters have the right to settle on public land under government regulation with a view to acquiring title, and such had been the case when the freedmen had created the Brick Hill community. Their rights had long been abrogated, however, and the blacks had become Fordham's tenants. When he put his land on the market, the Brick Hill settlement would have to move.

Major McWhorter's 1892 court testimony provides the only extant evidence that a freedmen's settlement existed at Brick Hill during the 1880s: it was in Fordham's interest to make sure his property was classified as wild lands, and McWhorter was asked how he categorized the tract for tax purposes:

Q. Did you not return it with all the balance as Wild Lands?

A. Yes, sir, just as one tract of land.

Q. And in your return, you returned all of this property as the same, or Wild Land?

A. Yes, sir, and including the little piece down at the Brick Kiln, where some negroes live.

Q. Did you refer to that as Wild Land?

A. Yes, sir.

From the time of their purchase, Fordham and Shepard had rented portions within the tract to tenants—all, McWhorter said, persons of color—whose rent consisted of a portion of their crop.[31]

In the autumn of 1890 Brick Hill's residents learned of Fordham's development plans. Mason Burbank had lived at the North End since the mid-1870s, and in June 1890 he had acquired 5 acres at Martin's Fishing Bluff on High Point. In the late autumn of 1890, Brick Hill's residents sent an emissary to Burbank, and he divided the acreage into fifty-by-one-hundred-foot lots, which he sold to blacks. Some of the former farmers went to work for the Hotel Cumberland, while Dungeness employed others. In 1894 Primus Mitchell led a group of men, all of them from the Brick Hill community, in purchasing another lot, on which they established a church that still stands today.[32]

In 1891 a plat and deed were prepared to confirm the location and ownership of the High Point Cemetery. About sixty-five years earlier, Celia Clubb had designated an acre as a cemetery, and North End residents as well as strangers had been interred in this "Old Burial Ground." By the 1880s title to the land had become obscure, and a new deed redefining the acre had to be prepared. The cemetery site was sold for $1 to William R. Bunkley of St. Marys and George H. Fader of Cumberland Island, who would henceforth act as trustees. Furthermore, "they agree that the west segment or section may be used by the colored residents of Cumberland Island." During the 1870s Brick Hill residents had buried their dead near their own community, but they now sought the right to be buried in High Point Cemetery.[33] Their inclusion suggests that longtime residents were beginning to recognize a shared island identity.

TWELVE

Carnegie Homeland

An Imperfect Title

*A*s a result of the 1891 Fordham-Bunkley lawsuit, Lucy Carnegie's lawyers found certain defects in her title to land on Cumberland. William Page and Samuel C. Atkinson consequently set in motion a complicated legal process to eliminate these defects. An 1899 grant from the state of Georgia would quiet her title forever. Lucy's lawyers had researched her title for more than six years and concluded that any future claims by Stafford heirs would prove ineffectual.[1] Certain aspects of her title were deficient, however, and needed clarification.

In 1899 Lucy Carnegie had owned only two tracts on Cumberland. The deed to Dungeness had originally been made out in her name, so no problem existed regarding its ownership. Stafford Farm, however, was a different matter. Lucy was legal owner of a half interest in Stafford Farm as a result of her purchase of Walton Ferguson's half share (which he had bought from Leander Morris). Because she had inherited Stafford Farm as Tom's sole legatee, under Georgia law she did not own the other half interest. Tom's will had been recorded but not probated in Camden County. Furthermore, it was not executed in such a way as to convey real estate in Georgia. Only a couple of clever lawyers would have dreamed this up, but Dunwody was a clever Georgia lawyer.[2]

After the 1896 passage of the legislation restricting fishing privileges, off-island fishermen and oyster gatherers began to harvest from creeks further south on Cumberland. Page, who found it necessary to post streams on Carnegie land, inquired into the legality of such posting. In the spring of 1897 Atkinson and Harry Dunwody examined the law on this subject and were astonished to find that Lucy Carnegie's title to Dungeness Plantation and Stafford Farm might be imperfect. Atkinson perplexedly wrote, "The inquiries made some time ago in reference to the fisheries and oyster privileges of the

Carnegie property on Cumberland Island has led us to an investigation which, at first, seemed quite easy to perform, but we have found it extremely difficult, and the questions have involved matters of grave importance to the rights of Mrs. Carnegie in the premises." The two lawyers found that she did not have the right to control use of Cumberland's waterways and that they were unable to complete a full title search. Although Atkinson and Dunwody were aware of the 1802 division of the two Cumberlands, even referring to it on one occasion, they were unable to determine exactly how Nathanael Greene and Thomas Lynch had acquired the islands. The lawyers thought that Greene's title might have emanated from South Carolina and attributed their failure in proving title to the fact that this part of Georgia had once been claimed by the province of South Carolina—true but irrelevant. Consequently, Atkinson and Dunwody stated incorrectly that Lucy's title was imperfect.[3]

Rather than see their client victimized by unscrupulous claimants, Atkinson and Dunwody advised certain steps aimed at confirming her title, including petitioning the Georgia legislature for relief. The cost of preparing such a petition would be $5,500. Page immediately sent a $500 retainer. The firm prepared the language for a bill to be presented to the legislature. After the act's first reading in the Georgia Senate, it was sent to the General Judiciary Committee. On the motion of a committee member—Harry Dunwody—the bill was taken out of committee and read for a second time. It was read for the third time on 1 November 1897 and became law. The governor signed the act on 16 December 1897, and the provisional grant that quieted her title was published in Georgia at the end of the year.[4]

Such a legislative act had to be tested by a court case in order to become state law. Although she had no dispute with Silas Fordham and he was cited as merely a "party defendant" to the case, Lucy Carnegie therefore sued Silas Fordham in Camden County Superior Court. Fordham was then in his late seventies and apparently did not understand why he was being sued. Page, who found it difficult to communicate with Fordham, made unflattering references to his mental capacities. Dunwody wanted an up-to-date map of Carnegie's island property to submit to the court, so Page engaged a surveyor, E. A. Meader.[5]

Fordham again retained Walter B. Hill as attorney. On 6 August 1898 Hill wrote to Atkinson asking if Lucy Carnegie wished to purchase Fordham's interests on the island: "An army friend of Mr. Fordham, General Catlin, has expressed the opinion that the High Point tract is the best place on the coast for a hospital." Suggesting that federal ownership might be "unacceptable" to adjacent owners, Hill set a possible price of $30,000. The offer was rejected. The Bunkleys offered $5,000 for Fordham's land. Certain that Lucy wanted his land, Fordham again offered to sell her his tract in December 1898. Page's one-sentence answer was haughty: "Mrs. Lucy C. Carnegie does not care to make an offer for the property adjoining hers on the North belonging to Mr. Fordham."[6]

Fordham died sometime in February or March 1899 (even his attorney was not certain when), and Hill, who was one of his executors, thus became a party to the suit. Fordham's 1898 will required that nearly all of his very considerable real estate holdings be sold to finance the legacies with which he wished to favor a large number of people. The test case subsequently proceeded smoothly. No defendants challenged Carnegie's claim. On 11 July 1899 the jury of Camden's Superior Court found for the plaintiff, thereby perfecting her title under Georgia law. The court decreed that all the land described in Lucy Carnegie's original petition shall "be in her legal possession and that she has been in legal possession of the property for a period exceeding fourteen years, and it is further decreed that a grant" be issued to her.[7]

In August Atlanta newspapers reported that Atkinson was in the city to secure the grant from Secretary of State Philip Cook Jr.: "Aside from the natural interest felt in the estate on Cumberland . . . the grant by the state made yesterday is unique for . . . it is the first of the kind to be made under the special act of the legislature governing control of land in Camden County." On 10 August 1899, for a fee of $39.20, Governor Allen D. Candler granted the "immense estate" to Lucy Carnegie.[8]

Lucy Carnegie now had undisputed title to Dungeness estate and Stafford Farm, and the two tracts became as one. Atkinson mailed the perfected grant to Page by 14 August 1899, immediately followed by a bill for $5,000. In his opinion, wrote Page to his patron, the lawyers' work had been exemplary: he recommended prompt payment.[9]

In a related matter, Lucy clarified her children's spouses' status for purposes of inheritance. Since several of her children had married, Lucy was contemplating a trust fund for future maintainance of her island property. On 4 February 1899 eight of her children, all described as residents of Pittsburgh but temporarily of Camden County, signed a deed of release in which they agreed to sell to their mother all their potential interests in Stafford Place. Because of "the natural love and affection they bore their mother," they sought "to further carry into effect the testamentary desires of their father." Each child received $10 to make the release legal. Their signatures were subsequently witnessed by bona fide Georgia residents and recorded in the county records.[10]

Some observers have misinterpreted this deed of release, calling it a matri-archal effort at control.[11] The true reason for the releases was to eliminate con-flict between the inheritance laws of Georgia and those of other states. Lucy was securing the integrity of the Cumberland Island property by preventing her children from dispersing the land to their spouses. It was a significant fac-tor in her thinking.

By the end of 1899 Hill was authorized by the terms of Fordham's will to offer his tract at public sale. Atkinson advised Lucy Carnegie to buy the tract for $6,000 and avoid waiting for an auction. On 18 December Page wrote to Atkin-son that Lucy was prepared to purchase the Fordham tract provided the price did not exceed $8,000. Page instructed the lawyer to act as a straw buyer. There were no other offers to buy the tract, and in July 1900 Lucy Carnegie bought all 3,400 acres of Fordham's land at auction for $6,000, just $1,000 more than Ford-ham and Shepard had paid for the property thirty years earlier.[12]

Burial Ground

Long before Lucy Carnegie's death, all was in readiness for her burial in a Carnegie family cemetery on the island. The idea of a family cemetery was not new, but its evolution into a burial ground on Cumberland casts light on Lucy's changing attitudes. The Carnegies originally had intended to be buried in Pittsburgh: Tom Carnegie was interred in the Coleman plot in Allegheny Cemetery, as was Thomas Carnegie Ricketson, an infant son of Oliver Ricket-son and Retta Carnegie Ricketson who died in 1898. But as Lucy's identifica-tion with Cumberland grew, she decided to be buried on the island. Burial in the Greene family cemetery would be inappropriate, although there is some evidence that she considered it.[13]

On 6 August 1911, after a long illness compounded by syphilis, Lucy's son, Coleman, died at Raquette Lake, New York, at the age of thirty-one. His death caused the family to review its thoughts for a cemetery on the island. Coleman was interred on Cumberland at a site that the Carnegies selected for a family cemetery. At that time the cleared plot lacked decoration and landscaping. The fact that there had been no particular provision for a family cemetery on the island before 1912 explains why the remains of Martha Gertrude Carnegie,

Will's wife, who died suddenly at home in 1906, had been buried in the garden next to Stafford House. She was subsequently reinterred in the new family cemetery.

In June 1912 John Reid of New York City's J. L. Mott Iron Works, which had done a good deal of ornamental work for Dungeness House, wrote to Page that a bronze cemetery gate was being designed at the request of Lucy Carnegie, who had visited him while passing through New York. Page approved the design but said that the width of the gate would have to be increased to accommodate an electric runabout in which Lucy frequently traveled because she had become very stout. If the requisite width was too great for a single gate, double gates would be required. And 1881, the date of the Dungeness purchase, would be part of the gate's design. Page also pointed out that the cemetery wall would have to be at least four to six feet high to keep out deer and cattle. By 1913 the cemetery walls and the double gate were in place.[14]

By 1915 Lucy Carnegie's health had begun to decline. Because of her increasing weakness and mental disorganization, her children decided that she and her nurse, Matilda Loughran, should be taken to the McLean Hospital, a famous private institution near Boston. Two of Lucy's married children, Retta Ricketson and Andrew Carnegie, lived in the area and would be able to look after her. Lucy's final departure from Dungeness was sad. She had for many years proudly worn a nautical cap that dated from her glory days as a member of the New York Yacht Club. She had tremulously agreed to enter the hospital. As she was dressing for the train journey, she placed her sailor's hat on top of her large pompadour. Becoming aware that her granddaughter, Nancy Carnegie, was staring, Lucy began weeping and said, "Oh, child, do not remember me like this!"[15]

During the fall of 1915, two of Lucy's sons, Thomas Morrison Carnegie Jr. (known as Morris) and Andrew Carnegie, suggested to Page that Dungeness be rented for a sum of between $5,000 and $10,000, with the tenant paying operating expenses and electricity. To his credit, Andrew subsequently changed his mind and opposed the idea, quoting a doctor's prediction that Lucy's health would improve. Andrew's opposition to renting Dungeness was echoed by his sister, Florence Perkins. All of the Carnegie children agreed to keep a "lid on expenses."[16]

On 16 January 1916 Lucy Carnegie died of cerebral arteriosclerosis at the age of seventy. Present at Lucy's death were two of her children, Andrew Carnegie II and Nancy Carnegie Johnston, as well as Nancy's husband, Marius E. Johnston, and Loughran. The other members of Andrew's family had influenza, as did Retta Ricketson. Only Nancy and her husband could accompany her mother's body to Dungeness, where Lucy's other children joined them. By this time, the younger Carnegies were residing all over the eastern United States: William and Florence in Pittsburgh; Frank and Morris in New York; Andrew in Manchester, Massachusetts; George on Cumberland Island; Retta in Washington, D.C.; and Nancy in Lexington, Kentucky.[17]

Lucy had signed her will on 15 June 1912, adding various codicils a year later. On 4 March 1916 the will was probated at the office of the Register of Wills of Allegheny County, Pennsylvania. Five of her children—Frank, Andrew, Morris, George, and Retta—were named as her executors and as trustees for two trusts created by the will, the Carnegie Office Building Trust and the Cumberland Island Trust. If any of the trustees were to die, resign, or refuse to act, Lucy's will specified that the next oldest child should assume the position.[18]

The trustees apparently did not fully understand or embrace their responsibilities. On 25 March 1916, just three months after Lucy's death, Morris wrote to Page in an effort to change the clause of her will that excluded her children's spouses from inheriting any share of her estate. Morris envisaged a ten-year trust arrangement, writing to ask what his wife should do if he were to die within ten years. Page forwarded the letter to the Pittsburgh law firm handling the estate, which responded, "We regret to have to advise you that we see no way in which the failure to make provision for the surviving wives of sons leaving children can be altered." Correspondence between Page and Morris in 1916 showed that Morris did not understand the difference between accounts of the estate of Lucy C. Carnegie, for which the executors were liable, and the accounts of the Carnegie Office Building, which was charged with Page's salary and a few incidental office expenses. The costs of running the island were to be paid from income received from the office building but were not chargeable to it. As a result, the individual heirs were responsible not only for the residences in which they lived but also for the enormous Dungeness House. Page also wrote to Morris that because Will was not one of Lucy's executors, he was exempt from financial responsibility for island administration. Page's letter evidently infuriated Morris, who felt that it was unfair that Will was free of the burden of running his share of the island.[19]

The Cumberland Island Trust was to be maintained out of the general income of the Carnegie Office Building Trust, which stipulated that all of Tom and Lucy's children who wished to live in their Cumberland houses could do so without paying rent. All residents would pay the expenses for administering their houses. The heirs were not excused from payment of any sum charged on the books against them: such amounts were to be deducted, without interest, before payment of any portion of her estate was made to that individual.[20] This bookkeeping method was simply a continuation of the accounting system Page and Campbell had used since 1896.

Any of the children who wanted to sell their interests in the island could do so with the written assent of the majority of the others, but no physical division of the property could take place until the death of the last surviving child. This prohibition on physical division would safeguard the rights of those heirs who wanted to continue living on the island in the same manner they had always known. If there was no sale to outsiders and if all the heirs agreed, the five trustees were empowered to divide the land among the heirs and to prepare conveyances for them. If the majority of the heirs wanted to sell all or part of the island, the trustees were empowered to do so, with the proceeds divided among the heirs or their surviving children. Spouses were excluded: none of Lucy's children could transfer their interest to their husbands or wives.[21]

The first charge on the Carnegie Office Building Trust was to support the building. Any income surplus could be distributed among the children. If the Cumberland Island Trust were terminated—for example, by the sale of the island—the office building trust was to continue, with its revenues distributed among her heirs or their surviving children until sale of the building and the land on which it stood. Such a sale could take place with the written assent of a majority of her children living at the time of the sale.[22]

Lucy's island property was not appraised at the time. The Carnegie Office Building was assigned a fictitious value of $1,155,222.45 solely for the purposes of depreciation (although the commissioner of internal revenue allowed this valuation). Johnston and Page appraised Lucy's Georgia personal property at $29,300. Lucy's personal property in Pennsylvania, which consisted mostly of real estate, was assessed at $1,000,000. Her assets in New Jersey were not made public.[23]

An addendum to Lucy's will requested that her children make the following gifts: $1,000 to each of her grandsons; $1,000 annually to her brother, William H. Coleman; $1,500 to Annie Meekin and $1,000 to Patrick Malony, longtime servants; and $1,000 to G. W. Yates, captain of the *Missoe*. Lucy also canceled the remaining $6,000 of Page's debt to her and asked her children to give him $10,000 "in appreciation of his faithful devotion to the interests of myself and my family."[24]

A reduction of Cumberland Island expenses began almost immediately after Lucy's death. By 19 March 1916 Page had begun to let men go, and as extra mules and cows were sold, he planned to dismiss more employees. On 12 April 1916 Page wrote that eight black men remained on the Dungeness payroll but that there would be only five by May. Of the four men still at Stafford, only one would be retained by May. The blacksmith had been let go, as had William Bealey. The income from the Carnegie Office Building rental paid the estate's operating expenses, including Page's salary.[25]

Lucy's will and codicils indicate that the Cumberland Island real estate was foremost in her thoughts. She sought to maintain the huge island property with its magnificent setting and separate residences for the benefit of her children. The income from the Carnegie Office Building Trust was to provide funds for maintaining the island property during her children's lives, until division in kind, or until sold at their request.[26]

Shortly after Lucy's death, members of her family ordered tombstones from Tiffany's in New York. Most of the Carnegies asked for flat stones that would lie directly on the ground, like Coleman's gravestone, but the markers for Tom and Lucy Carnegie were raised, like those in the old Greene-Miller graveyard at Dungeness. The two raised stones now stand alone at one end of the cemetery, their superior height indicating respect. At their feet lie numerous flat stones, indicating proliferation and adoration.[27]

On 27 March 1917 Tom Carnegie's remains were moved from Pittsburgh to Cumberland Island, where his body joined those of his wife; his son, Coleman; and his daughter-in-law, Martha, in the Carnegie family cemetery. Frank Carnegie died unexpectedly of pneumonia in 1917 and became the fifth person to be buried in the new graveyard.[28]

Andrew Carnegie's wife, Louise, wrote of her sister-in-law's death, "The whole family revolved around her, and life can never be quite the same to any of us." In the autumn of 1916, Page sadly wrote to Will Carnegie, "It is terribly lonesome here. When the time of year comes for the houses to fill up, and they don't fill up, you feel it more than in the summer when they have always been empty."[29]

Above: New steamroller for the Stafford golf course, later used for the island roads. Courtesy of Dollie Whitby Mclaren

Left: Four golf caddies at Stafford.

Margaret Thaw Carnegie at golf in 1906.

Left: Remains of a silo from Stafford Farm.
Courtesy of David Rosa.

Below: Fishing at Beach Creek, ca. 1911.
From the Nancy C. Rockefeller Collection.

Martha Gertrude Carnegie ringing bell for golf caddies.

Lucy R. Ferguson and friend at the Duck House, dressed for a cold day.

GAME RULES

The Estate of
Lucy C. Carnegie
Cumberland Island
Georgia

1 No game is to be hunted or shot from an automobile.
2 Only Turkey Gobblers shall be shot.
3 No shore birds, plover or any bird not classed as a game bird, or bear or alligators shall be shot.
4 Open season on duck is governed by the Federal Game Laws. (Closed season on wood or summer duck all year.)
5 Ashley Pond is a sanctuary for all game the year around.
6 No game is to be hunted at night with lights.
7 Guests will please observe the above rules and the following Federal and State bag limits.

Duck	15	daily limit
Turkey Gobblers	2	season limit
Deer	2	season limit

8 Guests will please not hunt with a rifle without special permission.
9 Employees of the families and employees of guests are not to hunt without permission of a trustee, and then only in company with their employer or a member of the family.
10 Fishing in Whitney Lake is closed until further notice.
11 No turtle eggs shall be dug or their nests disturbed.
12 Persons smoking will please take every precaution to prevent fire, especially when riding in automobiles. Put butts out on floor of car.

Game notice.

A hand ferry, thought to have served to cross Lake Whitney on Cumberland.

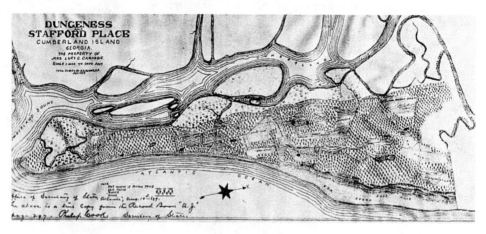

The 1898 Page-Meader map.

The proposed subdivision (1891) by Fordham and Shepard at Cumberland's North End.
Georgia Department of Archives and History, folder 11-1-010.

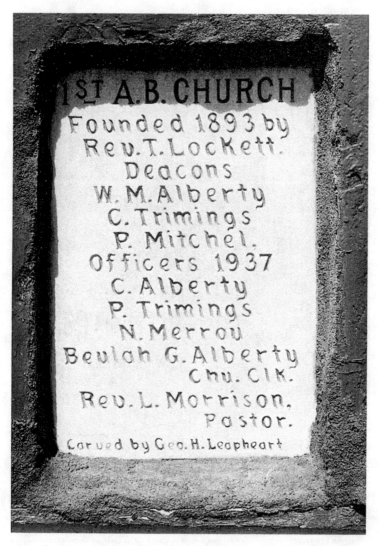

Cornerstone of the First African Baptist church, High Point.
Photo by Anne Wyman.

Left: Decayed grave plot,
High Point cemetery, ca. 1960.
Photo by Roy C. Craven Jr.

Below: High Point cemetery,
cleaned up by descendants.
Photo by Burt Rhyne.

The Carnegie family cemetery upon its completion (1913).
Georgia Dept. Archives and History, AC 69-501, box 57, folder 11-3-05.

Cumberland's Main Road has changed little in 250 years. Photo by Anne Wyman.

The Manager's House (1960s).

The Casino in ruins. Photo by Emily Runge.

Dungeness House burning, 1959. Photo by Homer Hail.

The ruins of the Carnegies' Dungeness. Photo by David Rosa.

An abandoned boat at High Point dock. Photo by Roy C. Craven Jr.

Sand dunes encroaching upon the Duck House.
Photo by Roy C. Craven Jr.

George Merrow and his wife, Audrey Holzendorf Merrow, at their house, High Point, 1980s. Courtesy of George and Audrey Merrow.

Horses cooling off at Stafford Shoals. Photo by Tracy Napert.

THIRTEEN

Planning for
the Future

A Separate Country

*O*n 1901, two of Lucy Carnegie's sons, Morris and Andrew II, dissuaded her from continuing with Peabody and Stearns as she planned further improvements for the Dungeness estate. William Page wrote to the firm that Lucy Carnegie had decided not to proceed with some of her plans. This correspondence shows contention developing between Page and the Carnegie children. Page, the perfect employee, interpreted and followed only Lucy's wishes, and as she aged, she became garrulous and expansive, embarrassing her children. The estate accounts mystified the younger Carnegies, and Page's dignified decorum on the subject annoyed Morris and Andrew, who believed that their mother was spending too much money. In 1913 Frederick Winslow, a young auditor, was invited to improve Dungeness estate's bookkeeping system, and the ever-polite Page agreed to follow Winslow's recommendations, with the result that Lucy's children were charged for certain estate expenses without fully approving them.[1]

Dungeness maintained its own roads. In addition to the Main Road, the estate kept up small but useful routes such as Wreckers Road, an access road to the beach, and various hunting trails, including the Roller Coaster Road. All Cumberland residents benefited from the Carnegie estate's keeping up its share of the Main Road. The estate paid not only for roadwork but also for the board of road laborers. Each Carnegie house supported its own roadways: for example, George Carnegie was charged $100 for crushed shell laid down on Plum Orchard roads, and in 1921 Frank MacLaren, manager at Plum Orchard, was charged $28 for "board of men on wood and roads." Visitors and island residents were not charged for using the estate roads.[2]

Because the estate maintained its own road system, the Carnegies rarely considered upkeep of mainland roads. As early as the 1820s, Cumberland's resi-

dents had been outraged at being compelled to send their slaves to the mainland for county roadwork. Since that time, Cumberland's road system had not
been considered a county responsibility. As a result, Page was reluctant to pay
a Camden County road tax. In 1904 Camden's collector of road taxes sent notices to George Carnegie and five estate employees, T. W. Godley, Henry Miller,
T. G. Brock, G. W. Yates, and Page—evidently the only Dungeness estate residents who could be taxed. Page asked Lucy Carnegie's attorney, Samuel C.
Atkinson, to intervene with the county road commissioner, writing crossly, "Of
course there are no roads in this district on which the county does any work."
Although Page was correct, his reasoning was insular and impolitic.[3]

Dungeness had become increasingly autocratic in its relationship with the
county, calling on Atkinson to arrange special favors on behalf of the estate and
its employees. In 1902 Page asked Atkinson to intervene on behalf of William
Bealey, "an engineer in our power house," who was called for jury duty. Wrote
Page, "It is essential to us that he be excused."[4]

No issue divided Dungeness estate from Camden County more sharply than
a 1926–27 school tax dispute. A special supplementary tax for the St. Marys
Consolidated School District was levied in 1925, and in 1926 the Board of Edu-
cation consolidated Cumberland Island into the St. Marys School District. In
January 1926 Morris Carnegie received four tax notices. Trustees Morris and
Andrew considered the notices unreasonable and protested the consolidation,
but the board refused to change its decision. The new estate attorney, C. B.
Conyers, reminded the school board that "such taxes are not collectible." While
Dr. A. K. Swift, board chairman, acknowledged that Conyers was correct, he
told the lawyer that the school board "will let the people of that district pay
them as far as they are willing to pay them."[5]

Swift next called on Isaac F. Arnow, who was acquainted with Morris and
Andrew through their shared interest in Cumberland's history. Well respected
in Camden County, Arnow wore many hats: proprietor of Riverview Farms,
deputy tax collector, president of the Board of Trustees of the St. Marys Consolidated School District, and chairman of the Camden County Board of Tax
Equalizers. On 15 March 1926 Arnow wrote to Andrew, acknowledging that
Conyers could keep the matter in the courts for a long time but expressing cer-
tainty that once the Carnegies understood how the special tax benefited school-
children, the family members would agree that it was necessary since nothing
had retarded Camden County's development as much as lack of education.
Arnow wrote, "You would have been proud to have attended the exhibition of

the negro schools on March 1." To equalize the school tax burden, St. Marys had abolished its city school system and replaced it with five consolidated districts, each of which would levy a supplementary tax. "The school district in which Cumberland Island lies, has the lowest rate in the county, and by the way, among the lowest in the state," Arnow continued.[6]

Next came the iron fist in the velvet glove. Arnow also wanted to explain "the unfortunate turns the matter of taxes might take." He reminded Andrew that waterfront property had increased in value and stated that it was wiser to increase the school tax rate from time to time than to reassess land values. Because two members of the school board were major county landholders, "None of us wish the matter of taxes in this county agitated any more than we can possibly avoid. . . . If you contest it you will not only deprive innocent children of what they most need at the present time, but, win or lose . . . you open up the matter of values, assessments and rates."[7]

Nonetheless, Andrew and Morris Carnegie strongly opposed payment. Morris wrote that he felt the supplementary school tax was "unjust" because Cumberland Island received no benefit from it. Reluctantly acceding to his client's request, Conyers formally protested the legality of the tax on 20 March 1926, adding that his clients had been unaware of the consolidation.[8]

On 27 March 1926 Arnow answered Conyers in a powerful, two-page, single-spaced letter. Both Arnow and Conyers recognized the value of education for the local citizenry, both admitted that Camden County fell behind, and both welcomed wealthy northerners for the economic benefits they could bring. Arnow intended to pressure Conyers, who sympathized with the county position, urging that he recommend to his clients that they pay not only the special levy but all other regular school taxes. Arnow wrote that the Carnegies' was the only protest he had heard: "The North American Investment Co., owners of Little Cumberland, have paid the tax, as has the Cumberland Island Club and all of the negroes owning property on Cumberland."[9]

Conyers recommended that his clients pay voluntarily, and in April the two trustees obtained a vote from the "scattered heirs" to pay the tax "as a voluntary act." But the matter did not end there. In May Morris and Andrew requested that Conyers petition the Board of Education to have Cumberland Island separated from the St. Marys Consolidated School District. In June Conyers asked if his clients realized that such an action would require the building of a new school, underwritten by the taxpayers of a new Cumberland School District. Arnow's next letter really struck home: in his capacity as chairman of the Board of Tax Equalizers, he asked for the names of all heirs of the estate of Lucy C. Carnegie. The estate had been liquidated by January 1926, and the tax equalizers were now considering taxing all real estate owned by nonresident heirs.[10]

Conyers's letters became increasingly testy, especially when he realized that neither Andrew nor Morris was taking the matter seriously. On 14 June Conyers wrote that the heirs must adjust their tax returns upward: "The courts may be called upon to investigate the possibility that the steel bonds might be taxable in Camden County." The Carnegies paid the supplementary school tax in June 1926, but the ill feeling did not end. Almost fifty years later, Burwell Atkinson, a descendant of Samuel C. Atkinson, remembered that "the Carnegies were well-known to live in a separate county, where they paid separate taxes."[11]

Lucy's Will

The integrity of the Dungeness property had been discussed at least as early as 1894. Lucy's purchase of land in Pittsburgh ensured Dungeness's future as a privately held estate. Her lawyer, Willis F. McCook, understood her wishes in this matter and thought about the future of the Dungeness estate. In 1894 McCook recommended that her executors be directed to sell all her real estate, with the exception of the Carnegie Office Building, so that a distribution could be made to her heirs within a given time. He recommended that the office building be placed in trust to collect the rent, distributing it to her children. Thus, the office building would serve as a financial umbrella for the island.[12]

McCook was less certain, however, on the subject of a future division of Dungeness estate: "The greatest objection I imagine on your part . . . will be in relation to the Island and the home at Homewood. [Homewood] is capable of subdivision in such a way that your children could buy portions of it from the executors thus enabling each of them to keep such portion of it as he may wish. The Island, however, is more embarrassing. It would hardly do to split it up into pieces and yet no one of your heirs could likely afford to own it and keep it up." McCook recommended that Lucy authorize her executors to sell the island, giving them plenty of time in which to sell, so that it need not be sacrificed.[13]

There was no doubt that the Dungeness property was expensive to run. At the time of her death, her holdings consisted of 16,500 acres of land on an island without a bridge to the mainland. The principal residential area consisted of one large mansion with a power plant, service quarters for white and black help, a separate large home for the estate manager, a roomy cottage for the boat captain, stables, a recreational building, and two docks. The property included five other residential dwellings, each with its own support and recreational facilities: Plum Orchard, Greyfield, the Cottage, Stafford House, and the Grange.

Page died on 11 September 1922 after a two-day illness. He had lived in Georgia for thirty of his sixty years. He was buried in the Carnegie family graveyard. Long before his death, his wife, Eleanor, had become a morphine addict, which Page knew but was unable to control.[14] Eleanor, too, is buried in the family cemetery.

Florence Carnegie Perkins subsequently moved into the Grange, and by 1924 all the estate homes were occupied by Lucy and Tom Carnegie's children and grandchildren. Not all of the estate buildings were kept in good repair, however. By the mid-1940s there were more than three hundred structures on the Cumberland Island property, including old stables, swimming pools, an abandoned laundry, doghouses, and poultry sheds.[15]

The trustees had the power to sell the Dungeness estate, and they began actively to seek customers. As early as 1923 Morris had created a file that he called "Sales and Rentals," with inquiries from potential buyers. He was flattered by these requests for information, and, like General W. G. M. Davis, anxious to show the island to interested parties. Nearly all correspondents spoke in terms of a friendly association of like-minded people, anxious not to degrade Cumberland Island. Two New Yorkers, A. A. Ainsworth and Mrs. H. Willis McFadden, were among the most persistent potential buyers. Morris also responded enthusiastically to queries from wealthy Midwestern industrialists, but no sale took place. In 1924 Morris wrote to Ainsworth that since there had been "a family change" (a reference to the 1921 death of George Carnegie and his widow's departure from Plum Orchard), another part of the island might now interest Ainsworth. Morris was seeking a tenant for Plum Orchard.[16]

Although Morris and Andrew told the general public that the land was not for sale, they were eager to show it to interested parties. R. L. Philips, president of the Brunswick, Georgia, Golf Club, wrote to say that he had heard from a New York friend that the Carnegie property was for sale. He sought an option on the Fordham-Shepard tract but was refused. In 1926 Andrew suggested renting the "Brickill Tract" to the High Point Club, thereby enlisting the club's aid in catching poachers: "We of course keeping privilege of hunting & traveling over as usual." J. B. Pound, proprietor of "a chain of hotels in the South," sought an appointment to see Dungeness in March 1924 but failed to appear. The chief reasons for the trustees' failure to find customers were the Crash of 1929 and the ensuing Great Depression. At least as important, however, was their failure to search for purchasers in a systematic fashion.[17]

In January 1936 Morris, with Andrew's approval, had sought advice from a New York law firm, Patterson, Eagle, Greenough, and Day, in connection with his protest of a federal ruling regarding deductible expenses. To answer some of the firm's questions, Morris prepared a long handwritten memorandum:

> Sale
>
> The Island is only saleable as a whole. Like practically all the other Sea Islands of Georgia its value is as a shooting preserve for a rich man or a club. It is also very valuable for its remarkably fine beach, its live oak and pine forests and views over the river and marshes. Its only other value is as a farm, cattle and hog range. The Estate owns between 16,000–17,000 acres. The Trustees make a small income from cattle, hogs, tung oil and such crops as are grown in this section of Georgia. The value of the buildings belonging to the Estate is about $500,000 or more. The Island is well known to be for sale. We value it at $2,000,000 at the low estimate, looking to the future.[18]

In 1936 Oliver G. Ricketson Jr. sent a long open letter to his relatives. He divided his audience into members of the first generation and members of the second generation. The first generation consisted of the four legatees who were directly concerned with Lucy's testamentary provisions regarding Cumberland Island (Andrew Carnegie II, T. Morrison Carnegie, Florence Carnegie Perkins, and Nancy Carnegie Johnston). The second generation consisted of the fourteen children of the members of the first generation, including Ricketson. Ricketson reminded the family of its tacit agreement that Stafford, Greyfield, the Cottage, Plum Orchard, and the Grange each was "home" to the family unit then occupying it. Nevertheless, the houses and their grounds did not legally belong to the occupants, as they knew, and they could not sell or lease the property. He suggested that each of these five houses be called a home place and allotted 500 acres. Dungeness House remained unoccupied. By Dungeness was meant the mansion; the Pool House; all utility buildings lying north and east of the stables, including the servants' dormitory; and the office (the Tabby House). Ricketson believed that if leased or sold, Dungeness Place could become a source of income that would materially affect the ultimate disposition of the island. Ricketson noted that nine of the members of the second generation could not permanently reside in their home places—five married women who would travel where their husbands went and four men with jobs: "Will all of these nine be in favor of retaining this relatively expensive playground rather than receive a direct cash payment from the COB [Carnegie Office Building], for the income of the COB would be paid to them in cash as soon as it is no longer used to defray Island expenses? An actual vote on that question would be very significant."[19]

Ricketson suggested that when the trust terminated, the five home places should be deeded to their occupants. The balance of the property, including Dungeness Place, should become the property of a company to be called Cumberland Island Associates that would have five voting members—the four surviving members of the first generation with rights to Cumberland and trustee Margaret C. Ricketson's two heirs (Oliver and his sister, Lucy Ricketson Ferguson), each of whom would have a half vote. He concluded by pointing out the advantages of his plan: flexibility in regard to getting rid of Dungeness and stability for the householders in the five home places.[20]

Ricketson also facetiously suggested that his family solicit the interest of the federal government: "How about a few political wire-pullings whereby [Cumberland] is sold to the Government as a bird and game preserve and a National Park . . . perhaps . . . with the proviso that all members of the family now living could live there until their death (that would include our children!)?"[21]

Ricketson's long memorandum had been prompted chiefly by the second generation's anxiety. The grandchildren perceived a lack of will and energy on the part of the two surviving trustees. Morris and Andrew never quite reconciled themselves to their mother's will and from the beginning had grumbled about their duties, especially the clerical work. After Page's death, fifty-three-year-old Andrew wrote to his brother, "With Page gone it would take one of us to be on the job continually and I am not fit or willing to assume much responsibility." The talented and opinionated members of the second generation were often seriously at odds with the two trustees, who were hostile to their nieces' and nephews' desire to own homes on the island. In addition to failing to provide leadership in the management of the island property, Morris and Andrew also failed to follow good management practices: Andrew told Ricketson that Morris had "borrowed" $3,000 from the estate funds and that the accounts were a mess. The second generation was dismayed to learn that Andrew, without family consultation, had ordered the sale of all island cattle on the grounds that his physician had told him he had an allergy to livestock. Since open-range cattle grazing helped control second- and third-growth timber on the island, this decision shook the younger generation's confidence in the trustees' administrative ability. Furthermore, Lucy and Tom's grandchildren lacked legal assurance that they would ever own their home places, particularly since the trustees were actively seeking to sell the entire property.[22]

World War II halted island planning. During the conflict, the Coast Guard, stationed at the Duck House, patrolled Cumberland's beaches. All the Carnegie men served in foreign theaters, and all returned. After the war ended, the Carnegie descendants renewed serious consideration of how to divide the estate when the trust ended. Morris Carnegie died in 1944. On 27 December 1946 seventy-six-year-old Andrew Carnegie II, the last remaining trustee, appealed to the Orphans Court, Allegheny County, Pennsylvania, to resign his powers as a result of ill health. Andrew suggested that the Peoples First National Bank and Trust Company of Pittsburgh be appointed to act in his stead. Advised that the bank was not qualified to act as a trustee in respect to the Georgia property, he then suggested Robert D. Ferguson, a Pittsburgh lawyer and vice president of the bank's trust department. Judge Trimble of the Orphans Court accepted Andrew's resignation on 16 January 1947 and the next day appointed the bank as the successor trustee for the Carnegie Office Building Trust and Ferguson as successor trustee for the Cumberland Island Trust. The bank intended to handle the two trusts as one joint matter except that separate accounts would be kept.[23]

Ferguson's appointment marked the beginning of a new era for Cumberland Island. More changed under his eight-year administration than in the previous thirty years of Carnegie trusteeship.

Decay

Ferguson immediately formed a trust committee composed of James D. Harlan of the bank's trust department; Leo Larkin, liaison between the bank's operations and financial departments; and William F. Knox of Moorhead and Knox, attorney for the trustee. The four men traveled to inspect the island in late January 1947. The committee found many tasks that needed immediate attention, the most pressing of which was finding a new estate manager. After residing on the island for forty-three years, Frank MacLaren was anxious to retire to a home he had purchased in Fernandina. Wrote Ferguson, "It appears that the ideal manager should be mature, experienced in similar work and married. He should be primarily an executive rather than a handy man and should have some bookkeeping ability. He should be able to oversee and direct the efforts of others who may be employed for their particular knowledge of such matters as cattle raising or lumbering or other activities as may be undertaken on the Island. He should preferably be a Southerner." On 14 May Ferguson wrote to the heirs that he had employed George Marsden Wallis, formerly manager of Biltmore, the fabulous Vanderbilt estate near Asheville, North Carolina, and more recently manager of a Florida ranch. As soon as suitable housing was found at Dungeness, Wallis's wife, who would act as bookkeeper, and their son would take up residence.[24]

Another important item on Ferguson's agenda was a solution for what the heirs viewed as the most pressing problem. To this end, Ferguson met with family representatives in the Pool House on 19 February 1947. The heirs felt that rundown conditions on the island, although partly attributable to Andrew's old age and illness, resulted primarily from improper care of the island's natural resources. Some heirs felt that timber cutting and reforestation were foremost considerations. Ferguson hired a professional forestry company run by Richard Tift and Herbert L. Stoddard of Thomasville, Georgia, to assess the condition of Cumberland's forests. Tift and Stoddard used the McKinnon map and reported, "After a careful study of the large map of the Island made in 1802, that shows the pine areas of that time, we are impressed with the fact that the present day growths of old pine timber occupy approximately the same areas." They recommended drainage ditches and supervised cutting as well as a forestry-livestock approach to land development that included cattle raising, a forestry program whose profits could be plowed back into purchasing a breeding herd, and controlled burning.[25]

An unexpected, important consideration suddenly appeared in July. Ferguson asked for a family meeting in late summer to determine policy on insuring Cumberland's buildings and water tanks. He felt that additional insurance should be purchased before 1 September, when higher rates set by the state of Georgia were to take effect. The meeting was held in New York on 12 August, and new evaluations were put in place. Nearly all the family members in attendance declared that they feared a forced sale of the island property at a time when the postwar depression would reduce prices: "It would seem criminal to let the Island suddenly come on the market at such a time, that is, the market at large, when such a depression would be an ideal time for the Island to change hands at a private sale." Family members privately talked about the need to get rid of Dungeness Place. The New York meeting provided a forum in which the heirs stated their feeling that Cumberland Island was too great an expense. There were too many buildings, many of them barely habitable or long disused. Roads were inadequate for the automobile age. There was a general feeling that with a new trustee and a new manager, improved administrative policies should be initiated.[26]

Wallis gave notice in October 1948. As the bank struggled to find good superintendents, employee morale sagged. Wallis wrote to Larkin that the major problem facing J. Pat Kelly, the incoming manager, was the quality of estate personnel. Larkin agreed and urged Wallis not only to meet with Kelly but also to remain at Dungeness for a short while to guide him through the estate problems.[27]

Kelly arrived in December 1948. At first he was confident that the estate could become self-supporting "within a few months." Soon, however, the physical circumstances of the job caused him to change his mind: "I have never seen a place so completely run-down and dilapidated as this one is. This applies to buildings, grounds, furnishings and equipment." The labor force was an "inferior type, slow, lackadaisical, and ignorant." "The quarters both white and colored, are unkempt, in fact, filthy." Kelly ordered an immediate cleanup of the living quarters and kitchen. On one occasion, some mainland workmen, stymied by incessant rain, began a poker game in the Pool House. At midnight an estate employee, Aubrey Hayes, began a noisy and inebriated search for Kelly, seeking funds to stay in the game. Kelly was absent on a "poacher hunt" organized by Lucy Ricketson Ferguson and three Camden County game wardens. He returned home, exhausted, at two o'clock in the morning and went to bed, only to be awakened an hour later by drunken workmen threatening one another. Kelly just rolled over and went back to sleep: it was still raining, and he had "a hopeless feeling." Hayes was dismissed in the morning, and the contractor's crew was told to leave the island within thirty minutes.[28]

The manager frequently received mysterious orders from the heirs. Florence Carnegie Perkins sent a telegram to Kelly ordering him to remove hogs from her place, the Grange. At the same time, Lucy Ricketson Ferguson received a telegram accusing her of ordering hog pens, medication, and slaughtering of hogs at the Grange. Kelly denied knowledge of this episode; he could not determine whether hogs had ever been butchered at the Grange.[29]

When Kelly prepared his first set of statements to be sent to Pittsburgh, he wrote, "I experienced the same difficulty in preparing them that I have had with everything on the Island. . . . the typewriter went out of commission. John Hazelton and I after about a week, have it running again. This is done by one person holding the paper in place while the other one . . . pecks out the letter on the keyboard." In a later letter he reported, "It is extremely difficult to do anything with such equipment as is available. I have worked with worn-out patched-up equipment until I see screwdrivers, wooden pegs, rusty nails and wire in my dreams. I am now trying to use a typewriter that has a wooden peg holding it together and a couple of yards of fishing line holding the balance in place."[30]

The bank wrote in July 1950 that because of expenses and pressure from the heirs, it had become necessary to decrease the island labor force. Kelly resigned, and on 25 August 1950, Major Norman T. "Pat" Collett became manager. Among his first requests was for authorization to purchase rain gear for island employees. The estate could provide only two oilskins, three sou'westers, and one pair of hip boots for all employees. Wallis had reported two years earlier that there were no lights in the office, and Collett wrote that there was still no electricity. He had window screens installed in the men's quarters, but the icebox in the men's kitchen would not keep perishables. Since the physical conditions for employment were thoroughly unsatisfactory, Collett was not surprised when employees rebelled at the beginning of October. Caesar Bullard led a delegation demanding wages at least equal to those on the mainland. Collett reported that he had told the mutineers that although negotiations on the subject were possible, the workers could leave if that was their intention. He wrote to Pittsburgh, "The employees, white and colored, had been having life easy— fishing and riding over the Island."[31]

Part of the difficulty was the awful food provided for the employees. Collett urged replacement of the cook, David "Pappy" Livingston, who had served at Dungeness since 1901. This was the managers' third reference to Livingston in eighteen months: he was constantly drunk, he always overstayed his leave on his weekends off, and his cooking was greasy and dirty. But the Carnegies felt a loyalty to many employees, including Livingston. The matter was soon resolved because the unfortunate Livingston became very sick with cancer. The Carnegies paid all of Livingston's medical bills and gave him a $50 monthly pension.[32]

Collett knew it was important to keep island roads open for fire protection and to please the heirs, but he was obliged to repeat again and again that road clearing and building were difficult: "As you know I have a large territory, many emergencies, worn out and inadequate machinery, badly worn transportation and a small . . . crew."[33]

Both Kelly and Collett complained that they spent a substantial amount of their time in bookkeeping regarding house maintenance and provisioning for the heirs, matters that had, in the now remote past, been tactfully and efficiently handled by Page. Family members who visited their houses on Cumberland still expected the manager to purchase their supplies and transport them to the island, especially when they arrived for a long visit. Larkin instructed Collett to inform local storekeepers that they should send their bills directly to the families involved. Although most family members had asked that their Fernandina or St. Marys bills be sent directly to them, in many cases they had forgotten exactly what repairs had been made to their home places or what they had ordered. Payment was often delayed while they indignantly queried the island manager about some minor outlay made months earlier. The manager's answers depended greatly on the reports of the estate employees who had performed the work. Labor turnover was so great that the manager could not always obtain prompt reporting. This turnover was caused primarily by low pay and a competitive mainland job market. Each manager in the 1950s mentioned the pulp mills and the pogey plant in Fernandina.[34]

On 25 January 1950 Ferguson sent the heirs an agenda for the next annual meeting that emphasized the need for stringent cutbacks in island expenditures. At that meeting on 8 February he dropped a bombshell. Ferguson reported that he believed an arrangement could be made for a sale of the Carnegie Office Building to its tenant, U.S. Steel, at the price of $1,750,000: $275,000 in cash and $1,475,000 in first-mortgage 5.5 percent bonds due on the same date as the termination of the present lease. Annual interest on these bonds would amount to $81,125. In addition, the steel company agreed to refund to the holders of the steel bonds a percentage of the personal property, or ad valorem, tax. Ferguson wanted the family members' reaction right away, and he urged the heirs to answer by 1 April. By 1 May it was clear that they were not interested.[35]

Many family members were beginning to feel the trusts had outlived their usefulness. On 14 November 1950 the Carnegie heirs met by themselves to discuss the state of Georgia's plans for Cumberland. The head of the Atkinson Dredging Company, which had just completed a causeway to Jekyll Island, told Ricketson that he understood that plans for a Cumberland Island causeway had entered the blueprint stage.[36]

On 3 May 1951 Ferguson announced that U.S. Steel had renewed its offer, up-
ping the price to $1,800,000, of which $1,500,000 would be issued in 5.5 percent bonds, and agreeing to cover the expenses (up to $15,000) of petitioning
the Orphans Court of Allegheny County. This time, the Carnegie heirs agreed.
By 15 August 1951 their petition to sell the Carnegie Office Building had been
filed. Although the primary source of income for administering the island had
gone, the heirs agreed that the proceeds would go to a successor trust to be administered by the Peoples First National Bank and Trust Company.[37]

Bird Roosts

Popular feeling, especially after World War II, decried private ownership of
such a large and valuable holding as Cumberland. So few people were living
there that it did not take much to whip up popular sentiment against the Carnegies. Easily represented as elitist, their relationships with native Georgians
were increasingly unfriendly. Mainland critics had long said that ownership of
Cumberland Island by rich Pennsylvania industrialists would end Georgians'
access to the island. As far back as the Fordham-Shepard purchase in 1900, local headlines criticized the Carnegies:

MRS. CARNEGIE BUYS ISLAND

RUMOR SAYS CUMBERLAND IS NOW HERS—WILL CLOSE THE RESORT

THE RICH WOMAN WILL MAKE AN IDEAL PLACE OF THE FAMOUS ISLAND[38]

Even when Lucy chose not to buy land, the press criticized her. When the
Bunkley resort was offered for sale in 1901, the *Brunswick Evening Call* wrote,

PURCHASER UNKNOWN—MRS. CARNEGIE NOT A BIDDER

HER ATTORNEYS SAY SHE OWNS AS MUCH OF CUMBERLAND AS SHE WANTS

Tomorrow a portion of Cumberland Island will be sold by the sheriff, to satisfy
creditors of the Cumberland Island Company. . . . There is [a] rumor too which
says that Mrs. Carnegie who already owned three-fourths of the island will purchase the property. . . . If this be the case, one of the most famous watering places
on the South Atlantic Coast will be closed forever to the people of Georgia; for if
the Carnegies buy it, the place will be transformed into private grounds, and
Georgians can no longer get the benefit of the magnificent surf.[39]

The issue of access to the barrier islands became more urgent after World
War II. Highway improvement brought increased traffic to rural areas.

Tourism was beginning to be viewed as an interstate industry. Georgia's coastal counties wanted to use their beautiful barrier islands to lure visitors and their money. In the late 1940s motorists had to pay county fees to cross the area's numerous rivers on narrow, rickety toll bridges or ferries.

The state of Georgia was also interested in exploiting the barrier islands. At the end of World War II, the Jekyll Island Club, a private body organized in 1886, faced a shaky future. Its precarious finances forced its board to consider sale of Jekyll real estate to a private hotel group from St. Simons Island. In August 1946 Georgia Revenue Commissioner Melvin E. Thompson hatched a plan to have the state purchase one of the Sea Islands for use as a public park and persuaded Governor Ellis Arnall to appoint Thompson to head a special state beach park committee. Proponents downplayed the probability that purchase of the island would have to be through condemnation—that is, the state's power to seize property for public use. By creating an atmosphere of public "agitation for acquisition," the state could declare that it was prepared to proceed "by condemnation or otherwise." Only a few scattered editorials condemned the takeover as "unjust, confiscatory, undemocratic, and un-American." Georgia acquired Jekyll Island by condemnation in 1947 for $675,000. Thompson, now Georgia's governor, announced that the island "had become a playground that now belongs to every Georgian." Within weeks, hundreds of convicts were brought to the island to begin the process of preparing it for state use.[40]

In the early 1950s the Scenic Highway Committee of the Commissioners of Roads and Revenue, Glynn County, published a booklet entitled *The Challenge of Georgia's Coast.* The authors fulminated against the continued existence of enormous, privately owned island estates that served primarily as bird roosts. The committee declared that "the Rip Van Winkle era of Coastal Georgia must pass" and that the area's "tremendous wealth potential" must be made available to the people of Georgia:

> A Scenic Highway down the Coast of Georgia which would permit linking the other barrier islands to the mainland with short causeways, would bring about the exposure and discovery of this last great Island frontier of America. . . . Beach frontage could be valued up to a quarter of a million dollars per mile, with home and hotel improvements eventually totaling many times this figure. Wild acreage would become subdivisions and as the population increased, paved roads would criss-cross the islands and follow the beautiful wooded bluffs of the mainland. The navigable riverfront sites would command a high premium, and pleas-

ure craft owners could enjoy some of the finest fresh and salt water fishing in the country.[41]

If such a highway were constructed, urged the pamphlet, the people of Georgia would have "fashioned the key of accessibility to Georgia's Golden Coast [and] the gold miners would gather on a scale unequalled since . . . the Miami boom. They would flock to the coast . . . to make their strike, they would come by Cadillac with fat cigars, and they would bring much . . . investment capital to expend along its course." The committee spelled out what it considered the first step toward solution of this problem of underdevelopment: "If such a highway were completed under a Scenic Highway Authority, with equal representation from the six coastal counties of Georgia, the eventual accumulation of excess toll receipts would finance short spur highways, out to every coastal island from Savannah to the Florida line. The birds would move over, and the tourists would come in great flocks."[42] The state's interest in the Sea Islands was closely tied to that of local developers and businessmen.

FOURTEEN

A Park in Progress

Breaking the Trust

*L*ucy Ricketson Ferguson had long desired to break the trust. She wanted to partition the Dungeness estate to obtain full control of Greyfield, her home place. In 1955 she initiated a court battle against nearly all of her relatives, who in turn had wished to ensure the island's integrity. On 30 January 1955 a Florida newspaper reported that "even though one of Lucy's children, Mrs. Florence (Carnegie) Perkins, still lives, a granddaughter . . . has filed suit in the Federal District Court of Brunswick, Georgia, and in the Superior Court of Camden County, to have the trust ended and the estate divided among thirteen relatives." Defendants included Perkins; Thomas M. Carnegie III of St. Augustine; Carter Carnegie of Palm Beach; Nancy Carnegie Rockefeller of Greenwich, Connecticut; and seven other relatives as well as Robert D. Ferguson, trust officer of the Peoples First National Bank and Trust Company of Pittsburgh. "In her suit Mrs. Ferguson (and some of the defendants have technically joined her) charged that trust officer Ferguson (no relation) was acting under color of authority from a court without jurisdiction." A hearing was to be held in Pittsburgh on 11 February to audit the accounts of the trustee and determine jurisdiction. A temporary injunction prevented the beneficiaries from proceeding further in the Georgia courts until after that hearing. Observed the newspaper, "If the local trustees lose out, the island apparently will be split up in a dozen ways and perhaps sold to other parties, or even opened up to the public, which has been excluded since about 1890. . . . If Cumberland Island is partitioned, as Mrs. Ferguson demands, and the unity of the place violated, a jewel of irreplaceable splendor will be gone forever from the face of America."[1]

The court determined that the Georgia real estate should be overseen by a Georgia trustee, while the Pittsburgh trustee should continue to administer the

Pennsylvania investments.[2] This determination satisfied no one except the plaintiff. Lucy Ferguson's cousins soon saw that the island's interests would be best served by not listening to her.

In April 1955 A. Myddleton Harris, president of the First National Bank of Brunswick, Georgia, became the new trustee of the Lucy C. Carnegie estate. One of the bank's vice presidents, Edward Gray, flew to Pittsburgh to discuss with his Pennsylvania counterpart the accounting methods used to run the island portion of the trust. The Brunswick bank established three priorities for efficient administration: setting up a new accounting system, supervising the manager, and establishing contact on a regular basis with the heirs. Gray soon met with the manager, Hugh Sloss, whom the Brunswick bank had inherited from the Pittsburgh administration. Gray quickly noted that Sloss and his wife drank fairly heavily and that Sloss stayed close to his house after dark, apparently afraid to go out.[3]

The possibility of a mineral lease was the first large-scale topic to engage the new trustee. An attempt to raise money for estate administration by utilizing the island's natural resources, it was certainly the most ambitious. Between 1955 and 1957 various mining companies became interested in strip-mining for titanium and ilmenite, ores found in the sands of the Sea Islands. Extraction of these natural resources would have ensured retention of the property by the Carnegie heirs, but strip-mining, which turns soil into a sandy wasteland, would have radically changed the topography and floral and faunal habitats.[4]

According to a map prepared by American Smelting and Refining Company, the southern limit of the principal ore body was an east-west meridian running through the area known as Old House Creek. Its northern limit was at the Carnegie-Candler fence line. Within this 7,000-acre area, however, was a much smaller area described as "assured ore" that was tapered at its southern end, about two hundred yards north of Stafford Plantation's ruined slave chimneys. Assured ore would have been found in New Swamp Field, Old Swamp Field, Yankee Paradise, a pine hill section, Oyster Pond and Oyster Pond Field, Ray Field, Kill Man Field, and west of Lake Whitney. The companies would have mined in both assured ore and probable/low grade ore areas, meaning that almost 6,000 acres would have been subjected to extensive hydraulic mining. The high bidder was Glidden Company of Cleveland, which planned to spend $9 million on its installation. Glidden planned to employ a hundred persons and build a 150-acre village at Brick Hill Bluff. The settlement would have seventy residences and would be completely fenced to keep employees from trespassing on the estate. A system of guards would be maintained. The mining lease was to extend for twenty years.[5]

Glidden promised a minimum of $2.25 million in royalties. Experts retained by the new trust officer promised that the Carnegie owners would get about $4.25 million. Glidden offered to recontour and reforest the devastated land at up to $50 per acre. The project promised to be profitable but at the expense of 7,000 acres of island habitat. Both Harris and Gray favored the leasing of land on Cumberland to a mineral company, but Coleman Perkins, an heir, objected to the mining, and his intervention halted further negotiations.[6]

As the result of litigation brought by Nancy Carnegie Rockefeller, Glidden's offer to lease was finally refused. The most important single reason against acceptance of the lease was the court's decision that the trustee had no right to enter into an agreement for such a long period of time. By 1957 Lucy's last surviving child was an elderly woman, and the court declared that because a twenty-year lease would extend beyond the life of the trust, such a lease was invalid.

Harris and Gray were sorely disappointed. The court's decision, however, was pivotal, leading nearly all the heirs to consider what they wanted to have happen to the island: they did not want to cut it up into little pieces, and they did not want to devastate the land. Private discussions among the Carnegies followed. They decided to prepare for the trust termination and to prepare for land division before the trust terminated.

Meanwhile, the Georgia legislature was opportunistically attentive to what it thought was a family quarrel. On 17 February 1955 the state created the Cumberland Island Study Committee:

> Since it was brought to the attention of the Governor of Georgia that the largest of the Golden Isles was still undeveloped and that a great interest by the people of Camden County and of the State at large had been demonstrated, it was decided in a conference composed of the Governor and Administration leaders, including the representative from Camden County, that some study, thought, and consideration should be given to the possible procurement of all or part of Cumberland Island and to the feasibility and plausibility of its development as a state park and/or public beach and recreational area.[7]

The committee was chaired by John D. Odum, state representative from Camden County, and included Robert Harrison from Wayne County, Cleve Mincy from Ware County, John Drinkard from Lincoln County, Benson Matheson from Hart County, and Roscoe Denmark from Liberty County. The committee was to investigate the size and land evaluations of the island, its accessibility to the mainland, approximate cost of highway and bridge construction, any benefits to the people of Georgia, the owners' attitude toward sale of their property, and acquisition costs against possible returns and benefits.[8]

After cruising the Inland Waterway, the committee found that a causeway to Cumberland Island could be joined to a paved rural road at Harriett's Bluff, with only about two and a half miles of marsh to cross and with only one bridge of any consequence. The members noted with pleasure that with authority financing, literally thousands of lots could be sold for residential purposes at prices within reach of the average Georgia family's income. Experts and engineers expressed amazement that such an island had remained in the hands of private owners without development for public use. The committee found that approximately two-thirds of the island was owned by the Carnegie estate and another third was owned by the Candler estate. The committee did not mention other landowners, perhaps because their acreage was too small to be of concern.[9]

Lucy Ricketson's husband, Robert W. Ferguson, a former state representative for Camden County who was familiar with the workings of state-appointed committees, spoke to the committee on behalf of the heirs. But he did so without their approval, and his statements later aroused a good deal of resentment. He went on record as saying that he completely agreed with the committee's mission. Not only did he feel that a bridge to Cumberland Island would be highly beneficial to the heirs, but he was sure that they could work out an amicable solution with the state. The study committee unanimously found that the state's acquisition of Cumberland Island would probably be the greatest achievement in the history of beach and island development.[10]

Ferguson was certain a state authority could obtain most of Cumberland Island. The Jekyll Island Authority was well known, however. This state-supported oceanfront resort was a continuing financial fiasco, and the authority bore the blame for the island's almost-complete denudation for construction of golf courses and motels. In 1957 the Jekyll Island Authority's critics, including Governor Marvin Griffin, urged an infusion of private capital to improve the shoddy development. In light of the Jekyll Island situation, Ferguson's public statements did not sit well with many of the Carnegies, who believed that the state of Georgia could not run a boat ramp without graft.[11]

After witnessing the First National Bank of Brunswick's support of a mineral lease, few Carnegies trusted its judgment on conservation. When the state began to express its interest in the island, the heirs realized they would need to create an entity separate from the trustee and its administrative concerns. As a result, family members incorporated the Cumberland Island Company on 8 January 1960 under the laws of Georgia. Shares were offered only to Carnegie heirs and represented each heir's undivided fractional interest in the land. Because the island real estate as well as its mineral rights were owned in common by a large group of heirs, land division was one of the first topics to be discussed.[12]

The Cumberland Island Company had held an organizational meeting during the previous October at the Trust Department of the Pittsburgh National Bank. Coleman C. Perkins was chosen as president, Joseph C. Graves Jr. was selected vice president, and Putnam B. McDowell became secretary-treasurer. Priorities and future agendas were discussed. A high priority was placed on analyzing the twin threats presented by Congress and the National Park Service (NPS), each anxious to present Cumberland as a desirable public seashore. Federal intrusion, with its threat of condemnation, was perceived as a great menace to the company's plans. As the first meeting unrolled, however, the top requirement turned out to be the development of a plan of division.[13]

By 9 August 1960 a map had been completed, showing a division of the island that could at least be considered suitable for the heirs' consideration. This process of land allotments was slow and was impeded by different opinions within the Carnegie family. Several members of the Johnston family, whose home place was Plum Orchard, were anxious to see a NPS bill put through as soon as possible, ensuring that Cumberland would eventually become a national park, never to be commercialized. They also sought an immediate and acceptable buyer for part of their shares and stated that they preferred the NPS over other purchasers, even at a sacrifice in price. The NPS was interested in finding out how many landowners would sell: the Candler family at the North End, for one, was not interested in selling any land and had so informed the NPS.[14]

Most members of the Carnegie family did not feel any compulsion to sell their shares. Nancy Carnegie Rockefeller and her sister, Lucy Carnegie Rice; Perkins and his sister, Peggy Perkins Laughlin; and Lucy Ferguson hoped that their cousins would not sell. Most of the other heirs, who were unlikely ever to live on the island, saw great merit in a park bill that would create a ready market for their shares without involving private developers. Although accused of disloyalty, many of the younger Carnegie heirs were willing to contemplate selling their shares to outside parties, especially if they were not developers. It was apparent to all that those who wanted to hold onto the land could not and would not offer to buy out those who wanted to sell.

For more than a year, the issue of hold or sell dominated discussions while the NPS fine-tuned its offer. The heirs' decisions about which tract to choose were suddenly complicated by a new communication from the NPS saying it would accept "land reserves," an option that provided an answer for owners who wanted to hold. At an April 1961 meeting of the company, Graves distributed copies of a bill drafted by the NPS calling for establishment of a national seashore reserve on Cumberland. The bill would authorize acquisition of parcels of land on the island as the various owners wished to sell. Only after a considerable amount of land had been accumulated would a seashore recreational area be set up. The secretary of the interior would have the right to invoke condemnation to prevent any land use that would destroy the island's park potential. The heirs would retain mineral rights.[15]

In 1961 the Cumberland Island Company's officers established a management plan to which thirteen of the fifteen heirs assented. The plan provided that the company officers would supervise management of the estate for one year to give the heirs time to accomplish a voluntary property division. The plan obligated the participants to back a loan to the company to provide funds for a year's operation.[16]

The company urged the family members to consider carefully the various options. The heirs were to remember that although there were probably alternatives, land division should be accomplished quickly. McDowell wrote that all mechanics for management were in place, including authorization by the heirs, a bank loan agreement, and a timetable for financing. A division plan acceptable to the heirs could be in place by the end of 1962.[17]

On 15 April 1962 Florence Perkins died, and the Cumberland Island Trust was terminated. Conditions changed radically, and the entire family convened in New York. Since the undivided interests in land and mineral rights were still owned in common, each of the heirs owned a proportional interest in some very valuable property. The estimated value of Cumberland Island was $4,000,000, and minerals, if mined, would be worth between $50,000 and $80,000.[18]

On 6 July 1964 the heirs of the estate of Lucy Coleman Carnegie divided their Cumberland Island property into ten tracts. In this way all heirs were assured of owning shares in the ore body, located in the northern portion of the island, as well as shares in land that would never be strip-mined (the southern portion). Each of the five families received two tracts, one in the north and one in the south.[19]

The Burning of Dungeness

In 1954 Francis L. Ellis, owner and operator of Duroc Farm, one of Florida's largest swine ranches, sought a contract to round up and transport to the mainland Cumberland Island's numerous wild hogs. "Have several ideas regarding the raising of hogs on the Island," he wrote to Leo Larkin, a Pittsburgh bank officer, on 7 December 1954. Larkin responded that a contract was already in effect with a Camden County man named J. B. Peeples, an employee who served generally as a gamekeeper on the island. On 15 May 1956 the Brunswick bank instructed Peeples to meet with island manager Sloss to discuss hog-hunting operations. The bank made it clear that it sought close supervision of Peeples, and he was to detail how much time he spent in "efforts to apprehend poachers on the Island." In spite of Peeples's attempts to patrol the island, poaching increased, and over the next three years, his encounters with illegal hunters sharpened a mutual animosity. Friends of island landowners repeatedly reported hearing Ellis threaten the "uncooperative" Carnegies. To everyone's delight, one of the Carnegies named a hog *Francis*.[20]

Hostility peaked on 6 May 1959, when Peeples saw what appeared to be some illegal hunters at Old House Creek and fired at one of them. Although Peeples could not positively identify the men, later that night a Florida resident named A. L. Hickox was brought to a Fernandina doctor after having been shot in the back of the neck with seven buckshot. Camden County Sheriff Willie Smith and Deputy Sheriff John A. Bodine of Fernandina, jointly investigating the case, went to the island and found blood in the area indicated by Peeples.[21]

Eight days later, before the shooting had been fully investigated, someone attempted to sink the island ferry and mail boat: "the *Dungeness* was [found] drifting and sinking off Fernandina Beach jetties Tuesday around 5 AM by a shrimp boat owned by L. R. Church. The boat had been cut loose and five holes found in the boat showed evidence of the hull being shot or bored which would have caused the boat to sink." Since the privately owned *Dungeness* was administered by a bank corporation, the incident represented an attempted theft of bank property, and Federal Bureau of Investigation personnel soon joined local authorities in trying to determine who had damaged the boat and whether there was any connection to the shooting. On 18 June various local newspapers carried an advertisement offering a $1,000 reward for information. The notice was signed by the First National Bank of Brunswick as trustee for the estate of Lucy C. Carnegie. No indictment was ever made, although speculation and some evidence pointed to a Florida source.[22]

On 24 June 1959 Dungeness House was in the news for the final time:

OLD LANDMARK ON CUMBERLAND ISLAND DESTROYED BY
FIRE LAST THURSDAY PM

Fire completely destroyed the old Carnegie mansion on Cumberland Island . . . leaving waste the 44-room structure which was completed in 1884 . . . said Joseph Graves, one of the heirs. . . . The fire apparently began on the third floor of the mammoth structure around 6 PM and was discovered by workers on the island while they were eating supper. It burned furiously until around 12 midnight.[23]

At that time no telephonic communication existed between island and mainland. Two members of the Civil Air Patrol were the first to verify the fire, flying over the site at 10:30 P.M. One of them, M. M. Tindale, advertising manager and staff writer for the *Fernandina News-Leader*, reported, "Like a gigantic Christmas tree decoration the flaming structure sent a red glow into the sky until early this morning. The building was a total loss." Air patrol radios crackled as they spread the news to Fernandina, St. Marys, Jacksonville, and Brunswick. The bank was notified at midnight. By 5 A.M. on 25 June Ed Gray had landed at the little Stafford airstrip, soon followed by Camden County's sheriff and deputies, to conduct lengthy interviews with the workers at Dungeness. Homer Hail, an island resident, recalled the fire:

[We] were at Plum Orchard getting ready to have dinner when one of the Dungeness workmen came racing up to inform us of the fire. We sped down to the building and of course we immediately observed that it was completely out of control and there was no hope of anybody doing anything about it. . . . My impression was that the fire had perhaps started somewhere in the area around the elevator shaft. . . . I actually drove around to the kitchen service entrance of the house, entered from the delivery area and walked up to the kitchen and pushed open the swinging door that led to the main hall that went into the center of the house.

Hail noted that all the workmen seemed awestruck by the fire's immensity, unable to beat out the flames engulfing nearby trees until Graves persuaded the workers to cut down at least a half dozen of the large trees burning profusely at their tops: "some people, shortly after we arrived on the scene, arrived from the mainland. I regret I cannot remember the man's name but he was one of those old Georgia 'swamp-rats' who as I recall at the time had a very bad reputation and who had been causing a lot of trouble on the Island."[24]

It was clear that the fire had been deliberately set. The bank fired Sloss the next day. Although the Federal Bureau of Investigation sent agents to the area and the Coast Guard held a hearing on the matter, no one was ever charged with torching the property.[25] By 1959 Dungeness House was vacant, empty of furniture, and had not been used for years. There was no insurance on the building. Regardless of who initiated the burning of Dungeness House, the action was almost certainly meant to strike at the heart of the Carnegie family. But the new generation of heirs no longer saw Dungeness House as a symbol of domestic virtue; instead, they saw the whole island as their home and continued to look toward the difficult questions of conservation and accessibility.

Competition for Purchase of Cumberland

By 1966 support for a national seashore was strong enough for Interior Secretary Stewart L. Udall to push for congressional authorization to acquire Cumberland. The Cumberland Island Company initially hailed Georgia Congressman J. Russell Tuten's sponsorship of a Cumberland Island bill. However, even at that date, Tuten's bill faced a major obstacle in Camden County's opposition to federal acquisition of the island. In 1966 Georgia Governor Lester Maddox challenged the federal government's acquisition of Wassaw Island, near Savannah, as a wildlife refuge. The state wanted to set aside the sale to pave the way for Wassaw's commercial development. Camden County wanted to see Cumberland developed either by the state, à la Jekyll Island, or by commercial interests. On 6 February 1966 Tuten stated that he believed it best to construct a causeway to Cumberland Island from the Camden County mainland. The county would have to agree, however, before he would go forward with any plan for a national seashore. In April 1967 another Georgia congressman, William S. Stuckey Jr., announced that he was drafting legislation for this purpose, hoping to obtain approval from Camden County representatives. But although Tuten, Stuckey, and Camden County officials favored a bridge, the Department of the Interior supported a ferry system. Stuckey pulled his bill from further consideration by Congress in October, when he found that the Department of the Interior was adamant that no causeway be built to the island.[26]

In 1968 an energetic new player appeared: short, unsmiling real estate developer Charles E. Fraser of Hilton Head Island, South Carolina. The first bridge to Hilton Head Island was constructed in 1956, and the island became nationally known as a resort for the affluent, winning numerous awards for excellence in land use.

Fraser was not the first purchaser of Carnegie land on Cumberland. On 26 September 1967 Carnegie heir Oliver G. Ricketson III sold 103 acres to Robert L. Davis of St. Marys for $66,000. The second Carnegie sale, however, consisted of 3,117 acres in two separate tracts, each with beach frontage and marsh. Fraser bought the two parcels from Henry Carter Carnegie, Thomas M. Carnegie IV, and Andrew Carnegie for $1.55 million, much of it in cash, on 15 January 1969. Fraser immediately began a campaign to explain why his planned resort would meet the aims of the most ardent conservationists: "Cumberland Island, the most magnificent island on the United States coast, deserves a master plan— a plan which will incorporate, with intelligence and sensitivity, the most advanced and thorough land-use planning, conservation programs, and architectural controls." To prevent any Carnegies from holding out, Fraser warned that he would proceed with his plans only if all owners of 60 or more acres on Cumberland would enter into some form of agreement with him. Over the next two years Fraser tried unsuccessfully to persuade the rest of the Carnegies to sell to him.[27]

Fraser's idealism did not match the realities of coastal Georgia. Local businessmen would not respond to the same high-minded stand about conservation he had taken with the Carnegies. When Fraser sought financial support, he was obliged to forgo arguments favoring ecology to avoid the "elitist" tag already attached to the Carnegies. Fraser had once said that he envisioned a $750,000 system of towers, cables, and aerial gondolas to carry people back and forth from his development to the mainland. In 1968 Fraser stated publicly that his projected development would include not only houses but rental apartments, marinas, a hospital (he had noticed at Hilton Head that buyers hesitated until they knew more about the medical facilities), airstrips, helicopter pads, security and service quarters, shopping facilities, and numerous athletic and amusement facilities. Fraser's plans required allies among local businessmen and legislators. State Representative Robert W. Harrison Jr., a St. Mary's attorney, gave a dinner for Fraser's Cumberland Island Holding Company on 31 January 1969. The holding company followed with an Atlanta luncheon for the county commissioners at which Fraser announced, "We hope to see a Cumberland Island

Recreation Authority established by the Georgia Legislature" to operate a ferry service and to build a private airstrip on Cumberland. The *Atlanta Journal* lampooned the controversy with a cartoon on its editorial page that showed a hapless Cumberland Island overwhelmed by a buccaneer speculator with a banner, "The Almighty Dollar." Early in 1969 Representative Harrison introduced Georgia Resolution 688, which was designed to allow a local land company to develop Cumberland. The bill failed when it became known that Fraser was one of Harrison's clients.[28]

Never monolithic, by the 1960s the Carnegie family held a wide variety of viewpoints. Some heirs rarely visited the island, and one or two disliked it, partly because its shabby appearance offered a depressing contrast to their memories of happier days. But family members generally agreed in their distrust of Fraser and his unholy alliance with mainland business interests.

Fraser saw the Carnegie landowners as representing all the hypocrisy of modern ecologists, contemptuously terming such people "druids" and dismissing their ecological objectives by calling them selfish, rich upstarts. Fraser scolded the Carnegie family for having no sense of history: "They think the history of the island is the history of their occupancy. They think history began when they arrived. . . . The family of my friend, Brailsford Nightingale, in Savannah, owned parts of this island when the Carnegies were still herding sheep. The Nightingales have been elegant for more generations than you can count. They are descendants of General Greene."[29]

Cumberland's small landowners were eager to cooperate with Fraser. The North End, never close to the South End, saw his proposed development in a positive light:

> A strip of land between Dungeness and Greyfield had been acquired in the sale
> and here Fraser built his headquarters. . . . Laurence A. Miller . . . was the engi-
> neer in charge of drawing plans. Two roads across the island from the river to the
> beach were cleared. . . . The development was called Cumberland Oaks. Plans
> were made for a club house, airport, lots for sale, golf course, etc. Lake Whitney
> would be . . . a playground for children with canoes and docks for fishing. . . .
> [Fraser's] vision included many activities such as . . . beach development, swings
> from the great oaks, watermelon vendors in summer, and roasted oysters in win-
> ter with sky vans to bring in food and supplies.[30]

Georgia's legislators joined in a swelling antielitist chorus. Populists saw the federal government as an intruder. A Byzantine array of subterranean arrangements soon arose among members of the Georgia legislature, Camden County officers, developers from other states, and lawyers. In vain did Congressman Stuckey hope for a reconciliation of views among the people of Camden County, the elected officials, and the owners.

In early March 1969 the Georgia General Assembly considered a bill to establish a development authority for the purpose of condemning private holdings on Cumberland Island. No owners were named. Any private landowners who refused to sell their land to development interests would find their property condemned and then sold for development. The authority would give the county commissioners power to condemn. Not surprisingly, Fraser and other development interests were instrumental in introducing this legislation.[31]

On 11 March an amendment to an act creating the North Georgia Mountains Authority was introduced in the Georgia Senate. Attorney Thornton W. Morris wrote to his Carnegie clients,

> The Authority at present has the power of eminent domain and its activities are exercised in the mountain area of North Georgia. Senate Bill 260 would . . . expand the jurisdiction of the Authority so that it might "engage in the business of its projects anywhere within the territorial boundaries of the State of Georgia." I know of the close relationship between the director of the Authority and Fraser. It appears to be an attempt to gain by amendment to an existing authority that which he was unable to get through the establishment of the Camden Recreation Authority.

The press quickly realized that Cumberland was the undeveloped area that Georgia's General Assembly had in mind. Some reporters began to connect Fraser with the legislature's manipulations, and the legislature backed off amid a storm of unfavorable publicity.[32]

Although chastened, the 1969 Georgia General Assembly created an eighteen-member special interim group, the Georgia Coastal Island Study Committee, with a mandate to visit all the Georgia Sea Islands and hold public discussions. The committee was composed of members of the Senate and House; Bill Jones Jr., son of the head of the Cloisters, a resort hotel on Sea Island; and Morris, a Carnegie attorney. It was clear to the press that Cumberland was again the committee's target.[33]

Early in October this committee arrived in Camden County to begin a three-day study of the feasibility and desirability of state acquisition of Cumberland Island for use as a state park. The committee was given an island tour. Almost none had ever visited Cumberland, and they were fascinated. Clearly preoccupied with the rundown appearance of many estate buildings, a committee member, State Representative Francis Scarlett, inquired: "Why does the Dungeness Estate have so many abandoned stables?" A long silence followed. Finally there came a gentle response: "We don't use horses anymore."[34]

After holding two coastal hearings and one large public hearing in Atlanta, the Coastal Island Study Committee recommended that the state float a $36 million bond issue to purchase and preserve some of the Sea Islands. The commission also recommended the creation of the Georgia Coastal Islands and Marshlands Planning Commission, with power to regulate the use of undeveloped areas remaining in private ownership. Although the landowners were criticized for "foot-dragging," the press generally commented that theft of land constituted a violation of property rights: "The ultimate aim, it is reported, is for Camden County to lease or sell the land back to the developer who would then go ahead with his plans." Georgia's legislature approved the committee's recommendations, with State Senator Roscoe Dean of Camden among those voting against the state's further involvement.[35]

In mid-January 1970 the Georgia legislature made its final attempts to seize control of Cumberland, considering a bill to establish the Georgia Coastal Islands and Marshlands Planning Commission as well as a measure to extend the jurisdiction of the Jekyll Island State Parks Authority. Both bills were defeated on 20 March.[36]

The Carnegies began to see that neither Fraser's promises nor his threats could be taken seriously. His choice of allies, his vituperative language, and his double-dealing gave rise to grave suspicions about his ability to "preserve Cumberland's natural beauty," which led to more serious examination of his financing. Fraser had assured the Carnegies as well as members of the legislature that the money he needed for current and future purchases was to be put up by Travelers Insurance Company. But he had greatly exaggerated the extent to which he had arranged his financing. Officers at Travelers privately told the Cumberland Island Company that Fraser's statement was not quite true.[37]

In March 1970 Fraser hired bulldozers to work on his Cumberland property, informing anyone who asked that he was constructing a firebreak and nothing more. By April it was clear that Fraser had instead constructed a very good road around the entire perimeter of his property. In the course of its construction, his "firebreak" had dammed and drained a number of freshwater ponds. Despite his preservationist claims, Fraser also had gouged out a clearing for an airport, as his employees freely admitted.[38]

Inquiries made by the Georgia Conservancy and the press revealed that on 3 March 1970, "Fraser . . . recorded a mortgage on the property of his Cumberland Island Holding Company for a new loan in the substantial amount of $5.3 million from Diversified Mortgage Investors—A Massachusetts Business Trust." Its chairman and managing trustee, D. A. Holladay of Coral Gables, Florida, told the Georgia Conservancy that he was unaware that a bill had been introduced in Congress to declare Cumberland Island a national seashore or that the NPS proposed administering the island in its natural condition. William Griffin, chairman of the Georgia Conservancy's Coastal Areas Committee, stated, "The amount of this loan and the clandestine treatment that its existence has so far received raises many disturbing questions concerning the future of Cumberland Island, especially its future as a National Seashore for all the people of Georgia and the United States, rather than the moneyed few who can afford to fly a jet airplane there."[39]

"Everyone Seems to Covet This Island": Conservation Interests

In the mid-1950s, Lucy Ricketson Ferguson looked back at the previous two decades and commented, "Everyone seems to covet this island." In 1935 the NPS inventoried the available unspoiled shoreline areas of the Atlantic and Gulf Coasts and recommended the purchase and preservation by the federal government of some 450 miles to be dedicated to public recreation. Although World War II interrupted the Department of the Interior's progress in land acquisition, the survey was updated in 1953, when the department proposed a "National System for Island Trusts." According to the 1953 survey, only 800 of the nation's 60,000 miles of coastline were publicly owned and available for recreation. Only 240 miles of the Atlantic and Gulf Coasts were federally or state owned. Seven national seashores had been set aside for public use, the oldest being Cape Hatteras and Cape Lookout National Seashore on North Carolina's Outer Banks. The NPS operated the national seashores, patrolling the surf, providing camping spots, and, in some areas, offering guided tours.[40]

Representatives from the Department of the Interior visited Cumberland as early as 1950. In early July 1954 Park Service representatives made an air and ground reconnaissance of Cumberland Island. Sloss showed the three visitors around the island and was told that the NPS was making an evaluation survey for a possible national or state park. On 1 October 1954 two more NPS employees made another survey of the island, offering no further explanation other than that they were there in the interest of sea-coast recreation.[41]

The Pentagon was also interested in Cumberland's future. In 1953 the U.S. Army initiated plans to take over part of Cumberland Island as a buffer zone for an ammunition depot to be located at St. Marys. The area was desirable for such purposes because of its isolation in sparsely populated south Georgia. At the same time that NPS representatives were surveying for a possible national park, the War Department was sending representatives to evaluate a portion of Cumberland. On 2 August 1954 Claud S. Hart of the Savannah District Office of the Corps of Engineers visited the island to gauge that portion of Cumberland to be included in the buffer zone around the Kings Bay ammunition project. Hart told Sloss that the plan was not yet definite and that this was a preliminary, informational survey. The buffer zones on Hart's maps consisted of concentric circles with diameters that differed by about two hundred yards based on the size of the ships to be loaded. Wrote the manager, "The boundary line of the largest circle, the 10-ton capacity, took in Stafford, just missed the Chimneys, took in all of Greyfield, and swung back across the Dungeness area including the Cottage, the Big Dock, and the Captain's House, missing the Dungeness building, the Grange, and the work areas. The lesser buffer zones would miss Stafford and Dungeness but would include Greyfield." Hart told Sloss that if the project were undertaken, federal procedure would be to offer a fair price for the land but to take it by condemnation if necessary. Restrictions would prohibit habitation within the buffer zones, but people would be free to come and go as long as no more than twenty-five persons congregated at any one time. The original owners would receive options to buy back their property if the project were abandoned. Hart said that no ammunition storage was planned for Kings Bay, and he assured Sloss that the Pentagon had not yet made its decision.[42]

Land acquisition for the installation began in 1953, and Kings Bay, a large coastal area near St. Marys, became an ammunition depot. The location seemed a curious choice for an ocean terminal. To provide ocean access, the army dredged a ten-mile-long, two-hundred-foot-wide, thirty-two-foot-deep channel. Construction began in 1956 and was completed in 1958 at a cost of $21 million. Because there was no immediate operational need for the installation, it was placed in an inactive ready status, a condition from which it never emerged.[43]

Private conservation agencies also became involved in the fight for Cumberland. The Avalon Foundation, established in 1940 by Ailsa Mellon Bruce, and the Old Dominion Foundation, established in 1941 by her brother, Paul Mellon, were deeply interested in conservation. In 1952 each foundation had contributed generously to enable the NPS to acquire the Cape Hatteras Recreation Area in North Carolina, which was officially dedicated as the first U.S. national seashore in 1958. In the 1950s the foundations jointly financed a series of coastal surveys, one of which was intended to drum up congressional support for the public acquisition of Cumberland. On 18 June 1955 Mellon, NPS Director Conrad Wirth, and other officials visited the island, with the NPS seeking money from the Mellon Foundation to purchase the island. The island's divided ownership made its acquisition seem impossible, but Wirth continued to keep the Old Dominion Foundation well informed about any negotiations with island landowners.[44]

The Mellon visit had not constituted a formal inquiry because none of the Carnegies had been contacted. As the 1955 court case proceeded, Wirth and his associates realized that since some of the Carnegies opposed fragmentation of the island, the family should be contacted. On 10 February 1956 the NPS telephoned one of the heirs, Margaret Johnston Wright, who visited Washington, D.C., within two weeks to confer with Park Service officials. An NPS representative spoke at the 5 April island meeting of the heirs. Most Carnegie heirs subsequently supported NPS efforts to acquire the island. On 28 June 1967 the Cumberland Island Conservation Association (CICA) was formed, with members including virtually all of the heirs. Until its formal termination on 25 August 1970, CICA sought to influence legislation favoring the Department of the Interior.[45]

In 1969 the Avalon and Old Dominion Foundations merged to form a new body, the Andrew W. Mellon Foundation (AWMF). In 1970 George B. Hartzog, the new NPS director, approached the AWMF for possible funding for the acquisition of Cumberland and received a favorable response. The Nixon administration had issued a "no new parks" edict, so the AWMF worked through the National Parks Foundation (NPF), which would hold the land in trust until federal funds were again available.[46]

The AWMF donated $5.5 million to the NPF in 1970 for the purchase of a major portion of Cumberland and an additional $1.15 million in 1971. Although the foundation had originally hoped to purchase the whole island, some owners still did not intend to sell their land. The AWMF decided to offer the owners fair market value, to negotiate with individuals wishing to sell, and to avoid an all-or-nothing approach. With this strategy in place, three key agreements to sell came quickly and proved to be enough to start the process. Coleman C. Perkins of the Table Point Company, the Johnston family of Plum Orchard, and Fraser signed options to sell in early August 1970. With the AWMF donation and the sell options in hand, in October 1970 Secretary of Interior Walter J. Hickel announced the purchase of about 8,300 acres on Cumberland Island, to be held in trust by the NPF pending congressional action on proposals to establish a national seashore on the island. After the authorization bill became law, the island would be turned over to the Department of the Interior, which would preserve the island for public use under controlled circumstances. The NPF would also continue to seek more land. Sellers would be permitted to retain life tenancies, to bring their vehicles, and to use existing roads, and the NPS agreed to follow the Carnegies' wishes in regard to the family cemetery.[47]

On 3 February 1970 Congressman Stuckey introduced legislation to create the Cumberland Island Seashore, and the measure was enacted on 23 October 1972. Cumberland Island opened as a national seashore in the summer of 1975. During the first twelve months of its administration, the NPS carried 13,800 tourists to the island, and demand to visit became so great that visitors were limited to around 40,000 per year. The Cumberland Island National Seashore had 40,022 visitors in 1995, 43,182 in 1996, and 44,125 in 1999, with 2,108 tourists in December alone. In 1997 the reservations office answered more than 120 calls per day. Camping reservations must now often be made a year in advance. Those who come to the island have a broad variety of reasons for their sojourns and a sense of historical perspective.[48]

Commerce, Tourism, and the Otter

Who benefits from the Cumberland Island National Seashore's policy of land acquisition? The island has been underpopulated for more than seventy years. In 1926 Andrew Carnegie II said that Cumberland's population consisted of fifty people, eleven of them children. In 1974 only fourteen people were full-time residents of the Cumberland Island National Seashore, and in 1997 its population numbered about twenty, many of them caretakers. Cumberland Island has not been agriculturally self-sufficient since Reconstruction. The last black men to live and work on the island were a descendant of Quash of Brick Hill, George Merrow, who died in 1995, and Nate Lane, who died in 1991. The

Carnegie family cemetery has seen a few additional family burials, as has the High Point cemetery. No market economy exists except for the Greyfield Inn, a small hotel. Although open for services, the only remaining church, First African Baptist, remains empty most of the time.[49]

The failure of Fraser's development on Cumberland Island rankled many people in Camden County for years. The Okefenoke Rural Electrification Membership Corporation, a cooperative that for decades supplied the county's electrical needs, was bitterly disappointed. For more than a decade, mainland businessmen pressed for increases in the national seashore's visitation levels. In 1993 State Representative Charles C. Smith Jr. of St. Marys publicly demanded that 200,000 people be admitted yearly. Smith was not concerned with the fragility of the island ecosystem: he declared that increased visitation would enable citizens of Camden County to recoup some of the losses incurred when the island was appropriated by the federal government: "There ought to be a way for Camden County to get a few crumbs."[50]

The NPS's most important aim for the past twenty-five years has been to acquire more acreage to prevent commercial development. The Wilderness Act of 1982 established 8,840 acres of wilderness and 11,718 acres of potential wilderness on Great Cumberland. The NPS continues looking for options to buy remaining acreage from island landholders. The price per acre, including marshland, has appreciated markedly. After more than a decade of negotiations, the Candler family at High Point sold 2,190 acres to the NPS in 1982 for $9.6 million. With this acquisition, only 1,700 acres of privately held land remained, and much of that has since become part of the national seashore. In 1999 the National Parks and Conservation Association purchased 1,148 acres of oak forest, marshland, and Atlantic beach from the Greyfield Corporation for $11.5 million.[51]

Two factors have protected Cumberland Island from overdevelopment. First is the fact that no causeway was ever built to the island. Although mainland businessmen clamored for vehicular access to the island in 1967 and 1968, the Department of the Interior, U.S. Navy, and U.S. Army opposed the building of a causeway, which would have prevented submarines from accessing Kings Bay. A causeway would have created an influx of traffic to the island and a demand for automobile facilities. But as things have turned out, Kings Bay Submarine Base has greatly added to the county's economy, and Cumberland's fragile ecosystem has been preserved.

The second factor is the island's relatively small size. Although it is the largest of the Sea Islands, its water and highland resources are limited. Great Cumberland was once supposed to encompass more than 24,000 acres, exclusive of marshland. Over time, definitions of land have changed. During the 1970s, under the leadership of Dr. Eugene Odum and the Georgia Fish and Game Commission, the state of Georgia realized that its coastal marshes were vulnerable to degradation and defined its jurisdiction to prevent their overdevelopment. The present total acreage of Great and Little Cumberland, including their marshes, is measured at 36,415 acres. Even though the standards of measurement have changed, the island remains a small, contained landscape. Cumberland has never been a city-state, a county, or even a separate school district. Its integrity is easy to experience. Walkers can go from one end of the island to the other in a few hours, thereby creating a close, even intimate, relationship to the island.[52]

Cumberland's most persistent and difficult foes may be those who would profit financially from its exploitation. Luckily, their numbers are diminishing. Visitors appreciate the island's unspoiled appearance. "It's a beautiful island, a real treasure, and I sure don't want to see it destroyed," said Representative Smith in 1996, just three years after his call for an eightfold increase in the number of visitors permitted to the island.[53]

If Cumberland's worst enemies are humans, then perhaps its best friends are the powers of nature. The island's size, location, isolation, and weather all work against comfortable residential patterns. Until the termination of the life estates, as many as three hundred part-time residents have the right to stay in island homes. But it is hard to live on Cumberland now. Everyone brings their own supplies from the mainland, and everyone carries their waste back. Improvements such as telephones and septic tanks benefit those persons who live, play, and work there, but island residents find it increasingly difficult to market, to educate children, or to attend church. The NPS is under congressional mandate not to allow any use of NPS land that would be a derogation of the values for which the park was established or be incompatible with the public interest. On Cumberland, this must be balanced with the unique rights of the twenty-two retained rights estates present. The Okefenoke Rural Electrification Membership Corporation delivers power to the island by single pole transmission lines that cross Cumberland River and marsh. At present, no rights-of-way exist for the electrical power supplied to the island.[54]

The residents do not inhabit the land as did their forebears. The environment is more fragmented for modern residents than for previous inhabitants. Erosion, weathering, fire, and flooding slowly destroy humans' best efforts at comfort. The Duck House (now burned) has slowly filled up with sand from the ever-migrating dunes. In 1981 uncontrolled forest fires started by lightning strikes rampaged through more than 1,600 acres of pine and threatened homes and water sources. As a result of decay and dampness, Plum Orchard is falling down. Although automobiles regularly drive over the Main Road, now categorized as a "historic trace," it receives minimal maintenance.

Humans have long defended Cumberland against other humans. Where hostile Indians or privateers were once the enemy, in the 1950s and 1960s the foe wore a developer's hat. At that time it seemed that an elite group of private owners was fighting Georgia's populist tendencies, which declared that the state was working for the public good by promoting access to the island. With the passage of the Wilderness Act of 1982 came a new idea: the island's best protection from uglification is the removal of human residents. This place, it is argued, needs protection from humankind's natural desire to exploit. In effect, such reasoning supports a new kind of game preserve. Wildlife preserves and protected areas have created islands of preservation where humans are usually invited to look but not to touch.[55] Both elitist and populist decry any interference with their values. Tension between them may be perpetual. But Cumberland Island needs humans.

Geopathology is the experience of place as an unresolvable conflict between home and exile, belonging and alienation. *Home* is the so-called abiding place of the domestic affections, the habitat. Because of the arguments brought up in defense of and in opposition to the Wilderness Act, the two meanings seem antithetical. On Cumberland Island, overvisitation and overbuilding threaten the island's ecosystem. But it is the human sense of place that preserves landscape, a portion of land which can be viewed pictorially. Over the years, specialists from a myriad of professions have learned that the ability to read the landscape enhances the understanding and appreciation of that landscape and its associations. The process called returning to nature threatens the visual quality of the island's resources. Cumberland was always more than a beautiful landscape. As ecologists and historians say, "Agricultural landscapes were also social ones, where the flow of water and the flow of human and natural power converged in a unique set of environmental, productive, and social relations."[56]

Cumberland Island is a social space. Landscapes exist because of their social values. From the point of view of the otter, this interpretation is ridiculous: he knows the landscape exists for otters. But it is humans who have memory of the past landscape. Only we bring beauty and value to the landscape. We endow the landscape with these qualities through memory, music, and poetry. Without humans, history lacks meaning, can no longer be remembered, and dies. When that happens, the landscape becomes memorialized, leading quickly to Disneyfication. Who will remember the bugles and bosuns' whistles at Dungeness during the War of 1812? Who will remember Quash and the bear in the dark of night on the Main Road? On the Georgia coast, in a place of great natural energy, nature and culture have flowed together. Who will remember Primus Mitchell and the culture from which he came? Without the human presence, there can be no history. Without figures, there can be no landscape.

APPENDIX: METHODOLOGY

Title search, if carried back far enough, ought to result in the discovery of the original grant descriptions. Although there has been relatively little subdivision of Cumberland Island, it is difficult to find grant information because the original descriptions appear in Georgia's colonial records. There are three categories of archival records that can be used to determine who petitioned for land in Georgia. Most important are the petitions themselves, which are generally found in the minutes of the Governor's Council. However, the minutes were rarely specific about the location of the requested land, unless the petitioner asked for an entire island. The second category is the records of survey, now kept by the surveyor-general of the state of Georgia. However, petitioners sometimes failed to have their land surveyed and plats drawn, instead settling on tracts for a time and then moving on. Furthermore, most plats were so crudely drawn that distinctive topographic features are almost completely lost to modern eyes. Only three original plats for Cumberland Island have survived the ravages of time and revolution. In addition, there is a fourth plat of a resurvey made after the American Revolution.

The third body of records consists of Georgia's colonial conveyances, which correspond to present-day registers of deeds. The conveyances often contain the name of the original owner as well as information about exchanges by sale, gift, or inheritance or about any other subsequent method by which land changed hands. The conveyances give tract boundaries in words rather than drawings and use a wide variety of topographic and descriptive phrases, including "marked by the white post"; "bounded by the Narrows"; "corner marked at ye Notched Tree"; linear measurements given in chains and rods; specific features such as already named swamps, creeks, or rivers; and sometimes the names of abuttors.

Although most of the original Cumberland Island land grants extended to the sea beach, the tract descriptions provided no topographical information. I generally found the names of all abuttors (except for the first grant, where there were no abuttors). By using the four plats, all written abuttors, and the names of the grant petitioners (including a few who did not receive grants) and with my title search completed, I have identified the location of each Crown grant on Cumberland. Because the island has changed little physically since the eighteenth century, it is possible to see what those petitioners saw when they plotted their strategies for obtaining land on the island.

NOTES

Abbreviations

CER	Carnegie Estate, Records of Cumberland Island, AC 69-501, Georgia Department of Archives and History, Atlanta
CRG	*The Colonial Records of the State of Georgia*
DAB	*Dictionary of American Biography*
EFP	East Florida Papers, P. K. Yonge Library of Florida History, University of Florida, Gainesville
GDAH	Georgia Department of Archives and History, Atlanta
JCC	James C. Campbell
LC	Library of Congress, Washington, D.C.
LCC	Lucy C. Carnegie
NA	National Archives, Washington, D.C.
OGR Jr.	Oliver G. Ricketson Jr.
ORN	*Official Records of the Union and Confederate Navies*
PKY	P. K. Yonge Library of Florida History, University of Florida, Gainesville
RCCG	Records of Camden County, Georgia, Camden County Courthouse, Woodbine
RDF	Robert D. Ferguson
RG	Record Group
SCA	Samuel C. Atkinson
S-G	Records of the Surveyor-General's Office of the Department of State, Georgia Department of Archives and History, Atlanta
TMC Jr.	Thomas Morrison Carnegie Jr.
TMC Sr.	Thomas Morrison Carnegie Sr.
WEP	William E. Page

Preface

1. Lawrence Durrell, *Reflections on a Marine Venus* (New York: Penguin Books, 1978), 15.

CHAPTER ONE. Cumberland: A Sea Island

1. Leatherman, *Barrier Island Handbook*, 5, 13, fig. 20.

2. Jonathan Bryan, *Journal.*

3. Benjamin Hawkins to Antoine-Rene-Charles-Mathurn, Compte de La Forest, 9 April 1785, Hawkins Papers, *Addition,* Coll. 322, folder 4, Southern Historical Collection, Wilson Library, University of North Carolina at Chapel Hill.

4. John Ehrenhard, pers. comm. 16 July 2002; Virginia Wood, pers. comm. 12 July 2002.

5. Kimber, *A Relation,* 7–10. Spanish naval officers vividly described some difficulties and hazards of the Inland Navigation in the journal of the Marquess of Casinas, written after the 1742 Spanish attempt to attack the British Fort Frederica. Two squadrons of naval vessels were dispatched from St. Augustine for the attack: a sea fleet took to the open ocean, and an inland fleet went up through the Inland Passage. Although the two squadrons were ordered to remain on the same parallel, the "inland flotilla," wrote the marquess, "can only proceed when the tide is favorable, at intervals of six hours and a few minutes" ("Orders to the Commanding Officers of the Fleet," in *Spanish Official Account*).

6. "A Map of South Carolina and a Part of Georgia, Containing the Whole Sea-Coast Composed from Surveys Taken by the Hon. William Bull, Esq., Lieut-Governor; Captain Gascoign; Hugh Bryan, Esq.; and the author [William Gerard DeBrahm]," engraved by Thomas Jeffery (London, 1757), Special Collections, University of Georgia, Athens, cat. G 3910, 1757, D4.

7. Hillestad et al., *Ecology,* 25–26.

8. "Orders to the Commanding Officers of the Fleet," in *Spanish Official Account,* 51. A bane to sailors, St. Andrew Sound was evidently a haven for another species. The Spanish called this body of water the Bay of Whales, although the length of time over which they used this name is unknown. The aborigines of the southern Georgia and Florida coasts hunted sea mammals, including whales and porpoises, as evidenced by bones recovered from middens in the coastal area. On the Georgia coast, bones of cetaceans have been found in sites on Cumberland and Sapelo Islands. Indian methods of whale hunting were well documented in early Spanish accounts.

9. Pendleton, "Short Account."

10. *Narrative of a Voyage.*

11. Nagle, *Nagle Journal,* 294.

12. Setzler, "Salvaging." In 1580 Spanish officer Menéndez Marques was trying to

track down some survivors of a 1577 French shipwreck. He learned that some of them were west of the Appalachian Mountains, and the French captain was brought from a distance of about 480 miles. This episode shows that coastal tribes could travel safely among the Cherokee. Coastal Indians traded captives, cassena, salt, fish, shells, and medicines. They are known to have traveled by canoe as far south as St. Augustine and as far north as Cape Fear (Waddell, *Indians*, 20–22).

13. In 1564, for example, two Indians in a canoe told a Spanish captain in St. Helena Sound that a man from a ship remained at their Indian village. The captain gave the Indians a homemade cross, and within a day or so, in response to this Christian symbol, Guillaume Rouffi, a French sailor on Captain Jean Ribaut's ship, arrived, clothed like the Indians (Waddell, *Indians*).

14. Milanich, "Western Timucua," 59–63.

15. Deagan, "Cultures in Transition," 89; Hann, "Twilight," 1–24.

16. Hann, "Twilight," 1–24.

17. Larson, *Aboriginal Subsistence Technology*, 195.

18. Milanich et al., "Georgia Origins."

19. Turner Bushnell, *Situado*, 66. San Pedro evidently was loaded with sassafras, for its Indian name was *Wissoe* (often printed as *Missoe*), which meant "sassafras." The Indian name persisted on maps and charts well into the eighteenth century. In 1602 a frigate provisioning St. Augustine received permission to continue to San Pedro Mocama to pick up 12,500 pounds of sassafras for which the ship's master had already contracted. Turner Bushnell, *Situado*, 66, quoting Lopez (1602); Hann, *History*, 161–62.

20. Turner Bushnell, *Situado*, 66.

21. Magnaghi, "Sassafras and Its Role," 10–21; Manning and Moore, "Sassafras and Syphilis," 473–75; Waddell, *Indians*, citing Thomas Ashe (1682) and Nicolás Monardes (1569–71), 50–51; Sauer, *Sixteenth Century North America*, 211, 226–27, 252, 283; Quinn, *Roanoke Voyages*, 2:764; Turner Bushnell, *Situado*, 66; Hann, *History*, 161–62.

22. Lowery, *Spanish Settlements*, 2:271–79.

23. Ibid.

24. Quinn, *Roanoke Voyages*, 2:802–15.

25. Ibid.

26. Ibid., 2:802–15; Thomas, "Saints and Soldiers," 95, 105, 108. See also Hudson and Tesser, *Forgotten Centuries*, fig. 4 and p. 291. Although planned for refugees who had fled Santa Catalina de Guale in the 1680s, the mission on Isla de Santa María was never built.

27. Thomas, "Saints and Soldiers"; Hudson and Tesser, *Forgotten Centuries*.

28. Ibid.

29. Ibid.

30. Thomas, "Saints and Soldiers," 107, 108.

31. Ibid.; Hudson and Tesser, *Forgotten Centuries*.

32. Milanich et al., "Georgia Origins," 47; Larson, *Aboriginal Subsistence Technology*, 215; Larson, "Guale Indians," 122.

33. Lanning, *Spanish Missions of Georgia;* Turner Bushnell, *Santa María,* 2–11.

34. Milanich, *Laboring,* 144–45. See also Turner Bushnell, *Situado.*

35. Worth, *Struggle,* 23, appendix A; Milling, *Red Carolinians;* Hudson, *Southeastern Indians.*

36. Milling, *Red Carolinians;* Hudson, *Southeastern Indians.*

37. Worth, *Struggle,* 23, appendix A; Turner Bushnell, *Situado,* 171, 210.

38. Hann, *History,* 21.

39. Milling, *Red Carolinians,* 156 n.69.

40. Connor, *Colonial Records,* 1:291, 293, quoting de Prado's memorial, "Memorial on Four Forts of Florida Presented to His Majesty by Captain Antonio de Prado," from cédula 2-1-1/27, no. 5, R3, Madrid, 16 November 1569; Chatelain, *The Defenses of Spanish Florida,* 14–38, 80–90.

41. "Descripcion Geographica de la parte que los Espanoles poseen actualmente en el continente de la Florida," Ms. No. 17,648, British Museum, copy in LC; Lyon, "San Pedro"; Connor, *Colonial Records,* 1:291, 293. Governor Pedro Menéndez Marques sent López de Velasco, cosmographer to Spain's King Philip II, a drawing that delineated the Florida coast. López utilized this sketch map for his own work, which contains his description of the fort—he never saw it himself.

42. Milanich, "Franciscan Missions," 296–98.

43. Worth, *Struggle,* 100–102.

44. Ibid., 6.

45. Ibid.

46. Ibid.

47. Ibid.

48. Ibid., 43, 46.

49. Ibid., 51 n.2; Gannon, "New Alliance," 329, citing modern anthropologists whose demographic work subverts conventional wisdom that European dietary practices benefited the natives.

CHAPTER TWO. San Pedro Gives Way to St. George

1. St. Georges Point (Punta San Jorge) was the name of a small Sea Island between St. Johns River and Amelia Island, separated from the latter by a narrow creek. By 1686 the uneducated referred to the entire Georgia and Carolina coasts north of this point as "San Jorge." After construction of a few English fortifications, the island became known as Fort St. George, the name it bears today. (Jonathan Bryan, *Journal,* n.105; Worth, *Struggle,* esp. testimonials [1680] before notaries, 154. See also Turner Bushnell, *Situado,* 164, fig. 15.1, for map of Florida [1683] showing "Puerto y Población de San Jorge de la Nación Ynglesa.")

2. Stevens, *History,* vol. 1; Thomas Spalding, "Sketch," 239; Kenneth Coleman,

Colonial Georgia; Robert Wright, *Memoir;* McCall, *History,* vol. 1; Phinizy Spalding and Jackson, *Oglethorpe in Perspective,* esp. chaps. 2–3; Phinizy Spalding, *Oglethorpe in America,* 80–90; Ettinger, *Oglethorpe.*

3. Juricek, *Georgia Treaties;* Jonathan Bryan, *Journal,* nn.1, 67; *CRG,* vol. 28, pt. 1A, p. 325. On Anglo-Creek traders and the British Board of Trade, see Marion R. Hemperley, letter to author, 1967.

4. Juricek, *Georgia Treaties;* Jonathan Bryan, *Journal,* nn.1, 67; *CRG,* vol. 28, pt. 1A, p. 325.

5. "Oglethorpe's Introductory Discourse to the Colony of Georgia," letter dated 11 October 1739, Phillipps Collection of Egmont Manuscripts, vol. 14204, 132; "Impartial Inquiry," 182. The trustees' stud assuredly bred with Indian horses already on the island: in 1597 the Spanish had rewarded Governor Don Juan, cacique of San Pedro Mocamo, for his loyalty in subduing the rebellion of that year by giving him a large sum of money, European cloth, and a good horse (Hann, *History,* 143).

6. Kimber, *A Relation,* 8.

7. Anderson, "Genesis," 266; Lane, *General Oglethorpe's Georgia,* 1:251; Cate, "Fort Frederica," 113–30; Frederick Nichols, *Architecture,* 22–26; *CRG,* 2:15, 32:499 (testimony of Philip Delegal Sr., 11 March 1740), 30:244 (letter dated 29 December 1739), 35:437 (Oglethorpe to Verelst, received 29 March 1742); "Fort St. Andrews/Fort Prince William," 22–24; *Pennsylvania Gazette,* 24 June 1736; Ivers, *British Drums,* 13.

8. Robert Wright, *Memoir;* 127.

9. *CRG,* 21:121–22 (Oglethorpe to Broughton, 28 March 1736).

10. Ivers, *British Drums;* Kenneth Coleman and Gurr, *Dictionary,* 2:671–72. Piraguas were enlarged, shallow-draft versions of dugout canoes, with deeper hulls, lengths sometimes in excess of thirty-five feet, and usually small cabins aft. The piragua was better suited to carrying cargo than was the boat-canoe and was faster. Because of their speed, the dugouts later came to be used as scout boats: by the time war erupted with Spain, Oglethorpe had a fleet of almost a dozen. Usually powered by oars, piraguas were often fitted with two-masted sailing rigs; however, if travel was taking place on rivers, the crew often struck these rigs, considering oars and strong backs more dependable than sails on rivers and creeks (Jonathan Bryan, *Journal,* nn.33, 34, 35; Fleetwood, *Tidecraft,* 31–43).

11. Ivers, *British Drums,* 51, 100; Oglethorpe, "Letters," 20 October 1739, 90–100.

12. Francis Moore, "A Voyage," 122–23.

13. A March scouting trip had passed Jekyll, Cumberland, and Amelia Islands (*CRG,* 35:36). On 28 March 1736 Oglethorpe wrote to Broughton, "I called the New Fort St. Andrew's and the Island it stands [on] the Highlands" (*CRG,* 21:121–22). Historian William Ramsey believes that the letter referred to an abortive effort to build a fort and that construction actually began on 19 April (Ramsey, "Final Contest," 500).

14. Charles Jones, *Historical Sketch,* 82; Ivers, *British Drums.*

15. Ivers, *British Drums*, chap. 4; *CRG*, 34:479–88 (depositions of Samuel Augsbourguer, 26 August 1739; Charles Dempsy, 11 March 1739; William Thomson, 26 August 1740). Fort St. Andrews's original Crown reserve was probably 200 acres. Jonathan Bryan's grant, dated 7 April 1767, specifically included 100 acres described as "the place whereon Fort St. Andrews formerly stood" (see chap. 3). As of 1770 the general area was defined as a Crown reservation. At the end of the revolution, the reserve became state property and was subsequently granted on a warrant to Jacob Weed and James Finley. McGillis's plat, dated 22 March 1798, is marked, "Fort St. Andrew, 100 acres, Jacob Weed." (For more on McGillis's plat, see chap. 5.) Weed, an enterprising land speculator, acquired half of the fort reserve. By 1798 Camden County tax officials no longer knew exactly how much acreage was considered public land (the fort reserve). Weed called his purchase "Town of St. Andrews" and sold shares in it. Only one buyer seems to have appeared: William Clubb bought two lots on 22 April 1807, thereby making the Clubbs the island's oldest residents. Although the governor and council may have intended to retain 200 acres as Crown property, after 1770 it appears that no one was able to define *fort* or *military reserve*.

16. Charles Jones, *Dead Towns*, 59–60; McCall, *History*; Ivers, *British Drums*, 58.

17. "Plan d'un Petit Fort." When carefully examined, the plan shows a clear, although faint, delineation of Fort St. Andrews's star-work configuration.

18. Egmont, *Diary*, 2:286–87, 289–91.

19. Kenneth Coleman, *Colonial Georgia*.

20. Ivers, *British Drums*, 78; Meroney, "London Entrepôt Merchants."

21. Ivers, *British Drums*, 79–84; W. R. Williams, "British-American Officers," 189.

22. Ivers, *British Drums*, 79.

23. *CRG*, 31:38, 247; Robert Wright, *Memoir*, 203–5; McCall, *History*, 1:123–25; Charles Jones, *Dead Towns*, 73–74; Hewatt, *Historical Account*, 2:70–71; Stevens, *History*, 1:154–55; Egmont, *Diary*, 3:6; Ivers, *British Drums*, 82–84.

24. Oglethorpe to Harman Verelst, 22 November 1738, in Lane, *General Oglethorpe's Georgia*, 2:368–71.

25. Robert Wright, *Memoir*, 203–5; McCall, *History*, 1:123–25; Charles Jones, *Dead Towns*, 73–74; Hewatt, *Historical Account*, 2:70–71; Stevens, *History*, 1:154–55; Egmont, *Diary*, 3:6; Ivers, *British Drums*, 82–84. Personal animosity between Colonel Cochran and Captain Mackay might have laid the groundwork for the outbreak at Fort St. Andrews. A keen rivalry existed between the two officers, and when, in early 1739, it broke out into an open quarrel—Cochran struck Mackay with a heavy stick—both men were immediately arrested. Cochran returned to England to face court-martial for his role in the quarrel, and Mackay enthusiastically sailed home to testify against his colonel (*CRG*, 4:294; Egmont, *Diary*).

26. *Spanish Official Account*, 11, 16.

27. Ibid., 10–11.

28. Oglethorpe to trustees, 29 December 1739, in Oglethorpe, "Letters," 100.

29. Bemis, *Diplomatic History*, 8.

30. Ibid.

31. Jonathan Bryan, *Journal*, 82–83 n.92; Kimber, *A Relation*, xxii–xiv.

32. Ivers, *British Drums*, chap. 11; Cate, "Fort Frederica," 113–30.

33. Ivers, *British Drums*, chap. 11; Cate, "Fort Frederica," 113–30; "Ranger's Report," 218–36; *CRG*, 35:26.

34. Ivers, *British Drums*, chap. 11; Cate, "Fort Frederica," 113–30.

35. Cate, "Fort Frederica," 163. McKinnon's map shows the exact location of this building: Angus Mackay, a grantee, chose "the suttles" for his 50 acres (see chap. 3).

36. Marques de Casina's account, in Arredondo's Journal, 26 July 1742, in *Spanish Official Account*, 65–87.

37. Cate, "Fort Frederica," 164.

CHAPTER THREE. Early British Settlements

1. Harman, *Trade and Privateering*, 2, 47–49.

2. *CRG*, 1:448.

3. Ibid., 5:523–24.

4. "Relación del Yndio," 261.

5. Oglethorpe to Harman Verelst, 22 November 1738, in Lane, *General Oglethorpe's Georgia*, 2:369; *CRG*, 35:531; Logan, "William Logan's Journal," 179. See also "Impartial Inquiry," 181, 182.

6. Jonathan Bryan, *Journal*, 28.

7. Charles Jones, *Dead Towns*, 246; Candler and Evans, *Cyclopedia*, 132.

8. Stevens, *History*, 1:406; Kenneth Coleman, *Colonial Georgia*, 181, 225; Jonathan Bryan, *Journal*; for description, see pp. 4, 24, 25, 26, 28, nn.28, 34, 75, 78, 79; for fire, see nn.80, 82, 84, 87, 92, 96.

9. *CRG*, vol. 27, pt. 1A, p. 216; vol. 28, pt. 1A, pp. 252, 272 (Ellis to Board of Trade, 20 May 1758, 28 January 1759, 1 March 1759); Hawes, "Proceedings," 333, 335–36; Kenneth Coleman, *Colonial Georgia*, 225. A British Quaker, Dr. Samuel Fothergill (1715–72), visited Virginia and the Carolinas in 1754–56. Writing from Charleston in February 1755, on the verge of going to Georgia, he said he had been invited to visit the Sea Islands but "found a prohibition" on such a trip (Fothergill, *Memoirs*).

10. Marguerite Hamer, "Edmund Gray," 1–12.

11. Ramsey, "Final Contest," 514.

12. *CRG*, vol. 27, pt. 1A, p. 216 (Ellis to Board of Trade, 20 May 1758); Ramsey, "Final Contest," 515.

13. Harman, *Trade and Privateering*, 33–34, 51–70, 12–14, 72, 91.

14. *CRG*, vol. 28, pt. 1A, pp. 19–20 (Ellis to Board of Trade, 5 May 1757).

15. Ibid.

16. Ibid., vol. 27, pt. 1A, p. 216 (Ellis to Board of Trade, 20 May 1758).

17. Ibid., vol. 28, pt. 1A, 252–54 (Ellis to Board of Trade, 28 January 1759).

18. Ibid., vol. 28, pt. 1A, p. 275.

19. Ibid., 8:569 (15 September 1761); Marguerite Hamer, "Edmund Gray," 8–9.

20. *CRG*, 8:690.

21. Harman, *Trade and Privateering*, 61–63. There is no record of the outcome of the charges brought against Piles.

22. *CRG*, vol. 28, pt. 2A, pp. 419–20.

23. Ibid., 9:313; *Savannah Georgia Gazette*, 25 October 1798. John Cane and John Cane Jr. were among the heads of families at Gray's settlement on 1 February 1759 (*CRG*, vol. 28, pt. 1A, p. 275). For John Cain, see also "Land Warrants, 1761–1766," 5 March 1765, S-G. James Woodland had acquired a large plantation tract in the present-day Kings Bay area of St. Marys.

24. Marguerite Hamer, "Edmund Gray," 12 n.33; Harman, *Trade and Privateering*, 61–63.

25. Pat Bryant, *English Crown Grants*, intro.

26. Warren and Jones, *Georgia Governor and Council Journals, 1761–1767*, vii.

27. Ibid.

28. Cadle, *Georgia Land Surveying*, 29–34.

29. Ulrich B. Phillips, editorial note, in Habersham, *Letters*, 10; Habersham to William Knox, 6 April 1763, 19 April 1763, 24 November 1763, in Habersham, *Letters*, 11–14. Author has silently corrected Habersham's punctuation.

30. Georgia Colonial Conveyances, Grant Book S, 363–65; Pat Bryant, *English Crown Grants*, 83.

31. Warren and Jones, *Georgia Governor and Council Journals, 1761–1767*, 103; Lilla Hawes, letter to author, November 1976, citing Bulloch, *History and Genealogy*. See also Northen, *Men of Mark*, for Archibald Bulloch, son of Rev. James; and Archibald Bulloch entry in Kenneth Coleman and Gurr, *Dictionary of Georgia Biography*.

32. Both of Bulloch's petitions are found in "Land Warrants, 1761–1766," S-G. The grant appears in colonial Grant Book E, 163, GDAH (also published in Pat Bryant, *English Crown Grants*).

33. Georgia Colonial Conveyances, Grant Book S, 360.3, GDAH.

34. Jonathan Bryan, *Journal*, 57–58 n.2, 1–15; Gallay, *Formation*.

35. Jonathan Bryan, *Journal*.

36. Ibid.

37. Ibid.

38. Laurens to Bryan, 4 September 1767, in Philip Hamer, Rogers, and Chesnutt, *Papers*, 5:288–91.

39. *CRG*, 9:441; "Land Warrants, 1761–1766," S-G. This Dungeness was almost cer-

tainly named after a headland by the same name on the southeastern coast of England, projecting into the Strait of Dover, that presented a serious navigational hazard for sailing vessels. Experienced English mariners would have recognized Cumberland's Dungeness as a hazard for ships. Dungeness is not mentioned in Ellis's or Wright's reports of their visits to Cumberland, and Bryan's petition seems to be the first recorded instance of the term's use in this context.

40. *CRG*, 9:541; Warren and Jones, *Georgia Governor and Council Journals, 1761–1767*, 135.

41. Pat Bryant, *English Crown Grants*, 8; Ramsey, "Final Contest"; Ramsey, "Last Days."

42. Pat Bryant, *English Crown Grants*, 8.

43. Gallay, *Formation*, 103.

44. Colonial Grant Book P, 256; Plat Book C, 330, both in Pat Bryant, *English Crown Grants*, 10. For Smith's sale, see Georgia Colonial Conveyances, Grant Book S, 363.5, Microfilm Library, GDAH, drawer 40, box 20.

45. *Savannah Georgia Gazette*, 10 February 1768, p. 3; Georgia Colonial Conveyances, Grant Book S, 357–59.

46. *Charleston South Carolina Gazette*, 26 July 1770, p. 4; Georgia Colonial Conveyances, Grant Book U, 292–96. Lynch and Rose held the two islands as tenants in common, meaning that each of the new owners owned an undivided interest. They were eager to divide their property and in November 1770 petitioned the Georgia governor and council for permission to divide the island into two halves, with Lynch taking the northern half and Rose the southern half. They pleaded that "loose and disorderly Persons" were taking advantage of the Crown reservations (public land) and were destroying livestock. Their petition was rejected (*CRG*, 11:178). The great events of the American Revolution swept away petty considerations of land division on Cumberland, and Lynch and Rose remained tenants in common until after the war. Lynch was active in colonial agitation leading to the American Revolution, participating in the 1765 Stamp Act Congress. He also served as a member of the First and Second Continental Congresses (*DAB*; Moultrie, *Memoirs*, 1:65).

47. *DAB*.

48. Bryan genealogy, Bryan Papers; Jackson, "Carolina Connection," 147–72; Gallay, *Formation*; Harrold, "Colonial Siblings," 707–44; *Abstracts*, 20–21; Georgia Writers' Project, *Savannah River Plantations*, 391–418; Kenneth Coleman and Gurr, *Dictionary of Georgia Biography*, 1:128–30.

49. "Land Warrants, 1761–1766," S-G; Colonial Grant Book E, S-G, 331; *CRG*, 9:417, 430. Hester's Bluff is the present-day Plum Orchard Landing, a long, low bluff facing on Brick Hill River. Its name may indicate the location of a settlement once occupied by William and John Hester, members of Edmund Gray's community.

50. Plat Book C, S-G, 330.

51. For Lachlan McIntosh, see Jackson, "General Lachlan McIntosh," 27; Plat Book C, 225, in Pat Bryant, *English Crown Grants;* Warren and Jones, *Georgia Governor and Council Journals, 1761–1767,* 108–9. For George McIntosh, see *CRG,* 9:337. For John Houstoun McIntosh and Houstoun-McIntosh relationships, see Johnston, *The Houstouns of Georgia,* 366. For Camden County resurvey and tract of Thomas Williams, see "Camden County Field Notes, 1796–1816," RCCG, 64.

52. Oglethorpe Regt. File, "Captain James Mackay," citing Phillips Coll., #14208, 101, Mackay to Oglethorpe, September 1735, Cate Collection.

53. *Savannah Georgia Gazette,* 12 January 1764, p. 2.

54. Ibid., 8 December 1763.

55. *CRG,* 9:519; Plat Book C, S-G, 218; Colonial Grant Book H, 11, GDAH; tax collector's sale, *Columbian Museum and Savannah Advertiser,* 2 March 1798, p. 6. For county surveyor, see "Map and Survey of the Islands of Cumberland. The Property of the Heirs of Lynch and General Greene. Executed 22nd March 1798, by R[andolph] McGillis," CER, folder 11-1-001.

56. *CRG,* 22:367, 24:393–94.

57. Ibid., 9:307; McLendon, *History,* 19.

58. Warren and Jones, *Georgia Governor and Council Journals, 1761–1767,* 106, 141.

59. *DAB,* 8:68–70. For Habersham's will, see Will Book E, Records of Chatham County, Savannah, 124.

60. "Land Warrants, 1761–1766," S-G; Colonial Grant Book F, 83, in Pat Bryant, *English Crown Grants;* Georgia Colonial Conveyances, Grant Book S, 366, GDAH.

61. Georgia Colonial Conveyances, Grant Book F, 256; Plat Book C, 330, in Pat Bryant, *English Crown Grants,* 10; Georgia Colonial Conveyances, Grant Book S, 363.5–365.

62. Pat Bryant, *English Crown Grants,* 83.

63. Colonial Grant Book F, 83, in Pat Bryant, *English Crown Grants;* Georgia Colonial Conveyances, Grant Book S, 290.3, 291–93; Warren and Jones, *Georgia Governor and Council Journals, 1761–1767,* 155.

64. Warren and Jones, *Georgia Governor and Council Journals, 1761–1767,* 4 December 1764, 282-R.

65. Ibid., 98, 157.

66. Ibid., 157; Colonial Grant Book F, 79, 80 (2 grants), in Pat Bryant, *English Crown Grants; CRG,* 9:730.

67. Deed Book II, RCCG, 730–31; *Gazette of the State of Georgia,* 25 September 1788, p. 2.

68. Colonial Grant Book G, 34–36, in Pat Bryant, *English Crown Grants,* 9.

CHAPTER FOUR. Cumberland's First Plantations

1. Robin L. Smith et al., *Coastal Adaptations;* Owsley, *Plain Folk;* Larson, *Aboriginal Subsistence Technology;* Reitz, "Spanish and British Subsistence Strategies"; Reitz, "Spanish Colonial Experience."

2. William Bartram, *Travels,* 43.

3. Jonathan Bryan, *Journal,* 28; Hermione Ross Walker memoir, in possession of Preston Stevens; Robin L. Smith et al., *Coastal Adaptations;* Owsley, *Plain Folk;* Larson, *Aboriginal Subsistence Technology;* Reitz, "Spanish and British Subsistence Strategies"; Reitz, "Spanish Colonial Experience."

4. Jonathan Bryan, *Journal,* 28; Hermione Ross Walker memoir, in possession of Preston Stevens; Robin L. Smith et al., *Coastal Adaptations;* Owsley, *Plain Folk;* Larson, *Aboriginal Subsistence Technology;* Reitz, "Spanish and British Subsistence Strategies"; Reitz, "Spanish Colonial Experience."

5. Gregorios del Castillo to Zéspedes, 10 November 1787, EFP, reel 45, bnd. 119 B 10, doc. 1787-142; Milanich, *Laboring,* 146–47.

6. Hermione Ross Walker, "Poverty," 43; Mary Miller, "Growing Up," 7–8; Robert W. Ferguson Jr., conversation with author, Cumberland Island, mid-1930s; Kemble, *Journal,* ed. Scott, 173.

7. Hann, *History,* 143; Oglethorpe, "Letters"; Kimber, *A Relation;* Robin L. Smith et al., *Coastal Adaptations.*

8. Bullard, *Abandoned Black Settlement,* 76–77 n.72. For information about swimming horses, I am grateful to Franklin Bass, Woodbine, Georgia; the late J. B. Peeples, Coleraine, Georgia; and a horse trainer I met at a 1976 auction near Folkston, Georgia.

9. Samuel Gray to McIntosh, 5 February 1789, McIntosh Papers, item 5. I cannot identify Hockings Island, unless Gray meant Hawkins Island, a marsh island lying north of Gascoigne Bluff on St. Simons Island.

10. See Butler and Hare, *Annals,* 308–9, Appendix 2, for personal account of Major Patrick Murray. See also Hanson and Karstad, "Feral Swine"; Ambrose, *An Analysis of Feral Horse Population Structure;* Bjork, *1995 Feral Horse Population Survey;* Goodloe, "Genetic Variation"; Monica Turner, "Simulation and Management Implications"; and Bonner, *History of Georgia Agriculture,* 25–31.

11. Carney, "Rice, Slaves, and Landscapes"; "Proceedings," 72. Descended from Black Angus stock, *black cattle* referred to beef cattle rather than dairy cattle and did not reflect the animals' color.

12. Gray, *History of Agriculture,* esp. "Rice and Indigo"; Schöpf, *Travels,* 157–60; Hewatt, *Historical Account,* 2:138–44; General [John] Floyd, "On the Cultivation and Preparation," 105–8, 154–62; Drayton, *View,* 123–25; Hilliard, "Tidewater Rice Plantation."

13. Doar, *Rice and Rice Planting;* Hilliard, "Tidewater Rice Plantation."

14. Ibid.

15. Hilliard, "Tidewater Rice Plantation"; McCallie, "Preliminary Report."

16. Georgia Colonial Conveyances, Grant Book V, 290.6–291, GDAH.

17. Virginia Wood, *Live Oaking*, 4–12.

18. Ibid.

19. Ibid.

20. Ibid.

21. Ibid., 107; *Columbian Museum and Savannah Advertiser*, 7 December 1798, p. 4.

22. Georgia Colonial Conveyances, Grant Book V, 290.6–291, GDAH.

23. Bullard, "Uneasy Legacy."

24. RCCG, "Superior and Inferior Court Papers, 1779–1827." Sheriff Samuel Smith issued two warrants attaching Belin's property, one in 1791, the other on 24 October 1794. Belin, a member of an old Huguenot South Carolina rice-planting family, resided on Great Cumberland Island. He was an inventor who interested himself in improving hydraulic systems for rice plantations. Sometime in the late 1780s the Lynch family invited Belin to work for them. While he lived on Cumberland, Belin must have employed slave labor to operate one of his water-powered mills for beating rice. When he departed Cumberland, probably in 1791, Belin left behind enough property—a house with furniture, farm equipment, and livestock—for it to have been attached by the sheriff in 1794 for nonpayment of taxes (Drayton, *View*, 121–25; author's file on Belin).

25. Hewatt, *Historical Account*, 2:144; De Vorsey, *Report*, 72.

26. Potash (or a lime derivative) eventually replaced urine as the catalyst. See Gray, *History of Agriculture*, esp. "Rice and Indigo."

27. Gray, *History of Agriculture*, esp. "Rice and Indigo"; Winberry, "Reputation," 242–50.

28. Landers, "Spanish Sanctuary," 296–97 and 310–11. Landers was a doctoral candidate when she wrote this carefully documented article, which remains excellent. The problem of supervision was of long duration. In 1790, some new edicts (17 May 1790) of the Spanish governor, Zéspedes, showed that he was bowing to the U.S. government by suspending the Spanish "century-old policy of sanctuary for fugitive slaves."

29. Gray, *History of Agriculture*, esp. "Rice and Indigo"; Leland, *Indigo*.

30. Jacob Blamey, "Plan de la Barre et de l'entrée de la Rivière de Nassau," Special Collections, University of Georgia, Athens, Map G 3922. Blamey's 1775 map is an almost exact copy of William Fuller's 1769 map ("A Chart of the Entrance into St. Mary's River," Special Collections, University of Georgia, Athens), drawn one year before Bryan's sale to Lynch and Rose. The Fuller map, dedicated to John, Earl of Egmont, and published by Thomas Jefferys, Geographer to the King, is often referred to as the "Egmont map" or the "Jefferys' map."

31. Hill, "'Masked Acquisition,'" 308. See also Bullard, "Uneasy Legacy," 769–73 and 775–76.

CHAPTER FIVE. The American Revolution

1. James Johnson, *Militiamen, Rangers, and Redcoats*, 43.

2. Searcy, *Georgia-Florida Contest*, 22; "Proceedings," 51.

3. Searcy, *Georgia-Florida Contest*, 22–23, 167.

4. Ibid., 46.

5. J. Leitch Wright, *Florida*, 37.

6. McCall, *History*, 349; Vanderhill, "Alachua–St. Marys Road," 50–67; Chalker, "Highland Scots," 35–42; Searcy, *Georgia-Florida Contest*, 46.

7. Searcy, *Georgia-Florida Contest*, 34; "Proceedings," 51.

8. Searcy, *Georgia-Florida Contest*.

9. Ibid., 35–36, 44–51.

10. Ibid.

11. Ibid., 44.

12. Journal of the Council of Safety, 5 July 1776, *Revolutionary Records of Georgia*, 1:151–52.

13. Searcy, *Georgia-Florida Contest*, 47.

14. Ibid., 47–48.

15. Ibid., 49–50.

16. Ibid., 55, 61–62.

17. Ibid., 56, 62, 63; *CRG*, 1:193; "Proceedings," 102–3.

18. Searcy, *Georgia-Florida Contest*, 68–69, 70.

19. McCall, *History*, 347; J. Leitch Wright, *Florida*, 42–43; Kenneth Coleman, *American Revolution*, 89.

20. J. Leitch Wright, *Florida*, 44.

21. Elbert to Col. Habersham, 30 May 1777, 31 May 1777, *Collections of the Georgia Historical Society*, vol. 5, pt. 2; Elbert, *Order Book*, 33–35, 45; Moultrie, *Memoirs*, 336. "The Continentals resorted to Cumberland's South Point to rest their sick, because of its accessibility and its fresh water. When the Rebels came forward to this province, they left on Cumberland Island three hundred men sick of a bad, infectious fever." Governor Tonyn, St. Augustine, to Viscount George Keith Elphinstone, on the St. Johns River, mid-July 1778, cited in *The Keith Papers*, Navy Records Society, 62 (London, 1927).

22. Elbert, *Order Book*, 45.

23. Ibid., 25; *CRG*, 9:352; index to headright and bounty grants, Colonial Grant Book F, 418, GDAH; *Abstracts of Colonial Wills*, 31. For a Clubb genealogy, see Cate Collection. For East Florida, see "A Return of Refugees with Their Negroes Who Came to the Province of East Florida in Consequence of the Evacuation of the Province of Georgia," C.O. 5/560, 481, Manuscript Division, LC. For map, see "Map of the Coast of Georgia, Bordering on Camden and Glynn Counties, Showing Also the Course and

Soundings of the Alatamaha, Turtle, Crooked, St. Marys, Great Satilla, and Little Satilla Rivers," Acc. #73-691562, Map and Geography Division, LC. See also Bullard, *Abandoned Black Settlement*, 13 n.14. A legal advertisement in the late 1780s warned Raymond Demere's creditors that he was no longer responsible for the debts of Mary Clubb, because she had left his bed and board. His notice concluded peevishly by saying they were never legally married. On 10 July 1777 Georgia's treasury was ordered to pay "Mary Clubb in full of her account" the sum of 23 pounds 17 shillings 5¼ pence ("Minutes of the Executive Council," 28).

24. Elbert, *Order Book*, May 18, 1777.

25. Siebert, *Loyalists*, 1:73; Kenneth Coleman, *American Revolution*, 120–21.

26. Kenneth Coleman, *American Revolution*, 119.

27. Siebert, *Loyalists*, 1:73.

28. Ibid., 1:73; Butler and Hare, *Annals*, 308–9.

29. Kenneth Coleman, *American Revolution*.

30. Stevens, *History*, 2:370.

31. George Washington Greene, *Life*, vol. 1.

32. *DAB*.

33. Ibid. The legislature also ordered that the general receive a plantation called Boones Barony on the south side of the Edisto River and a credit with which he could buy some of its slaves. Greene later had to sell Boones Barony to meet his personal debts.

34. Thayer, *Nathanael Greene*, 414.

35. Banks, Burnet, and Greene to McQueen, 7 August 1783, Miscellaneous Records, vol. WW, pt. 1, pp. 225–28, South Carolina Department of Archives and History; rerecorded by McQueen, 31 July 1786, Nathanael R. Greene Papers, Rhode Island Historical Society; certificate of Major Robert Forsyth, 7 September 1793, Greene Papers, estate box 2. Forsyth, a member of the general's official family, was testifying about what he knew about the 1783 transaction. Forsyth's certificate was a preface to a thirteen-page document reviewing these transactions. His testimony was abstracted by Phineas Miller in Charleston, 22 March 1794. Burnet had also been an aide to the general until he resigned his commission in 1783 to become Banks's partner. For the complete title search for the two Cumberland Islands up to 11 August 1783, see Bullard, "Cumberland Islands." For the division of the two islands, see Bullard, "Uneasy Legacy," 757–88. McQueen may have started this risky venture by offering to buy supplies if Greene lent McQueen the money. In that case, McQueen would have been required to post bond, and the deed known as Greene's purchase deed should instead be thought of as a security deed, somewhat like the performance bond required of contractors today.

36. *DAB*; Thayer, *Nathanael Greene*, 413–20; Moultrie, *Memoirs*, 2:336–44; McCrady, *History*, 4–5, 677–80; George Washington Greene, *Life*, 3:458–66.

37. Deed Book D, RCCG, 97–120, 86–96, 128–34. The fact that Banks and Burnet bound themselves to pay Greene instead of being paid by him clearly indicates that

they put up the tracts as a form of security in a promise-to-pay arrangement. Failure on the part of Banks and Burnet to pay the consideration did not invalidate the instrument (Cadle, *Georgia Land Surveying*, 356–57).

38. Thayer, *Nathanael Greene;* "Claim for Losses Sustained by Major General Greene in Procuring Supplies for the Southern Army, in 1782," in *American State Papers*, no. 23, 33–49.

39. Bullard, "Uneasy Legacy," 776. Phineas Miller (1764–1803) was the son of Isaac and Hannah Miller of Middletown, Connecticut, and a 1785 graduate of Yale College. Upon the recommendation of Yale's president, Greene hired Miller immediately after his graduation and took him to Georgia, where he combined tutoring the Greene children with his official duties. Miller and Eli Whitney later became partners. Because Miller died at Dungeness, the absence of any grave marker for him at the Greene-Shaw cemetery has puzzled researchers. His will indicates that he was survived by numerous brothers and sisters in Connecticut, so his remains may have been returned to Middletown (Murdoch, "Letters and Papers," 54:270; Richard Showman, letter to author, 1986; Stegeman and Stegeman, *Caty;* Mirsky and Nevins, *World*).

40. Torres, *Historic Resource Study*, 66–75; *Revolutionary Records of Georgia*, 2:730–31; Lockey, *East Florida*, 315.

41. Tanner, *General Greene's Visit*, 10–11.

42. Torres, *Historic Resource Study*, 71.

43. Ibid.

44. Ibid., 70–71 n.16.

45. William Johnson, *Sketches*, 2:355–75, 435–37; Bullard, "Uneasy Legacy," 776.

46. Deed Book AB, RCCG, 5–6, with scraps of preceding pages, and Deed Book A, RCCG, 8. These documents were originally recorded in Deed Book AB, possibly earlier than 1786. Seagrove and Weed's appointments were reconfirmed in Deed Book A on 30 June 1788. Deed Book AB is the first register of deeds for Camden County. Probably because of its deteriorated condition, it was replaced at an unknown date by Deed Book A, now viewed as the county's first register of deeds.

47. Deed Book AB, RCCG, 18.

48. Bullard, "Uneasy Legacy," 778.

CHAPTER SIX. Legacy of War

1. Bullard, "Uneasy Legacy," 778.

2. Ibid.; Kurtz, *Presidency*, 305–6, 336–37, 359; Dauer, *Adams Federalists*, 145–51; *Annals*, 8:3758–59, 3778–85; *Republican and Savannah Evening Ledger*, 1 January 1813, p. 4. The Evaluation Act was amended in 1802. By that date, although the two legal entities known as the Estate of General Greene and the Heirs of Lynch were still frequently listed as tax delinquents, the Greenes were beginning to be solvent again.

3. Miller to Whitney, 17 February 1799, typescript of letter at Georgia Historical Society, Eli Whitney Papers; Deed Book 1-W, Records of Chatham County, Savannah, 279–84.

4. Virginia Wood, *Live Oaking*, 35, 36–38.

5. CER, folder 11-1-001. This "Map and Survey of the Islands of Cumberland. The Property of the Heirs of Lynch and General Greene. Executed 22nd March 1798 by R. McGillis" is now housed at GDAH.

6. *Columbian Museum and Savannah Advertiser*, 6 April 1798, p. 3; Camden County Deed Books D–H, drawer 71, box 20, Microfilm Library, GDAH.

7. Minutes, Superior Court, October term, 1799, RCCG, n.p.

8. "Superior and Inferior Court Papers, 1779–1827," n.p., RCCG, Microfilm Library, drawer 27, box 69, GDAH; "Surveyor's Field Notes, 1796–1816," RCCG, 88–102.

9. *Columbian Museum and Savannah Advertiser*, 28 January 1800, p. 4.

10. Ibid., 18 February 1800, p. 2.

11. Bullard, "Uneasy Legacy," 782.

12. Torres, *Historic Resource Study*, 79; Cornelia Greene to Margaret Cowper, 3 May, 6 August, 10 October 1800, Mackay-Stiles Papers.

13. Deed Book K, RCCG, 196.

14. CER, folder 11-1-002. The McKinnon map is now housed at GDAH.

15. Gritzner, "Tabby," 32, 104; Blunt, *American Coast Pilot*; map, "Coast of Florida: Little Cumberland Island to South Lagoon," [ca 1821?], map 1396, PKY; Bailey Family Papers. Gritzner calls Dungeness a three-story house, but she may have overlooked the basement, which does not show well in the photographs available to her in 1978. Cumberland Island National Seashore literature correctly calls Dungeness a four-story building.

16. S. G. W. Benjamin, "Sea Islands," 848–50; *Columbian Museum and Savannah Advertiser*, 6 April 1798; Torres, *Historic Resource Study*, 83; Ober, "Dungeness," 12.

17. Pierson, *American Buildings*; Whiffen and Koeper, *American Architecture*; Wayne Andrews, *Architecture*. At least three of Dungeness's architectural elements would have been too difficult for Miller and Sands to have designed by themselves: the roof treatment (there may have been a balustrade around the hipped roof), central staircase, and decorative ornamentation for its windows and the front entrance. In 1805 Thomas Spalding built a tabby home on Sapelo Island, employing Roswell King, a young New England carpenter and building contractor, to finish the woodwork. Miller and Sands may similarly have sought the services of Isaiah Davenport, a Rhode Island carpenter who became a famous Savannah builder. Davenport is supposed to have arrived in that city in 1803, but his whereabouts for the preceding two years are unknown (Raley, "Daniel Pratt," 425–32; Carol Juneau, letter to author, February 1986; Karen E. Osvald, letter to author, 23 January 1986).

18. "Map Representing Dungenness Plantation Situated on the South End of Missoe Island, known as Cumberland, in Camden County, Georgia. The Property of the

Estate of Mrs. Eliza H. Molyneux, and Containing a Total of Eighteen Hundred and Ninety-one acres," resurveyed 5 September 1878, by John R. Tebeau, CER, folder 11-1-003.

19. Robert G. Neiley, letters to author, 1990.

20. Darlington, *Reliquiae Baldwinianae,* 112.

21. For height of high land, see "Map of South End, Cumberland Island, Showing Break in Beach with Protection Dike, and High and Low Water levels," prepared by U.S. Army Corps of Engineers, 1903–7. See WEP correspondence and graphics, CER, ser. 7 and ser. 11; and folder 11-1-006, "United States Army Corps of Engineers, Cumberland Island South End Survey Blueprint, 1912"; Ober, "Dungeness," 241–49; Milanich, "Tacatacuru," 290; Hale Smith and Bullen, *Fort San Carlos,* 34–36.

22. Bailey Family Papers, folder 2, item 28; Torres, *Historic Resource Study,* 89. See also S. G. W. Benjamin, "Sea Islands," 848–50.

23. Ober, "Dungeness," 241–49; Garrett, *At Home;* Torres, *Historic Resource Study,* 98–101; see also his illustration 8.

24. Poesch, *Titian Ramsey Peale,* 21; Cornelius H. Longstreet diary, 7 March 1865, University of Florida, George A. Smathers Libraries; George Washington Greene, *Life,* 1:445–46.

25. Ober, "Dungeness," 241–49. Louis Torres, National Park Service historian, suggests that Ober was guided through the house by someone who knew it well. Torres is correct, but Ober's guide was probably not a member of the immediate Nightingale family, since their ownership of Dungeness had terminated in 1870. Torres, *Historic Resource Study,* 85.

26. *Savannah Republican,* 13 April 1825. The entire Greene family may have been interested in cultivating oranges at Dungeness. In 1800 Cornelia Greene asked a friend to send flower and fruit seeds for propagation. Cornelia particularly asked for oranges, saying that it did not matter if they arrived rotten since she wanted the seeds (Cornelia Greene to Margaret Cowper, 10 October 1800, Mackay-Stiles Papers). Phineas Miller died in 1803, allegedly of lockjaw after puncturing his finger on an orange thorn (Murdoch, "Letters and Papers," 270; Nightingale, "Dungeness," 376; *Columbian Museum and Savannah Advertiser,* 14 December 1803).

27. Ober, "Dungeness," 14.

28. Du Pont, *Civil War Letters,* 1:358–59, 2:68–70; Longstreet diary, 1864–65, University of Florida, George A. Smathers Libraries.

29. Wiedemann, "Architectural Preservation," 38; extract from Account of Titian Peale's Journey, 1817–18, folder 3; Floyd diary, 23 June 1834, Charles Rinaldo Floyd Papers, folder 1, item 1; John McQueen to Enrique White, 3 October 1801, bundle 135 E 11 (reel 56), doc. 1801-245, EFP.

30. According to Gray, Sea Island cotton commanded top prices since the delicate fibers were suitable for the production of fine thread, lace, and silky cloth. Gray, *History of Agriculture,* 731, cited by Robin L. Smith et al., *Coastal Adaptations,* 169–72.

31. George F. Clarke's map, 1811, acc. 1507, PKY; Eloise Bailey, *Pathway*, 8. The islands also housed smuggled slaves. U.S. customs officers suspected Garvin of reselling slaves off-loaded from ships in Spanish waters. The Steam Saw Mill at St. Marys existed as of 3 April 1803. It was referred to in a deed of sale between John Chevalier and William Pitt Sands, dated 20 April 1803, recorded 19 May 1805, Deed Book F, RCCG, 298–301.

32. CER, folder 11-1-002. The overseer almost certainly was Thomas Stafford. Upon his death, Isham Spalding Sr. took the job and eventually married Stafford's widow. On McKinnon's map, Spalding's house is shown in tract 3, within land purchased by Lucy Stafford before her remarriage.

33. CER, folder 11-1-002. Also residing in tract 5, but at a different home site, was Mrs. "Dilliworth," widow of Captain John Dilworth, the previous superintendent. Said to have been a British naval officer, the captain may have been hired by a Greene-Lynch combine to oversee the cutting of live oak (see Bullard, *Robert Stafford*, 313–14).

34. Division of property, 24 April 1810, Deed Book H, RCCG, 184; Stegeman and Stegeman, *Caty*, 117. On 12 March 1814 in a prenuptial agreement, Louisa placed her property in trust, including this lot (Deed Book I, RCCG, 195). The Stegemans provide no sources for their contention that Skipwith partnered with Miller and Nightingale.

35. Mart Stewart, *"What Nature Suffers to Groe,"* 117.

36. William Henry Capers, "Culture of Sea-Island Cotton," *Southern Agriculturist* 8 (1835): 402–15; Gray, *History of Agriculture*, 731.

37. Capers, "Culture of Sea-Island Cotton," 402–15.

38. Ibid.

39. Ibid.

40. Gray, *History of Agriculture*, 350.

41. Capers, "On the Cotton Caterpillar," 203–9.

42. Gray, *History of Agriculture*, 737–38; Peggy Stanley Froeschauer, interview by author, Cumberland Island, 1988; Froeschauer, "Interpretation."

43. Torres, *Historic Resource Study*, 112; Murdoch, "Letters and Papers," 53:500, 54:102; Melish, *Travels*, 27.

44. Division of property, 24 April 1810, Deed Book H, RCCG, 184–87. Camden County records lack an 1814 inventory of Catharine Miller's estate. When she died, British warships were cruising off the southeastern Georgia coast, and her will was probated on 4 January 1815, the day before the British invasion. During the British occupation of Cumberland (January–March 1815) court and executors were hindered in their duties by the naval invasion (see "Minutes of Camden County Inferior Court, 10 April 1815, Justices Miller, Gibson, Ross presiding," RCCG). An appraisal of her estate was made on 17 April 1815, a month after the British squadron's departure. The only copy of this appraisal is in the National Archives. More than half of the Greene slaves departed with the British; approximately eighty slaves were forcibly returned by the

British admiral in compliance with his interpretation of the Treaty of Ghent (see Bullard, *Black Liberation*).

45. Testimony of Nathanael Greene, RG 76, entry 190, claim 493, doc. 13, NA. See Bullard, *Black Liberation*, 100 n.124.

46. Various estate inventories, RCCG. See Bullard, *Abandoned Black Settlement*, 1 n.1.

47. Kolodny, *Land*, 47.

48. Stevens, *History*, 2:360; Lamplugh, "Politics," 55.

49. Patrick Carnes to Vicente Emanuel de Zéspedes, 1 August 1789, bundle 120 C 10, doc. 1789-161, EFP.

50. *CRG*, vol. 19, pt. 2, pp. 165–66 (5 August 1782). In February 1783 Georgia's governor and council were presented with a plan to allow East Florida loyalists to settle between the St. Marys and Altamaha Rivers. The plan's anonymous author pointed out that southeast Georgia was nearly deserted and needed new settlers. The project failed to win approval ("Minutes, Governor and Executive Council," 25 February 1783, file East and West Florida, 1764–1850, GDAH).

51. *CRG*, vol. 19, pt. 2, p. 459.

52. Elbert to Lachlan McIntosh, 19 September 1785; Elbert to Montfort, 19 September 1785, in Samuel Elbert, *Letter Book*, 218. The surveyor acknowledged on 25 August 1785 that surveys were made at the two Cumberland reserves before receipt of an order to the contrary from the Governor's Council. Montfort told Governor Elbert that he had warned petitioners for Wright's Fort that they must promptly incorporate into a town or risk legislative inquiry.

53. Henry Osborne to Samuel Elbert, 8 April 1785, Henry Osborne File, file 1. "En el punto norte de la Ysla de Cumberland tiene establecido su almacén de efectos y víveres, el americano d[o]n Alexandro Semple" (On Cumberland's north point is now a store belonging to the American Alexander Semple where he sells general merchandise and provisions) (Parker, "Men without God," 135–55, n.43, from a Spanish lieutenant's report of 1785). Semple's store at the High Point sold salted and almost fresh meat, ham, flour, potatoes, butter, rice, and English and small crackers. From other unspecified merchants on Cumberland in 1785, residents from Spanish East Florida sailed in to buy their *beautiful guns* (Spaniard's emphasis), powder, gunflints, and riding saddles for both men and women.

54. Elbert, *Letter Book*, 204. Osborne's deed was recorded in June 1785 before surveyor Montfort arrived with new instructions. Osborne's warrant was confirmed in 1787 by a grant from Governor George Mathews. For their appointments to justices of the peace, see "Statutes, Colonial and Revolutionary, 1774–1805," *CRG*, vol. 19, pt. 2, pp. 469, 524. Osborne was admitted to practice in Georgia courts on 13 February 1786. For warrant executed by Solomon Pendleton, 20 June 1785, see "Headrights and Plats, 1785–1849," Superior Court, Book A, RCCG, 43. For the grant, see colonial Grant Book

MMM, 114; Plat Book D, 28, registered 29 January 1787; both in GDAH. Governor George Mathews confirmed the warrant to Henry Osborne, 24 January 1787. In 1802 Congress passed a resolution directing the construction of a "sufficient" lighthouse on South Point, Cumberland Island. Congress ordered the state of Georgia to cede this land. The resolution, acknowledging that there was a difficulty because Georgia had already granted all public land at South Point to private individuals, ordered the secretary of the treasury to purchase sufficient land if no other method of acquisition was possible. Congress ordered the U.S. attorney general to look into this matter. In 1804 Georgia agreed to cede jurisdiction over 6 acres at South Point, provided the United States construct a lighthouse on that tract. Attorney Archibald Clarke later attempted to sell this 6-acre tract to the U.S. government for a lighthouse site, but litigation over its ownership delayed the sale. Osborne's heirs must have succeeded in making their claim to ownership because on 19 July 1820, while the lighthouse was under construction, the heirs of Henry Osborne transferred to the United States 6 acres on South Point for $600 (Clayton, *Compilation*, 197, 675; Torres, *Historic Resource Study*, 222).

55. Osborne later became a Superior Court judge in Camden County. In 1792 he was impeached and stripped of his office after being convicted by the state House of Representatives of suppressing returns from Camden and Glynn Counties during the hotly contested 1790 congressional election between General Anthony Wayne and James Jackson. Wayne, who was a Federalist and a friend of General and Mrs. Greene, ran against Jackson, an antigovernment man, and Judge Osborne was accused of having reopened the polls after they were legally closed. General Wayne, asking in the U.S. House of Representatives (1792) for more time to justify himself, said he found it impossible to collect his evidence or to send it "over a space of 200 miles of difficult roads in the most inclement season, the inhabitants of Cumberland Island being separated by a dangerous sound." Prosecution's evidence showed that after the fall of darkness on Election Day, Judge Osborne, whose plantation lay on Satilla River, received a boatload (in the case, a galley or dugout canoe, rowed by slaves) of Federalist Cumberland Islanders, accompanied by two soldiers. *Georgia Gazette*, 12 April 1792, 2; *Federal Gazette* (Philadelphia), 8 February 1792, 13, 28; George R. Lamplugh, "Thomas Carr and the Camden County 'War' of 1793," *Atlanta Historical Bulletin* 20, no. 2 (fall 1976), 37–45; Lockey, *East Florida;* Siebert, *Loyalists in East Florida*, 1:208; Troxler, "Loyalist Refugees"; Kenneth Coleman, *American Revolution*, 240–43; Parker, "Men without God."

56. Michaux, "Journal," 38–39; Chappell, *Miscellanies*, 37–41; *DAB;* James Seagrove to George Matthews, 20 December 1795, Matthews Collection; Kenneth Coleman, *American Revolution*, chap. 15 (for Indian relations with Georgia, 1785–89); James Jackson to David Blackshear, 18 June 1799, in Stephen F. Miller, *Bench and Bar,* 1:405–6; Milfort, "Memoir"; Fuller, *Purchase,* 60–75; Murdoch, *Georgia-Florida Fron-*

tier (citing Captain Andrew Atkinson, of the Spanish East Florida militia, reporting suspected American activity in fortifying the southern end of Cumberland in 1794); Murdoch, "Elijah Clarke," 173–90; Hays, *Hero* (a detailed, sympathetic biography of Clarke); Murdoch, "Citizen Mangourit," 522–40; Hill, "Masked Acquisition"; Coatsworth, "American Trade," 243–66, esp. 240–51 (for U.S. trade with French West Indies).

57. Stephen F. Miller, *Bench and Bar*, 1:46–51, 67, 70, details regarding the Camden County militia; Lamplugh, "Politics," esp. chaps. 5 and 6.

58. Bundle 118 A 10 (reel 44), doc. 1786-93, EFP.

59. Camden County File II, GDAH. Most of the men on the grand jury for this case had either lived on South Point or did business there, including James Woodland, Alexander Semple, Isham Spalding, and Langley Bryant.

60. William Maxwell to Governor Vicente Manuel de Zespedes, East Florida, ca. 1 April 1785; Lockey, *East Florida*, 489–90; Lt. Randolph McGillis, Light Horse, Camden Regt. Militia at St. Marys, to his commanding officer at Savannah, 4 April 1794, GDAH, Folder "Pre-1900," File II, Box 7, "Randolph McGillis."

61. Randolph McGillis to his commanding officer at Savannah, 4 April 1794, GDAH, Folder "Pre-1900," File II, Box 7, "Randolph McGillis."

62. Murdoch, "Correspondence," 7; Maclay, *History*, 338–39, 7–8; Swanson, *Predators*, chaps. 1–3. Cray Pratt, a longtime resident of St. Marys and eventual employee of the Carnegies, provided the information about the origins of the name "Wreckers Road."

63. *Savannah Georgia Gazette*, 25 October 1764, p. 2; 29 March 1775, p. 2; 24 March 1796, p. 1.

64. *Columbian Museum and Savannah Advertiser*, 4 May 1809, p. 3; WEP to Mrs. Emma Sweetland (who lost her father and her brother in *Lizzie Heyer*), November 1898, and WEP to Captain Fader (who was reported to have seen *Lizzie Heyer* broken up on Stafford Shoals), November 1898, in CER, folder 2-2-042.

65. Robert Mackay to Eliza Anne McQueen, 3 September 1799, in Mackay, *Letters*, 11.

66. Committee of Officers to Lyman Hall, draft, February 1783, in McIntosh, *Papers*, 119.

67. McIntosh to Nathanael Greene, 30 October 1782, in ibid., 103.

68. Miller to Eli Whitney, 12 May 1797, Greene Papers.

69. Miller to McQueen, 6 March 1801, bundle 135 E 11, docs. 1801-77, 1801-78, EFP.

70. Jameson, *Privateering and Piracy*, 586; Chappell, *Miscellanies*, 37–41; James Seagrove to George Matthews, 20 December 1795, Matthews Collection; Upton, *Law*, 287–300; Keber, "Planters"; Bushnell, *República*, esp. 14–16, 19–34; Pierre Ordronaux, "To the Public," *Savannah Georgia Republican*, 12 September 1806, p. 2 (a privateer of a large brig protests decisions by a St. Marys ad hoc arbitration commission); Cabot,

"Defensa"; Cabot, "Ultimos Años"; McMaster, *Life,* vol. 2 (for effects of Embargo Acts and Nonimportation Acts on St. Marys); Tornero, *Relaciónes,* esp. 80–84, 108–18, 19–20 (for a mention of Cumberland Island).

71. McQueen to Enrique White, 31 October 1801, bundle 135 E 11, doc. 1801-245, EFP.

72. U.S. naval officers commanded the *St. Marys,* but the remainder of its crew was composed of local recruits. The galley was transferred to the Revenue Cutter Service in 1802, where its duties were to intercept smugglers and their customers. Abstracted from *Columbian Museum and Savannah Advertiser,* 25 December 1798, in *Georgia Genealogical Magazine* no. 5 (July 1962); *Dictionary of American Naval Fighting Ships,* 6:249–50.

73. Savannah *Public Intelligencer,* 3 June 1808, p. 3 (item dated 27 May 1808); *Republican and Savannah Evening Ledger,* June 2, 1808, p. 2, c. 1 (item dated 24 May 1808).

74. *Republican and Savannah Evening Ledger,* 2 June 1808, p. 2 (item dated 24 May 1808).

75. Ibid., 15 April 1809 (extract from Savannah admiralty court, Minute Book B, 429–31, recorded 12 April 1809).

76. *Columbian Museum and Savannah Gazette,* 23 July 1818, p. 2; 11 August 1818, p. 2.

77. For correspondence regarding Thomasson/Thompson/Tomasini, see bundle 123 F 10, doc. 1793-328; bundle 125 H 10, docs. 1794-154, 1794-219; bundle 127 J 10, docs. 1794-1059, 1794-[December]; bundle 128 K 10, docs. 1795-[January], 1795-41, and 1795-90, all in EFP. Howard's letter regarding the *José María* was dated 18 January 1795. For Thomasson's marriage see "Chattham County Marriages, 1805–1852," abstracts, Historical Research Projects, WPA (Georgia), at GHS. For Thomasson as French vice-consul, see GHS, Coll. 359, Folder 1. For sponsor for Catholic children, see "Parish Register of the Church of St. John the Baptist, 1796–1816," archives of Cathedral of St. John the Baptist, Savannah, 261.

78. For tract purchase by "Francis Le Roy," see Deed Book H, RCCG, 40, deed dated 23 April 1809, recorded 30 June 1809. It was described as a tract of 300 acres, for which LeRoi paid $2400. For sale of the tract see Paul P. Thomasson, Adm. of Estate of Francois Thomas Leroy, to Ethan Clarke, Trustee for Nathaniel R. Greene, land put up for sale at public auction, Ethan Clarke the high bidder at $1450. Deed Book K, RCCG, 166, deed dated 20 March 1819.

LeRoi may have been in Camden County as early as 1801. "Frances Leroy" was one of three witnesses to Phineas Miller's will, dated 1797, when Miller rewrote it in Camden County. Miller's will was originally prepared in Chatham County, where Mulberry Grove is located, and he had to rewrite the document when he took up residence in another county. The date of rewriting is uncertain, but Miller's will was recorded on

19 July 1804, as part of the probate process after his death in 1803 (will dated 11 December 1797, probated 11 May 1804, recorded 19 July 1804, Will Book A, RCCG). "Francis Le Roy" was listed as a voter in 1803, which required proof of a two-year residency (Superior and Inferior Court Papers, 1797–1827, RCCG, drawer 27, box 60, voters' list).

For LeRoi's slaves see Blair, *Some Early Tax Digests of Georgia.* He had ten slaves in 1809. In 1816, a few months before his death, LeRoi testified before Ray Sands, J.P., that six Negroes left him and went off with the British forces on Cumberland in 1815 and had never been returned to him. GDAH, File 2, Camden Co., Folder "Insolvent Lists," doc. signed by Francois Le Roy, 13 July 1816. The slaves were Mingo, 60-year-old male, valued at $150; Hannah, 36-year-old female, $350; Lewis or Levi, 26-year-old male, $400; Dick, 26-year-old male, $350; William, 60-year-old male, $180; and Philip, 40-year-old male, $350. Spoliation Claims, NA, RG 76. LeRoi's claim is misfiled and placed within Claim 18, made by Remy Brunette (another one of the St. Marys Frenchmen). LeRoi's claim for compensation was presented by Paul P. Thomasson of Savannah, Adm. of LeRoi's Estate. In 1828, Leroi's claim was rejected. NA, RG 76, Claim #1004, "LeHoy's" [sic] claim.

Le Roy's gravestone is in Oak Grove Cemetery, St. Marys, Georgia. For his will see Will Book A, RCCG, 105, will dated 8 September 1810, recorded 20 February 1811.

Spelling of Le Roy reflects court record inconsistencies.

79. "Part of Cumberland Island and Vicinity," U.S. Coast Survey (1870), in Torres, *Historic Resource Study,* illus. 63, facing p. 260. Torres (p. 79) speculated that the dam was constructed to improve cotton field irrigation; Meader's 1898 map, *RCCG,* Plat Book 2, 137; McKinnon map, GDAH, folder 11-1-002. For McIntosh Creek and its tidal pull, see Hillestad et al., *Ecology,* 62.

80. Hunter, *Waterpower; Long Island Wind and Tide Mills;* Terry S. Reynolds, *Stronger Than a Hundred Men,* 67; John Reynolds, *Windmills and Watermills,* 19; Rawson, *Little Old Mills,* 17–20, 95–97. According to Hunter, stone was necessary to make the millstones. France sold good buhr millstone, but Georgia was specifically mentioned as a source (Hunter, *Waterpower,* 108 n., citing *Appleton's Dictionary of Machines,* 2:385). Stone was also necessary in building the causeway that would support the mill house. On southern coasts, stone was hard to find. For causeway construction, LeRoi and La Furque could have used ballast stone.

81. "On the Cultivation of Reclaimed Salt Marshes," *Southern Agriculturist* 1 (18 September 1828): 20–24.

82. Bullard, *Black Liberation,* 1–12.

83. Ibid., 120–21.

84. Ibid., 1; *Niles Weekly Register,* 11 June 1814, p. 242.

85. Bullard, *Black Liberation,* 1–12.

86. Ibid., 30 n.13.

87. Ibid., 54–61.

88. Ibid., 78; "Letters Sent, 1815–16, 21 July–19 June [sic], Miscellaneous," Cockburn Papers, vol. 26.

89. Bullard, *Black Liberation*, 83–89.

90. Ibid., 85–90, 122–25.

91. Ibid., 85–90.

92. Ibid., 91 n.112, 92.

93. Ibid., 97 n.121.

94. Ibid., 91–92.

95. Ibid., 58–60; Bullard, *Robert Stafford*, 58. Stafford and Hawkins likely married in Georgia or Bermuda in 1815, and their only child, Thomas Drew Hawkins, was born in London on 16 March 1816. Hawkins died in 1818, and Susannah's brother, Robert Stafford, brought her and her son back to Cumberland Island.

CHAPTER SEVEN. Slavery, Freedom, and Interdependence

1. Bullard, *Robert Stafford*, 17, 32–33 n.45, 33–35 n.48; Bullard, *Black Liberation*, 30 n.13, 31 n.15, 33, 37 n.18, 42 n.23, 100–101 n.124; for instrument of agreement dated 24 April 1810, recorded 26 April 1810, see Deed Bk. H, RCCG, 184–87; Stegeman and Stegeman, *Caty*, 207; Greene and Clarke, *Greenes;* for sale of slaves of Martha Nightingale, see *Republican and Savannah Evening Ledger*, 21 February 1811, p. 2; for sale of tract 3, see Deed Bk. I, RCCG, 94–95; Murdoch, ed., "Letters"; for "runaway match" (marriage took place on Cumberland Island), see Robert Mackay to Eliza Anne Mackay, 4 June 1810, in Mackay, *Letters*, 112–13; Charles Rinaldo Floyd Papers, coll. 257, I, p. 79, GHS. A Greene family history gives Martha's death date as 1840. Henry Turner died in Savannah in 1862. His tombstone states that Martha died in June 1839 and was buried at Dungeness. Her death date is now generally accepted as 1839.

2. Du Pont, *Civil War Letters*, 1:359n; Ethelyne N. McKinnon, letter to author, 1974; Greene and Clarke, *Greenes;* John C. Nightingale's gravestone at the Springs (present-day Greyfield); Bernard N. Nightingale, letter to author, 1974.

3. Charles Jones, "Reminiscences," 616–27.

4. Bullard, *Black Liberation;* Shaw's war claims, dated 18 June 1823, RG 76, E185, folder 25, NA.

5. *Savannah Georgian*, 27 November 1827, p. 3; Coulter, *Thomas Spalding*, 89–91; for Phineas Nightingale's first appearance on poll tax record, see 1827 tax digests, Captain Miller's district, RCCG.

6. Notes from Cate Collection; Thomas Spalding to A. F. Wilcox, 14 March 1848, quoted in unpublished manuscript in possession of Alfred W. Jones; *Southern Cultivator*, 17 January 1868; *Savannah Gazette*, 8 December 1827, p. 2; *Savannah Georgian*, 27

November 1827, p. 3; Rudolphus Bogart to WEP, 13 December 1809, Couper Papers, folder 1; Worrell Druggist's Receipt Book; *Savannah Republican*, 13 April 1825.

7. Robert Worrell, Druggist's Receipt Book, GHS; Cresap, "History of Florida Agriculture"; Downing, *Fruits*; Gray, *History of Agriculture*; Henry Phillips, *Companion*, "Lemon, Lime, and Citrus"; Edward Cutbush, *Observations on the Means of Preserving the Health of Soldier and Sailors* (Philadelphia: Thomas Dobson, 1808); Sir Gilbert Blane, *Observations on the Diseases of Seamen*, 3rd ed. (London: J. Callow, 1803); Stewart and Guthrie, eds., *Lind's Treatise on Scurvy*; William Johnson, *Nugae Georgicae*, 22; J. C. Loudon, "Fixed Structures for Growing," *The Suburban Horticulturist* (London, 1842), 220–23; L. H. Bailey, *The Standard Cyclopedia of Horticulture*, s.v. "orange"; *Hortus Third: A Concise Dictionary of Plants Cultivated in the United States and Canada* (New York and London, 1976), s.v. "citrus fruits." See also the series of articles by Florida planter George J. F. Clarke in *The Southern Agriculturist and Register of Rural Affairs, adapted to the Southern Section of the United States*, edited by J. D. Legare (Charleston, S.C., 1828–1836), 3:73, 558–91, 4:19–24, 67–71, 613, 6:147, 251–52, 8:323–24, 350, in which Clarke discusses coastal Georgia and Florida orange cultivation as he practiced it in the 1830s.

8. Will dated 1829, recorded 3 May 1831, Will Book B, RCCG, 7–14. Will Book B is no longer extant. A copy of Shaw's will may be found in the Ravenel Papers; a second copy is in Mackay-Stiles Papers, folders 44, 45.

9. Deed of sale and mortgage dated 27 May 1831, recorded 26 March 1832, Deed Book M, RCCG, 37–38. Mortgage marked paid, 30 October 1843, Deed Book M, RCCG, 58–59. For details of Lynch-Nightingale sale, see Bullard, "Uneasy Legacy," 757–88. See also Mary R. Bullard, "Title Search for Great and Little Cumberland Island" (unpublished manuscript, copyright November 1, 2001, on file at GDAH, Atlanta; Southeastern Archaeological Center, Tallahassee; and Bryant-Lang Historical Library, Woodbine, Georgia), pp. 10–11 under "land disposition" and tracts 4, 6, 7, 10, and 11 under "title search."

10. Bullard, *Robert Stafford.*

11. John Mackay to his mother, 9 April 1836, Mackay-Stiles Papers, folder 70; Charles Rinaldo Floyd diary, various entries, Charles Rinaldo Floyd Papers.

12. Downing, *Fruits*, 542–43. A bowdlerized version of this letter appeared in Stern, *Robert E. Lee*, 144.

13. Bullard, *Robert Stafford*, 206–13; J. K. Johnson, *Affectionately Yours*, 8–9, 40–45; *Savannah Daily Georgian*, 3 July 1840, in Cate Collection. Special mention was made of olive, orange, citron, lemon, and lime groves, and the 3,680 acres to be sold were described as capable of subdivision into three tracts, each with its own landing.

14. Holmes, *"Dr. Bullie's" Notes*, 134–35, 137, 147, 150, 201; Johnston, "The Kollock Letters," 66, 144; Charles Rinaldo Floyd diary, various entries, Charles Rinaldo Floyd Papers; "The Steam Packet *Pulaski*," in Stick, *Graveyard*; Lovell, *Golden Isles*, 156–82;

Conrad, "Reminiscences," 13; *Savannah Georgian*, 10 October 1835, p. 2; 19 June 1835, p. 2; *Savannah Daily Georgian*, 13 February 1836, p. 2; John A. King draft letter to Phineas M. Nightingale, 5 December 1848—"John A. King Papers, box 1," courtesy of the New York Historical Society. Although the draft is unsigned, the handwriting matches King's other communications.

15. Bullard, *Robert Stafford*, 93–96, 98–101, 103–6.

16. White, *Statistics*, 139.

17. From a copy made by William and Gertrude Carnegie based on a description given by Cray Pratt and entitled "Mr. Pratt's Account," recorded before 12 February 1899, in Stafford House Guest Book, in possession of Nancy McFadden Copp. "Mrs. ————" was probably Sarah Clubb Frohock. Author has silently corrected spelling, punctuation, and capitalization.

18. 1840 U.S. Census, Population Schedules, Camden County, Georgia. For Pratt as postman, see interview with William E. Meyers, 11 September 1995, in Seward, "Oral History," at Cumberland Island National Seashore. For details regarding Pratt's personal life, see Muriel Williams, interview by author, St. Marys, Georgia, 1978.

19. Bullard, "Title Search for Great and Little Cumberland Islands."

20. Poll tax and probate records (1827–66) and tax records for all Cumberland Islanders, 1830, 1840, 1850, 1860, RCCG; 1850 and 1860 U.S. Censuses, Slave Schedules, Camden County.

21. Tax records for all Cumberland Island residents, real property and slave property, 1830, 1840, 1850, 1860, RCCG.

22. Bundle 120 C (reel 46), doc. 1790-159; bundle 122 E 10 (reel 47), docs. 1792-235, 1793-582, and 1793-598, all in EFP.

23. Bullard, *Robert Stafford*.

24. Stafford's will, made in 1867, omitted any reference to his Georgia property either because his lawyer advised him to do so or because the U.S. War Department had confiscated his island properties in 1865. Bullard, *Robert Stafford*.

25. Bullard, *Robert Stafford*. Peter Bernardey is buried at Plum Orchard on Cumberland Island in the same grave plot as his mother. Her executor, Robert Stafford, paid for a brick wall to be placed around the two graves. RCCG, "Letters of Administration, Executors, and Guardians," Book D, "1854–1858," 4–5.

26. Bullard, *Robert Stafford*. In 1827 a planter from the mainland saw Gray on Election Day in St. Marys: "Lord Gray . . . from Cumberland was both drunk and valiant all day. He assaulted the people indiscriminately" (Charles Rinaldo Floyd diary, 23 June 1834, Charles Rinaldo Floyd Papers). Cumberland's earliest settlers had named his tract Indian Spring, after its large artesian spring; Gray called it Spring Garden Plantation. (The Carnegies subsequently renamed it Greyfield.) Gray purchased the land from William Craig, a doctor from Edinburgh who was naturalized in 1824 (Deed Book L, RCCG, 211). Craig apparently had been practicing on Cumberland Island, where he

met and married a young Camden County widow named Mary Elliott, who had inherited the Spring. In 1825 Dr. Craig and his wife moved to Honduras. An extraordinary midcentury advertisement reported that he died in that country in 1826 and that
his widow eventually moved back to the United States, first to St. Marys and then to
Tallahassee, where she remarried. Robert Stafford placed the newspaper notice on behalf of Mary Craig in an effort to catch the eye of John Elliott, her son, thought to be a
seaman, with whom she had lost contact (*Savannah Daily Georgian*, 25 April 1827, p. 3;
Tallahassee Floridian, 29 November 1845, p. 4).

27. 1850 U.S. Census, Population Schedules, Camden County.

28. Bullard, *Black Liberation*, table I; White, *Statistics*, 139.

29. Franklin, "Southern History," 9; Gutman, *Black Family*, 26; Bullard, *Robert
Stafford*.

30. Information on estate inventories, deeds of sale of Negroes, deeds of gift, and
mortgages derived from Records of Camden County; U.S. Census, Population Schedules, 1800–1860; U.S. Census, Slave Schedules, 1850 and 1860; and the National
Archives in Washington, D.C. County tax records show reported slave ownership in that
county. Camden's tax records do not show a given landholder's ownership in other counties, yet those slaves called Cumberland their home. One source gives Cumberland's
1837 population as thirty whites and two hundred blacks (Adiel Sherwood, *Gazetteer
of the State of Georgia*, quoted in Torres, *Historic Resource Study*, 129). Another source
gives Cumberland's 1837 population as five hundred total ("Mr. Pratt's Account"). In
1846, Cumberland's population was thirteen white men, eight white women, eight
white boys, seven white girls, and four hundred Negroes (White, *Statistics*). And in
1861, when Phineas Miller Nightingale wrote Governor Brown of Georgia asking for
military protection, he stated that Cumberland Island had five white men and about
four hundred slaves (Bullard, *Robert Stafford*, 214 n.1).

31. Tax records, 1830, 1840, 1850, 1860, RCCG. Archaeological work undertaken in
1999 shows some cabin centralization at Stafford's plantation (David Brewer and J. E.
Cornelison, *Report Brief*, August 1999, SEAC, National Park Service, Tallahassee). One
two-room cabin with chimneys at either end may have been occupied by the two free
persons of color, and a nearby single cabin may have been occupied by the third free
person of color. Stafford was required to report his ownership of slave houses, but he evidently chose not to report cabins occupied by free blacks.

32. Bullard, "Title Search for Great and Little Cumberland Islands."

33. John McWhorter, "Afro-American Englishes: Genesis, History, and Future,"
lecture, John Carter Brown Library, Providence, 19 April 1999; John McWhorter,
Towards a New Model of Creole Genesis (New York: P. Lang, 1997). McWhorter stresses
the importation of plantation creoles (namely, languages) from West African trade
settlements, where slave traders spoke Portuguese and Spanish. In a *New York Times*
interview (30 October 2001), McWhorter pointed out syntax and case attributes that

were close to Latin. Also see Peter H. Wood, "Gullah Speech: The Roots of Black English," in Wood, ed., *Black Majority.*

34. Superior and Inferior Court Papers, March term, 1818, RCCG. Downes's sworn testimony dated 28 October 1818; Belton Copp, attorney for plaintiff.

35. Bullard, *Robert Stafford.*

36. Ibid.

37. Ibid.

38. Frank Moore, *Civil War,* 117–18.

39. Deed Book I, RCCG, 117–19; Bullard, *Robert Stafford,* 68–70.

40. "Fleet Orders, January–April 1815," Cockburn Papers, 46:12.

41. Deed Book M, RCCG, 191, deed of sale dated 2 April 1834, recorded 27 May 1834.

42. Moore, *Civil War,* 117–18; Ascher and Fairbanks, "Excavations," 3–17.

43. Polydore McNish had at least one son, Adam, whose great-granddaughter, Althea McNish, now lives in London with her husband, John Weiss. In January 1994 Polydore's descendants gathered in Trinidad. It is rare to find such a well-documented genealogical line from a slave who responded to British efforts to enlist slaves during the War of 1812 (Bullard, *Black Liberation,* 65; John Weiss, letters to author, beginning 14 April 1994; John Stewart, "Mission and Leadership," 17–25).

44. Bullard, *Black Liberation;* John Weiss, letters to author, beginning 14 April 1994; John Stewart, "Mission and Leadership."

45. Georgia Writers' Project, *Drums and Shadows,* 161–63; Will Book A, RCCG, 122–28. For variant spelling, see Parrish, *Slave Songs,* 24–27. Parrish and the Writers' Project interviewed the same person. One prominent coastal Muslim slave was Thomas (Salih Bilali), foreman for the Coupers in Glynn County. Zephaniah Kingsley, a Florida slave owner in the 1820s, referred to Thomas as one of two Muslim drivers who prevented slaves from deserting to Admiral Cockburn in 1815 (Kingsley, *Treatise,* 13–14; see also Charles Spalding, "Some Happy Memories," and Charles Spalding Wylly, "Sapeloe," typescripts in possession of Alfred Jones; John Sawyer to David Blackshear, 27 January 1815, in Stephen F. Miller, *Bench and Bar,* 1:455–56; Gomez, "Muslims," 689, 694; Lyell, *Second Visit,* 1:266–67; Conrad, "Reminiscences," 13).

46. Will of Louisa G. Shaw, Ravenel Papers. When Shaw died, she possessed 151 slaves, appraised at $275 per head, for a total of $41,525 (appraisal and inventory of estate of Louisa G. Shaw, made by John W. Gray, Robert Stafford, and Newton Chapelle, dated 9 May 1831, recorded 14 January 1835, "Inventory and Appraisements of Estates, 1832–1851," RCCG, 12–15).

47. Will of Louisa G. Shaw, Ravenel Papers.

48. Mrs. C. A. Taft to Mackay, 7 December 1856, Mackay-Stiles Papers, folders 44, 45. Ben Sullivan, a descendant of Couper slaves, mentioned Thomas as having gone from St. Simons to Dungeness "tuh trade in slabes." He "nebuh was seen again." The

Nightingales may have sent Thomas, who would have been very old at the time, with Abu to Hartford. Aging slaves were a problem, and Hartford was home to the African Mission School, which trained blacks to be missionaries, catechists, and schoolmasters in Africa. The school attracted Arabic-speaking participants, some of them former slaves. The records of the African Mission School Society do not extend beyond 1830, but a sympathetic friend or minister may have suggested to the Nightingales that Thomas's Arabic would make him useful in Hartford (for a full description of Thomas, see Austin, *African Muslims,* 309–408, esp. 313, 324–25, 392; for the African Mission School Society, see Gerald M. Cruthers, letter to author, autumn 1994; Alford, *Prince among Slaves,* 158; Brewer, *History,* 243–46).

49. Nightingale, "Dungeness," 376, citing Ober and Vocelle, neither of whom knew much about the Greene-Nightingale family; RG 76, claim 493, doc. 1, p. 3, NA; "Admiralty List of Slaves Carried off by British Forces," RG 76, entry 185, folder 57, NA. In reality, the Shaw slaves had not remained loyal; rather, the admiral returned those slaves who had not yet boarded British warships.

50. EFP, bnd. 150 G 12, docs. 1814–94 and 1814–97, documents dated 8 and 15 May 1814. A report (24 February 1807) was made to Spanish authorities in East Florida that stolen Negro slaves were being received on Tiger Island, of which Samuel Meers (American) was the chief resident. Numerous similar reports showed that tiny settlements along the marshy waterways of Tiger River, Spanish Creek, Bells Creek, and Amelia River were being used for illegal importation of slaves into Georgia (EFP, bnd. 109 E 9, doc. 1807–9). Martins Island, David Garven's marsh island, was cited as being particularly troublesome. See also Edwin Williams, "Negro Slavery in Florida," 93–110; Landers, "Spanish Sanctuary," 296–313; and Parker, "Men without God," 135–55.

51. Mackay, *Letters,* 223–24, 230.

52. Georgia Writers' Project, *Drums and Shadows,* 192. In 1976 Hubert Barber of Woodbine, Georgia, and his son, Perry, told the author that a few years earlier they had seen a blowout of the sandy shore at Beach Creek, not far from Dungeness, that revealed door sills and brick foundations of small frame buildings. Sand has since recovered the site. In 1874 the St. Marys City Council, trying to replace an earlier site on the North River, decreed that a new quarantine site be established between Beach Creek and Cumberland Island's South End (Marjorie Waters, "Mayor and Aldermen Passed Quarantine Law in Early 1800s," *Camden County Tribune,* Bicentennial Edition, 26 November 1987, 2C). The council's choice may have derived from an undocumented use of Beach Creek as a site for a lazaretto.

53. Orders, 23 January 1815, Cockburn Papers; Will Book A, RCCG, 547–49; RG 76, claim 44, NA.

54. *Savannah Daily Georgian,* 4 January 1828, p. 2.

55. For purchase of Norris, 10 March 1801, see Deed Book F, RCCG, 75; for her reg-

istration, see Ordinary, Camden County, "Free Persons of Color, 1819–1843," Microfilm Library, GDAH.

56. *Darien (Ga.) Timber Gazette*, 21 August 1886, 3, C4. I am indebted to Kenneth H. Thomas Jr. for this notice. One of Charles Jackson's brothers was named Amasa, after whom Martha and John Nightingale named their eldest son, Amasa Jackson Nightingale.

57. NA, RG 76, Entry 185, Folders 57 and 59. See Bullard, *Black Liberation*, 82–83, for explanation and identification of the Clubb family.

58. Clubb family Bible (publication date 1817, inscribed on last page by "John Club," 1818), in possession of Lawrence Miller, St. Simons Island, Georgia. Loose papers within give birthdates for certain named persons born in servitude. See also Bullard, *Abandoned Black Settlement*, 52–57, and appendix A for a genealogy.

59. Bullard, *Abandoned Black Settlement*, 53 n.45.

60. Deed of gift to Miller, dated 10 February 1831, recorded 12 November 1831, Deed Book M, RCCG, 27.

61. Torres, *Historic Resource Study*, 101, illustration 8. There are occasional references to Miller's slave property (see, for example, Bell, *Major Butler's Legacy*, 167 n.35), but the slaves in question probably belonged to his wife.

62. Deed of sale of land and slaves, dated 2 April 1834, recorded 27 May 1834, Deed Book M, RCCG, 191–94.

63. Bullard, *Robert Stafford*, 256–59; David M. Hammond to Douglas G. Risley, 23 January 1868, RG 105 (Bureau of Refugees, Freedmen, and Abandoned Lands), E-801, subheading 1, NA.

64. 1880 U.S. Census, Population Schedules, Camden County, Georgia. For personal recollections, I am indebted to the late Mary Miller, Brunswick, Georgia, and the late George Merrow, Kingsland, Georgia, a descendant of Mitchell.

65. Mason Burbank to William Alberty, Charles Trimmin[g]s, Thomas Alberty, and Primas Mitchell, Trustees, Lot 16, 9 May 1894, Deed Book V, RCCG, 425; Lucy R. Ferguson, personal communication with author, Greyfield, Cumberland Island, 1968. For the year of Primus Mitchell's death and other personal recollections, I am indebted to Nancy Carnegie Rockefeller, who placed a marker on Mitchell's grave.

66. Genovese, *Roll, Jordan, Roll*, 255–56; Hermione Ross Walker memoir, in possession of Preston Stevens.

CHAPTER EIGHT. The Civil War and Its Aftermath

1. From loose papers in Torres File, Cumberland Island National Seashore, under "Plantation Period," with extracts from printed material published in the *Camden County Tribune*, 24 April 1953. Letters were described as part of the Lang Collection.

2. 1860 U.S. Census, Slave Schedules, Camden County, Georgia.

3. Corgada, "Florida's Relations," 42–52.

4. *War of the Rebellion*, 53:155–56.

5. Bullard, *Robert Stafford*, 218.

6. Richard Martin, "*New York Times*," 418; Stedman, *Civil War Sketchbook*, 66, 67, 68. Stedman, a surgeon who was aboard one of the gunboats, said that the entire Union flotilla grounded on the Dividings. This would have greatly amused the watching locals, one of whom must have been Robert Stafford, who had a spyglass and a house with a cupola (Bullard, *Robert Stafford*, 328).

7. Du Pont, *Civil War Letters*, 1:347–49.

8. Ibid., 1:349; DuPont to secretary of the Light-House Board, 5 March 1862, *ORN*, 12:582; list of keepers of the Little Cumberland Island Lighthouse, RG 26 (Records of the U.S. Coast Guard), NA. Clubb was keeper on Little Cumberland from 1859 to the outbreak of the war. See Torres, *Historic Resource Study*, 221–27, for an overview of the lighthouses on Little and Great Cumberland Islands.

9. Du Pont, *Civil War Letters*, 1:347.

10. *Savannah Daily Morning News*, 19 March 1862 (item from Gainesville, Florida).

11. Bullard, *Robert Stafford*, 221.

12. Ibid., 223 n.22.

13. Memorandum by Captain Drayton concerning two contrabands from Thunderbolt, Georgia, 18 February 1863, *ORN*, 13:671.

14. Bullard, *Robert Stafford*, 221.

15. Du Pont, *Civil War Letters*, 2:23, 77.

16. Bullard, *Robert Stafford*, 230–31.

17. Ibid., 231.

18. Percival Drayton to S. F. DuPont, 4 April 1862, Du Pont Papers.

19. Bullard, *Robert Stafford*, 226–28.

20. Hewett, *Supplement*, 478, 27 December 1861. I am grateful to Sam Graham, Cartersville, Georgia, for making this information available to me.

21. Thomas Belden and Belden, *So Fell the Angels*, 254; Schuckers, *Life and Public Services*, 322–24; Hart, *Salmon Portland Chase*, 225–27.

22. Acting British Consul Fullerton to John Russell, 10 October 1861, quoted in Price, "Ships," 105; Hart, *Salmon Portland Chase*, 227; Donald, *Inside Lincoln's Cabinet*, 147, 155–56.

23. Shapiro, *Confiscation*, 51–52; A. Sellew Roberts, "Federal Government and Confederate Cotton," 262–75.

24. Bullard, *Robert Stafford*, 234.

25. Ibid., 235.

26. Ibid., 236.

27. "Lieut. Col. Gardiner, 7th C.V., is to be arrested, we learn, for complicity with the Connecticut Copperheads" (Diary entry of George R. Durand, dated 11 April 1863,

"Naval History Society Collection," courtesy of the New York Historical Society). On 7 May Gardiner received orders to resign within twenty-four hours or face dishonorable discharge, and he resigned on 19 May (*Record*).

28. Bullard, *Robert Stafford*, 238–39.

29. Ibid., 239–40.

30. RG 393, Records of the Army Continental Commands, Records of the Provost Field Organizations, E-1599, Letters Received by the Provost Marshal, Oath #83, NA.

31. Du Pont, *Civil War Letters*, 2:345.

32. Bullard, *Robert Stafford*, 246–48.

33. Carol Juneau, letter to author, 1976; Myers, *Children*, 1627; Kenneth Thomas, "Sapelo," 1, 4, 6; Cimbala, "Terms," 272–72; T. Bryan, *Confederate Georgia*, esp. chap. 5. Three weeks after the firing on Fort Sumter, Richard Arnold sold his land and slaves in Georgia to his son, Thomas Clay Arnold, and returned north to Newport, Rhode Island, where he remained for the duration of the war. Arnold was, as he told others, a "Union man although a Southern planter" (Hoffmann and Hoffmann, "North by South," 32–35).

34. Reminiscences of Vernon D. Mitchell, in possession of Virginia Rowland; *ORN*, 12:584; Mercer diary, 3:17.

35. Bullard, *Robert Stafford*, 244.

36. Frank Moore, *Civil War*, 117; Mercer diary, 4:61; 1870 U.S. Census, Population Schedules, Camden County, Georgia. The Camden Chasseurs were undoubtedly punishing "recalcitrants" at Stafford's tracts.

37. Westwood, "Sherman Marched," 49; Bentley, *History*, 134, 144–46.

38. Bullard, *Robert Stafford*, 247–48.

39. Ibid., 247.

40. Eaton to C. P. Ketchum, 25 August 1865, RG 105, E-1018 ("Savannah, Ga. ADC. Letters sent by C. P. Ketchum, May–October 1865"), NA.

41. W. F. Eaton, "Report of Abandoned Lands," in "Captain A. P. Ketchum's Records, Abandoned Land Reports, August 1865–December 1868," RG 105, M-869, roll 33, NA. See also Bullard, *Robert Stafford*, 249–53.

42. During the Civil War some Cumberland Islanders persecuted the Spalding family because of its members' independent views regarding slavery (Bullard, *Robert Stafford*, 228–29 n.27). As late as 1929, Billy Spalding, then an old man living in the Okefenokee Swamp, told visitors that his family had not "rated" in the island community because it was poor and did not own slaves. His Confederate father had showed federal gunboats "the way to places on the Georgia coast." I am indebted to Chris Trowell for this information from the field notebooks of Dolores B. Colquitt, Marmaduke H. and Dolores B. Floyd Papers. Even in the 1940s Stockwell and Spalding descendants were apt to fight each other on school playgrounds.

43. RG 105, M798, roll 34, 2–3, NA. Special Orders 3 were also published in *Senate Documents,* 39th Cong., 1st sess., 1866, Ex. Docs, no. 27, 105–6, but without the five names.

44. Bullard, *Robert Stafford,* 256–57.

45. Ibid., 254–62, appendix B.

46. Ibid. Although the exact date on which Stafford's land was restored to him is not known, it was probably during the first half of 1866. Sometime before June of that year Stafford was offered $100,000 in gold for 8,000 acres on Cumberland, excluding his house and adjacent land. The offer was made by "Mr. Friend" of New York City, who represented a German colonization society. Friend stated that the company would put three hundred German farmers on Cumberland, mainly for the purpose of growing cotton (*New York Times,* mid-June 1866; *New York Daily Tribune,* 13 June 1866; *Savannah Morning News,* 12 July 1866). By mid-1866 Stafford apparently felt legally free to accept such an offer.

47. Lucy Ricketson Ferguson, letter to author, 1948; Knight, *Georgia's Landmarks,* 1:12. A passenger named William McAdoo saw the building looming above the trees when his steamer passed Dungeness on 23 April (Bailey Family Papers, folder 2, item 28).

48. Bullard, *Robert Stafford,* 267–68, 271.

49. Nightingale to Sanger, 4 July 1870, 17 June 1870, Ravenel Papers.

50. "Plan for the Organization of the Hotel Dungeness Company," formerly in Bernard N. Nightingale Papers, copy and transcription in GDAH, present location of original unknown.

51. Ibid.; Sanger to Nightingale, 7 May 1870, Ravenel Papers.

52. Cited in Torres, *Historic Resource Study;* judgment (1871) recorded 27 September 1879; action of ejectment and demesne, 9 October 1879; and sworn statement, William Nightingale, 26 November 1879, Deed Book R, RCCG, 404.

53. Bullard, *Abandoned Black Settlement,* 71–74, 77 (see also n.69); Penniman Reminiscences, 2:37.

54. "Orders and Circulars Issued and Received, 1865–1869," RG 105, M-798, roll 34, 2–3, Special Orders issued by General Davis Tillson; RG 105, E-638, NA; Bullard, *Robert Stafford,* 261.

55. Bullard, *Robert Stafford,* 261–62.

56. Ransom and Sutch, "Impact," 1–28; Temin, "Patterns," 661–74; Foner, *Reconstruction,* 52–54, 405, 407, 535–37; Powell, *New Masters,* 99–103; Vlach, *Back of the Big House;* Babson, "Archaeology," 20–28; Brown and Cooper, "Structural Continuity," 7–19; Prunty, "Renaissance," 460–62, 464–66, 470, 472, 474, 479–80, 489–91; Shlomowitz, "Squad System," 266–67, 272–73; Orser, "Toward a Theory," 313–24; Singleton, "Archaeological Framework," 361–64. It is fairly clear that land tenure arrange-

ments on Cumberland Island following the war followed a distinctive settlement pattern called the squad system. The squad system was a share collective composed of former slaves related by kinship. Squad members lived in clustered settlements, as they had as slaves, but at some distance from the landlord.

57. Orser and Nekola, "Plantation Settlement," 68–70.

58. Bullard, *Abandoned Black Settlement*, 83–87; Margaret Downes to Douglas G. Risley, 24 May 1867, "Unregistered Letters Received 1867–1868," RG 105, item 1002, NA. Germain may have taken his name from G. I. Germond, a bookkeeper employed by Alberti (Germond diary, in possession of Kathleen E. Davis).

59. *ORN*, 12:584; reminiscences of Vernon D. Mitchell, in possession of Virginia Rowland. In April 1864 the Confederates burned "Mr. German's house and mill at Kings Ferry to prevent the lumber from going to the Yankees" (Fisher diary).

60. Bullard, *Abandoned Black Settlement*.

61. Bullard, *Robert Stafford*, 263.

62. Angele C. Davis, 20 May 1882, in *Cincinnati Commercial*, 24 June 1882, quoted in *Brunswick (Georgia) Advertiser and Appeal*, September 1882; Bullard, *Abandoned Black Settlement*, 115–19.

CHAPTER NINE. The Beginning of Visitors on Cumberland

1. Virginia Wood, *Robert Durfee's Journal; Savannah Republican*, 13 April 1825.

2. Mary Miller, *Cumberland Island*, 82, chaps. 3 and 4.

3. Carmichael, "Brown Family."

4. Candler and Evans, *Cyclopedia*, 540.

5. *Brunswick (Georgia) Advertiser and Appeal*, 26 May 1875. Clubb advertised that he was opening a hotel at the north end of Cumberland Island. For Burbank's purchase of the "Occidental Hotel on the old Clubb Place" see *Fernandina Florida Mirror*, 20 November 1880: 8, col. 2. On another page, same date, Burbank solicited investment in his new hotel, "to be built at the High Point" of Cumberland. The use of "occidental" and "oriental" reflected the familiarity of pilots with charts, where these terms were commonly used for "east" and "west."

6. *Fernandina Florida Mirror*, 20 November 1880, p. 8. The post office at the North End was occasionally called the High Point Post Office (map of Georgia post offices, 1889, S-G). The sale was not recorded until after the 1881 death of Rebecca Miller Clubb, but since Burbank's daughter, Nellie, married on the island in 1880, it seems that her family was living there at that time (Mary Miller, "Innkeeping," 2).

7. Mary Miller, "Innkeeping."

8. See Torres, *Historic Resource Study*; and Bullard, "Title Search." Bunkley and his partners, some of whom were from Macon and some of whom were his family members, formed the Cumberland Island Company to raise capital for the enlargement

of the hotel and resort (for indenture of mortgage and deed, both dated 11 November 1890, see Deed Book U, RCCG, 169–73, 204–6).

9. Hermione Ross Walker, "Cumberland Island," 35.

10. Ibid., 37.

11. Candler and Evans, *Cyclopedia*, 540; Mary Miller, "Innkeeping."

12. Mary Miller, "Innkeeping," 14.

13. Ibid.; Hermione Ross Walker, "Cumberland Island"; Bullard, "Title Search."

14. Deed Book U, RCCG, 93–94.

15. Mary Miller, *Cumberland Island*, "Entertainment," "Growing Up," "Innkeeping," and *On Christmas Creek*. Either the total or the payment plan seems to be in error; no clarification could be found.

16. Ibid.

17. Ibid.

18. The Jekyll Island Club of New York City was founded in 1886. The DuBignon family, owners of this Georgia Sea Island, faced financial disappointments in 1884 and began discussing its real estate possibilities. Through the medium of Newton Finney, a son-in-law residing in Manhattan, a private association was established to obtain a charter in 1885. Finney organized a campaign that sent hundreds of solicitations recommending the club's speculative possibilities. Assiduous advertising drew an enthusiastic response from American industrialists, and by 1900 their investment was referred to as the most exclusive club in the world. *The New Georgia Guide* (Athens: University of Georgia Press, 1996), 690–91; McCash and McCash, *Jekyll Island Club*.

19. Ibid.

20. Angeline Reddick, *Pen Portraits*.

21. Wall, *Andrew Carnegie*; Hacker, *World*.

22. *Encyclopedia of Pennsylvania Biography*, 2:283–84; Durant, *History*, 179–80; information provided by Professor John Ingham; Wall, *Andrew Carnegie*; Hacker, *World*; Hendrick, *Life*; Casson, *Steel*; LCC daybook, in possession of James S. Rockefeller.

23. 1880 U.S. Census, Population Schedules, Allegheny County, Pennsylvania.

24. Obituary notices of TMC Sr., in Carnegie family scrapbooks; Wall, *Andrew Carnegie*, 359–60; Casson, *Steel*, 94.

25. Wall, *Andrew Carnegie*, 360, 473.

26. In 1842 Charles Dickens wrote of Pittsburgh, "furnace fires and clanking hammers on the banks of the canal warned us that we approached. . . . Pittsburgh is like Birmingham in England. . . . It certainly has a great quantity of smoke hanging about it" (*American Notes*, 74). Nine years later, the Rev. C. C. Jones wrote that Pittsburgh was "a city well called the City of Smoke, full of iron furnaces and factories, and every fire made with bituminous coal. There hangs over the city a dense cloud of smoke, and

the tops of the houses are colored black, and all the buildings are dingy and black, and even the fences and bodies of the trees are blackened. The houses lately built look sixty years old. Wash your face and walk out and come home, and your handkerchief is soiled as you use it" (Myers, *Georgian*, 129).

27. Ober, "Dungeness," 241–49; newspaper clipping, Greyfield scrapbook, [1880]. Frederick Albion Ober (1849–1913), who also published under the name of Fred Beverly, came from Obers Point, Beverly, Massachusetts. Ober later went to Cuba to cover the Spanish-American War. He became something of an expert on ornithology and the sportsman's life (*DAB*, 8:606–7). In his article, Ober stated without proof that General James Edward Oglethorpe had once built a hunting lodge called Dungeness on Cumberland Island. Some Georgia historians believe that such a building actually existed (see Vanstory, *Georgia's Land;* Lovell, *Golden Isles;* Torres, *Historic Resource Study*, 33–34 [although Torres notes that several such statements lack proof]).

28. Torres, *Historic Resource Study;* Marmaduke H. Floyd to Edith Duncan Johnston, 26 January 1929, Marmaduke H. Floyd and Dolores B. Floyd Papers, box 6, p. 57. On 26 January 1929, M. H. Floyd told Edith Duncan Johnston that he had obtained stereographs of Dungeness House and the "Greene milk house" from Miss Emily Noyes, an old lady who lived in Fernandina, and that Noyes told him about the Johnstons. "Mr. Johnston" may have been the son of Emily Greene Turner and George Houstoun Johnston. Emily was one of the daughters of Martha Washington Greene and her second husband, Dr. Henry E. Turner, and was therefore a half-sister of Phineas M. Nightingale. The Turners lived in Savannah and frequently visited Dungeness before the Civil War. The dates when "Mr. Johnston" resided at Dungeness correspond with the period between Nightingale's final illness and death (1873) and the advent of a new owner (1879).

29. Deed Book S, RCCG, 66–68; *Florida Law Journal* 23 (February 1949): 300; catalog, PKY; *St. Joseph Times*, 15 October 1839, p. 1; *Florida News* (Fernandina), 3 March 1858, and subsequent issues; *East Floridian and Florida News* (Fernandina), summer and fall 1859; Wakelyn, *Biographical Dictionary; Charleston Mercury*, 7 April 1859, p. 2; *Fernandina Florida Mirror*, 20 March 1880, p. 3 (reprinting private letter published in the *Savannah News*). Davis was born on 9 May 1812 in Portsmouth, Virginia. On 15 October 1839 he advertised that he was prepared to attend to legal business with the firm A. G. Semmes and W. G. M. Davis in St. Joseph, Florida. When the Civil War came, Davis had become a successful Tallahassee lawyer. On 10 January 1861 in an open convention of sixty-eight persons, Davis was among the first to sign the Ordinance of Secession on behalf of the people of Florida. Davis immediately offered his services and his fortune to the cause of the Confederacy. His gift of $50,000 made possible the raising of the First Florida Cavalry, of which he was elected colonel. On 4 November 1862 he was promoted to the rank of brigadier general. On 6 May 1863 Davis resigned his commission in the Confederate army to move to Richmond, Virginia, where for the rest

of the war he operated a very successful fleet of blockade-runners. He died in 1900 and was buried in Remington, Virginia.

30. All correspondence in Rockefeller Collection.

31. *Fernandina Florida Mirror*, 8 January 1881; Davis to Carnegie, 6 May 1881, Rockefeller Collection. According to the newspaper, Bernard Davis's remains were interred at Dungeness on 2 January 1881. His exact burial site is unknown, although there is an unmarked vault in the Greene-Miller cemetery that is a likely locale. As of July 1996 the Cumberland Island National Seashore had discovered a previously unknown vault inside the Greene-Miller cemetery. No gravestones remain. It would have been natural for General Davis to have installed a vault for his family's use, never expecting a second death so soon.

32. Davis to Carnegie, 17 May 1881, Rockefeller Collection.

33. Ibid.

34. *Fernandina Florida Mirror*, 15 January 1881, last page; 21 January 1880, p. 3; 4 December 1880, p. 1.

35. "Cumberland Island Legal Papers, 1857–1902," CER, folder 1-1-7. Other records dealing with the purchase, obviously from the same files, were in the possession of Nancy Carnegie Rockefeller, who clearly had taken papers from the office on Cumberland Island: the records complement one another perfectly.

36. *Fernandina Florida Mirror*, 11 June 1881, last page.

37. *Jacksonville Florida Dispatch*, 8 May 1882; *Fernandina Florida Mirror*, 21 May 1881, last page; undated newspaper article in Carnegie family album, evidently from a British newspaper since prices were given in pounds. Although few people noted Carnegie's razing of the old mansion at the time, its demolition was long resented by those who loved the past. Seventy years later, Isaac Arnow, a prominent local historian, lamented its loss: "In 1880, Thomas Morrison Carnegie . . . leveled the tabby home that General Greene had planned and that should have stood for many generations as a monument to his greatness, and upon the ruins, built the Big House" (Arnow, "History," chap. 46).

38. *Fernandina Florida Mirror*, 1 April 1882, p. 7.

39. Ibid., 26 November 1881–18 November 1882; Deed Book S, RCCG, 308–10.

40. Bullard, "Title Search"; Stafford, *Growth of a Planter*, 270–71 and n. 33.

41. Statement of Leander M. Morris's account, in TMC Sr.'s investment acct. 12, 1883–85, CER, folder 1-1-08.

42. Numerous friends from Pittsburgh were present. Mr. Paterson represented the contractors, McKenzie & Paterson, of Quincy, Massachusetts. Peebles, the architect, made a long and grandiloquent speech. With an orator's flourish Peebles declared that in Dungeness the general had found a rural haven: "[H]ere to this beautiful Cumberland Island came General Greene, happy to escape from the turmoil of a public life to the quiet seclusion of its sea-girt shores."

At the conclusion of Peebles's speech, M. W. Vandervort of Pittsburgh responded on behalf of Mr. and Mrs. Carnegie. The cornerstone was then tapped by Mrs. Carnegie and pronounced to be "plumb, square and level, and truly laid." The party adjourned to luncheon in a little cottage "now temporarily occupied by the family." This cottage was built either by Nightingale or by the Dungeness Hotel Association, probably to house a caretaker and his family, or for Nightingale's sons. It was the house in which the general's son lived. Tom and Lucy evidently took it over while their house was under construction.

Paterson showed the completed drawings to the press. The structure was to be built in the Queen Anne Gothic style. (*Fernandina Florida Mirror*, 1 March 1884, clippings in Carnegie family albums; newspaper clipping, Greyfield scrapbook, item 18.)

43. Ibid.

44. *Fernandina Florida Mirror*, beginning 4 April 1885, clippings in Carnegie family albums. When Nancy Carnegie Rockefeller asked her uncles where they stayed while Dungeness House was under construction, they answered in unison, "We stayed in the stable!" (Rockefeller, letter to author, 1980). The stable is the carriage house to which Davis alluded in his 17 May 1881 letter. In later years, the cottage apparently housed Catharine Rikart, Dungeness's first housekeeper. After Rikart's death in 1911, the cottage was razed and replaced by a dormitory for white female employees (OGR Jr., circular letter to his cousins; for mimeographed copies, see CER, folder 8-5-002). A photograph in a Carnegie family album shows a large two-story frame house, probably built by Nightingale or Davis, in the Dungeness area, although Rockefeller had no recollection of it.

45. Torres, *Historic Resource Study*, 167; *Fernandina Florida Mirror*, beginning 4 April 1885, clippings in Carnegie family albums.

46. *Fernandina Florida Mirror*, beginning 4 April 1885, clippings in Carnegie family albums.

47. Ibid.

48. Ibid.

49. Ibid.

50. Ibid.

51. Ibid.; LCC daybook, in possession of James S. Rockefeller. For breakdown of costs, see "TMC Sr., Cash Transactions, 1883–86," CER, folders 2-1-003–4. The 1886 obituary notices for TMC Sr. gave $200,000 as the cost of building Dungeness House. The Carnegie papers have no account book or filing system to show construction costs per se. My estimate is corroborated by an 1887 evaluation of Lucy Carnegie's Georgia properties that put the total value of Dungeness House at $285,000 (CER, folders 2-1-003–4).

52. Torres, *Historic Resource Study*, 275; *Fernandina Florida Mirror*, 15 March, 29 March, and 17 May 1884, p. 8.

53. LCC daybook, 28 December 1885, in possession of James S. Rockefeller.

54. Wall, *Andrew Carnegie;* Durant, *History;* Carnegie, *Autobiography;* Hacker, *World.* In 1887 Frank and Andrew Carnegie attended Pennsylvania State College, an agricultural school (CER, folder 2-1-020; the folder also contains a receipt, 7 October 1887, from John A. Heston, State College principal). They were the only Carnegie boys to attend college.

55. Wall, *Andrew Carnegie,* 418–19.

56. The will of Thomas M. Carnegie is located in Allegheny County (Pennsylvania), Will Book, vol. 31, p. 24, and at RCCG, Will Book C, 163–72. Recorded in Pennsylvania and Georgia, 29 October 1892. See also Hacker, *World,* 411–12; Wall, *Andrew Carnegie,* 353–54 and 488–91.

57. CER, folders 2-1-005–7, 2-1-010. According to Nancy Carnegie Rockefeller, "Grandmother always hated Phipps" (letter to author, 18 June 1987).

58. Wall, *Andrew Carnegie,* passim; LCC and the Carnegie Steel Company Records, 1871–1907, TMC Sr., "Estate Account Book, 1886–87," CER, folder 2-1-003. Valuable records regarding the life of Tom and Lucy Carnegie from 1871 to 1889 are found in CER, ser. 1, "Early Papers, 1800–1901," and ser. 2, "Lucy C. Carnegie and the Carnegie Steel Company Records, 1871–1907." See also subser. 1-1, "Pittsburgh Records, 1849–1889," and subser. 1-2, "Cumberland Island Legal Documents, 1800–1901," especially folders 1-2-001–3 and 1-2-005–7; and subser. 2-1, "Carnegie Steel Company Records, 1871–1907," esp. folders 2-1-001–7, 2-1-035, and 2-1-042.

59. LCC to Jones, 29 October 1886, in private possession. According to Carnegie family lore, Will was "the only one who ever went to work" (OGR Jr. to daughter, Mary B. Ricketson, 1950).

60. Newspaper clipping, ca. winter 1886–spring 1887, Greyfield scrapbook, item 18.

61. Allen Thomas, *Biographical Catalogue.* Harvard University's Fiftieth Anniversary Report for its Class of 1882 (published in 1932, after Page's death) stated incorrectly that Page had became the boys' tutor in 1892. LCC wrote to Francis T. F. Lovejoy on 3 April 1891 that Page was to take Beugnet's place as Dungeness manager (CER, folder 2-1-031).

62. Newspaper clipping, Greyfield scrapbook item 18; Casson, *Steel,* 196; McCook to LCC, 10 June 1892, 25 June 1892, CER, folder 2-1-026.

63. John Walker to LCC, 1894, CER, folder 2-1-026; Lorant, *Pittsburgh,* 471–72.

64. JCC to LCC, 25 January 1896, "Lucy C. Carnegie Letterbook No. 1, 1888–1890 and 1894–1897," CER, folders 2-1-067 and 2-1-071.

65. WEP to Franks, 22 February 1902, "Lucy C. Carnegie Personal Income and Disbursement Memorandum Book, 1901–1903," CER, folder 5-1-003. When Andrew

Carnegie sold Carnegie Steel to J. P. Morgan's syndicate, there was no longer a family business in Pittsburgh to manage Lucy's accounts. Franks, Andy's private secretary, took over these responsibilities (Wall, *Andrew Carnegie*, 491; CER of Cumberland Island Inventory, intro. to ser. 2-1: "Carnegie Steel Company Records, 1871–1907," 114 folders; see inventory, pp. 9–21).

66. WEP to SCA, 31 March 1905, "Atkinson and Dunwody Law Offices, Correspondence with William E. Page, 1904–1905," CER, folder 4-006; WEP to SCA, 28 April 1902, CER, folder 4-004.

67. SCA to WEP, 30 April 1902; WEP to SCA, 2 May 1902, CER, folder 4-004.

68. Lorant, *Pittsburgh*, 212–15. See also Winkler, *Incredible Carnegie;* Casson, *Steel;* and Wall, *Andrew Carnegie*, chap. 19.

69. Winkler, *Incredible Carnegie*, 255.

70. Ibid., 259. Winkler stated incorrectly that Lucy's interest in the company had been Tom's: she had held a 1.5 percent share in the company in her name.

71. Wall, *Andrew Carnegie*, 789; Winkler, *Incredible Carnegie*, 274–76; Casson, *Steel*, 196; JCC to WEP, 6 March 1901, CER, folder 2-2-043.

72. WEP to JCC, 8 July 1899, CER, folder 2-2-042.

73. LCC, Hudson Trust Company, and WEP Records, 1887–1928 and n.d., CER, folder 5-1-002. CER, folder 5-1-001, "Lucy C. Carnegie Private Statements #2, 1899–1912"; folder 5-1-002, "[LCC] Private Journal #2, 1901–1913"; folder 5-1-003, "[LCC] Personal Income and Disbursement Memorandum Book, 1901–1903"; folders 5-1-008–14, "[WEP]'s Open Accounts B, C, D, and E"; folder 5-1-066, "Expense Accounts, 1902–1906"; folder 5-2-014, "[LCC] Authorization for her children's allowances, 1911."

74. OGR Jr. Papers, 1913, based on statistics for 1912, private collection.

CHAPTER TEN. The Canon of Domesticity

1. Winkler, *Incredible Carnegie*, 290.

2. JCC to LCC, 24 July 1900, CER, folder 2-1-074, in which Campbell asked for clarification of Will's outstanding note. Lucy answered that the note had been intended to be "a wedding present" (CER, folder 2-1-074). She evidently intended to give her son a start in life by lending him money his father had earned.

3. Clifford Clark, *American Family Home*, chaps. 2 and 4.

4. CER, folders 5-2-014, 2-1-051, 2-1-060, 2-1-065–68, 2-1-074.

5. LCC letter book, 21 May 1896, CER, folder 2-1-067; WEP to JCC, 21 May 1896, CER, folder 2-1-076; William E. Page Letterbook, 1896–1897, CER, folder 2-2-040.

6. WEP to JCC, 21 May 1896, CER, folder 2-1-076.

7. The property was called Dungeness Estate. For almost seventy-five years this

letterhead appeared on the property's business stationery and bills of lading. After the death of her husband, the landholding was referred to as "Property of Lucy C. Carnegie," and its return address was always given as Fernandina, Florida. The return address has fooled several eminent historians. In his excellent biography of Andrew Carnegie, Joseph Wall said Andrew's sister-in-law had an estate in Florida. Wall, *Carnegie*, 954.

8. Wharton, *Italian Villas;* "Cumberland Island, Georgia," architectural drawings, n.d., Boston Public Library. When the author viewed these drawings in June 1986, the collection was uncataloged, some drawings were stuck together, and some rolls had been mislabeled. See Torres, *Historic Resource Study*, 278–80, for listing of items. I am indebted to Henderson, *Architectural Data Section*, for his interpretation of these architectural drawings. As originally planned, Plum Orchard and its outbuildings bore a remarkable resemblance to specific Italian Palladian villas, with Brick Hill River substituting for the Brenta Canal.

9. LCC to James B. Zahm, 8 May 1892, CER, folder 2-1-027. Will used part of the money he received from his mother to invest in Pittsburgh real estate. Mrs. Carnegie explained to Francis Lovejoy that her purchase of two houses in Pittsburgh extinguished her loan to their ex-owner. Her son, Will, was purchasing them from her, and their purchase price was to be deducted from his wedding present of $10,000. LCC to [Francis] Lovejoy, 31 July 1891, CER, folder 2-1-051.

10. LCC to Peabody and Stearns, 27 May 1898, CER, folder 3-003; WEP to Peabody and Stearns, 1 December 1898, CER, folder 3-002.

11. WEP to Peabody and Stearns, 27 January 1899, CER, folder 3-003; WEP to Morris Carnegie, July 1899, WEP to George Carnegie, August 1899, CER, folder 3-003.

12. Lucy Ricketson Ferguson, interview by author, Cumberland Island, 1980; WEP to MacClure and Spahr, 13 April 1901, CER, folder 3-003. Page wrote that "any departure from this simplicity will ruin the effect of the house in the opinion of the owners." Oliver Ricketson's desire for a simple house may have been a reaction to his mother-in-law's pretentious Dungeness House. Ricketson opened a bank account in Fernandina in late spring. Contractors began work on 1 June. In September 1901 WEP informed accountants that he was opening a new account in Lucy Carnegie's name. This "Greyfield Account" "will cover a new house and barn which are being built for Mrs. Ricketson. Mrs. Carnegie will pay $10,000 toward this account" (CER, folders 5-1-003–4). The Ricketsons originally planned to obtain all their water from a windmill-powered pump, but Page suggested supplementary use of the artesian spring at Gray's Field Bluff. This bountiful spring was the origin of the eighteenth-century site name "Indian Spring."

13. CER, "Accounting Records, 1899–1913" and "Lucy C. Carnegie Private Journal #2, 1901–1913," folders 5-1-002–4.

14. After Lucy's death, Andrew and his family stayed at Stafford House, which Will

had rebuilt. Andrew used his wedding money to build a home in Manchester, Massachusetts. Andrew later said "that his mother had given him some money and that he had built a house in Manchester and that it seemed rather unfair that the houses on the Island with such money should go to the benefit of him and the others who had not built them" (John M. Bullard to OGR Jr., 10 August 1936, privately held).

15. Information furnished by Richard B. Trask, town archivist, Danvers, Mass.; Elinor S. Hearn, letter to author, 20 August 1987; Allen Thomas, *Biographical Catalogue;* LCC to Francis T. F. Lovejoy, 3 April 1891, CER, folder 12-1-002; Coleman Perkins, conversation with author, 1940s.

16. Barbara Lutz, letter to author, 19 October 1988; Sharpe, "Historic Furnishing Plan"; Elinor S. Hearn, letter to author, 20 August 1987; Ruth Jones, letter to author, 29 October 1988; Jeane L. Richardson, letter to author, 23 August 1988; Frank E. Fuller, letter to author, 14 September 1988; John F. Burke, letter to author, 21 November 1988; author's files on WEP; Knowlton, *Inventory,* index.

The Victorians fancied medieval terms, and nineteenth-century America enjoyed romanticizing its European heritage. In Old English *grange* meant "the house of the farm-steward." Probably Page suggested it in a graceful allusion to his status. Although the house was called by its formal name in a few records, it was more commonly known simply as "Mr. Page's House."

17. TMC Sr. to W. G. M. Davis, 24 May 1881, and W. G. M. Davis to TMC Sr., 2 August 1881, CER, folders 1-2-001–2.

18. LCC daybook, 51, 166, in possession of James S. Rockefeller; TMC Sr. to Davis, 24 May 1881; Davis to TMC Sr., 2 August 1881, CER, folders 1-2-001–2.

19. CER, folders 2-1-006–7, 2-1-015, 12-2-001–3.

20. LCC daybook, 51, 166, in possession of James S. Rockefeller; 1890 U.S. Census, Population Schedules, Nassau County, Florida; Knowlton, *Inventory,* 43–44. In 1895 Beugnet was a clerk living with his wife and three children in Fernandina (Sixth Florida State Census).

21. Thompson, *Plantation Societies,* esp. chap. 13, "The Natural History of Agricultural Labor in the South," 213–63.

22. Dorothy Dodd, *Florida, the Land of Romance* (Tallahassee: Florida Department of Agriculture, Peninsular Publishing Service, 1957), 61; Amelia Island Fernandina Restoration Foundation, *Centre St. Fernandina* (Helen Gordon Litrico, 1976), 10, 22–23; John Ferreira, interview by author, Fernandina, Fla., June 1976; Helen G. Litrico, interview by author, Fernandina, Fla., June 1976; *Fernandina Florida Mirror,* years 1878–1881 (all) and 29 October 1891–1 September 1894; *Fernandina Mirror,* 14 January 1882–27 August 1887; *Fernandina Observer,* 31 July 1875–June 1895; "Fernandina at the End of the Nineteenth Century," *Fernandina News-Leader,* April 1957.

23. TMC Sr., "Estate Account Book, 1886–87, Cash Transactions, 1 November 1886–31 October 1887," CER, folders 2-1-003, 2-1-035, 12-1-003; WEP to Yates, 17 July 1901, folder 2-2-056. By 1910 Page was supervising the care and overhauling of some

seventeen vessels owned by the Dungeness Estate or by LCC's sons. Transportation to the mainland became one of the manager's priorities.

24. WEP to SCA, June 1902, CER, folders 4-004–5; see also folder 5-4-007.

25. Winkler, *Morgan*, 135. The Dilworth family may have resided on Cumberland Island from prerevolutionary times. Through his great-grandfather, Dilworth was descended from settlers of Edmond Gray's community on Cumberland Island. From 1886 to 1887 Dilworth served Glynn, Camden, and Charlton Counties as a state senator. See Margaret D. Cate, *Our Todays and Yesterdays;* U.S. Censuses, Population and Agricultural Schedules; NA, RG 105 Entry 805, "Letters Rcvd. by Agent, July 1867 to December 1868"; civil records of Camden County: and CER. In July 1868 Dilworth, then Camden County's tax collector, encountered difficulty in collecting taxes from the new freedmen's settlement at Elliott's Bluff.

26 Willie Miller, interview by author, 1973; Willie Miller interview, *Fernandina Beach (Florida) News Leader,* 4 April 1974. See also CER, 6:15 and folders 2-2-049 and 2-2-033.

27 Dollie Whitby MacLaren, interview by author, Fernandina, Florida, 1973; Lucy Ricketson Ferguson, interview by author, Greyfield, Cumberland Island. 1976.

28 Dudden, *Serving Women,* 54; telegram in Carnegie family album in possession of Retta Ferguson McDowell. With the responsibilities that accrued as her family grew and with the Carnegies' increasing wealth, Lucy was later able to hire domestic help

29 Knowlton, Inventory, index; author's files.

30. CER, folders 5-1-009–10, 12-1-001–7; Knowlton, *Inventory,* index; author's files. For further discussion of immigrant women as domestics, see Sutherland, *Americans and Their Servants.*

31. CER, folders 5-1-009–10, 12-1-001–7; Emma Roberts Bealey, interview by author, St. Marys, Georgia, 19 August 1974.

32. CER, folder 5-1-009. Nancy Carnegie eloped with Hever, a horse trainer and head of the Dungeness stables. Despite press articles publicizing her "misalliance," her uncle, Andrew Carnegie, said that he was "glad that his niece had married an honest man instead of a dissolute duke." After Hever's death in about 1910, Nancy married Dr. Marius Johnston of Lexington, Kentucky, in April 1912 (Rockefeller, *Carnegies,* 59–60, 152).

33. Dudden, *Serving Women,* chaps. 3, 4, 7; "Payroll and Personnel Records, 1890–1958," CER, folders 12-1-001–3, 12-1-009–20.

34. WEP to Samuel C. Atkinson 16 July 1903, re: seeking a carpenter for "isolated work," CER, folder 13-2-11. Sidney Vernon Brock and Lucille Brock McLean, interview by author, Folkston, Georgia, 1989. Sidney and Lucille Brock had lived at Brick Hill with their parents, Joseph Brock and Mary Gowen Brock. Lucille McLean vividly remembered that despite the Brocks' isolated position, they had numerous High Point and mainland visitors who were anxious to see Cumberland Island.

35. "Payroll and Personnel Records, 1890–1958," CER, folders 12-1-001–3, 12-1-009–20.

36. Emma Roberts Bealey, interview by author, St. Marys, Georgia, 19 August 1974.

37. CER, "Carnegie Estate Rules and Regulations, Publications, 1901–1904, and n.d." (Jacksonville: H. and W. S. Drew, n.d.), folder 5-2-040; CER, "William E. Page, Letterbook, June, 1900–mid-July 1901," folder 2-2-043, p. 104; Emma Roberts Bealey, interview by author, St. Marys, Georgia, 19 August 1974.

38. CER, folders 5-1-009–10, 12-1-001–7.

39. Emma Roberts Bealey, interview by author, St. Marys, Georgia, 19 August 1974.

40. Emma Roberts Bealey, interview by author, St. Marys, Georgia, 19 August 1974; unidentified woman, conversation with author, Cumberland Island, 1975.

41. "Dungeness Payroll Records, July–August 1890," CER, folders 2-1-005–6, and payroll records for 1887 and 1891, CER. In 1868, following an outbreak of petty crime, St. Marys's black community petitioned the city council to appoint a black police force. Laurance Tompkins, city marshal, was appointed its captain, and Chance Johnson was appointed subchief. Tompkins resigned in protest after one of the black policemen was fined for nonpayment of taxes and deprived of his badge. The black police unit broke up as a result (Arnow, "History," chap. 44). Johnson remained with the Carnegies as late as 1910.

42. "Dungeness Payroll Records, August 1896," CER, folders 2-2-049–50.

43. WEP to SCA, 17 April 1897, CER, folder 4-002; "Atkinson and Dunwody File," CER, folder 4-006; tax bill, 27 April 1896, and 1897 correspondence regarding tax bill, CER, folder 4-002.

44. WEP to SCA, 17 April 1897, CER, folder 4-002.

45. "Atkinson and Dunwody File," CER, folder 4-006. Here is a statement of Lucy's taxable property in Camden County in 1896: 100 acres improved land, Dungeness; 200 acres improved land, Stafford Place; 7,980 acres uncultivated land; 2,000 acres marsh

assessed value of acreage:	$82,440
personal property:	$3,400
farm animals:	$4,150
farm equipment:	$450
boats, etc.:	$1,500
new total:	$91,940

46. CER, folders 2-1-031, 2-1-042, 2-1-56.

47. Letter originally in the private possession of Nancy C. Rockefeller, now at the GDAH. A handwritten addendum on the letter said that it was answered on 31 October 1887. See also Beugnet's correspondence in CER, folders 2-1-031 and 2-1-042.

48. Hillestad et al., *Ecology*, 45–52; McCallie, "Preliminary Report"; J. Richardson, *The Negro*, 45 and 47–48.

49. WEP to William B. Scaife and Sons, 18 September 1897, CER, folders 2-2-040–41.

50. WEP to G. W. Mudd, 25 May 1901, CER, folder 2-2-042.

51. WEP to C. Herschel Koyl, 14 March 1901, and WEP to Morse, Williams, and Company, 19 June 1896, 31 August 1896; William E. Page Letterbook, 1896–1897, CER, folder 2-2-040. Page's statement that the car frame would be paneled on Cumberland indicates that there were some local cabinetry workers. In another letter, Page referred to skilled local carpenters using wood from Dungeness's olive trees to make a parquet dining room floor for the Addition. The remains of a woodworking shop existed until recently.

52. CER, folder 2-2-040.

53. CER, folder 2-2-040.

54. CER, folder 2-2-042.

55. CER, folder 2-2-042.

56. Cummings, *American Ice Harvests;* Feay Coleman, *Nostrums,* 29; WEP to Remington Machine Company, 1900, CER, folder 2-2-042.

57. *Rules and Regulations.*

58. James, *American Scene,* 447.

59. McCash and McCash, *Jekyll Island Club,* 27; CER, folder 5-2-056.

60. Rockefeller, *Carnegies.*

61. Gilkes, *Cora Crane.* Howorth later married novelist Stephen Crane.

62. Letter, 1 April 1898, formerly in possession of the late Retta Johnston Wright, present location unknown.

63. Fitch, *The Steel Workers,* 141, table C, pp. 351–53; Reischauer, *Samurai and Silk,* 324.

64. Blandy, "Dungeness—A Winter Home," part 2.

65. Arnow, "History," chap. 47.

CHAPTER ELEVEN. Conflicts in Land Usage

1. Powell, *New Masters,* 100; *Digest News and Herald* (Savannah), 3 January 1868, 1; U.S. Congress, Senate, *Report of the Committee on Agriculture and Forestry,* 1–2: 354.

2. Minutes of Superior Court, Minute Book C, RCCG, 1–13.

3. Stafford House Guest Book, in possession of Nancy McFadden Copp. The guest book begins with Lucy Carnegie's entry and was kept until 22 March 1906, four days before Martha Gertrude Carnegie died suddenly at Stafford. Pages have been torn out of the volume through 26 December 1908. There are few entries between 1908 and 1910 except for a Nancy Patton, who appeared frequently—perhaps a housekeeper. The next series of regular entries began with Andrew Carnegie and Bertha Sherlock Carnegie and their daughters, Nan and Lucy; their 1910–11 entry referred to a "very happy winter at Stafford."

4. *Brunswick (Georgia) Observer,* 19 November 1895, 2 January 1896, both in Miller-Frazier abstracts, in possession of author.

5. WEP to James Doig, 2 December 1897, CER, folders 2-2-040–42.

6. Otto, "Origins," 117, 119; Otto, "Open-Range Cattle-Herding," 317–34; Hahn, *Roots*, 61.

7. *Acts, 1874*, acts 347, 378.

8. Fite, *Cotton Fields*, 8–9; Hahn, *Roots*, 58–63; Elliott, *Carolina Sports*, 254–58.

9. *Fernandina Florida Mirror*, 2 April 1881, last page; 19 February 1881, last page; McCash and McCash, *Jekyll Island Club*, 19; W. E. D. Stokes to WEP, 19 February 1895; WEP to Peter Duryea, 28 July 1896, 6 October 1896, CER, folder 2-2-045; for telegram to Page, see family albums; for shipment of ponies and riding of horse into Greyfield, see CER, folder 7-5-012.

10. WEP, possibly to J. P. Freeman, 1898, letter seeking a laborer, CER, folder 2-2-041.

11. Newspaper clipping, Greyfield scrapbook.

12. LCC daybook, 28 December 1885, 228, in possession of James S. Rockefeller; "Camden County, Georgia, Hunting Club," constitution (1815), rules, and membership lists (Marmaduke H. and Dolores B. Floyd Papers, box 21, folder 213). Wild bull hunting was an accepted coastal Georgia sport, although few practiced it (Hopkins, "Wild Bull Spearing," 397).

13. Blandy, "Dungeness—A Winter Home," part 1.

14. Veblen, *Theory*, 170–72.

15. Elliott, *Carolina Sports*, 174.

16. *Fernandina Florida Mirror*, 5 March 1881, last page; Mrs. Thomas M. Carnegie daybook, in possession of Nancy Johnston Butler; Carnegie family albums; conversation with Robert W. Ferguson Jr., ca. 1970. The Cumberland Island National Seashore recently has endeavored to reestablish bobcats on the island.

17. Bangs, "Land Mammals," 219.

18. Stafford House Guest Book, 26 December 1898, in possession of Nancy McFadden Copp; CER, folder 13-2-11; WEP, 15 March 1898, CER, folders 2-2-041–42.

19. CER, folder 2-2-040, "William E. Page Letterbook, 1896–1897"; CER, folder 13-2-12, WEP to S. C. Atkinson (1905); CER, folders 7-5-022–23, "Visitors to island correspondence." The Carnegies did permit a few men to hunt or trap on Carnegie land. For example, Camden County's Punch Godley and a friend would come to the island each year to trap raccoon, otters, and occasionally mink, selling the skins. When Godley's quota was reached, the men returned to the mainland and sent their catch to a wholesaler (Jack Godley, interview by author, Woodbine, Georgia, 11 September 1973).

20. CER, folders 1-1-008, 1-2-005; WEP to Beugnet, 2 April 1901; WEP to SCA, 2 April 1901; WEP to Bunkley, 13 April 1901, all in CER, folder 2-2-043.

21. The head of the dead bull was found on the beach, and its identification was made by Punch Godley, William Alberti, Nelson Merrow, and Will Merrow. The Merrows testified they had refused to assist Adams in butchering the bull. Nelson knew

Adams's two head of cattle, apparently free-ranging on Cumberland, and this wasn't one of them. CER, folders 4-003, 4–005.

22. House Bill 301, enacted 24 December 1896, *Journal of the House*, 499; *Fernandina Florida Mirror*, 5 March 1881, last page.

23. Cross-examination of Silas Fordham by defense attorney Samuel C. Atkinson, 23 March 1892. Bill in Equity, U.S. Circuit Court, Eastern Division, Southern District, Ga., #156, Doc. 11, p. 18.

24. Deed Book Q, RCCG, 211; Finn Papers.

25. Plat of High Point Cumberland Island Company, filed 4 July 1891, recorded 29 July 1891, Deed Book U, RCCG, 348–49. For Hunter, see Bullard, *Abandoned Black Settlement*.

26. The Bunkleys produced as testimony the original will of Winifred Downes, dated 7 April 1855. Her will was recorded in Will Book B, a county record that was destroyed by fire.

Walter Barnard Hill (1851–1905) began practicing law in Macon, Georgia, in 1871. He became president of the Georgia Bar in 1887 and served as an occasional professor at Mercer University's Law School and as president of the Southern Educational Association. Hill was familiar with Cumberland Island through his acquaintance with Fordham, through the Macon Company, or because of his background as a prominent Georgia educator. He was elected chancellor of his alma mater, the University of Georgia, on 13 July 1899, serving until his death.

27. Suit in Equity, Case #156, *Fordham and Hunter v. Miller, Bunkley, et al.*, U.S. Fifth Circuit Court Records, Eastern Division, Southern District of Georgia, testimony filed 23 March 1892. When I visited the Federal Records Center, the decision for this case could not be located. Records of Camden County, a subsequent sale to Lucy Carnegie, and Hill's papers at the University of Georgia show that Fordham retained ownership of the tract.

28. Hermione Ross Walker, "Poverty," 49.

29. SCA to WEP, 13 October 1900, CER, folders 4-002–3.

30. Bullard, *Abandoned Black Settlement*.

31. Ibid.

32. Ibid.

33. Deed Book U, RCCG, 251–52; Bullard, *Abandoned Black Settlement*, 110–11.

CHAPTER TWELVE. Carnegie Homeland

1. In 1907 LCC was startled by the unexpected appearance of two claimants to Robert Stafford's estate. See Bullard, *Robert Stafford*, 306, 315–16.

2. Harry F. Dunwody to WEP, 24 May 1906, CER, folder 4-007. By 1906 Atkinson had left the firm.

3. SCA to WEP, 30 June 1897, Atkinson and Dunwody to WEP, 11 August 1899, both in CER, folder 4-002. Not until 1993 did anyone fully explain how Greene had acquired his interest in the Cumberlands: see Bullard, "Uneasy Legacy," 773–75.

4. *Journal of the Senate*, 99; *Acts, 1897*, 574–75.

5. Minutes, Superior Court, March term, 1898, Minute Book C, RCCG, 1–13; WEP to Fordham, 19 February 1898, CER, folder 2-2-041; WEP Letterbook, 1896–1897, CER, folder 2-2-040.

6. Walter B. Hill to SCA, 6 August 1898, WEP to SCA, 6 January 1899, both in CER, folder 4-002. General Catlin may have had a genuine interest in creating a lazaretto on Cumberland Island. The army was actively discussing the need for improved port quarantine in Georgia. After several decades of examining flea- and rat-infested holds, medical authorities had begun ordering disinfection of suspicious ballast. During the Spanish-American War, troops returning from Cuba were placed in quarantine as a preventive measure against yellow fever, and after 1881 all infected vessels were required to proceed to Blackbeard Island (Voelker, "Port Quarantines").

7. Silas Fordham's will, dated 1898, recorded 17 March 1899, Will Book C, RCCG, 173; decree of the Superior Court, Camden County, Georgia, 11 July 1899, RCCG.

8. *Atlanta Constitution*, 4 August 1899, p. 9; 11 August 1899, n.p.

9. WEP Letterbook, 1898–1900, CER, folder 2-2-042.

10. Deed of release dated 4 February 1899, recorded 3 July 1899, Deed Book W, RCCG 572–75. The ninth child, Nancy, still at school near Hartford, had her signature witnessed in Connecticut.

11. Torres, *Historic Resource Study*, 161. Torres misunderstood the purpose of the deeds and erred in the number of signatories.

12. Deed Book X, RCCG, 76–79; WEP Letterbook, 1898–1900, CER, folder 2-2-042.

13. Obituary notice; plat of lot 18, section 20, owned by William Coleman, TMC Sr., and Margaretta Fuller, furnished by Allegheny Cemetery Historical Association. William Carnegie, Tom's father, was buried in Uniondale Cemetery on 29 September 1855 but was reinterred in the Coleman plot at Allegheny Cemetery on 12 April 1890 (H. Harriss, letter to author, 25 August 1987).

14. Reid to WEP, 25 June 1912, WEP to Reid, 29 June 1912, in possession of author; family photographs in a dated scrapbook.

15. Nancy Carnegie Rockefeller, interview by author, Greenwich, Connecticut, 1976.

16. Family records in private collection of the author.

17. *Pittsburgh Bulletin*, 22 January 1916, p. 13.

18. LCC's will, dated 15 June 1912, first codicil dated 7 January 1913, second codicil dated 17 May 1913; probated 4 March 1916, Register of Wills, Allegheny County, Pennsylvania; copy probated 1916, Camden County, Georgia. In 1912 widower Will Carnegie

had married Alice Bell in Pennsylvania. His mother thoroughly disapproved of his re-marriage and as a result excluded him as an executor and trustee. He was not disin-herited, however, and he maintained friendly relationships with his family and with Page until Will's death in 1944.

19. TMC Jr. to WEP, 25 March 1916; bank to WEP, 29 March 1916; WEP to TMC Jr., 9 June 1916, CER, folder 7-1-026.

20. LCC's will.

21. Ibid.

22. Ibid.

23. Summary, Prescott, Bullard, and McLeod, 1946, in Papers of OGR Jr.; Trustees' Account, Patterson, Crawford, Miller, and Arensberg, Attorneys, to WEP, 28 March 1916, CER, folders 7-1-004–6, 7-1-008, 7-1-010–12.

24. Document signed by LCC, 17 May 1912, and attached to a copy of her will, in possession of author. On 9 July 1916 WEP wrote to LCC's executors that certain items belonging to the principal of her estate had been paid in.

25. CER, folders 7-1-025–26.

26. Opinion of the Court, Ownership of Carnegie Building, Orphans Court, Al-legheny County, Pennsylvania, 9 February 1955, item A, Opinion of Court re. Owner-ship and Jurisdiction. Allegheny County Courthouse.

27. WEP to Tiffany Studios, 18 October 1916, CER, folder 5-2-035; WEP to Andrew Carnegie II, 18 May 1916, 18 October 1916, 11 March 1917, CER, folder 7-1-030; Will Carnegie to WEP, 19 November 1916, CER, folder 7-3-001; Andrew Carnegie II to WEP, 11 November 1916, CER, folder 7-1-030. The Carnegie children specifically asked that their parents' gravestones be "table-stones . . . like those in the old graveyard at Dun-geness." Tiffany did not design Coleman's gravestone.

28. Plat, Allegheny Cemetery Historical Association; WEP to Will Carnegie, 17 March 1917, CER, folder 7-3-001. Moving Tom's remains from Pittsburgh to the Greene-Miller Cemetery was considered at one time. Instead, Lucy had a plaque in memory of her husband bolted to the wall of the Greene cemetery.

29. Wall, *Andrew Carnegie*, 1032; WEP to Will Carnegie, CER, folder 7-3-001.

CHAPTER THIRTEEN. Planning for the Future

1. WEP to Peabody and Stearns, November 1901, CER, folder 3-003.

2. Family records in private collection of the author.

3. "Accounts receivable," 31 December 1921; "1916, reimbursement of working fund"; WEP to SCA, 30 December 1904, CER, folders 8-6-002, 7-2-001, 4-006. For Cumberland's nineteenth-century road commissioners, see Bullard, *Robert Stafford*, 195–99.

4. WEP to SCA, 11 March 1902, CER, folder 4-004.

5. CER, folder 8-2-010; Knowlton, *Inventory,* 111.

6. Ibid.

7. Ibid.

8. Ibid.

9. Ibid. The Macon Company failed in the 1910s. Although it had acquired the Cumberland Island Hotel, and although Lee Shackelford was running it successfully, the Macon investors began to lose interest as newer and more accessible Florida resorts opened. The Bunkley family retained ownership of the hotel and gradually turned to a new class of businessmen from nearby Brunswick, Georgia, who preferred hunting to visiting the beach and who could easily reach Cumberland for long weekend visits. The Cumberland Island Hotel became known as a hunting lodge, open only during the fall deer season and winter. Overcome by debt and mortgages, however, the Bunkleys sold their property on 7 December 1920 to the Cumberland Island Club, another organization of businessmen interested in hunting. In the early 1930s the club sold the tract at depression prices to Charles Howard Candler, a prominent Atlanta businessman, who used the land as a seaside estate for his family. The Candler property extends west from the beach and Long Point to the terminus of what used to be called the Old Bunkley Road (formerly the "road to the suttles") (Torres, *Historic Resource Study,* 192–215).

10. CER, folder 8-2-010; Knowlton, *Inventory,* 111.

11. Conyers to Thomas Morrison Carnegie Jr., 14 June 1926, CER, folder 8-2-010; Burwell Atkinson, interview by author, Camden County, Georgia, 1974; Knowlton, *Inventory,* 111. The Carnegie children's opposition to taxes was not limited to local jurisdictions. Like hundreds of other wealthy U.S. citizens, they were appalled by the federal income tax, which Lucy apparently had not anticipated when she signed her will in 1912 ("The original Will creating the Estate was made in 1912 . . . in ignorance of the future imposition of large income taxes" [W. S. Whitney (for TMC Jr.) to Andrew Carnegie II, 11 October 1935, in possession of author]).

12. CER, folders 7-1-026–27, 7-1-030.

13. Willis F. McCook to LCC, 15 December 1894, privately held.

14. Obituary, *Boston Transcript,* 12 September 1922, CER, folder 7-3-006. Eleanor remained in Florida under the care of nurses until her death in March 1941. She was subsequently buried in the same grave as her husband. The Dungeness estate had paid her a pension of $3,000 and footed the bill for her funeral (Knowlton, *Inventory,* 37, 87, 98, 110, 126, 154).

15. Opinion of the Court, Ownership of Carnegie Building, Orphans Court, Allegheny County, Pennsylvania, 9 February 1955, item A from Opinion of Court re. Ownership and Jurisdiction. Allegheny County Courthouse.

16. Letters from John Frident, CER, folder 8-8-005, "Land Sales Correspondence," dated mostly 1923; McFadden correspondence, CER, folder 8-7-015; A. A. Ainsworth correspondence, CER, folder 8-7-001. Other correspondence dealing with land sales

and rentals can be found in CER, folder 8-8-005, dated 1923–1925. Yet another group of letters involving a "national" chain of hotels is in CER, folder 8-7-015. Thomas M. Carnegie's veiled reference to the possibility that Plum Orchard might be available for rent appears in several folders in series 8. It was not available for rent, and he was doing his widowed sister-in-law a grave injustice.

17. Correspondence from file of TMC Jr. to A. A. Ainsworth and others, 1923–26, CER, folder 8-7-001.

18. TMC Jr., draft memorandum, n.d.; typewritten copy from estate of LCC, Dungeness, Cumberland Island, to Patterson, Eagle, Greenough, and Day, New York, 21 January 1936, CER, folder 8-1-019. Author has silently corrected punctuation.

19. Ricketson, "Suggestion." Margaret had died in 1927, and only Andrew and Morris were trustees ("A paper dated March 23, 1917, is on file at Orphans' Court of Allegheny County, No. 156 May Term, 1917, signed by Florence C. Perkins and Nancy C. Johnston reciting the death of Frank Morrison Carnegie and renouncing their right to succeed [Frank] as Trustees and agreeing that Andrew, Thomas, George, and Mrs. Ricketson, the then surviving Executors and Trustees, continue to act as such in the administration of the Estate of Lucy C. Carnegie" [memorandum prepared by law firm Crapo, Clifford, Bullard, and Prescott, New Bedford, Massachusetts, 3 August 1946, in possession of the author]). Two codicils to LCC's will effectively eliminated Will Carnegie from any interest in or enjoyment of the island property. He did, however, receive one-eighth of the net income from the Carnegie Building (before it was applied to the island property) before its sale and one-eighth of the proceeds when it was sold (Report of the Guardian ad Litem and Trustee ad Litem in re. the Account of Robert D. Ferguson, Successor Trustee u/w of Lucy C. Carnegie for Her Cumberland Island Property, in re Estate of Lucy C. Carnegie, Deceased, Orphans' Court of Allegheny County, Pennsylvania, no. 1510A of 2942, 18 July 1952, p. 3).

20. Ricketson, "Suggestion." At this time, Florence Carnegie Perkins and her family occupied the Grange; Thomas Morrison Carnegie and his family occupied the Cottage; Margaret Carnegie Ricketson and her family occupied Greyfield; Andrew Carnegie II and his family occupied Stafford; and Nancy Carnegie Johnston and her family occupied Plum Orchard (Brief on Behalf of Robert D. Ferguson, Trustee, in Support of His Petition for Permission to Use Insurance Funds for Rebuilding Purposes, in re Estate of Lucy C. Carnegie, Deceased, no. 1510 of 1941, in the Orphans Court of Allegheny County, Pennsylvania, 14 February 1950, pp. 5–8). The Cottage was destroyed by fire in January 1949, and Morris's two sons were seeking funds to build a replacement house.

21. Ricketson, "Suggestion." The idea of a "game preserve" would die hard. As late as 1950 Lucy Johnston Graves wrote to her cousin, Oliver Ricketson, "I wonder if [Dungeness estate] couldn't become a Federal Park and Game Preserve in memory of grandfather and [grand]mother" (Graves to OGR Jr., 28 January 1950, OGR Jr. Papers).

22. Andrew Carnegie II to TMC Jr., 22 February 1923, privately held; OGR Jr. to Lucy Ricketson Ferguson, 19 April 1936, privately held.

23. Petition for Leave of Sole Surviving Testamentary Trustee to Resign and Be Discharged and for the Appointment of Successor Trustees, in Orphans' Court of Allegheny County, Pennsylvania, in re Estate of Lucy C. Carnegie, Deceased, 16 January 1947; Moorhead and Knox to OGR Jr., 10 January 1947; RDF to OGR Jr., 29 January 1947, all in possession of author. The bank itself could not act as a trustee because Georgia prohibited foreign corporations from holding more than 5,000 acres of land.

24. RDF to OGR Jr., 21 January 1947; OGR Jr. to family associates, 28 January 1947; "Memorandum with reference to operation of Cumberland Island," RDF to family members, 17 March 1947; James D. Harlan to OGR Jr., 3 April 1947; RDF to OGR Jr., 14 May 1947. All in possession of author.

25. "Memorandum, on July 8–10, 1947, Examination of Cumberland Island," Richard Tift, Albany, Georgia, and Herbert L. Stoddard, Thomasville, Georgia, in possession of author.

26. Robert W. Ferguson (husband of Lucy Ricketson Ferguson), memorandum, 14 May 1947, OGR Jr. Papers; RDF to OGR Jr., 25 July 1947; RDF "To the Life Tenants and Remaindermen of the Estate of Lucy C. Carnegie," 12 August 1947, both in possession of author.

27. Kelly to RDF, 25 January 1949; Kelly to Leo Larkin, 14 February (two letters), 27 March 1949; Kelly to RDF, 1 August 1949; RDF to J. Pat Kelly, 25 January 1950, all in CER, box 42, folders 9-1-003–9.

28. Kelly to RDF, 25 January 1949.

29. Ibid.

30. Ibid.; Larkin to Wallis, telegram, 17 December 1948; Kelly to RDF, 14 February 1949 (two letters), 27 March 1949, 3 April 1949, and 1 August 1949, CER, folders 9-1-003–9.

31. RDF to Kelly, July–August 1950, CER, box 42, folder 9-1-004; Collett correspondence with Estate Trustee, CER, box 42, folder 9-1-005.

32. RDF to Kelly, July–August 1950; Collett to RDF, September 1950, 21 September 1950, 2 October 1950, 5 October 1950, "Estate Trustee Correspondence with Manager J. Pat Kelly, 1948–1949," "Estate Correspondence with Manager J. Pat Kelly, 1950," and "Estate Correspondence with Manager Norman (Pat) T. Collett, 1950," CER, folders 9-1-003, 9-1-004, and 9-1-005; RDF newsletter to family, 2 July 1953, in possession of author.

33. Collett to Larkin, 17 November 1950, CER, folders 9-1-005–6.

34. Kelly to RDF, March 1949, box 42, folder 9-1-003; Collett correspondence with Estate Trustee; Larkin to Collett, August 1950, CER, box 42, folder 9-1-005.

35. OGR Jr. Papers, in possession of author.

36. Weldon Shouse to Thomas Morrison Johnston Jr., 11 November 1950, OGR Jr. Papers.

37. OGR Jr. Papers, in possession of author.

38. *Brunswick (Georgia) Evening Call,* 24 July 1900.

39. Ibid., 6 February 1901.

40. McCash and McCash, *Jekyll Island Club,* chap. 12.

41. *Challenge of Georgia's Coast.*

42. Ibid.

CHAPTER FOURTEEN. A Park in Progress

1. E. E. Lewis, "Paradise of Golden Isles Periled," *Jacksonville (Florida) Sunday Sun-Telegraph,* 30 January 1955, p. 3.

2. E. E. Lewis, "Carnegie Will Fought in Court," *Jacksonville (Florida) Sunday Sun-Telegraph Pictorial Review,* 30 January 1955, pp. 3–4.

3. Edward Gray, interview by author, Darien, Georgia, 1983.

4. Lucy C. Graves and Margaret J. Wright to family, 28 February 1956, in possession of author; "Minutes of the Meeting of the Heirs of LCC, Cumberland Island," 5–6 April 1956, 10 December 1956, in possession of author; Oliver Prescott to Margaret R. Sprague, 11 December 1956, in possession of author; Jerry Bader, "Courts to Settle Squabble in Million Dollar Cumberland Leasing," *Brunswick (Georgia) News-Leader,* 1 April 1956, p. 3; U.S. District Court for the Southern District of Georgia, Brunswick Division, Civil Action no. 469, *Mrs. Nancy Carnegie Rockefeller v. The National Bank of Brunswick, et al.,* 9 April 1957; "Glidden Pact Approved," *Brunswick (Georgia) News-Leader,* n.d., 1957, p. 16; Edward Gray, interview by author, Darien, Georgia, 1989.

5. Lucy C. Graves and Margaret J. Wright to family, 28 February 1956, in possession of author; "Minutes of the Meeting of the Heirs of LCC," Cumberland Island, 5–6 April 1956, 10 December 1956, in possession of author; Oliver Prescott to Margaret R. Sprague, 11 December 1956, in possession of author; Jerry Bader, "Courts to Settle Squabble in Million Dollar Cumberland Leasing," *Brunswick (Georgia) News-Leader,* 1 April 1956, p. 3; U.S. District Court for the Southern District of Georgia, Brunswick Division, Civil Action no. 469, *Mrs. Nancy Carnegie Rockefeller v. The National Bank of Brunswick, et al.,* 9 April 1957; "Glidden Pact Approved," *Brunswick (Georgia) News-Leader,* n.d., 1957, p. 16; Edward Gray, interview by author, Darien, Georgia, 1989.

6. Lucy C. Graves and Margaret J. Wright to family, 28 February 1956, in possession of author; "Minutes of the Meeting of the Heirs of LCC, Cumberland Island," 5–6 April 1956, 10 December 1956, in possession of author; Oliver Prescott to Margaret R. Sprague, 11 December 1956, in possession of author; Jerry Bader, "Courts to Settle Squabble in Million Dollar Cumberland Leasing," *Brunswick (Georgia) News-Leader,*

1 April 1956, p. 3; U.S. District Court for the Southern District of Georgia, Brunswick Division, Civil Action no. 469, *Mrs. Nancy Carnegie Rockefeller v. The National Bank of Brunswick, et al.*, 9 April 1957; "Glidden Pact Approved," *Brunswick (Georgia) News-Leader*, n.d., 1957, p. 16; Edward Gray, interview by author, Darien, Georgia, 1989.

7. Georgia House of Representatives, Cumberland Island Study Committee, *Report.* See House Resolution No. 166 (1955).

8. Ibid.

9. Ibid.

10. Ibid., 2.

11. *Brunswick (Georgia) News*, 8 April 1957.

12. Oliver Prescott Jr. to Margaret Ricketson Sprague, Mary R. Bullard, and Oliver G. Ricketson III, 11 June 1959; Cumberland Island Company Inc., stock certificate, 8 January 1960, both in possession of author.

13. "Minutes of the Organization Meeting of the Board of Directors of Cumberland Island Company, Inc.," 12 October 1959, in possession of author.

14. Oliver Prescott Jr. to Margaret Ricketson Sprague, Mary R. Bullard, and Oliver G. Ricketson III, 9 August 1960, in possession of author.

15. "Minutes of the Meeting of the Heirs of LCC, Plaza Hotel, New York," 29 April 1961, in possession of author.

16. Coleman C. Perkins, Joseph C. Graves Jr., and Putnam B. McDowell to heirs of LCC, 9 June 1961, in possession of author.

17. Putnam B. McDowell to John Young, 1 August 1962, in possession of author.

18. These figures appeared in a May 1961 account Harris filed with the Camden County Superior Court. The Cumberland Island Company protested his estimates, contending that the bank had provided high valuations in an attempt to increase the trustee's termination fee. The court eventually awarded the First National Bank of Brunswick $100,000 as a termination fee, the highest such fee ever awarded in Georgia. A grandson of Lucy and Tom Carnegie, T. M. C. Johnston, led an appeal of the decision, and the State Supreme Court unanimously set aside the lower court's decision. Lucy Ferguson was bitterly blamed for having brought the First National Bank of Brunswick into the picture: "Had the trust remained in Pennsylvania there would have been no termination fee (under Pennsylvania law on real estate trusts)" (Oliver Prescott Jr. to Mary R. Bullard, 2 June 1961, in possession of author).

19. Camden Superior Court, case 1667, 6 July 1964, RCCG.

20. First National Bank of Brunswick to J. B. Peeples, 15 May 1956, CER, folder 9-6-09.

21. *Fernandina (Florida) News-Leader*, 7 May 1959, p. 1.

22. Ibid., 14 May 1959, p. 1; *Kingsland Southeast Georgian*, 18 June 1959, p. 1.

23. *Fernandina (Florida) News-Leader*, 24 June 1959, p. 1.

24. Ibid.; Homer Hail, letter to author, 6 September 1974.

25. In May 1959 the Georgia bank had reviewed insurance coverage on all structures on the island. Dungeness House was insured for $25,000, but because the house was abandoned, the bank proposed eliminating its insurance (A. M. Harris Jr. to Way, Peters, and Harris, 5 May 1955, in possession of author).

26. Margaret Shannon, "U.S. Starts Move to Acquire Cumberland Island as a Park," *Atlanta Journal*, 25 January 1966; *American Forests*, June 1966, p. 7.

27. Deed Book 882-5318, 26 September 1967, RCCG; Henry Carter Carnegie, Thomas M. Carnegie IV, and Andrew Carnegie to Cumberland Island Holding Company, 15 January 1969, RB 90, RCCG, 66; Charles E. Fraser to Mary R. Bullard, 5 November 1968, in possession of author.

28. McPhee, "Profiles," 53; *Atlanta Journal*, 3 January 1969, 22 January 1969, 7 February 1969; *Brunswick (Georgia) News*, December 1969; Schuck and Wellford, "Democracy and the Good Life," 58–61.

29. McPhee, "Profiles," 56.

30. Mary Miller, in *Mullet Wrapper* (National Seashore newsletter), January 1993.

31. Thornton W. Morris, "Memorandum to Cumberland Island Land Owners," 7 March 1969, in possession of author; *Atlanta Journal and Constitution*, 2 March 1969, p. 18-B.

32. Thornton W. Morris, "Memorandum to Cumberland Island Land Owners," 18 March 1969; Morris to Bullard, letter and memorandum, 27 September 1993, all in possession of author; *Savannah Morning News*, 10 December 1969, p. 1; *Atlanta Constitution*, 10 December 1969.

33. Thornton W. Morris, "Memorandum to Cumberland Island Conservation Association," 11 September 1969, in possession of author.

34. Thornton W. Morris, personal observation, October 1969.

35. David Nordan, "Bill to Preserve Cumberland Awaits Push from Rep. Stuckey," *Atlanta Journal*, late October 1969; Harry Murphy, "New Control Unit for Islands Mulled," *Atlanta Journal*, 10 December 1969.

36. *Savannah Morning News*, 11 December 1969, p. 2A.

37. Putnam B. McDowell to Mary R. Bullard, 10 March 1969; "Minutes of Land Owners," Cumberland Island, 29 March 1969; "Organizational Meeting of Cumberland Island Conservation Association," Cumberland Island, 30 March 1969, all in possession of author.

38. *Atlanta Constitution*, 9 April 1970.

39. *Georgia Conservancy Newsletter*, 22 April 1970.

40. *National Observer*, 5 January 1970; Hartzog, "Conservation and Management," 2.

41. CER, folders 9-1-003–5; People's National Bank, managers' correspondence, CER, folders 9-1-011–13.

42. People's National Bank, managers' correspondence, Hugh Sloss to Leo Larkin, 5 August 1954, CER, folders 9-1-011–13. The depot's buffer zone included thousands of acres of valuable timberland. Land acquisition on such a scale threatened the local pulpwood industry, and locals viewed the terminal with hostility.

43. Ted Rice (Senator Leverett Saltonstall's office) to Margaret and Howard Sprague, 22 September 1953, in possession of author; "Base History." Kings Bay was used on two occasions: as a station for small army boats during the Cuban Missile Crisis, and as a shelter for local residents during a 1964 hurricane ("Base History"). The terminal languished until 1975, when the U.S. Navy ordered an evaluation of more than sixty sites on the Atlantic and Gulf Coasts for a new submarine support base. The Secretary of the Navy selected Kings Bay as a new base in 1976, and in 1982 it became the present-day Naval Submarine Base, Kings Bay, changing forever St. Marys's rural nature (John J. Glisch, "Submarine Base Changes Rural Life in South Georgia," *Orlando [Florida] Sentinel*, 10 April 1989; Michelle Owens, "Kings Bay's Likely Growth Means Pressure on Area," *Jacksonville Florida Times-Union*, 19 April 1993, p. 1).

44. "Chronology"; Allen T. Edmunds to Hugh Sloss, 12 April 1955, CER, folder 9-2-001; *Our Vanishing Shoreline*. Mellon wore dark glasses, was not introduced, remained silent throughout his visit, and appeared uneasy if anyone spoke to him.

45. Graves, "Establishment."

46. Eric N. Lindquist and Janet E. Stewart, letter to author, 8 July 1988; Martha Wilder, "A New Playground near Jacksonville," *Jacksonville Journal*, 13 December 1970, p. H-1. The Nature Conservancy, a privately funded organization that acquires land for conservation, offered valuable advice to Cumberland landowners and in the late 1960s began considering how to raise money to purchase land and how to find possible allies. On learning of the AWMF's willingness to donate funds for land acquisition, the Nature Conservancy notified island landowners of its desire to withdraw.

47. Graves, "Establishment." I am especially indebted to Graves, a great-granddaughter of Lucy and Tom Carnegie, for her passages on life estates.

48. *Mullet Wrapper*, February 1997; Brian Peters, letter to author, 1 May 2000.

49. CER, folder 8-2-010; John Pennington, "Cumberland," 650. Few records remain of Cumberland churches. However, a Methodist mission was established on the island in 1848, with parishioners including Catharine Laen (Peter Bernardey's widow), Sarah Clubb, and Winifred Downes. After the Civil War, the North End became the site of a Methodist church known as the Union Church and the High Point Community Church. Also a school, the building was still standing in the early twentieth century (Mrs. Paul V. Proctor, letter to author, May 1976; Mary Miller, letter to author, June 1976; Eloise Y. Thompson, letter to author, July 1976).

50. S. M. Hillmer, "Cumberland Island Management," *Kingsland Southeast Georgian*, 11 August 1993, p. 8A.

51. *Savannah Morning News,* 21 January 1982; "Park News," *National Parks* magazine, March–April 1999, 12.

52. Leavell, *Legal Aspects.* Lucille McLean said that her mother, Mary Gowen Brock, well remembered how rapidly black women walked from High Point to Dungeness. They had a peculiar loping stride, carrying laundry, baskets, and even boxes on their heads (interview by author, Folkston, Georgia). Nate Lane remembered walking to High Point on Fridays after work at Dungeness (interview by author, Stafford, Cumberland Island). The presence of a still at High Point gave purpose to the long walk (Mary Miller, in *Mullet Wrapper,* autumn 1990).

53. Jingle Davis, "A Wilderness Noel on Cumberland Island," *Atlanta Constitution,* 25 December 1996, p. C2.

54. Water and Air Research, Inc., Gainesville, Fla., "Environmental Assessment of a Proposal to Provide Telephone Service on Cumberland Island Outside the Wilderness Area" (Telecom, Environmental Assessment Report #01-5678, September 2001, pp. 24–25).

55. Mart Stewart, *"What Nature Suffers to Groe,"* 252.

56. Chaudhuri, *Staging Place,* 259; Froeschauer, "Interpretation," 111, 144; Stewart, *"What Nature Suffers to Groe,"* 250.

BIBLIOGRAPHY

MANUSCRIPT COLLECTIONS, OFFICIAL RECORDS,
AND OTHER DOCUMENTS

Amistad Research Center, New Orleans. American Missionary Association Archives.
Cathedral of St. John the Baptist, Savannah, Georgia. Parish Register 1796–1816, 1816–1838.
Coastal Georgia Historical Society, St. Simons Island. Couper Family Collection.
Connecticut State Library, Hartford. Superior Court Records, Cases in Chancery, New London. Probate District of Groton. Groton Land Records. Groton Vital Records. Norwich Land Records. New London Land Records.
Cumberland Island National Seashore, National Park Service. Seward, Joyce. Interviews, "An Oral History of Cumberland Island, Georgia." Nathanael Greene letter to Ethan Clarke, East Greenwich, 1809.
Eleutherian Mills Historical Library, Greenville, Delaware. Samuel Francis Du Pont Papers, Winterthur Manuscripts.
G. W. Blunt White Library, Mystic Seaport, Connecticut. National Whaling Bank Collection.
Georgia Department of Archives and History, Atlanta. Carnegie Estate, Records of Cumberland Island, AC 69-501. Journal of Archibald Clark at Port of St. Marys, 1822–1840. "Clubs, Societies, and Lodges, Masons, Grand Lodges of Georgia." Grand Dutreuil Family Papers. Edmond Gray (microfilm). Beatrice Lang Collection. Henry Osborne File. Registration Oath Book, Senatorial District 4, vol. 22, Camden County, 1867. Returns of Qualified Voters, District 4, Camden County, vol. 13. Nancy Carnegie Rockefeller Collection. Surveyor-General, Office of the Secretary of State, Atlanta. Land Warrants, 1761–1766.
Georgia Historical Society, Savannah. Alexander Smith Atkinson Papers. Bailey Family Papers. William Baldwin Papers. James Vallence Bevins Papers. Jonathan Bryan Papers. Margaret Davis Cate Collection. Central Railroad of Georgia Collection. Luke Christie Papers. Charles Rinaldo Floyd Papers. Marmaduke B. Floyd and Do-

351

lores B. Floyd Papers. Forman-Bryan-Screven Papers. Fraser-Couper Papers. Harry
Frohock Papers. Isabel Caroline Hamilton Papers. Isaac Peace Hazard Papers. Jabez
Jackson Letters. Edith Duncan Johnston Papers. William Jones Papers. Remer Lane
Papers. John H. McIntosh Papers. Mackay-McQueen Couper Papers. George
Matthews Collection. Thomas Porcher Ravenel Papers. E. H. Steele Paper. Joseph
Frederick Waring Papers. Wayne-Stites-Anderson Papers. Eli Whitney Papers.
Robert Worrell, Druggist's Receipt Book.

Hargrett Special Collections, University of Georgia, Athens. Phillipps Collection of
Egmont Manuscripts.

Historical Society of Pennsylvania, Philadelphia. General Nathanael Greene, letters to
Lieutenant Colonel Henry Lee.

Jekyll Island State Authority, Jekyll Island, Georgia. Dubignon Binders.

Library of Congress, Washington, D.C. Sir George Cockburn Papers. William Drayton
Manuscript, Force Collection.

National Archives, Washington, D.C. Record Groups 76, 98, 105, 107.

New-York Historical Society, New York. Bagoe Collection, Print Department. George
R. Durand Diary. John Alsop King Papers. Nathaniel Pendleton Papers.

P. K. Yonge Library of Florida History, University of Florida, Gainesville. East Florida
Papers, Series 323 A, Census Returns (1784, 1787, and 1789) (copy in Library of Congress and in Public Records Office, London). James T. O'Neill Papers. Spanish Bor-
derland Collections.

Philadelphia Academy of Natural Sciences. Zaccheus Collins Collection. Account of
Titian Peale's Journey, 1817–18. Titian Ramsay Peale Papers. Thomas Say to P. V.
Melsheimer, 1818.

Rhode Island Historical Society, Providence. Nathanael R. Greene Papers.

South Carolina Department of Archives and History, Columbia. Miscellaneous Records.

Southern Historical Collection, Wilson Library, University of North Carolina at Chapel
Hill. William Audley Couper Papers. Couper Family Papers. James Hamilton Papers.
Benjamin Hawkins Papers, Addition. Julia Johnson Fisher Diary. Thomas Butler
King Papers. Mackay-Stiles Papers. George Anderson Mercer Diary. William Page
Papers. William Frederick Penniman Reminiscences. Thomas Porcher Ravenel Pa-
pers. John Rutledge Papers. Martha Schofield Diary. Aaron Wilbur Paper.

United States Fifth Circuit Court Records, Eastern Division, Southern District of Geor-
gia, Federal Records Center, East Point, Atlanta. Suit in Equity, Case #156, *Silas
Fordham and J. M. Hunter v. Charles A. Miller; Mrs. W. R. Bunkley, et al.* Suit in
Equity, Case #10335, *Nancy Stafford Gassman and Cornelia Stafford Williams v.
Lucy C. Carnegie.*

University of Florida, George A. Smathers Libraries, Special Collections. Typescript,
Extract from the Civil War entries, Cornelius H. Longstreet, Box 26, Miscellaneous
Manuscript Collection.

University of Georgia Libraries, Athens. Walter B. Hill Personal Papers.

William R. Perkins Library, Duke University, Durham, North Carolina. Herschel Vespasian Johnson Papers.

PERSONAL COLLECTIONS

Mary R. Bullard, South Dartmouth, Massachusetts

Nancy Johnston Butler, Lexington, Kentucky

Mary Lyman Cammann, Philadelphia, Pennsylvania

Nancy McFadden Copp, Memphis, Tennessee

Kathleen E. Davis, Fernandina, Florida

Lucy Ricketson Ferguson, Greyfield Corporation, Fernandina, Florida

Dora Frohock Finn, St. Marys, Georgia

Helen Harriss, in possession of the author

Alfred Jones, Sea Island, Georgia

Retta Ferguson McDowell, Fernandina, Florida

Mary Miller and Mildred Frazier, Brunswick and St. Simons Island, Georgia (copies in possession of the author)

Bernard N. Nightingale, Brunswick, Georgia

Oliver G. Ricketson Jr., in possession of the author

Oliver G. Ricketson III, in possession of the author

James S. Rockefeller, Camden, Maine

Virginia Rowland, Mattapoisett, Massachusetts

Howard B. Sprague and Margaret Ricketson Sprague, Prides Crossing, Massachusetts

Margaret Ricketson Sprague, in possession of the author

Preston Stevens, Atlanta, Georgia

Retta Johnston Wright, Lexington, Kentucky

BOOKS, ARTICLES, PAMPHLETS, AND MISCELLANEOUS WRITINGS

Abbott, W. W. *The Royal Governors of Georgia, 1754–1775.* Chapel Hill: University of North Carolina Press, 1959.

Abstracts of Colonial Wills of the State of Georgia, 1733–1777. [Hapeville, Ga.?]: Atlanta Town Committee of the National Society Colonial Dames of America in the State of Georgia, 1962.

Ackerman, James S. *Palladio.* Harmondsworth, Eng.: Penguin, 1966.

Acts and Resolutions of the General Assembly of the State of Georgia, Passed at the Regular January Session, 1874. Savannah, Ga.: J. H. Estill, 1874.

Acts and Resolutions of the General Assembly of the State of Georgia, 1897. Atlanta: Franklin Printing and Publishing, 1898.

Adams, William Hampton, ed. *Historical Archaeology of Plantations at Kings Bay,*

Camden County Georgia. Gainesville: University of Florida Department of Anthropology, 1987.

Akin, Edward N. *Flagler: Rockefeller Partner and Florida Baron.* Kent, Ohio: Kent State
University Press, 1988.

Aldrich, Mark. "Flexible Exchange Rates, Northern Expansion, and the Market for
Southern Cotton, 1866–1879." *Journal of Economic History* 33 (June 1973).

Aldrich, Nelson W., Jr. *Old Money: The Mythology of America's Upper Class.* New York:
Knopf, 1988.

Alford, Terry. *Prince among Slaves.* New York: Harcourt Brace Jovanovich, 1977.

Ambrose, Jonathan. *An Analysis of Feral Horse Population Structure on Cumberland Island.* National Park Service and University of Georgia Cooperative Park Studies
Unit Technical Report 1, 1983.

American State Papers. 1st session, 1st Congress, to 2nd session, 17th Congress, March 4,
1789–March 3, 1823. Washington, D.C.: Gales and Seaton, 1834.

American State Papers: Claims. Washington, D.C.: Gales and Seaton, 1834.

Anderson, Jefferson Randolph. "The Genesis of Georgia." *Georgia Historical Quarterly* 13 (1929).

Andrews, Evangeline W., and Charles McL. Andrews, eds. *Jonathan Dickinson's Journal; or, God's Protecting Providence Being the Narrative of a Journey from Port Royal
to Philadelphia between August 23, 1696, and April 1697.* New Haven: Yale University
Press, 1945.

Andrews, Sidney. *The South since the War as Shown by Fourteen Weeks of Travel and Observation in Georgia and the Carolinas.* Boston: Ticknor and Fields, 1866.

Andrews, Wayne. *Architecture, Ambition, and Americans: A Social History of American
Architecture.* New York: Free Press of Glencoe, 1964.

Annals of Congress. 42 vols. Washington, D.C.: n.p., 1834–56.

Appleton's Dictionary of Machines, Mechanics, Engine Work, and Engineering. New
York: Appleton, 1852.

Arnow, Isaac F. "History of St. Marys and Camden County." *Camden County Tribune.*
1950–51. (Series of articles in albums at Bryant-Lang Library, Woodbine, Ga.;
St. Marys Public Library, St. Marys, Ga.)

Ascher, Robert, and Charles H. Fairbanks. "Excavations of a Slave Cabin: Georgia,
U.S.A." *Historical Archaeology* 5 (1971).

Aslet, Clive. *The American Country House.* New Haven: Yale University Press, 1990.

Austin, Allan D. *African Muslims in Antebellum America: A Sourcebook.* New York:
Garland Publishing, 1984.

Babson, David W. "The Archaeology of Racism and Ethnicity on Southern Plantations." *Historical Archaeology* 24, no. 4 (1990).

Bailey, Eloise Yancey. *Pathway: Proctor Kith and Kin.* Kingsland, Ga.: E. Y. Bailey, 1978.

Bailey, L. H. *The Standard Cyclopedia of Horticulture.* Vol. 2. New York: Macmillan,
1935.

Bangs, Outram. "Land Mammals of Peninsular Florida and the Coast Region of Georgia." *Proceedings, Boston Society of Natural History,* vol. 28, no. 7 (1898).

Bardaglio, Peter W. *Reconstructing the Household: Families, Sex, and the Law in the Nineteenth-Century South.* Chapel Hill: University of North Carolina Press, 1995.

Bartram, John. *Diary of a Journey through the Carolinas, Georgia and Florida, from July 1, 1765, to April 10, 1766.* Annotated by Francis Harper. Philadelphia: American Philosophical Society, 1942.

Bartram, William. *Travels.* Ed. Francis Harper. New Haven: Yale University Press, 1958.

"Base History." Kings Bay, Ga.: Department of the Navy, Public Affairs Office, Naval Submarine Base, 1987. Press release.

Beirne, Francis F. *The War of 1812.* New York: Dutton, 1949.

Belcher, Max, Beverly Buchanan, and William Christenberry. *House and Home: Spirits of the South.* Andover, Mass.: Addison Gallery of American Art, 1994.

Belden, Louise Conway. "Entertaining in America in the Nineteenth Century." *Antiques* 130 (December 1986).

Belden, Thomas Grahm, and Marva Robins Belden. *So Fell the Angels.* Boston: Little, Brown, 1956.

Bell, Malcolm, Jr. *Major Butler's Legacy: Five Generations of a Slaveholding Family.* Athens: University of Georgia Press, 1987.

Bemis, Samuel Flagg. *A Diplomatic History of the United States.* Rev. ed. New York: H. Holt, 1942.

Benjamin, Asher. *The American Builder's Companion.* 6th ed. 1827; reprint, New York: Dover, 1969.

———. *The Country Builder's Assistant.* Greenfield, Mass.: T. Dickman, 1797.

Benjamin, S. G. W. "The Sea Islands." *Harper's New Monthly* 57, no. 342 (November 1878).

Bentley, George R. *A History of the Freedmen's Bureau.* New York: Octagon Books, 1970.

Berlin, Ira. "From Creole to African: Atlantic Creoles and the Origins of African-American Society in Mainland North America." *William and Mary Quarterly,* 3d ser., 53 (April 1996).

———. *Many Thousands Gone: The First Two Centuries of Slavery in North America.* Cambridge, Mass.: Belknap Press of Harvard University Press, 1998.

Bigelow, John. *Breaches of Anglo-American Treaties: A Study in History and Diplomacy.* New York: Sturgis and Walton, 1917.

Bjork, Jennifer. *1995 Feral Horse Population Survey.* National Park Service Report, 1995.

Blair, Ruth. *Some Early Tax Digests of Georgia.* Atlanta: Georgia Department of Archives and History, 1926.

Blake, Janice Gayle, comp. *Pre-Nineteenth Century Maps in the Collection of Georgia Surveyor General Department: A Catalogue.* Atlanta: State Printing Office, 1975.

Blandy, F. Graham. "Dungeness—A Winter Home." Pts. 1 and 2. *The Sportsman Tourist,* [ca. 1898].

Blassingame, John W. *The Slave Community: Plantation Life in the Antebellum South.* Rev. and enl. ed. New York: Oxford University Press, 1979.

Blunt, Edmund M. *The American Coast Pilot.* 10th ed. New York: E. M. Blunt, 1822.

Bonner, James C. *A History of Georgia Agriculture, 1732–1860.* Athens: University of Georgia Press, 1964.

Braden, Susan R. "Florida Resort Architecture: The Hotels of Henry Plant and Henry Flagler." Ph.D. diss., Florida State University, 1987.

Braund, Kathryn E. Holland. *Deerskins and Duffels: The Creek Indian Trade with Anglo-America, 1685–1815.* Lincoln: University of Nebraska Press, 1993.

Breckinridge, H. M. *History of the Late War between the United States and Great Britain.* Baltimore: Schaeffer and Maund, 1818.

Brentnall, Margaret. *The Cinque Ports and Romney Marsh.* London: Gifford, 1972.

Brewer, Clifton Hartwell. *A History of Religious Education in the Episcopal Church to 1835.* New Haven: Yale University Press, 1924.

Brown, Kenneth L., and Doreen S. Cooper. "Structural Continuity in an African-American Slave and Tenant Community." *Historical Archaeology* 24, no. 4 (1990).

Bryan, Jonathan. *Journal of a Visit to the Georgia Islands of St. Catherines, Green, Ossabaw, Sapelo, St. Simons, Jekyll, and Cumberland, with Comments on the Florida Islands of Amelia, Talbot, and St. George, in 1753.* Ed. Virginia Steele Wood and Mary R. Bullard. Macon: Mercer University Press, 1996.

Bryan, T. Conn. *Confederate Georgia.* Athens: University of Georgia Press, 1953.

Bryant, Pat. *English Crown Grants for Islands in Georgia, 1755–1775.* Atlanta: State Printing Office, 1972.

Bryant, William Cullen, and Sidney Howard Gay. *A Popular History of the United States.* 4 vols. New York: Scribner's, 1886.

Buck, Paul H. *The Road to Reunion: 1865–1900.* Boston: Little, Brown, 1937.

Buckingham, J. S. *The Slave States of America.* 2 vols. 1842; reprint, New York: Negro Universities Press, 1968.

Buckley, Roger Norman. *The British Army in the West Indies.* Gainesville: University Press of Florida, 1998.

Bullard, Mary R. *An Abandoned Black Settlement on Cumberland Island.* South Dartmouth, Mass.: M. R. Bullard, 1982.

———. *Black Liberation on Cumberland Island in 1815.* South Dartmouth, Mass.: M. R. Bullard, 1983.

———. "The Cumberland Islands: Their Division between the Heirs of Lynch and the Estate of General Greene." Typescript, Georgia Historical Society, 1979.

———. "In Search of Cumberland Island's Dungeness: Its Origins and English Antecedents." *Georgia Historical Quarterly* 76 (spring 1992).

———. *Robert Stafford of Cumberland Island: Growth of a Planter.* Athens: University of Georgia Press, 1995.

———. "Title Search for Great and Little Cumberland Islands, Camden County, Georgia." South Dartmouth, Mass.: M. R. Bullard, 2001.

————. "Uneasy Legacy: The Lynch-Greene Partition on Cumberland Island, 1798–1802." *Georgia Historical Quarterly* 77 (winter 1993).

Bulloch, J. G. B. *A History and Genealogy of the Families of Bulloch, Stobo, De Veaux*. Savannah, Ga.: J. G. B. Bulloch, 1892.

Burnett, E. C., ed. *Letters of Members of the Continental Congress*. Vol. 1. Washington, D.C.: Carnegie Institution of Washington, 1921.

Bushnell, David, comp. *La República de las Floridas: Text and Documents*. Mexico City: Pan American Institute of Geography and History, 1986.

Butler, Lewis [William George], and Stewart Hare. *The Annals of the King's Royal Rifle Corps*. Vol. 1, *The Royal Americans*. London: J. Murray, 1913.

Cabot, Ramón Romero. "La Defensa de Florida en el Segundo Periodo Español, 1783–1821." Master's thesis, University of Florida, 1982.

————. "Los Ultimos Años de la Soberanía Española en la Florida, 1783–1821." Ph.D. dissertation, University of Florida, 1983.

Cadle, Farris W. *Georgia Land Surveying: History and Law*. Athens: Unversity of Georgia Press, 1991.

Camden's Challenge: A History of Camden County, Georgia. Comp. Marguerite Reddick, ed. Eloise Bailey and Virginia Proctor . [Jacksonville]: Camden County Board of Commissioners, Camden County Historical Commission, 1976.

Camplin, Jamie. *The Rise of the Rich*. New York: St. Martin's Press, 1979.

Candler, Allen D., and Clement A. Evans. *Cyclopedia of Georgia*. Vol. 1. Atlanta: State Historical Association, 1906.

Capers, C. W. "On the Cotton Caterpillar." *Southern Agriculturist* 1 (1828).

Carawan, Guy, and Candie Carawan, eds. *Ain't You Got a Right to the Tree of Life? The People of Johns Island, South Carolina: Their Faces, Their Words, and Their Songs*. Rev. ed. Athens: University of Georgia Press, 1989.

Carmichael, Allie Brown. "The Brown Family of the Sand Hills." In *Pen Portraits: Stories of Pioneer Camden Women*, comp. Angeline Lang Reddick. Kingsland, Ga.: *Southeast Georgian*, 1969.

Carnegie, Andrew. *Autobiography of Andrew Carnegie*. Boston: Houghton Mifflin, 1920.

Carney, Judith. "Rice, Slaves, and Landscapes of Cultural Memory." In *Places of Cultural Memory: African Reflections on the American Landscape*. [Atlanta]: U.S. Department of the Interior, National Park Service, 2001.

Cashin, Edward J. *Governor Henry Ellis and the Transformation of British North America*. Athens: University of Georgia Press, 1994.

Casson, Herbert N. *The Romance of Steel: The Story of a Thousand Millionaires*. New York: A. S. Barnes, 1907.

Cate, Margaret Davis. "Fort Frederica and the Battle of Bloody Marsh." *Georgia Historical Quarterly* 27 (June 1943).

————. *Our Todays and Yesterdays: A Story of Brunswick and the Coastal Islands.* Rev. ed. Brunswick, Ga.: Glover Brothers, 1930.

Catterall, Helen Tunncliff. *Judicial Cases Concerning American Slavery and the Negro.* Vol. 3, *Cases from the Courts of Georgia, Florida, Alabama, Mississippi, and Louisiana.* Washington, D.C.: Carnegie Institution of Washington, 1932.

Chalker, Fussell M. "Highland Scots in the Georgia Lowlands." *Georgia Historical Quarterly* 60 (spring 1976).

The Challenge of Georgia's Coast: A Realistic Analysis of Present Highway Problems[,] Undeveloped Resort Facilities, and a Blueprint for Unlocking the Golden Coast of Georgia. N.p.: Scenic Highway Committee of the Commissioners of Roads and Revenue, Glynn County, [ca. 1950].

Chandler, David Leon. *Henry Flagler: The Astonishing Life and Times of the Visionary Robber Baron Who Founded Florida.* New York: Macmillan, 1986.

Chappell, Absalom H. *Miscellanies of Georgia, Historical, Biographial, Descriptive, Etc.* Atlanta: J. F. Meegan, 1874.

Chatelain, Verne. *The Defenses of Spanish Florida: 1565 to 1763.* Publication 511. Washington, D.C.: Carnegie Institution of Washington, 1941.

Chaudhuri, Una. *Staging Place: The Geography of Modern Drama.* Ann Arbor: University of Michigan Press, 1995.

Chesnutt, David R. *South Carolina's Expansion into Colonial Georgia, 1720–1765.* New York: Garland Publishing, 1989.

"Chronology of Principal Contacts Made between Service Representatives and Carnegie Heirs . . . Regarding Cumberland Island." Mimeographed. N.p.: National Park Service, 1965.

Cimbala, Paul Alan. "The Terms of Freedom: The Freedman's Bureau and Reconstruction in Georgia, 1865–1870." Ph.D. diss., Emory University, 1983. Published as *Under the Guardianship of the Nation: The Freedmen's Bureau and the Reconstruction of Georgia, 1865–1870.* Athens: University of Georgia Press, 1997.

Clark, Clifford Edward, Jr. *The American Family Home, 1800–1960.* Chapel Hill: University of North Carolina Press, 1986

Clark, Murtie June. *Colonial Soldiers of the South, 1732–1774.* Baltimore: Genealogical Publishing, 1983.

Clark, R. H., T. R. R. Cobb, and D. Irwin. *The Code of the State of Georgia.* 2d ed. Atlanta: Franklin Steam Print House, 1867.

Clayton, Augustin Smith. *A Compilation of the Laws of the State of Georgia, 1800–1810.* Augusta, Ga.: Adams and Duyckinck, 1813.

Clifton, James M. "The Rice Driver: His Role in Slave Management." *South Carolina Historical Magazine* 82 (October 1981).

Coatsworth, John H. "American Trade with European Colonies in the Caribbean and South America, 1790–1812." *William and Mary Quarterly* 24, no. 2 (April 1967).

Cobb, Thomas R. R., comp. *A Digest of the Statute Laws of the State of Georgia in Force Prior to the Sessions of the General Assembly of 1851.* Athens, Ga.: Christy, Kelsea, and Burke, 1851.

―――. *An Inquiry into the Law of Negro Slavery in the United States of America; to Which Is Prefixed an Historical Sketch of Slavery.* 1858; reprint, New York: Negro Universities Press, 1968.

Cochran, Hamilton. *Blockade Runners of the Confederacy.* Indianapolis: Bobbs-Merrill, 1958.

Cody, Cheryll Ann. "Naming, Kinship, and Estate Dispersal: Notes on Slave Family Life on a South Carolina Plantation, 1786 to 1833." *William and Mary Quarterly* 39 (January 1982).

Cohn, David L. *The Life and Times of King Cotton.* New York: Oxford University Press, 1956.

Cohn, Jan. *The Palace or the Poorhouse: The American House as a Cultural Symbol.* East Lansing: Michigan State University Press, 1979.

Coker, William S. "John Forbes and Company and the War of 1812 in the Spanish Borderlands." In *Hispanic-American Essays in Honor of Max Leon Moorhead,* ed. William S. Coker. Pensacola: Perdido Bay Press, 1979.

Coleman, Feay Shellman. *Nostrums for Fashionable Entertainments: Dining in Georgia, 1800–1850.* Savannah, Ga.: Telfair Academy of Arts and Sciences, 1992.

Coleman, Kenneth. *The American Revolution in Georgia, 1763–1789.* Athens: University of Georgia Press, 1958.

―――. *Colonial Georgia: A History.* New York: Scribner, 1976.

Coleman, Kenneth, and Charles Stephen Gurr, eds. *Dictionary of Georgia Biography.* 2 vols. Athens: University of Georgia Press, 1983.

Coleman, Kenneth, and Milton Ready, eds. Original Papers of Governor John Reynolds 1754–1756. Vol. 27 of *Colonial Records of the State of Georgia.* Athens: University of Georgia Press, 1977.

Coles, Robert. *Privileged Ones: The Well-off and the Rich in America.* Boston: Little, Brown, 1977.

Colledge, J. J. *Ships of the Royal Navy: An Historical Index.* Newton Abbott, Eng.: David and Charles, 1969.

The Colonial Records of the State of Georgia. Atlanta and Athens: C. P. Byrd, Franklin-Turner, and University of Georgia Press, 1904–.

Connor, Jeanette Thurber, ed. *Colonial Records of Spanish Florida.* 2 vols. DeLand: Florida State Historical Society, 1927.

Conrad, Georgia Bryan. "Reminiscences of a Southern Woman." In *The Southern Workman.* Hampton, Va.: Hampton Institute Press, 1901.

Conway, Alan. *The Reconstruction of Georgia.* Minneapolis: University of Minnesota Press, 1966.

Conyngham, David Powers. *Sherman's March through the South.* New York: Sheldon, 1865.

Cook, Jeannine, ed. *Columbus and the Land of Ayllón: The Exploration and Settlement of the Southeast.* Valona, Ga.: Lower Altamaha Historical Society, 1992.

Copeland, Melvin Thomas. *The Cotton Manufacturing Industry of the United States.* Cambridge: Harvard University Press, 1912.

Corbitt, D. C. "The Return of Spanish Rule to the St. Mary and the St. Johns, 1813–1821." *Florida Historical Quarterly* 20 (July 1941).

Corgada, James W. "Florida's Relations with Cuba during the Civil War." *Florida Historical Quarterly* 59 (July 1980).

Corkran, David H. *The Creek Frontier, 1540–1783.* Norman: University of Oklahoma Press, 1967.

Coulter, E. Merton, ed. *The Journal of William Stephens.* Athens: University of Georgia Press, 1958.

———. "The Okefenokee Swamp, Its History and Legends." *Georgia Historical Quarterly* 48 (1964).

———. *Thomas Spalding of Sapelo.* University: Louisiana State University Press, 1940.

Crane, Verner W. *The Southern Frontier, 1670–1732.* 1928; reprint, Ann Arbor: University of Michigan Press, 1956.

Creel, Margaret W. *A Peculiar People: Slave Religion and Community-Culture among the Gullahs.* New York: New York University Press, 1988.

Cresap, Ida Keeling. "The History of Florida Agriculture: The Early Era." Unpublished paper, Florida Agricultural Experiment Station, Hume Library, University of Florida, Gainesville, 1937.

Cummings, Richard O. *The American Ice Harvests: A Historical Study in Technology, 1800–1918.* Berkeley: University of California Press, 1949.

Darlington, William, comp. *Reliquiae Baldwinianae: Selections from the Correspondence of the late William Baldwin.* Philadelphia: Kimber and Sharpless, 1843.

Dauer, Manning J. *The Adams Federalists.* Baltimore: Johns Hopkins Press, 1953.

Daugherty, Charles M. "The Cotton Seed Industry." In *Yearbook of the United States Department of Agriculture.* Washington, D.C.: U.S. Government Printing Office, 1920.

Davis, Charles T., and Henry Louis Gates Jr., eds. *The Slave's Narrative.* New York: Oxford University Press, 1985.

Davis, David Brion. *The Problem of Slavery in the Age of Revolution, 1770–1823.* Ithaca: Cornell University Press, 1975.

———. *The Problem of Slavery in Western Culture.* Ithaca: Cornell University Press, 1966.

Davis, Kathleen E. *We Remember: The Davis-Mizell Family.* Fernandina, Fla.: Privately printed, 1982.

Davis, Mary Lamar. "Brigadier General W. G. M. Davis, C.S.A." *Florida Law Journal* 23 (February 1949).

Davis, T. Frederick. "Digest of Florida Material in Niles' Register, 1811–1849." Typescript, P. K. Yonge Library of Florida History, University of Florida, Gainesville, 1939.

————. "Early Orange Culture in Florida and the Epochal Cold of 1835." *Florida Historical Quarterly* 15 (April 1937).

Davis, William Watson. *The Civil War and Reconstruction in Florida.* New York: Columbia University, 1913.

Dawson, William Crosby, ed. *A Compilation of the Laws of the State of Georgia.* Milledgeville: Grantland and Orme, 1831.

Deagan, Kathleen A. "Cultures in Transition: Fusion and Assimilation among the Eastern Timucua." In *Tacachale: Essays on the Indians of Florida and Southeastern Georgia during the Historic Period,* ed. Jerald Milanich and Samuel Proctor. Gainesville: University Presses of Florida, 1978.

————. "St. Augustine and the Mission Frontier." In *The Spanish Missions of La Florida,* ed. Bonnie G. McEwan. Gainesville: University Press of Florida, 1993.

————. "Sixteenth-Century Spanish-American Colonization in the Southeastern United States and the Caribbean." In *Columbian Consequences: Archaeological and Historical Perspectives on the Spanish Borderlands East, vol. 2,* ed. David Hurst Thomas. Washington, D.C.: Smithsonian Institution Press, 1990.

DeCanio, Stephen. "Cotton 'Overproduction' in Late Nineteenth-Century Southern Agriculture." *Journal of Economic History* 33 (September 1973).

Dennett, Tyler. *Lincoln and the Civil War in the Diaries of John Hay.* New York: Dodd, Mead, 1939.

De Pratter, Chester B., and J. D. Howard. "History of Shoreline Changes Determined by Archaeological Dating: Georgia Coast, U.S.A." *Transactions of the Gulf Coast Association of Geological Societies* 27 (1977).

Desmond, Harry W., and Herbert Croly. *Stately Homes in America from Colonial Times to the Present Day.* New York: Appleton, 1903.

De Vorsey, Louis, Jr. "Early Maps and the Land of Ayllón." In *Columbus and the Land of Ayllón,* ed. Jeannine Cook. Valona, Ga.: Lower Altamaha Historical Society, 1992.

————. "Indian Boundaries in Colonial Georgia." *Georgia Historical Quarterly* 54 (spring 1970).

————. *The Indian Boundary in the Southern Colonies, 1763–1775.* Chapel Hill: University of North Carolina Press, 1966.

————, ed. *Report of the General Survey in the Southern District of North America,* by John Gerar William De Brahm. Columbia: University of South Carolina Press, 1971.

Dickens, Charles. *American Notes and Pictures from Italy.* London: 1873.

Dickinson, Jonathan. *God's Protecting Providence.* 7th ed. London: James Phillips, 1790.

Dictionary of American Biography. New York: Scribner's, 1928–[58].

Dictionary of American Naval Fighting Ships. Washington, D.C.: Naval History Division, Department of the Navy, 1976.

A Digest of the Laws of the State of Georgia. Milledgeville, Ga.: Grantland and Orme, 1822.

A Digest of the Laws of the State of Georgia. 2d ed. Athens, Ga.: Oliver H. Prince, 1837.

Doar, David. *Rice and Rice Planting in the South Carolina Low Country.* Charleston, S.C.: The Charleston Museum, 1936.

Donald, David, ed. *Inside Lincoln's Cabinet: The Civil War Diaries of Salmon P. Chase.* New York: Longman's, Green, 1954.

Downing, A. J. *The Fruits and Fruit Trees of America.* New York: Wiley and Putnam, 1845.

Drayton, John. *A View of South Carolina as Respects Her Natural and Civil Concerns.* Charleston, S.C.: W. P. Young, 1802.

Dudden, Faye E. *Serving Women: Household Service in Nineteenth-Century America.* Middletown, Conn.: Wesleyan University Press, 1983.

Dumont, William H. *Colonial Georgia Genealogical Data, 1748–1783.* Washington, D.C.: National Genealogical Society, 1971.

Duncan, Russell. *Freedom's Shore: Tunis Campbell and the Georgia Freedmen.* Athens: University of Georgia Press, 1986.

Du Pont, Samuel Francis. *Samuel Francis Du Pont: A Selection from His Civil War Letters.* Ed. John D. Hayes. 3 vols. Ithaca: Cornell University Press for the Eleutherian Mills Historical Library, 1969.

Durant, Samuel W. *History of Allegheny County, Pennsylvania, with Illustrations Descriptive of Its Scenery, Palatial Residences, Public Buildings, Fine Blocks, and Important Manufactories.* Philadelphia: L. H. Everts, 1876.

Dusinberre, William. *Them Dark Days: Slavery in the American Rice Swamps.* New York: Oxford University Press, 1996.

Eaton, Clement. *The Waning of the Old South Civilization, 1860–1880s.* Athens: University of Georgia Press, 1968.

Egmont, John Perceval, First Earl of. *Diary of Viscount Perceval, afterwards First Earl.* London: H. M. Stationery Office, 1923.

————. *Journal of the Earl of Egmont: Abstract of the Trustees' Proceedings for Establishing the Colony of Georgia, 1732–1738.* Ed. with intro. Robert G. McPherson. Athens: University of Georgia Press, 1962.

————. *Journal of the Earl of Egmont, First President of the Board of Trustees, from June 14, 1738, to May 25, 1744.* New York: AMS Press, 1970.

Ehrenhard, John E. "Composite Mapping for Archeology." In *Transactions of the First Conference of Scientific Research in the National Parks,* vol. 1. Houghton: Michigan Technological University, 1977.

Ehrenhard, John E., and Mary R. Bullard. "The Chimneys." In *Stafford Plantation, Cumberland Island National Seashore, Georgia: Archeological Investigations of a Slave Cabin.* Tallahassee, Fla.: National Park Service, 1981.

Elbert, Samuel. *Letter Book of Governor Samuel Elbert, from January, 1785, to November, 1785.* In *Collections of the Georgia Historical Society,* vol. 5, pt. 2. Savannah: Wymberley Jones De Renne and The Morning News, 1902.

————. *Order Book of Samuel Elbert, Colonel and Brigadier General in the Continental Army. N.p.: Wymberley Jones De Renne, n.d.* In *Collections of the Georgia Historical Society,* vol. 5, pt. 2. Savannah: Wymberley Jones De Renne and The Morning News, 1902.

Elliott, William. *Carolina Sports by Land and Water, Including Devil-Fishing, Wild-Cat, Deer, and Bear Hunting, etc.* London: Richard Bentley, 1867.

Encyclopedia of Pennsylvania Biography. New York: Lewis Historical Publishing, 1914–63.

Epperson, Terrence W. "Race and the Disciplines of the Plantation." *Historical Archaeology* 24, no. 4 (1990).

Erickson, Charlotte. *Invisible Immigrants: The Adaptation of English and Scottish Immigrants in Nineteenth-Century America.* Coral Gables, Fla.: University of Miami Press, 1972.

Ettinger, Amos Aschback. *James Edward Oglethorpe, Imperial Idealist.* Oxford: Clarendon, 1936.

Fairbanks, Charles H. "The Kingsley Slave Cabins in Duval County, Florida, 1968." *Conference on Historic Site Archaeology Papers* 7 (1972).

————. "The Plantation Archaeology of the Southeastern Coast." *Historical Archaeology* 18, no. 1 (1984).

Fairbanks, Charles H., and Sue A. Mullins-Moore. "How Did Slaves Live?" *Magazine of Modern Archaeology* 2 (summer 1980).

Fallows, James M. *The Water Lords: Ralph Nader's Study Group Report on Industry and Environmental Crisis in Savannah, Georgia.* New York: Grossman, 1971.

Fitch, John A. *The Steel Workers.* Vol. 3 of *The Pittsburgh Survey: Findings,* ed. Paul Underwood Kellogg. New York: Charities Publication Committee, 1910.

Fite, Gilbert. *Cotton Fields No More: Southern Agriculture, 1865–1980.* Lexington: University Press of Kentucky, 1984.

Flanders, Ralph B. *Plantation Slavery in Georgia.* Chapel Hill: University of North Carolina Press, 1933.

Fleetwood, Rusty. *Tidecraft: An Introductory Look at the Boats of Lower South Carolina, Georgia, and Northeastern Florida, 1650–1950.* Savannah, Ga.: Coastal Heritage Society, 1982.

Floyd, General [John]. "On the Cultivation and Preparation of Indigo." *Southern Agriculturist* 2 (March 1829).

Floyd, Marmaduke. "Certain Tabby Ruins on the Georgia Coast." In *Georgia's Disputed Ruins,* ed. E. Merton Coulter. Chapel Hill: University of North Carolina Press, 1937.

Fogel, Robert William, and Stanley L. Engerman. *Time on the Cross: The Economics of American Negro Slavery.* Boston: Little, Brown, 1974.

Foner, Eric. *Reconstruction: America's Unfinished Revolution, 1863–1877.* New York: Harper and Row, 1988.

Fonseca, Isabel. *Bury Me Standing: The Gypsies and Their Journey.* New York: Knopf, 1995.

Ford, J. A., and Gordon R. Willey. "An Interpretation of the Prehistory of the Eastern United States." *American Anthropologist* 43 (July–September 1941).

"Fort St. Andrews/Fort Prince William." *Georgia Magazine,* August–September 1969.

Foster, John T., and Sarah Whitmer Foster. "Aid Societies Were Not Alike: Northern Teachers in Post–Civil War Florida. *Florida Historical Quarterly* 73 (winter 1995).

Fothergill, Samuel. *Memoirs of the Life and Gospel Labors of Samuel Fothergill, with Selections from His Correspondence.* New York: Collins, 1844.

Fowles, John. *Islands.* London: Cape, 1978.

Franklin, John Hope. "Southern History: The Black-White Connection. The 1986 Elson Lecture." *Atlanta Historical Journal* 30 (summer 1986).

Frazier, C. Craig. *Historic Structure Report: Architectural Data Section for Plum Orchard Mansion: Cumberland Island National Seashore, Camden County, Georgia.* Denver, Colo.: U.S. Department of the Interior, [1987].

Freidel, Frank, ed., with Richard K. Showman. *Harvard Guide to American History.* Cambridge: Belknap Press of Harvard University Press, 1974.

Froeschauer, Peggy Stanley. "The Interpretation and Management of an Agricultural Landscape: Stafford Plantation, Cumberland Island National Seashore, Georgia." Master's thesis, University of Georgia, 1989.

Fuller, H. B. *The Purchase of Florida, Its History and Diplomacy.* 1906; reprint, Gainesville: University of Florida Press, 1964.

Galbraith, John Kenneth. *The Scotch.* 2d ed. Boston: Houghton Mifflin, 1985.

Gallardo, José Miguel, trans. and ed. "The Spaniards and the English Settlement in Charles Town." *South Carolina Historical and Genealogical Magazine* 37 (October 1936).

Gallay, Alan. *The Formation of a Planter Elite: Jonathan Bryan and the Southern Colonial Frontier.* Athens: University of Georgia Press, 1989.

———. "The Search for an Alternate Source of Trade: The Creek Indians and Jonathan Bryan." *Georgia Historical Quarterly* 73 (summer 1989).

Gallois, R. W. *British Regional Geology: The Wealden District.* 4th ed. London: National Environment Research Council, Institute of Geological Sciences, 1965.

Gannon, Michael. "The New Alliance of History and Archaeology in the Eastern Spanish Borderlands." *William and Mary Quarterly* 49 (April 1992).

Garraty, John A. *The New Commonwealth, 1877–1890.* New York: Harper and Row, 1968.

Garrett, Elizabeth Donaghy. *At Home: The American Family, 1750–1870.* New York: H. N. Abrams, 1990.

Genovese, Eugene D. *Roll, Jordan, Roll: The World the Slaves Made.* New York: Vintage Books, 1976.

Georgia House of Representatives. Cumberland Island Study Committee. *Report to the 1956 Session of the General Assembly.* Atlanta, 1956.

Georgia Writers' Project, Works Projects Administration. *Drums and Shadows: Survival Studies among the Georgia Coastal Negroes.* 1940; reprint, Athens: University of Georgia Press, 1986.

————. *Savannah River Plantations.* Ed. Mary Granger. 1947; reprint, Spartanburg, S.C.: Reprint Company, 1972.

Gilbert, C. J. "Evolution of Romney Marsh." *Archaeologia Cantiana,* n.s., 45 (1933).

Gilkes, Lillian. *Cora Crane: A Biography of Mrs. Stephen Crane.* Bloomington: Indiana University Press, 1960.

Ginger, Ray. *Age of Excess: The United States from 1877 to 1914.* New York: Macmillan, 1965.

Girouard, Mark. *Life in the English Country House: A Social and Architectural History.* New Haven: Yale University Press, 1978.

————. *The Victorian Country House.* Oxford: Clarendon Press, 1971.

Golden, Claudia Dale. "The Economics of Emancipation." *Journal of Economic History* 33 (March 1973).

Gomez, Michael A. "Muslims in Early America." *Journal of Southern History* 60 (November 1994).

Goodloe, Robin. "Genetic Variation and Its Management Applications in Eastern U.S. Feral Horses." *Journal of Wildlife Management* 55, no. 3 (1991): 412–21.

Gordon, Robert. "Negro 'Shouts' from Georgia." In *Mother Wit from the Laughing Barrel: Readings in the Interpretation of Afro-American Folklore,* ed. Alan Dundes. Englewood Cliffs, N.J.: Prentice-Hall, 1972.

Grady, Henry W. *The New South and Other Addresses.* New York: Maynard, Merrill, 1904.

Graham, Thomas. "Flagler's Magnificent Hotel Ponce de Leon." *Florida Historical Quarterly* 54 (July 1975).

Graves, Margaret. "The Establishment of Cumberland Island National Seashore." Unpublished paper, Hotchkiss School, Connecticut, 1981.

Gray, Lewis C. *History of Agriculture in the Southern United States to 1860.* 2 vols. Washington, D.C.: Carnegie Institute, 1933.

Green, Harvey. *The Light of the Home: An Intimate View of the Lives of Women in Victorian America.* New York: Pantheon Books, 1983.

Greenberg, Kenneth S. *Honor and Slavery*. Princeton: Princeton University Press, 1996.

Greene, George Sears, and Louise Brownell Clarke. *The Greenes of Rhode Island*. New York: Knickerbocker Press, 1903.

Greene, George Washington. *Life of Nathanael Greene, Major-General in the Army of the Revolution*. 3 vols. New York: G. P. Putnam and Son, 1867–71.

Greene, Melissa Faye. *Praying for Sheetrock*. Reading, Mass.: Addison-Wesley, 1991.

Griffin, Martha M. *Geologic Guide to Cumberland Island National Seashore*. Atlanta: Department of Natural Resources, 1982.

Gritzner, Janet Bigbee. "Tabby in the Coastal Southeast: The Culture History of an American Building Material." Ph.D. diss., Louisiana State University and Agricultural and Mechanical College, 1978.

Grossberg, Michael. *Governing the Hearth: Law and the Family in Nineteenth-Century America*. Chapel Hill: University of North Carolina Press, 1985.

Gutman, Herbert. *The Black Family in Slavery and Freedom, 1750–1925*. New York: Pantheon, 1976.

Habersham, James. *The Letters of Hon. James Habersham, 1756–1775*. Vol. 6 of *Collections of the Georgia Historical Society*. Savannah, Ga.: Savannah Morning News, 1904.

Hacker, Louis M. *The World of Andrew Carnegie, 1865–1901*. Philadelphia: Lippincott, 1968.

Hahn, Steven. *The Roots of Southern Populism: Yeoman Farmers and the Transformation of the Georgia Upcountry, 1850–1890*. New York: Oxford University Press, 1983.

Hamer, Marguerite Bartlett. "Edmund Gray and His Settlement at New Hanover." *Georgia Historical Quarterly* 13 (March 1929).

Hamer, Philip M., George Rogers Jr., and David R. Chesnutt, eds. *Papers of Henry Laurens*. 10 vols. Columbia: University of South Carolina Press, 1968–85.

Handlin, David P. *The American Home: Architecture and Society, 1815–1915*. Boston: Little, Brown, 1979.

Hann, John H. *A History of the Timucua Indians and Missions*. Gainesville: University Press of Florida, 1996.

————. "Twilight of the Mocamo and Guale Aborigines as Portrayed in the 1695 Spanish Visitation." *Florida Historical Quarterly* 66 (July 1987).

Hanson, R. P., and Lars Karstad. "Feral Swine in the Southeastern United States." *Journal of Wildlife Management* 23, no. 1 (1959): 64–74.

Hardee, Charles Seton Henry. "Reminiscences of Charles Seton Henry Hardee." *Georgia Historical Quarterly* 12 (June–September 1928).

Hardeman, Nicholas P. *Shucks, Shocks, and Hominy Blocks: Corn as a Way of Life in Pioneer America*. Baton Rouge: Louisiana State University Press, 1981.

Harden, William. *A History of Savannah and South Georgia.* 2 vols. Atlanta: Cherokee Publishing, 1969.

———. "The Moravians of Georgia and Pennsylvania as Educators." *Georgia Historical Quarterly* 2 (March 1918).

Harman, Joyce Elizabeth. *Trade and Privateering in Spanish Florida, 1732–1763.* St. Augustine, Fla.: St. Augustine Historical Society, 1969.

Harrold, Frances. "Colonial Siblings: Georgia's Relationship with South Carolina during the Pre-Revolutionary Period." *Georgia Historical Quarterly* 73 (winter 1989).

Hart, Albert Bushnell. *Salmon Portland Chase.* Boston: Houghton Mifflin, 1899.

Hartridge, Walter Charlton, ed. *Letters of Don Juan McQueen to His Family, Written from Spanish East Florida, 1791–1807.* Columbia, S.C.: Bostick and Thornley, 1943.

Hartzog, George B., Jr. "Conservation and Management of Seashore and Underwater Areas for Public Enjoyment." Paper presented at the Latin American Conference on Conservation of Renewable Natural Resources, sponsored by the International Union for the Conservation of Nature and Natural Resources, San Carlos de Bariloche, Río Negro, Argentina, 27 March–2 April 1968.

Hawes, Lilla M. "Proceedings of the President and Assistant in Council, 1749–51, Part 1." *Georgia Historical Quarterly* 35 (1951).

Hays, Louise Frederick. *Hero of Hornet's Nest: A Biography of Elijah Clarke, 1733 to 1799.* New York: Stratford House, 1946.

Hemperley, Marion R. *English Crown Grants for Parishes of St. David, St. Patrick, St. Thomas, St. Marys in Georgia, 1755–1775.* Atlanta: Surveyor General Department, State of Georgia, 1973.

Henderson, David G. *Architectural Data Section, Historic Structure Report, Mansion Ruins, Dungeness Historic District, Cumberland Island National Seashore, Camden County, Georgia.* Denver: National Park Service, U.S. Department of the Interior, 1976.

Hendrick, Burton J. *The Age of Big Business.* New Haven: Yale University Press, 1921.

———. *The Life of Andrew Carnegie.* 2 vols. Garden City, N.Y.: Doubleday, Doran, 1932.

Hesseltine, William B. *Confederate Leaders in the New South.* Westport, Conn.: Greenwood Press, 1970.

Hewatt, Alexander. *An Historical Account of the Rise and Progress of the Colonies of South Carolina and Georgia.* 2 vols. London: A. Donaldson, 1779.

Hewett, Janet B., ed. *Supplement to the Official Records of the Union and Confederate Armies.* Part 2, *Record of Events,* vol. 5, ser. 17. Wilmington, N.C.: Broadfoot Publishing, 1994–98.

Higginbotham, A. Leon, Jr. *In the Matter of Color: The Colonial Period.* New York: Oxford University Press, 1978.

Higginson, Mary Thatcher, ed. *Letters and Journals of Thomas Wentworth Higginson, 1846–1906.* Boston: Houghton Mifflin, 1921.

Higginson, Thomas Wentworth. *Army Life in a Black Regiment.* Boston: Fields, Osgood, 1870.

Hill, Peter P. "'A Masked Acquisition'—French Designs on Cumberland Island, 1794–1795." *Georgia Historical Quarterly* 64 (fall 1980)

Hillestad, Hilburn O., John R. Bozeman, A. Sidney Johnson, C. Wayne Berisford, and J. I. Richardson. *The Ecology of the Cumberland Island National Seashore, Camden County, Georgia.* Skidaway Island: Georgia Marine Science Center, University System of Georgia, 1975.

Hilliard, Sam B. "The Tidewater Rice Plantation: An Ingenious Adaptation to Nature." In *Coastal Resources,* ed. H. J. Walker. Baton Rouge School of Geoscience, Louisiana State University, 1975.

Hirshson, Stanley P. *Farewell to the Bloody Shirt: Northern Republicans and the Southern Negro, 1877–1893.* Bloomington: Indiana University Press, 1962.

Hitz, Alex M. "The Wrightsborough Quaker Town and Township in Georgia." *Bulletin of Friends Historical Association* 46 (1957).

Hobson, Fred. *But Now I See: The White Southern Racial Conversion Narrative.* Baton Rouge: Louisiana State University Press, 1999.

Hoffman, Kathleen. "Cultural Development in *La Florida.*" *Historical Archaeology* 31, no. 1 (1997).

Hoffman, Paul E. "Lucas Vasquez de Ayllón." In *Columbus and the Land of Ayllón,* ed. Jeannine Cook. Valona, Ga.: Lower Altamaha Historical Society, 1992.

Hoffmann, Charles, and Tess Hoffmann. "The Limits of Paternalism: Driver-Master Relations on a Bryan County Plantation." *Georgia Historical Quarterly* 67 (fall 1983).

———. "North by South: The Two Lives of Richard James Arnold." *Rhode Island History* 43 (February 1984).

Holmes, James. *"Dr. Bullie's" Notes: Reminiscences of Early Georgia and of Philadelphia and New Haven in the 1800s.* Comp., ed., and intro. Delma Eugene Presley. Atlanta: Cherokee Publishing, 1976.

Holsoe, Svend E., and Bernard L. Herman. *A Land and Life Remembered: Americo-Liberian Folk Architecture.* Athens: University of Georgia Press, 1988.

Hopkins, Benjamin. "Wild Bull Spearing as Practiced in Georgia." *American Turf Register and Sporting Magazine* 5 (April 1834).

Howard, O. O. *Autobiography of Oliver Otis Howard.* New York: Baker and Taylor, 1907.

Howard, Warren S. *American Slavers and the Federal Laws, 1837–1862.* Westport, Conn.: Greenwood Press, 1963; reprint, 1976.

Hudson, Charles. *The Southeastern Indians.* Knoxville: University of Tennessee Press, 1976.

Hudson, Charles, and Carmen Chaves Tesser, eds. *The Forgotten Centuries: Indians and Europeans in the American South, 1521–1704.* Athens: University of Georgia Press, 1994.

Hunter, Louis C. *Waterpower in the Century of the Steam Engine.* Vol. 1 of *A History of Industrial Power in the United States, 1780–1930.* Charlottesville: University Press of Virginia for the Eleutherian Mills–Hagley Foundation, 1979.

Hurd, John Codman. *The Law of Freedom and Bondage in the United States.* 2 vols. N.p., 1858.

"An Impartial Inquiry into the State and Utility of the Province of Georgia." In *Collections of the Georgia Historical Society,* vol. 1. Savannah: Georgia Historical Society, 1840.

Ingham, John N. *The Iron Barons: A Social Analysis of an American Urban Elite, 1874–1965.* Westport, Conn.: Greenwood Press, 1978.

Inscoe, John C., ed. *Georgia in Black and White: Explorations in the Race Relations of a Southern State, 1865–1950.* Athens: University of Georgia Press, 1994.

Ivers, Larry E. *British Drums on the Southern Frontier: The Military Colonization of Georgia, 1733–1749.* Chapel Hill: University of North Carolina Press, 1974.

Jackson, Harvey H. "The Carolina Connection: Jonathan Bryan, His Brothers, and the Founding of Georgia, 1733–1752." *Georgia Historical Quarterly* 68 (summer 1984).

———. "General Lachlan McIntosh, 1727–1808: A Biography." Ph.D. diss., University of Michigan, 1973.

James, Henry. *The American Scene.* 1907; reprint, London: Rupert Hart-Davis, 1968.

Jameson, John Franklin. *Privateering and Piracy in the Colonial Period: Illustrative Documents.* New York: Macmillan, 1923.

Johnson, A. Sidney, Hilburn O. Hillestad, Sheryl A. Fanning, and G. Frederick Shanholtzer. *An Ecological Survey of the Coastal Region of Georgia: A Report to the National Park Service.* Athens: University of Georgia Press, 1971.

Johnson, Cecil. *British West Florida: 1763–1783.* New Haven: Yale University Press, 1943.

Johnson, Guion Griffis. *A Social History of the Sea Islands.* Chapel Hill: University of North Carolina Press, 1930.

Johnson, J. K., ed. *Affectionately Yours: The Letters of Sir John A. Macdonald and His Family, 1842–1891.* Toronto: Macmillan, 1969.

Johnson, James M. *Militiamen, Rangers, and Redcoats: The Military in Georgia, 1754–1776.* Macon, Ga.: Mercer University Press, 1992.

Johnson, William. *Nugae Georgicae: An Essay to the Literary and Philosophical Society of Charleston, South Carolina.* Charleston: J. Hoff, 1815.

———. *Sketches of the Life and Correspondence of Nathanael Greene.* Charleston: A. E. Miller, 1822.

Johnston, Edith Duncan. *The Houstouns of Georgia.* Athens: University of Georgia Press, 1950.

———, ed. "The Kollock Letters, 1799–1850, Part 3." *Georgia Historical Quarterly* (1947).

Johnstone, J. "Chart of Dungeness, East and West Bays" (London, 1806). In *Report of the Commissioners upon the Subject of Harbours of Refuge.* London: H. M. Stationery Office, 1844.

Jones, Charles Colcock, Jr. *Biographical Sketches of the Delegates from Georgia to the Constitutional Congress.* 1891; reprint, Spartanburg, S.C.: Reprint Company, 1972.

———. *The Dead Towns of Georgia, 1878.* 1878; reprint, Spartanburg, S.C.: Reprint Company, 1974.

———. *Historical Sketch of Tomo-Chi-Chi, Mico of the Yamacraws.* Albany, N.Y.: J. Munsell, 1868.

———. *Negro Myths from the Georgia Coast, Told in the Vernacular.* Boston: Houghton, Mifflin, 1888.

———. "Reminiscences of the Last Days, Death, and Burial of General Henry Lee." *Southern Review* 9 (1871).

Jones, George Fenwick, trans. "Commissary Von Reck's Report on Georgia." *Georgia Historical Quarterly* 47 (March 1963).

———. *The Georgia Dutch: From the Rhine and Danube to the Savannah, 1733–1783.* Athens: University of Georgia Press, 1992.

———, ed. "A German Surgeon on the Flora and Fauna of Colonial Georgia: Four Letters of Johann Christoph Bornemann, 1753–1755." *Georgia Historical Quarterly* 75 (winter 1992).

Jones, Jacqueline. *Soldiers of Light and Love: Northern Teachers and Georgia Blacks, 1865–1873.* Chapel Hill: University of North Carolina Press, 1980.

Jones, Rufus M. *The Quakers in the American Colonies.* London: Macmillan, 1911.

Jones, Sarah E. [pseud.]. *Life in the South: From the Commencement of the War by a "Blockaded British Subject."* London: Chapman and Hall, 1863.

Jones-Jackson, Patricia. *When Roots Die: Endangered Traditions on the Sea Islands.* Athens: University of Georgia Press, 1987.

Josephson, Matthew. *The Politicos: 1865–1896.* New York: Harcourt, Brace, 1938.

Journal of the House of Representatives of the State of Georgia, at the Regular Session of the General Assembly, at Atlanta, Wednesday, October 28, 1896. Atlanta: Franklin Printing and Publishing, 1896.

Journal of the Senate of the State of Georgia, at the Regular Session of the General Assembly, at Atlanta, Wednesday, October 27, 1897. Atlanta: Franklin Printing and Publishing, 1897.

Joyner, Charles. *Remember Me: Slave Life in Coastal Georgia.* Atlanta: Georgia Humanities Council, 1989.

———. *The Robber Barons: The Great American Capitalists, 1861–1901.* New York: Harcourt, Brace, 1934.

Juricek, John T., ed. *Georgia Treaties, 1733–1763.* Vol. 11 of *Early American Indian Documents: Treaties and Laws, 1607–1789,* ed. Alden T. Vaughan. Washington, D.C.: University Publications of America, 1979.

Keber, Martha. "Planters, Merchants, and 'Devil Ears.'" Paper presented at the Georgia Historical Society, Savannah, 10 June 1999.

Keeling, William B. "Cumberland Island as a National Seashore." *Georgia Business* 27 (April 1968).

Kemble, Frances Anne. *Journal of a Residence on a Georgian Plantation in 1838–1839.* New York: Harper and Brothers, 1863. Reprint, ed. John A. Scott. Athens: University of Georgia Press, 1984.

Kemp, Peter, ed. *The Oxford Companion to Ships and the Sea.* London: Oxford University Press, 1976.

Kennedy, N. Brent, with Robyn Vaughan Kennedy. *The Melungeons: The Resurrection of a Proud People. An Untold Story of Ethnic Cleansing in America.* Macon, Ga.: Mercer University Press, 1994.

Kicza, John E. "Native American, African, and Hispanic Communities during the Middle Period in the Colonial Americas." *Historical Archaeology* 31, no. 1 (1997).

Kimber, Edward. *Itinerant Observations in America, 1745–46.* 1878; reprint, Spartanburg, S.C.: Reprint Company, 1974.

———. *A Relation, or Journal, of a Late Expedition, etc.* Gainesville: University Presses of Florida, 1976.

King, Linda O. "Cotton Planters and Society in the Low Country, Post Civil War–1900." Unpublished paper given for the Center for Low Country Studies, Savannah, Georgia, 1987.

King, Spencer B., Jr. *Darien: The Death and Rebirth of a Southern Town.* Macon, Ga.: Mercer University Press, 1981.

Kingsley, Zephaniah. *A Treatise on the Patriarchal or Co-operative System of Society as It Exists in Some Governments, and Colonies in America, and in the United States, under the Name of Slavery with Its Necessity and Advantages.* 2d ed. 1829; reprint, Freeport, N.Y.: Books for Libraries, 1970.

Knight, Lucian Lamar. *Georgia's Landmarks, Memorials, and Legends...* 2 vols. Atlanta: Byrd Printing Company, 1913.

Knowlton, Elizabeth W., comp. and ed. *Carnegie Estate Records of Cumberland Island Inventory.* Atlanta: Georgia Department of Archives and History, Descriptive Services Division, 1999.

Kolodny, Annette. *The Land before Her: Fantasy and Experience of the American Frontiers, 1630–1860*. Chapel Hill: University of North Carolina Press, 1984.

Krakow, Kenneth K. *Georgia Place-Names*. Macon, Ga.: Winship, 1975.

Kurtz, Stephen. *The Presidency of John Adams: The Collapse of Federalism, 1795–1800*. Philadelphia: University of Pennsylvania Press, 1957.

Lader, Lawrence. *The Bold Brahmins: New England's War against Slavery, 1831–1863*. New York: Dutton, 1961.

Lamar, Lucius Quintus Cincinnatus, ed. *A Compilation of the Laws of the State of Georgia, 1800–1819*. Augusta: T. S. Hannon, 1821.

Lamb, Daniel Smith. *Howard University Medical Department: A Historical, Biographical, and Statistical Souvenir*. Washington, D.C.: R. Beresford, 1900.

Lambert, Robert S. "The Confiscation of Loyalist Property in Georgia, 1782–1786." *William and Mary Quarterly*, 3d ser., 20 (January 1963).

Lamplugh, George Russell. "Politics on the Periphery: Factions and Parties in Georgia, 1776–1806." Ph.D. diss., Emory University, 1973.

Landers, Jane. "Africans in the Land of Ayllón: The Exploration and Settlement of the Southeast." In *Columbus and the Land of Ayllón*, ed. Jeannine Cook. Valona, Ga.: Lower Altamaha Historical Society, 1992.

———. "Gracia Real de Santa Teresa de Mose: A Free Black Town in Spanish Colonial Florida." *American Historical Review* 95 (February 1990).

———. "Spanish Sanctuary: Fugitives in Florida, 1687–1790." *Florida Historical Quarterly* 62 (January 1984).

Lane, Mills, ed. *General Oglethorpe's Georgia: Colonial Letters, 1733–1743*. Savannah, Ga.: Beehive Press, 1975.

———, ed. *Neither More nor Less than Men: Slavery in Georgia: A Documentary History*. Savannah, Ga.: Beehive Press, 1993.

Lanning, John Tate. *The Spanish Missions of Georgia*. Chapel Hill: University of North Carolina Press, 1935.

Larsen, Clark Spencer. "On the Frontier of Contact: Mission Bioarchaeology in La Florida." In *The Spanish Missions of La Florida*, ed. Bonnie G. McEwan. Gainesville: University Press of Florida, 1993.

Larson, Lewis H., Jr. *Aboriginal Subsistence Technology on the Southeastern Coastal Plain during the late Prehistoric Period*. Gainesville: University Presses of Florida, 1980.

———. "Guale Indians and the Spanish Mission Effort." In *Tacachale: Essays on the Indians of Florida and Southeastern Georgia during the Historic Period*, ed. Jerald Milanich and Samuel Proctor. Gainesville: University Presses of Florida, 1978.

———. *A Guide to the Archaeology of Sapelo Island, Georgia*. Rev. ed. Carrollton, Ga.: West Georgia College, 1991.

———. "The Spanish on Sapelo." In *Sapelo Papers: Researches in the History and Pre-*

history of Sapelo Island, Georgia, ed. Daniel P. Juengst. Carrollton, Ga.: West Georgia College, 1980.

Leatherman, Stephen P. *Barrier Island Handbook.* Amherst: National Park Service, Cooperative Research Unit, Environmental Institute, University of Massachusetts at Amherst, 1979.

Leavell, Carroll. *Legal Aspects of Ownership and Use of Estuarine Areas in Georgia and South Carolina.* Athens: University of Georgia, Institute of Government, 1971.

Lee, Robert E., Jr. *Recollections and Letters of General Robert E. Lee, by His Son.* New York: Doubleday, Page, 1904.

Legare, J. D. "An Account of an Agricultural Excursion Made into the South of Georgia in the Winter of 1832." Pts. 1–9. *Southern Agriculturist* 6 (1833).

Leigh, Frances Butler. *Ten Years on a Georgia Plantation since the War.* London: R. Bentley and Son, 1883.

Leighton, Ann. *American Gardens in the Eighteenth Century.* Amherst: University of Massachusetts Press, 1981.

———. *American Gardens of the Nineteenth Century.* Amherst: University of Massachusetts Press, 1987.

Leland, Jack. *Indigo in America.* Parsippany, N.J.: BASF Wyandotte, n.d.

Leone, Mark P., and Parker B. Potter Jr., eds. *The Recovery of Meaning: Historical Archaeology in the Eastern United States.* Washington, D.C.: Smithsonian Institution Press, 1988.

Lindsay, Arnett G. "Diplomatic Relations between the United States and Great Britain Bearing on the Return of Negro Slaves, 1783–1828." *Journal of Negro History* 5 (October 1920).

Linley, John. *The Georgia Catalog, Historic American Buildings Survey: A Guide to the Architecture of the State of Georgia.* Athens: University of Georgia Press, 1982.

Little, William. *The History of Weare, New Hampshire, 1735–1888.* Weare, N.H.: Town of Weare, 1888.

Litwack, Leon F. *Been in the Storm So Long: The Aftermath of Slavery.* New York: Knopf, 1979.

———. *North of Slavery: The Negro in the Free States, 1790–1860.* Chicago: University of Chicago Press, 1961.

Lloyd, Christopher. *The Navy and the Slave Trade: The Suppression of the African Slave Trade in the Nineteenth Century.* New York: Longmans, Green, 1949.

Lockey, Joseph Byrne. *East Florida, 1783–1785: A File of Documents Assembled and Many of Them Translated.* Berkeley: University of California Press, 1949.

Logan, William. "William Logan's Journal of a Journey to Georgia, 1745." *Pennsylvania Magazine of History and Biography* 36 (1912).

Long Island Wind and Tide Mills: An Interim Report of a Study Conducted by the His-

toric American Engineering Record and the Society for the Preservation of Long Is-land Antiquities. [Washington, D.C.?]: Historic American Engineering Record, Office of Archeology and Historic Preservation, National Park Service, U.S. Department of the Interior, 1976.

Lorant, Stefan, ed. *Pittsburgh, the Story of an American City.* Garden City, N.Y.: Doubleday, 1964.

Lord, Walter. *The Dawn's Early Light.* New York: Norton, 1972.

Lossing, Benson. *Pictorial Field Book of the War of 1812.* New York: Harper and Brothers, 1868.

Lovell, Caroline Couper. *The Golden Isles of Georgia.* Boston: Little, Brown, 1933.

Lowery, Woodbury. *The Spanish Settlements within the Present Limits of the United States: Florida, 1562–1574.* 2 vols. New York: G. P. Putnam's Sons, 1905.

Lucas, Silas Emmett, Jr. *Index to the Headright and Bounty Grants of Georgia, 1756–1909.* Vidalia: Georgia Genealogical Reprints, 1970.

Ludlum, David M. *Early American Hurricanes, 1492–1870.* Boston: American Meteorological Society, 1963.

Lyell, Charles. *A Second Visit to the United States of North America.* 2 vols. New York: Harper and Brothers, 1849.

Lyon, Eugene. "The Failure of the Guale and Orista Mission, 1572–1575." In *Columbus and the Land of Ayllón,* ed. Jeannine Cook. Valona, Ga.: Lower Altamaha Historical Society, 1992.

———. "San Pedro de Tacatacuru." Paper presented at the Joint Conference of the Florida, Georgia, and Alabama Historical Societies, St. Augustine, Florida, 5 October 1990.

MacArthur, Robert H., and Edward O. Wilson. *The Theory of Island Biogeography.* Princeton: Princeton University Press, 1967.

MacFarlane, Suzanne. "The Ethnoarcheology of a Slave Community: The Couper Plantation." Ph.D. diss., University of Florida, 1975.

Mackay, Robert. *Letters of Robert Mackay to His Wife: Written from Ports in America and England, 1795–1816.* Ed. Walter Charlton Hartridge. Athens: University of Georgia Press, 1949.

Maclay, Edgar Stanton. *A History of American Privateers.* New York: B. Franklin, 1968.

Magdol, Edward. *A Right to the Land: Essays on the Freedmen's Community.* Westport, Conn.: Greenwood Press, 1977.

Magnaghi, Russell M. "Sassafras and Its Role in Early America, 1562–1662." *Terrae Incognitae* 29 (1997).

Mahon, John K. *The War of 1812.* Gainesville: University of Florida Press, 1972.

Malone, Ann Patton. "Piney Wood Farmers of South Georgia, 1850–1900: Jeffersonian Yeomen in an Age of Expanding Commercialism." *Agricultural History* 5 (fall 1986).

Manning, Charles, and Merrill Moore. "Sassafras and Syphilis." *New England Quarterly* 9 (September 1936).

Marbury, Horatio, and William H. Crawford, eds. *A Digest of the Laws of the State of Georgia, 1755 to 1800.* Savannah, Ga.: Seymour, Woolhopter, and Stebbins, 1802.

Marks, Stuart A. "Some Rituals and Riddles of Southern Venery: A Synopsis of Privileged Hunting Traditions in the Coastal Carolinas." In *Sea and Land: Cultural and Biological Adaptations in the Southern Coastal Plain,* ed. James L. Peacock and James C. Sabella. Athens: University of Georgia Press, 1988.

Marland, Frederick C. *Tides on the Georgia Coast.* Brunswick, Ga.: Department of Natural Resources, 1979.

Martell, J. S. *Immigration to and Emigration from Nova Scotia, 1815–1838.* Halifax: Public Archives of Nova Scotia, 1942.

Martin, B[radford] G. "Sapelo Island's Arabic Document: The 'Bilali Diary' in Context." *Georgia Historical Quarterly* 77 (fall 1994).

Martin, Harold H. *This Happy Isle: The Story of Sea Island and the Cloister.* Sea Island, Ga.: Sea Island Company, 1978.

Martin, Richard A. "The *New York Times* Views Civil War Jacksonville." *Florida Historical Quarterly* 53 (April 1975).

McAlester, Virginia, and Lee McAlester. *A Field Guide to American Houses.* New York: Knopf, 1984.

McAndrew, John. *The Open-Air Churches of Sixteenth Century Mexico: Atrios, Posas, Open Chapels, and Other Studies.* Cambridge: Harvard University Press, 1965.

McCall, Hugh. *History of Georgia.* 2 vols. Savannah, Ga.: Seymour and Williams, 1811–16.

McCallie, S. W. "A Preliminary Report on the Artesian-Well System of Georgia." *Geological Survey of Georgia* 7 (1898).

McCash, William Barton, and June Hall McCash. *The Jekyll Island Club: Southern Haven for America's Millionaires.* Athens: University of Georgia Press, 1989.

McCrady, Edward. *The History of South Carolina in the Revolution, 1780–1783.* New York: Macmillan, 1902.

McDaniel, George W. *Hearth and Home: Preserving a People's Culture.* Philadelphia: Temple University Press, 1982.

McEwan, Bonnie G. "Hispanic Life on the Seventeenth-Century Florida Frontier." In *The Spanish Missions of La Florida,* ed. Bonnie McEwan. Gainesville: University Press of Florida, 1993.

———, ed. *The Spanish Missions of La Florida.* Gainesville: University Press of Florida, 1993.

McFeely, William S. *Yankee Stepfather: General O. O. Howard and the Freedmen.* New Haven: Yale University Press, 1968.

McIntosh, Lachlan. *The Papers of Lachlan McIntosh, 1774–1779.* Ed. Lilla M. Hawes. Vol. 12 of *Collections of the Georgia Historical Society.* Savannah: Georgia Historical Society, 1957.

McKelvey, Blake. *The Urbanization of America, 1860–1915.* New Brunswick, N.J.: Rutgers University Press, 1963.

McLaurin, Melton A. *Celia, a Slave.* Athens: University of Georgia Press, 1991.

McLendon, S. G. *History of the Public Domain of Georgia.* Atlanta: Foote and Davis, 1924.

McMaster, John Bach. *The Life and Times of Stephen Girard: Mariner and Merchant.* Philadelphia: Lippincott, 1918.

McPhee, John. "Profiles: Encounters with the Archdruid. Part 2: An Island." *New Yorker,* 27 March 1971.

McPherson, James M. *Battle Cry of Freedom: The Civil War Era.* New York: Oxford University Press, 1988.

Melish, John. *Travels in the United States of America in the Years 1806 and 1807, and 1809, 1810, and 1811.* 2 vols. Philadelphia: T. and G. Palmer, 1812.

Meriwether, Robert L. *The Expansion of South Carolina, 1729–1765.* Philadelphia: Porcupine Press, 1974.

Meroney, Geraldine. "The London Entrepôt Merchants and the Georgia Colony." *William and Mary Quarterly* 25, no. 2 (April 1968).

Michaux, André. "Journal of André Michaux, 1787–1796." *American Philosophical Society* 26 (19 October 1888).

Milanich, Jerald T. "A Deptford Phase House Structure, Cumberland Island, Georgia." *Florida Anthropologist* 26 (September 1973).

————. "Franciscan Missions and Native Peoples." In *The Forgotten Centuries: Indians and Europeans in the American South, 1521–1704,* ed. Charles Hudson and Carmen Chaves Tesser. Athens: University of Georgia Press, 1994.

————. *Laboring in the Fields of the Lord: Spanish Missions and Southeastern Indians.* Washington, D.C.: Smithsonian Institution Press, 1999.

————. "Tacatacuru and the San Pedro de Mocamo Mission." *Florida Historical Quarterly* 50 (January 1972).

————. "The Western Timucua: Patterns of Acculturation and Change." In *Tacachale: Essays on the Indians of Florida and Southeastern Georgia during the Historic Period,* ed. Jerald T. Milanich and Samuel Proctor. Gainesville: University Presses of Florida, 1978.

Milanich, Jerald, and Samuel Proctor, eds. *Tacachale: Essays on the Indians of Florida and Southeastern Georgia during the Historic Period.* Gainesville: University Presses of Florida, 1978.

Milanich, Jerald T., with Carlos A. Martinez, Karl T. Steinem, and Ronald L. Wallace. "Georgia Origins of the Alachua Tradition." *Florida Bureau of Historic Sites and*

Properties Bulletin No. 5 (1976). Division of Archives, History, and Records Management, Dept. of State, Tallahassee, Fla.

Milfort, Leclerc. "Memoir or Short Sketch of My Different Voyages and My Stay in the Creek Nation, 1775 to 1795. Trans. Oliver G. Ricketson Jr. Typescript, Georgia Historical Society, 1952.

Miller, David Hunter, ed. *Treaties and Other International Acts of the United States.* Vol. 2. Washington, D.C.: U.S. Government Printing Office, 1931.

Miller, Herman. *Riches, Class, and Power before the Civil War.* Lexington, Mass.: D. C. Heath, 1973.

Miller, Mary. *Cumberland Island: The Unsung Northend.* Darien, Ga.: Darien News, 1990.

————. "Entertainment at the Cumberland Island Hotel, Early 1900, One of a Number of Sketches of the North End of Cumberland Island." N.d. Mimeographed. Copy in possession of author.

————. "Growing Up on Cumberland Island." N.d. Mimeographed. Copy in possession of author.

————. "Innkeeping on the North End of Cumberland Island." 1986. Mimeographed. Copy in possession of author.

————. *On Christmas Creek: Life on Cumberland Island.* Darien, Ga.: Darien News, 1995.

Miller, Randall M., ed. *"Dear Master": Letters of a Slave Family.* Athens: University of Georgia Press, 1990.

Miller, Stephen F. *The Bench and Bar of Georgia: Memoirs and Sketches.* 2 vols. *Memoir of Gen. David Blackshear.* Philadelphia: J. B. Lippincott, 1858.

Milling, Chapman J., ed. *Colonial South Carolina: Two Contemporary Descriptions, by Governor James Glen and Doctor George Milligen-Johnston.* Columbia: University of South Carolina Press, 1951.

————. *Red Carolinians.* 2d ed. Columbia: University of South Carolina Press, 1969.

"Minutes of the Executive Council, May 7 through October 14, 1777, Part 2." *Georgia Historical Quarterly* 34 (March 1950).

Mirsky, Jeannette, and Allan Nevins. *The World of Eli Whitney.* New York: Macmillan, 1952.

Mitchell, Augustus. "Antiquities of Florida." In *Annual Report of the Board of Regents of the Smithsonian Institution.* Washington, D.C.: Smithsonian Institution, 1875.

Mohr, Clarence L. *On the Threshold of Freedom: Masters and Slaves in Civil War Georgia.* Athens: University of Georgia Press, 1986.

Moore, Clarence Bloomfield. "Certain Aboriginal Mounds of the Georgia Coast." *Journal of the Academy of Natural Sciences of Philadelphia* 11 (1897).

Moore, Francis. "A Voyage to Georgia Begun in the Year 1735." In *Collections of the Georgia Historical Society,* vol. 1. Savannah: Georgia Historical Society, 1840.

Moore, Frank, coll. and ed. *The Civil War in Song and Story, 1860–1865.* New York: P. F. Collier, 1892.

More, Timothy T. *Architectural Pattern Books in Eighteenth-Century America.* Providence, R.I.: John Carter Brown Library, 1990.

Morgan, H. Wayne, ed. *The Gilded Age.* Rev. and enl. ed. Syracuse, N.Y.: Syracuse University Press, 1970.

Morison, Samuel Eliot. *The Northern Voyages.* Vol. 1 of *The European Discovery of America.* New York: Oxford University Press, 1971.

Morton, Patricia, ed. *Discovering the Women in Slavery: Emancipating Perspectives on the American Past.* Athens: University of Georgia Press, 1996.

Moultrie, William. *Memoirs of the American Revolution So Far as It Related to the State of North and South Carolina, and Georgia.* 2 vols. New York: David Longworth, 1802.

Mowat, Charles Loch. *East Florida as a British Province, 1763–1784.* Berkeley: University of California Press, 1943.

Mueller, Edward A. "Steamboat Activity in Florida during the Second Seminole Indian War." *Florida Historical Quarterly* 64 (April 1986).

Mullins-Moore, Sue A. "The Antebellum Barrier Island Plantation: A Search for an Archaeological Pattern." Ph.D. diss., University of Florida, 1981.

———. "Social and Economic Status on the Coastal Plantation: An Archeological Perspective." In *The Archaeology of Slavery and Plantation Life,* ed. Theresa A. Singleton. Orlando: Academic Press, 1985.

Murdoch, Richard K. "Citizen Mangourit and the Projected Attack on East Florida." *Journal of Southern History* 14 (1948).

———. "Correspondence of French Consuls in Charleston, 1793–1797." *South Carolina Historical Magazine* 74 (1973).

———. "Elijah Clarke and Anglo-American Designs on East Florida, 1794–1798." *Georgia Historical Quarterly* 35 (December 1951).

———. *The Georgia-Florida Frontier, 1793–1796: Spanish Reaction to French Intrigue and American Designs.* Berkeley: University of California Press, 1951.

———, ed. "Letters and Papers of Dr. Daniel Turner: A Rhode Islander in South Georgia." *Georgia Historical Quarterly* 53–54 (1969–70).

Myers, Robert Manson, ed. *Children of Pride: A True Story of Georgia and the Civil War.* New Haven: Yale University Press, 1972.

———, ed. *A Georgian at Princeton.* New York: Harcourt Brace Jovanovich, 1976.

Myers, Walter Dean. *At Her Majesty's Request: An African Princess in Victorian England.* New York: Scholastic Press, 1999.

Nagle, Jacob. *The Nagle Journal: A Diary of the Life of Jacob Nagle, Sailor, from the Year 1775 to 1841.* Ed. John C. Dann. New York: Weidenfeld and Nicolson, 1988.

Narrative of a Voyage to the Spanish Main in the Ship "Two Friends," the Occupation of

Amelia Island by M'Gregor, etc.: Sketches of the Province of East Florida. Ed. John Griffin. Facsimile ed. 1819; Gainesville: University Presses of Florida, 1978.

Nichols, Charles H. *Many Thousands Gone: The Ex-Slaves' Account of Their Bondage and Freedom.* Leiden: E. J. Brill, 1963.

Nichols, Frederick Doveton. *The Architecture of Georgia.* Savannah: Beehive Press, 1976.

Nightingale, Bernard N. "Dungeness." *Georgia Historical Quarterly* 22 (December 1938).

Northen, William J., ed. *Men of Mark in Georgia.* 1907; reprint, Spartanburg, S.C.: Reprint Company, 1974.

Novak, Barbara. *Nature and Culture: American Landscape and Painting, 1825–1875.* New York: Oxford University Press, 1980.

Nugent, Walter T. K. *Money and American Society, 1865–1880.* New York: Free Press, 1968.

Oak Grove Cemetery Inscriptions. St. Marys, Ga.: Women's Club, 1953.

Ober, Frederick A. "Dungeness, General Greene's Sea-Island Plantation." *Lippincott's Magazine* 26 (August 1880).

Odum, E. P. "The Role of Tidal Marshes in Estuarine Production." *New York State Conservationist* (June–July 1961).

Official Records of the Union and Confederate Navies in the War of the Rebellion. Ser. 1. Washington, D.C.: U.S. Government Printing Office, 1901.

Oglethorpe, James Edward. "Letters from General Oglethorpe to the Trustees of the Colony and Others from October 1735 to August 1744." In *Collections of the Georgia Historical Society*, vol. 3. Savannah: Georgia Historical Society, 1873.

Olmstead, Frederick Law. *The Cotton Kingdom: A Traveller's Observations on Cotton and Slavery in the American Slave States.* Ed. Arthur M. Schlesinger. 1861; reprint, New York: Knopf, 1953.

Olson, Sarah. *Plum Orchard, Cumberland Island National Seashore, St. Marys, Georgia.* Historic Furnishings Report. Harpers Ferry. National Park Service, 1989.

Oré, Luis Jeronimo de. "Relation of the Martyrs of Florida" (ca. 1617). In *The Roanoke Voyages, 1584–1590: Documents to Illustrate the English Voyages to North America under the Patent Granted to Walter Raleigh in 1584*, ed. David B. Quinn, vol. 2. London: Hakluyt Society, 1955.

Orser, Charles E., Jr. "Toward a Theory of Power for Historical Archaeology: Plantations and Space." In *The Recovery of Meaning: Historical Archaeology in the Eastern United States*, ed. Mark P. Leone and Parker B. Potter Jr. Washington, D.C.: Smithsonian Institution Press, 1988.

Orser, Charles E., Jr., and Annette M. Nekola. "Plantation Settlement from Slavery to Tenancy: An Example from a Piedmont Plantation in South Carolina." In *The Ar-*

chaeology of Slavery and Plantation Life, ed. Theresa A. Singleton. Orlando: Academic Press, 1985.

Otto, John Solomon. "Artifacts and Status Differences: A Comparison from Planter,
Overseer, and Slave Sites on an Antebellum Plantation." In *Research Strategies in
Historical Archaeology,* ed. Stanley South. New York: Academic Press, 1977.

———. *Cannon's Point Plantation, 1794–1860: Living Conditions and Status Patterns in
the Old South.* New York: Academic Press, 1984.

———. "A New Look at Slave Life." *Natural History,* December 1978.

———. "Open-Range Cattle-Herding in Southern Florida." *Florida Historical Quarterly* 65 (January 1987).

———. "The Origins of Cattle-Ranching in Colonial South Carolina, 1670–1715."
South Carolina Historical Magazine 87 (April 1986).

———. "Slavery in a Coastal Community: Glynn County, 1790–1860." *Georgia Historical Quarterly* 64 (winter 1977).

———. "Status Differences and the Archeological Record: A Comparison of Planter,
Overseer, and Slave Sites from Cannon's Point Plantation (1794–1861), St. Simons Island, Georgia." Ph.D. diss., University of Florida, 1975.

Oubre, Claude F. *Forty Acres and a Mule: The Freedmen's Bureau and Black Land Ownership.* Baton Rouge: Louisiana State University Press, 1978.

Our Vanishing Shoreline. Washington, D.C.: U.S. Department of the Interior, National
Park Service, 1955.

Owsley, Frank L. *Plain Folk of the Old South.* Baton Rouge: Louisiana State University
Press, 1982.

Pack, James. *The Man Who Burned the White House: Admiral Sir George Cockburn,
1772–1853.* Annapolis: Naval Institute Press, 1987.

Parker, Susan R. "Men without God or King: Rural Settlers of East Florida, 1784–
1790." *Florida Historical Quarterly* 69 (October 1990): 135–40.

Parkman, Aubrey. *History of the Waterways of the Atlantic Coast of the United States.*
[Fort Belvoir, Va.?]: National Waterways Study, U.S. Army Engineer Water Resources Support Center, Institute for Water Resources, 1983.

Parrish, Lydia, comp. *Slave Songs of the Georgia Sea Islands.* Athens: University of
Georgia Press, 1992.

Parsons, Elsie Clews. "Folklore of the Sea Islands, South Carolina." *Memoirs of the
American Folk-lore Society* 16 (1923).

Patrick, Rembert W. *Florida Fiasco: Rampant Rebels on the Georgia-Florida Border,
1810–1815.* Athens: University of Georgia Press, 1954.

Patterson, Orlando. *Slavery and Social Death: A Comparative Study.* Cambridge: Harvard University Press, 1982.

Paullin, Charles. *Atlas of the Historical Geography of the United States.* Ed. K. Wright.
Washington, D.C.: Carnegie Institution, 1932.

Peacock, James L., and James C. Sabella, eds. *Sea and Land: Cultural and Biological Adaptations in the Southern Coastal Plain.* Athens: University of Georgia Press, 1988.

Pearson, Elizabeth Ware, ed. *Letters from Port Royal, 1862–1868.* Boston: W. B. Clarke, 1906.

Pearson, Fred Lamar. "Early Anglo-Spanish Rivalry in Southeastern North America." *Georgia Historical Quarterly* 58 supplement (1974).

Pease, William H., and Jane H. Pease. *Black Utopia: Negro Communal Experiments in America.* Madison: State Historical Society of Wisconsin, 1963.

Pendleton, Nathaniel. "Short Account of the Sea-Coast of Georgia in Respect to Agriculture, Ship-Building, Navigation, and the Timber Trade." Ed. Theodore Thayer. *Georgia Historical Quarterly* 41 (March 1957).

Pennington, John. "Cumberland, My Island for a While." *National Geographic* 152 (November 1977).

Pennington, Patience [pseud.]. *A Woman Rice Planter.* New York: Macmillan, 1922.

Perry, Bliss. *Life and Letters of Henry Lee Higginson.* Boston: Atlantic Monthly Press, 1921.

Phillips, Henry. *The Companion for the Orchard.* London: H. Colburn and R. Bentley, 1831.

Phillips, Martha Littlefield. "Recollections of a Washington and His Friends, as Preserved in the Family of General Nathanael Greene." *Century Magazine* 60 (January 1898).

Pierson, William H., Jr. *American Buildings and Their Architects.* 2 vols. Garden City, N.Y.: Doubleday, 1970.

Pitts, Walter F., Jr. *Old Ship of Zion: The Afro-American Ritual in the African Diaspora.* New York: Oxford University Press, 1993.

"Plan d'un Petit Fort pour l'Isle de St. André." In *Collections of the Georgia Historical Society,* vol. 3. Savannah: 1913.

Poesch, Jessie. *Titian Ramsey Peale, 1799–1885, and His Journals of the Wilkes Expedition.* Philadelphia: American Philosophical Society, 1961.

Powell, Lawrence N. *New Masters: Northern Planters during the Civil War and Reconstruction.* New Haven: Yale University Press, 1980.

Price, Marcus. "Ships That Tested the Blockade of the Georgia and East Florida Ports, 1861–1865." *American Neptune* 15 (April 1955).

"Proceedings of Georgia Council of Safety." In *Collections of the Georgia Historical Society,* vol. 5, pt. 1. Savannah: Georgia Historical Society, 1901.

Proctor, Madena. *Among Untrodden Ways: A Vignette of Delightful St. Marys, Georgia, 1915.* Woodbine, Ga.: privately published, 1980.

Proctor, Samuel, ed. *Eighteenth-Century Florida and the Caribbean.* Gainesville: University Presses of Florida, 1976.

Prunty, Merle, Jr. "The Renaissance of the Southern Plantation." *Geographical Review* 45 (October 1955).

Quinn, David Beers. *The Roanoke Voyages, 1584–1590: Documents to Illustrate the English Voyages to North America under the Patent Granted to Walter Raleigh in 1584.* 2 vols. London: Hakluyt Society, 1955.

Raley, Robert L. "Daniel Pratt, Architect and Builder in Georgia." *Antiques Magazine* 102 (September 1992).

Ramsey, William. "The Final Contest for the 'Debatable Land': Fort William and the Frontier Defenses of Colonial Georgia." *Georgia Historical Quarterly* 77 (fall 1993).

———. "The Last Days of the Debatable Land: A Study of the Colonial British Forts on Cumberland Island." Master's thesis, Valdosta State College, 1992.

"A Ranger's Report of Travels with General Oglethorpe in Georgia and Florida, 1739-1742." In *Travels in the American Colonies,* ed. Newton D. Mereness. New York: Macmillan, 1916.

Ransom, Roger, and Richard Sutch. "The Ex-Slave in the Post-Bellum South: A Study of the Economic Impact of Racism in a Market Environment." *Journal of Economic History* 33 (March 1973).

———. "The Impact of the Civil War and of Emancipation on Southern Agriculture." *Explorations in Economic History,* 2d ser., 12 (January 1975).

Rasico, Philip D. "Minorcan Population of St. Augustine in the Spanish Census of 1786." *Florida Historical Quarterly* 66 (October 1987).

Rawick, George P., ed. *The American Slave: A Composite Autobiography.* 17 vols. Westport: Greenwood Publishing, 1972.

Rawson, Marion Nicholl. *Little Old Mills.* 1935; reprint, New York: Johnson Reprint Corp., 1970.

Record of Connecticut Men in the Army and Navy of the United States during the War of the Rebellion. Hartford, Conn.: Case, Lockwood, and Brainard, 1889.

Reddick, Angeline Lang, comp. *Pen Portraits: Stories of Pioneer Camden Women.* Kingsland, Ga.: *Southeast Georgian,* 1969.

Reddick, Marguerite, comp. *Camden's Challenge: A History of Camden County, Georgia.* Ed. Eloise Bailey and Virginia Proctor. N.p.: Camden County Historical Commission, 1976.

Reed, John Shelton. *Southern Folk, Plain and Fancy: Native White Social Types.* Athens: University of Georgia Press, 1986.

Reichel, William C. *A History of the Rise, Progress, and Present Condition of the Moravian Seminary for Young Ladies, at Bethlehem, Pennsylvania.* 2d ed. Philadelphia: Lippincott, 1870.

Reid, Whitelaw. *After the War: A Southern Tour, May 1, 1865, to May 1, 1866.* Cincinnati: Moore, Wilstach, and Baldwin, 1866.

Reischauer, Haru Matsukata. *Samurai and Silk: A Japanese and American Heritage.* Cambridge: Belknap Press of Harvard University Press, 1986.

Reitz, Elizabeth J. "Spanish and British Subsistence Strategies at St. Augustine, Florida, and Frederica, Georgia, between 1565 and 1783." Ph.D. diss., University of Florida, 1979.

————. "The Spanish Colonial Experience and Domestic Animals." *Historical Archaeology* 26, no. 1 (1992).

"Relación del Yndio." In *Documentos Históricos de la Florida y la Luisiana, Siglos XVI al XVIII,* ed. Manuel Y Sanz Serrano. Madrid: V. Suárez, 1912.

Reynolds, John. *Windmills and Watermills.* London: H. Evelyn, 1970.

Reynolds, Terry S. *Stronger Than a Hundred Men.* Baltimore: Johns Hopkins University Press, 1983.

Rezneck, Samuel. "Distress, Relief, and Discontent in the United States during the Depression of 1873–1878." *Journal of Political Economy* 58 (December 1950).

Richardson, Joe M. *The Negro in the Reconstruction of Florida, 1865–1877.* Tallahassee: Florida State University Press, 1965.

Ricketson, Oliver G., Jr. "A Suggestion for the Future Disposition of Cumberland Island." 1936. Mimeographed. Copy in possession of author.

Riddell, William Renwick. "The Slave in Canada." *Journal of Negro History* 5 (July 1920).

Ritchie, G. S. *The Admiralty Chart: British Naval Hydrography in the Nineteenth Century.* New York: American Elsevier, 1967.

Roberts, A. Sellew. "Federal Government and Confederate Cotton." *American Historical Review* 32 (January 1927).

Roberts, Joan W. "Geologic Evolution of the South End of Cumberland Island, Georgia." Master's thesis, Smith College, 1975.

Rockefeller, Nancy Carnegie. *The Carnegies and Cumberland Island.* Greenwich, Conn.: Privately printed, 1993.

Roper, Laura Wood. *FLO: A Biography of Frederick Law Olmstead.* Baltimore: Johns Hopkins University Press, 1973.

Rose, Willie Lee. *Rehearsal for Reconstruction: The Port Royal Experiment.* Indianapolis: Bobbs-Merrill, 1964.

Rosenbaum, Art. *Shout Because You're Free: The African American Ring Shout Tradition in Coastal Georgia.* Athens: University of Georgia Press, 1998.

Rostlund, Erhard. "The Geographic Range of the Historic Bison in the Southeast." *Annals of the Association of American Geographers* 50 (December 1960).

Ruhl, Donna L. "Oranges and Wheat: Spanish Attempts at Agriculture in *La Florida.*" *Historical Archaeology* 31, no. 1 (1997).

Rules and Regulations Governing Employment on the Property of Mrs. Lucy C. Carnegie on Cumberland Island. Jacksonville, Fla.: H. and W. B. Drew, 1901.

Sauer, Carl O. *Sixteenth Century North America: The Land and the People as Seen by the Europeans.* Berkeley: University of California Press, 1971.

Saunders, Rebecca. "Architecture of the Missions Santa Maria and Santa Catalina de Amelia." In *The Spanish Missions of La Florida*, ed. Bonnie G. McEwan. Gainesville: University Press of Florida, 1993.

Saye, Albert Berry. *A Constitutional History of Georgia, 1732–1968.* Rev. ed. Athens: University of Georgia Press, 1970.

Schlesinger, Arthur M. *The Rise of the City, 1878–1898.* New York: Macmillan, 1933.

Schöpf, Johann David. *Travels in the Confederation, 1783–1784.* Trans. and ed. Alfred J. Morrison. New York: B. Franklin, 1968.

Schreiner, Samuel A., Jr. *Henry Clay Frick: The Gospel of Greed.* New York: St. Martin's Press, 1995.

Schuck, Peter, and Harrison Wellford. "Democracy and the Good Life in a Company Town [St. Marys, Georgia]." *Harpers Magazine*, March 1972.

Schuckers, J. W. *The Life and Public Services of Salmon Portland Chase.* New York: Appleton, 1874.

Schulz, Mark R. "Interracial Kinship Ties and the Emergence of a Rural Black Middle Class: Hancock County, Georgia, 1865–1920." In *Georgia in Black and White: Explorations in the Race Relations of a Southern State, 1865–1950*, ed. John C. Inscoe. Athens: University of Georgia Press, 1994.

Scott, J. T. *The First Families of Frederica: Their Lives and Locations.* Athens, Ga.: J. T. Scott, 1985.

Searcy, Martha Condray. *The Georgia-Florida Contest in the American Revolution, 1776–1778.* University: University of Alabama Press, 1985.

Senter, Nathaniel G. M. *A Vindication of the Character of Nathaniel G. M. Senter against the Charge of Being a Spy and a Traitor.* Hallowell, Maine: Goodale, 1815.

Sernett, Milton C. *Black Religion and American Evangelicalism: White Protestants, Plantation Missions, and the Flowering of Negro Christianity, 1787–1865.* Metuchen, N.J.: Scarecrow Press, 1975.

Setzler, F. M. "Salvaging an Aboriginal Dug-Out Canoe, Cumberland Island, Georgia." In *Explorations and Field-Work for 1932.* Washington, D.C.: Smithsonian Institution, 1933.

Shapiro, Henry D. *Confiscation of Confederate Property in the North.* Ithaca: Cornell University Press, 1962.

Sharpe, Townley M. "Historic Furnishing Plan, Containing Sections C, D, and E, Cumberland Island National Seashore, Tabby House, National Park Service, U.S. Department of the Interior." Draft, September 1978.

Sherman, William T. *Memoir of General William T. Sherman.* New York: Appleton, 1886.

Shlomowitz, Ralph. "The Squad System on Postbellum Cotton Plantations." In *Toward a New South? Studies in Post–Civil War Southern Communities*, ed. Orville V. Burton and Robert C. McMath Jr. Westport, Conn.: Greenwood Press, 1982.

Shofner, Jerrell H. "Andrew Johnson and the Fernandina Unionists." *Prologue* 10 (winter 1978).

———. *Nor Is It Over Yet: Florida in the Era of Reconstruction, 1863–1877*. Gainesville: University of Florida Presses, 1974.

Siebert, Wilbur H. *Loyalists in East Florida, 1774 to 1785: The Most Important Documents Pertaining Thereto.* 2 vols. Deland: Florida State Historical Society, 1929.

———. "Slavery in East Florida, 1776 to 1785." *Florida Historical Quarterly* 10 (January 1932).

———. "Slavery and White Servitude in East Florida, 1727–1776." *Florida Historical Quarterly* 10 (July 1931).

Silva, James S. *Early Reminiscences of Camden County, Georgia, by an Old St. Marys Boy in His Eighty-Second Year, 1914–1915*. Kingsland, Ga.: *Southeast Georgian*, 1976.

Singleton, Theresa A. "An Archaeological Framework for Slavery and Emancipation, 1740–1880." In *The Recovery of Meaning: Historical Archaeology in the Eastern United States*, ed. Mark P. Leone and Parker B. Potter Jr. Washington, D.C.: Smithsonian Institution Press, 1988.

———. "The Archaeology of Afro-American Slavery in Coastal Georgia: A Regional Perception of Slave Household and Community Patterns." Ph.D. diss., University of Florida, 1980.

Smith, Hale G., and Ripley P. Bullen. *Fort San Carlos*. Tallahassee: Department of Anthropology, Florida State University, 1971.

Smith, Marvin T. "Archaeological Evidence of the Ayllón Expedition." In *Columbus and the Land of Ayllón: The Exploration and Settlement of the Southeast*, ed. Jeannine Cook. Valona, Ga.: Lower Altamaha Historical Society, 1992.

Smith, Page. *The Rise of Industrial America*. Vol. 6 of *A People's History*. New York: McGraw-Hill, 1984.

Smith, Robin L. *An Archaeological Survey of Kings Bay, Camden County, Georgia*. Gainesville: University of Florida Department of Anthropology, 1978.

———. *Sea Island Cotton Culture*. Gainesville: University of Florida Department of Anthropology, 1978.

Smith, Robin L., Chad L. Braley, Nina T. Borremans, and Elizabeth J. Reitz. *Coastal Adaptations in Southeast Georgia: Ten Archeological Sites at Kings Bay*. Gainesville: University of Florida, 1981.

South, Stanley. "Santa Elena: Threshold of Conquest." In *The Recovery of Meaning: Historical Archaeology in the Eastern United States*, ed. Mark P. Leone and Parker B. Potter Jr. Washington, D.C.: Smithsonian Institution Press, 1988.

Spalding, Phinizy. *Oglethorpe in America*. Chicago: University of Chicago Press, 1977.

Spalding, Phinizy, and Harvey H. Jackson, eds. *Oglethorpe in Perspective: Georgia's Founder after Two Hundred Years*. Tuscaloosa: University of Alabama Press, 1989.

Spalding, Thomas. "Sketch of the Life of General James Oglethorpe, Written for the Georgia Historical Society." In *Collections of the Georgia Historical Society*, vol. 1. Savannah: Georgia Historical Society, 1840.

The Spanish Official Account of the Attack on the Colony of Georgia, in America, and of Its Defeat on St. Simons Island by General James Oglethorpe. Vol. 7, pt. 3 of the *Collections of the Georgia Historical Society*. Savannah: Georgia Historical Society, 1913.

Spencer, Ethel. *The Spencers of Amberson Avenue: A Turn-of-the-Century Memoir*. Pittsburgh: University of Pittsburgh Press, 1983.

Stanley, Amy Dru. *From Bondage to Contract: Wage Labor, Marriage, and the Market in the Age of Slave Emancipation*. New York: Cambridge University Press, 1998.

Starks, George L., Jr. "Singing 'bout a Good Time: Sea Island Religious Music." *Journal of Black Studies* 4 (June 1980).

The Statutes at Large, from the Ninth Year of the Reign of King George II to the Twenty-fifth Year of the Reign of King George II. London: Charles Eyre, 1786.

Stedman, Charles Ellery. *Civil War Sketchbook of Charles Ellery Stedman, Surgeon, United States Navy: Biography and Commentary*. San Rafael: Presidio Press, 1976.

Steers, J. A. *The Coastline of England and Wales*. Cambridge: Cambridge University Press, 1964.

Stegeman, John F., and Janet A. Stegeman. *Caty: A Biography of Catharine Littlefield Greene*. Providence: Rhode Island Bicentennial Foundation, 1977.

Sterling, Dorothy, ed. *The Trouble They Seen: Black People Tell the Story of Reconstruction*. Garden City, N.Y.: Doubleday, 1976.

Stern, Philip Van Doren. *Robert E. Lee: The Man and the Soldier*. New York: McGraw-Hill, 1963.

Stevens, William Bacon. *A History of Georgia, from Its First Discovery by the Europeans to the Adoption of the Present Constitution in 1798*. 2 vols. Savannah, Ga.: W. T. Williams, 1847.

Stewart, C. P., and Douglas Guthrie, eds. *Lind's Treatise on Scurvy: A Bicentenary Volume Containing a Reprint of the First Edition of* A Treatise on Scurvy. Edinburgh: University Press, 1953.

Stewart, John. "Mission and Leadership among the 'Merikin' Baptists of Trinidad." In *LAAG Contributions to Afro-American Ethnohistory in Latin America and the Caribbean*, comp. Norman E. Whitten Jr. Vol. 1 of *Contributions of the Latin American Anthropology Group*, ed. Peter Furst. Urbana: University of Illinois, 1977.

Stewart, Mart A. *"What Nature Suffers to Groe": Life, Labor, and Landscape on the Georgia Coast, 1680–1920*. Athens: University of Georgia Press, 1996.

Stick, David. *Graveyard of the Atlantic: Shipwrecks of the North Carolina Coast.* Chapel
    Hill: University of North Carolina Press, 1952.

Stilgoe, John R. *Common Landscape of America, 1580 to 1845.* New Haven: Yale Uni-
    versity Press, 1982.

Stoddard, Albert H. *Gulla Tales and Anecdotes of South Carolina Sea Islands.* N.p.: pri-
    vately printed, 1940.

———. "Origin, Dialect, Beliefs, and Characteristics of the Negroes of the South Car-
    olina and Georgia Coasts." *Georgia Historical Quarterly* 28 (September 1944).

Strasser, Susan. *Never Done: A History of American Housework.* New York: Pantheon
    Books, 1982.

Sullivan, Buddy. *Early Days on the Georgia Tidewater: The Story of McIntosh County
    and Sapelo.* Darien, Ga.: McIntosh County Board of Commissioners, 1990.

Surrency, Erwin C. "The First American Criminal Code: The Georgia Code of 1816."
    Georgia Historical Quarterly 64 (winter 1979).

Sutherland, Daniel E. *Americans and Their Servants: Domestic Service in the United
    States from 1800 to 1920.* Baton Rouge: Louisiana State University Press, 1981.

Swanson, Carl E. *Predators and Prizes: American Privateering and Imperial Warfare,
    1739–1748.* Columbia: University of South Carolina Press, 1991.

Swint, Henry Lee. *The Northern Teacher in the South, 1862–1870.* Nashville: Vanderbilt
    University Press, 1941.

Tanner, Helen Hornbeck, ed. *General Greene's Visit to St. Augustine in 1785.* Ann Arbor:
    William L. Clements Library, 1964.

———. "The Land and Water Communication Systems of the Southeastern Indians."
    In *Powhatan's Mantle: Indians in the Colonial Southeast,* ed. Peter H. Wood, Gregory
    A. Waselkov, and M. Thomas Hatley. Lincoln: University of Nebraska Press, 1989.

Taylor, Paul S. *Georgia Plan, 1732–1752.* Berkeley: Institute of Business and Economic
    Research, University of California, 1972.

Temin, Peter. "Patterns of Cotton Agriculture in Post-Bellum Georgia." *Journal of Eco-
    nomic History* 43 (September 1983).

Thayer, Theodore. *Nathanael Greene: Strategist of the American Revolution.* New York:
    Twayne, 1960.

Thomas, Allen C., ed. *Biographical Catalogue of the Matriculates of Haverford College,
    1833–1900.* Philadelphia: n.p., 1900.

Thomas, David Hurst. *Georgian Genesis: The Intercultural Beginnings.* Atlanta: Geor-
    gia Humanities Council, 1993.

———. "Saints and Soldiers at Santa Catalina: Hispanic Designs for Colonial Amer-
    ica." In *The Recovery of Meaning: Historical Archaeology in the Eastern United
    States,* ed. Mark P. Leone and Parker B. Potter Jr. Washington, D.C.: Smithsonian In-
    stitution Press, 1988.

———. "The Spanish Mission Experience in La Florida." In *Columbus and the Land of Ayllón: The Exploration and Settlement of the Southeast*, ed. Jeannine Cook. Valona, Ga.: Lower Altamaha Historical Society, 1992.

Thomas, David Hurst, Grant D. Jones, Roger S. Durham, and Clark Spencer Larsen. *The Anthropology of St. Catherines Island.* Vol. 1, *Natural and Cultural History.* New York: American Museum of Natural History, 1978.

Thomas, Hugh. *The Slave Trade: The Story of the Atlantic Slave Trade, 1440–1870.* New York: Pantheon Books, 1997.

Thomas, Kenneth H., Jr. "Sapelo from 1851 to 1861." Paper prepared for Georgia Department of Natural Resources Sapelo Island Project, 12 May 1984.

Thompson, C. Mildred. *Reconstruction in Georgia: Economic, Social, Political, 1865–1872.* New York: Columbia University Press, 1915.

Thompson, Edgar T. *Plantation Societies, Race Relations, and the South: The Regimentation of Populations.* Durham, N.C.: Duke University Press, 1975.

Thompson, Shirley Joiner. *The People of Camden County, Georgia: A Finding Index prior to 1850.* Kingsland, Ga.: *Southeast Georgian*, 1982.

Tinkler, William P. *Atlantic Intracoastal Waterway Project in Georgia: A Study of Its History, Maintenance, and Present Use.* Brunswick: Georgia Department of Natural Resources, 1976.

Todd, Richard Cecil. *Confederate Finance.* Athens: University of Georgia Press, 1954.

Tornero Tinajero, Pablo. *Relaciónes de Dependencia entre Florida y Estados Unidos (1783–1820).* Madrid: Ministerio de Asuntos Exteriores, Dirección General de Relaciónes Culturales, 1979.

Torres, Louis. *Historic Resource Study, Cumberland Island National Seashore, Georgia, and Historic Structure Report, Historic Data Section of the Dungeness Area.* Denver: Historic Preservation Division, National Park Service, U.S. Department of the Interior, 1977.

Trowell, C. T. *The Suwanee Canal Company in the Okefenokee Swamp.* Douglas, Ga.: South Georgia College, 1984.

Troxler, Carole Watterson. "Loyalist Refugees and the British Evacuation of East Florida, 1783–1785." *Florida Historical Quarterly* 60 (July 1981): 18–26.

Turner, Lorenzo Dow. *Africanisms in the Gullah Dialect.* 1949; reprint, Ann Arbor: University of Michigan Press, 1974.

Turner, Monica. "Simulation of Management Implications of Feral Horses Grazing on Cumberland Island, Georgia." *Journal of Range Management* 41, no. 5 (1988): 441–47.

Turner Bushnell, Amy. "A Peripheral Perspective." *Historical Archaeology* 31, no. 1 (1997).

———. *Santa María in the Written Record.* [Gainesville]: Florida State Museum, Department of Anthropology, 1986.

———. *Situado and Sabana: Spain's Support System for the Presidio and Mission Provinces of Florida.* Athens: University of Georgia Press, 1994.

Twining, Mary A., and Keith E. Baird. "Introduction to Sea Island Folklife." *Journal of Black Studies* 10 (June 1980).

Upton, Francis H. *The Law of Nations Affecting Commerce during War: With a Review of the Jurisdiction, Practice, and Proceedings of Prize Courts.* 1861; reprint, Littleton, Colo.: Rothman, 1988.

U.S. Congress. Senate. *Report of the Committee on the Agriculture and Forestry on the Condition of Cotton Growers, the Present Prices of Cotton, and the Remedy.* 53rd Cong., 3d sess., 1895. Rept. 986.

———. *Treaties, Conventions, International Acts, Protocols and Agreements between the United States of America and Other Powers, 1776–1909.* 61st Cong., 2d sess., 1910. Doc. 357.

U.S. National Park Service. Denver Service Center. *Draft Environmental Statement: General Management Plan, Wilderness Study, Cumberland Island National Seashore, Georgia.* Denver: Department of the Interior, National Park Service, Denver Service Center, 1978.

Vanderhill, Burke G. "The Alachua–St. Marys Road." *Florida Historical Quarterly* 66 (July 1987).

Vandiver, Frank E. *Rebel Brass: The Confederate Command System.* Baton Rouge: Louisiana State University Press, 1956.

Van Doren, Mark, ed. *Travels of William Bartram.* 1928; reprint, New York: Dover, 1955.

Vanstory, Burnette. *Georgia's Land of the Golden Isles.* Rev. ed. Athens: University of Georgia Press, 1981.

Veblen, Thorstein. *The Theory of the Leisure Class.* New York: Macmillan, 1899.

Vignoles, Charles Blacker. *The History of the Floridas, from the Discovery by Cabot, in 1497, to the Cession of the Same to the United States, in 1821.* Brooklyn, N.Y.: G. L. Birch, 1824.

Vlach, John Michael. *Back of the Big House: The Architecture of Plantation Slavery.* Chapel Hill: University of North Carolina Press, 1993.

———. *By the Work of Their Hands: Studies in Afro-American Folklife.* Charlottesville: University Press of Virginia, 1991.

Vocelle, James Thomas. *History of Camden County, Georgia.* 1914; reprint, Kingsland, Ga.: *Southeast Georgian,* 1967.

Voelker, Cecelia. "Port Quarantines on the Atlantic, Prototypes of Ellis Island." Research project, Clemson University School of Architecture, 1989.

Waddell, Gene. *Indians of the South Carolina Lowcountry, 1562–1751.* Spartanburg, S.C.: Reprint Company, 1980.

Wakelyn, Jon L. *Biographical Dictionary of the Confederacy.* Westport, Conn.: Greenwood Press, 1977.

Walker, George. *New Directions for Sailing along the Coast of North America and into Its Several Harbours Commencing at Halifax in Nova Scotia and Including the Whole Navigation to Cape Florida ... to Which Is Added a Particular Description of the Coast from New York to St. Augustine.* London: Robert Laurie and James Whittle, 1801.

Walker, George Fuller. *Abstracts of Georgia Colonial Book J, 1755–1762.* Ed. Frank E. Vandiver. Atlanta: R. J. Taylor Jr. Foundation, 1975.

Walker, Hermione Ross. "Cumberland Island" and "Poverty in Paradise." In *An Anthology of Historical Family Writings: Simri's Journal.* Simri Rose, ed. Preston S. Stevens Jr. and John D. Davenport. Bloomington, Ind.: privately published, 1999.

Walker, James W. St. G. *The Black Identity in Nova Scotia.* Halifax, Nova Scotia: University of Waterloo, Black Cultural Centre, Department of History, 1985.

Walkley, Stephen, comp. *History of the Seventh Connecticut Volunteer Infantry: Hawley's Brigade, Terry's Division, Tenth Army Corps, 1861–1865.* [Southington, Conn.: n.p., 1905].

Wall, Joseph Frazier. *Andrew Carnegie.* New York: Oxford University Press, 1970.

Wallenberg, J. K. *The Place-Names of Kent.* Uppsala: Appelbergs Boktryckeriaktiebolag, 1934.

Walsh, William F. *Monitoring Estuarine Shoreline Variability on Cumberland Island National Seashore, Georgia: An Interim Report.* Athens: University of Georgia, Department of Geography, 1988.

The War of the Rebellion: A Compilation of the Official Records of the Union and Confederate Armies. 70 vols. Washington, D.C.: U.S. Government Printing Office, 1880–1901.

Ward, Christopher. "The Commerce of East Florida during the Embargo, 1806–1812: The Role of Amelia Island." *Florida Historical Quarterly* 68 (October 1989).

Ware, John D. *George Gauld: Surveyor and Cartographer of the Gulf Coast.* Gainesville: University Presses of Florida, 1982.

Warren, Mary Bondurant, and Jack Moreland Jones. *Georgia Governor and Council Journals, 1753–1760.* Danielsville, Ga.: Heritage Papers, 1991.

———. *Georgia Governor and Council Journals, 1761–1767.* Athens, Ga.: Heritage Papers, 1992.

Weatherwax, Paul. *The Story of the Maize Plant.* Chicago: University of Chicago Press, 1923.

Weber, David J. *The Spanish Frontier in North America.* New Haven: Yale University Press, 1992.

Wecter, Dixon. *The Saga of American Society: A Record of Social Aspiration, 1607–1937.* New York: Scribner, 1970.

Weigley, Russell F. *Quartermaster General of the Union Army: A Biography of M. C. Meigs*. New York: Columbia University Press, 1959.

Weiss, John McNish. "The Great Escape." Paper presented at the conference on Mutiny: Narrative Event, and Context in Comparative Perspective, Columbus, Ohio, October 1998.

Westwood, Howard C. "Sherman Marched—And Proclaimed Land for the Landless." *South Carolina Historical Magazine* 85 (January 1984).

Wharton, Edith. *Italian Villas and Their Gardens*. New York: Century, 1904.

Wheat, James Clements, and Christian F. Brun. *Maps and Charts Published in America before 1800: A Bibliography*. New Haven: Yale University Press, 1969.

Whiffen, Marcus, and Frederick Koeper. *American Architecture, 1607–1976*. Cambridge: MIT Press, 1981.

Whipple, Henry Benjamin. *Bishop Whipple's Southern Diary, 1843–1844*. Ed. and intro. Lester Burrell Shippee. Minneapolis: University of Minnesota Press, 1937.

White, George. *Historical Collections of Georgia*. New York: Prudney and Russell, 1854.

———. *Statistics of the State of Georgia: Including an Account of Its Natural, Civil, and Ecclesiastical History*. Savannah, Ga.: W. Thorne Williams, 1849.

Wiedemann, Frederick W. "The Architectural Preservation of the Dungeness Site, Cumberland Island, Georgia." Master's thesis, University of Florida, 1975.

Wiley, Bell I. *Southern Negroes, 1861–1865*. New Haven: Yale University Press, 1938.

Williams, Edwin L., Jr. "Negro Slavery in Florida." *Florida Historical Quarterly* 28 (October 1949).

Williams, Mervyn R. "Song from Valley to Mountain: Music and Ritual among the Spiritual Baptists ('Shouters') of Trinidad." Master's thesis, Indiana University, 1985.

Williams, W. R., comp. "British-American Officers, 1720–1763." *South Carolina Historical and Genealogical Magazine* 33 (July 1932).

Williamson, Joel. *After Slavery: The Negro in South Carolina during Reconstruction, 1861–1877*. Chapel Hill: University of North Carolina Press, 1965.

———. "Black Self-Assertion before and after Emancipation." In *Key Issues in the Afro-American Experience*, ed. Nathan I. Huggins, Martin Kilson, and Daniel M. Fox. 2 vols. New York: Harcourt Brace Jovanovich, 1971.

Wilms, Douglas C. "The Development of Rice Culture in Eighteenth Century Georgia." *Southeastern Geographer* 12 (1972).

Winberry, John J. "Reputation of Carolina Indigo." *South Carolina Historical Magazine* 80 (July 1979).

Winkler, John K. *Incredible Carnegie: The Life of Andrew Carnegie*. New York: Vanguard Press, 1931.

———. *Morgan, the Magnificent: The Life of J. Pierpont Morgan (1837–1913)*. New York, Vanguard Press, 1930.

Wood, Peter H. *Black Majority: Negroes in Colonial South Carolina from 1670 through the Stono Rebellion.* New York: Knopf, 1974.

Wood, Peter H., Gregory A. Waselkov, and M. Thomas Hatley, eds. *Powhatan's Mantle: Indians in the Colonial Southeast.* Lincoln: University of Nebraska Press, 1989.

Wood, Virginia Steele. "After the War of 1812: Spoliation Claims of Georgia Residents." 1984. Manuscript.

———. *Live Oaking: Southern Timber for Tall Ships.* Boston: Northeastern University Press, 1981.

———, ed. *Robert Durfee's Journal and Recollections of Newport, Rhode Island.* Marion, Mass.: Belden Books, 1990.

Woodward, C. Vann. *Origins of the New South, 1877–1913.* Baton Rouge: Louisiana State University Press, 1951.

———. *The Strange Career of Jim Crow.* New York: Oxford University Press, 1955.

Works Progress Administration. *Annals of Savannah, 1850–1937: A Digest and Index of the Newspaper Record of Events and Opinions.* Athens, Ga.: n.p., 1937.

Worth, John E. *The Struggle for the Georgia Coast: An Eighteenth-Century Spanish Retrospective on Guale and Mocama.* New York: American Museum of Natural History, 1995; distributed by the University of Georgia Press.

Wright, Albert Hazen. *Our Georgia-Florida Frontier.* Vol. 1. Ithaca, N.Y.: A. H. Wright, 1945.

Wright, J. Leitch, Jr. *Florida in the American Revolution.* Gainesville: University Presses of Florida, 1975.

Wright, Robert. *A Memoir of General James Oglethorpe, One of the Earliest Reformers of Prison Discipline in England.* London: Chapman and Hall, 1867.

Wyllie, Irvin G. *The Self-Made Man in America: The Myth of Rags to Riches.* New Brunswick, N.J.: Rutgers University Press, 1954.

Youngman, Elsie P. *Summer Echoes from the Nineteenth Century: Manchester-by-the-Sea.* Rockport, Mass.: D. Russell, 1981.

INDEX

Abu (slave), 140–42

admiralty law, and salvaged ships, 46

African Baptist Church, First, 286

African Mission School Society, 320–21 (n. 48)

agriculture on CI: corn, 4, 48, 49, 67, 68; cotton cultivation, 4, 104–8, 118; diversification of, 107, 128; and financial credit, 95; garden produce, 42, 46, 48, 49, 67; and Indians, 17, 24; indigo, as crop, 4, 74–75; and itinerant farmers, 134; and land grants, 50; olive trees, cultivation of, 128, 183, 203, 317 (n. 13); orange trees and citriculture, 17, 127–30; rice cultivation, 52, 58, 70–72, 105, 107; Sea Island cotton, 104, 105–6, 225–27

Ainsworth, A. A., 255

Alabama, USS, 155

Alas, Esteban de las, 20

Alberti, Edwin, 168

Alberty, Rodgers, 168

Albion, HMS, 122, 142

Alexander, Ephraim, 46

"Altamaha project," 53–54

Altamaha River: and British settlement, 42, 49; and Guale Indians, 13

Amelia Dividings, 84

Amelia Inlet, 4

Amelia Island, 4, 31, 103; British fortification of, 35; and international trade, 10; map of, 6; during Revolutionary War, 82, 83; as scout station, 42; and Spanish mission settlement, 16, 19

Amelia Island Harbor, 9

American Revolution, 67, 70, 108, 119; and cattle raids, 79–86; and indigo market, 75; and Jonathan Bryan, 56; and Lachlan McIntosh, 58; and shipbuilding, 72–73; soldiers' desertion during, 84; and Thomas Lynch, 301 (n. 46)

American Smelting and Refining Company, 270

ammunition depot, and U.S. Army, 283

amnesty proclamation (May 1865), 161

Andrew W. Mellon Foundation (AWMF), 284, 348 (n. 46)

archaeological sites: mission church, St. Catherines Island, 17; slave settlement, Rayfield, 139–40; Stafford plantation, 319 (n. 31)

architectural traditions of CI: Dungeness House (Miller), 99–103, 308 (nn. 15, 17); Georgia vernacular, and Greyfield, 205; Italian Palladian style, Plum Orchard and Dungeness "Improvements," 203–4, 333 (n. 8); live-oakers, shelters for, 73; military fortifications, 31, 35–36, 37; Queen Anne Gothic style, Dungeness House (Carnegie), 185, 186–88, 203–4, 329–30 (n. 42); palmetto thatching, 43–44, 176–77; slave dwellings, 136, 147, 167; Spanish mission compounds, 16–17, 20

Panic of 1893, 221, 235

Panza, Sancho, as free black, 142

Pareja, Father Francisco, 18

Parker, Isaac, 143

Parker, John, 143–44

Patterson, Eagle, Greenough, and Day (law firm), 256

Peabody and Sterns (architectural firm), 204, 251

Peebles, Andrew, as architect of Dungeness House (Carnegie), 185, 201, 329–30 (n. 42)

Peeples, J. B., as gamekeeper, 275

Pendleton, Nathaniel, 9

Pennimen, William, 166

Peoples First National Bank and Trust Company (Pittsburgh), 258, 261, 263, 269

Perkins, Coleman C., 206, 271, 273, 285

Perkins, Florence Carnegie, 206, 245, 255, 256, 260, 269, 343 (n. 20)

pheasants, introduction of, 229, 231

Philips, R. L., 255

Phipps, Henry, Jr., 190–91, 193, 195, 196

Phipps, Henry, Sr., 179

picnics, at Dungeness, 219, 230

Piles, Samuel, 48

pilot whales, in St. Andrew Sound, 8, 294 (n. 8)

pilots: contraband slaves as, 154–55, 166; island inhabitants as, 6; of St. Andrews Bar, 132; of St. Mary's Bar, 54, 117

Pilots Town, on St. Johns River, 155

pine timber, 4, 9, 259

piraguas, as watercraft, 29, 35, 297 (n. 10)

pirates, 22–23, 68, 103, 113, 115. *See also* privateering

Pittsburgh National Bank, 273

Pittsburgh, Pa., 181, 327–28 (n. 26)

Pizarro (ship), 113

Plant, Henry B., 174

plantations: abandonment of, during Civil War, 155, 158, 160; administration of, 207; and cotton cultivation, 104–8; on CI, 132–34, 136; Dungeness as, 130; establishment of, 95–99; and financial credit, 95; and rice

cultivation, 53, 55, 70–72; and slavery, 55, 135–37, 166

Planters House, 133, 155, 226

planters, itinerant, 134, 143

Plum Orchard, 57, 63, 69, 288; and Carnegie family, 194, 204, 231, 251, 255, 256; construction of, 204, 333 (n. 8); electrical plant for, 218; and Johnston family, 273, 343 (n. 20); staffing and administration of, 209

Plum Orchard Bluff, 73

Plum Orchard Plantation, and Bernardey family, 108, 131, 134

poaching, of livestock, 260, 275

Polydore, a slave, 140, 320 (n. 43)

population estimates: for Camden County and St. Marys, 221; for CI, 3, 22, 49, 131, 135, 319 (n. 30)

Port Royal, 14, 20, 24, 28

Powers, E. B., 209, 226

Pratt, Cray, 131, 229, 313 (n. 62), 318 (n. 17)

Pratt, Natty, 209

Prevost, Augustine, 81, 85

Prevost, James Mark, 83–84, 86

Prevost, Mark, 85

Prince George (scout boat), 79

Princess Mary (schooner), 112–13

privateering, 112–17; and coastal trading, 46–47; and live oak timber, 72; and observation platform at Dungeness, 103; plantation raids, during Revolutionary War, 83; and slaves, as bounty, 20, 113–15; and state boundaries, 10

Propagation of the Gospel in Foreign Parts, 20

quail, hunting of, 229

Quakerism: and Gray's settlement, 44–45, 47; and Nathanael Greene, 86, 87

Quash (former slave), of Brick Hill, 68–69, 285

Queen Anne Gothic style, and Dungeness House, 185, 329–30 (n. 42)

Quesada, Juan de N., 117, 133

CPSIA information can be obtained
at www.ICGtesting.com
Printed in the USA
LVHW021941280720
661758LV00004B/46

9 780820 327419